SURFING YOUR

SOLAR CYCLES

A Lifetime Guide to Your Stars

Neil D. Paris

The Wessex Astrologer

Published in 2012 by
The Wessex Astrologer
4A Woodside Road
Bournemouth
BH5 2AZ
England

www.wessexastrologer.com

ISBN 9781902405827

A catalogue record of this book is available at The British Library

Cover design by Tania at Creative Byte, Bournemouth, England

Contents

For Mrs Brown
who told me that if I kept writing
I'd "go far"

and Eleanor Iley
who wanted to see this book finished
but couldn't

Acknowledgements

Russell Sveda and Victor Schachter
for filling my first moments in the USA
with Capricorn comfort and Cancer care

Randy,
for carving a road through snowy mountains

Eric Lee,
for Taurus stability and security in the big city

Linda Goodman,
for everything you've done and continue to do

Crystal and Kelly-Anne Bush,
for making a Dream come true

Adrian Quayle,
My fellow Fish who surfs beside me still through all tides

Jared DeCarlo, the Krabkat,
for your protective Cancer pincers, Scorpio strength during the dark,
the Leo lights of laughter and Love and for more than words can say

My clients,
for boldly living the stories that have shaped the telling of my own

The Family of Light,
who continue to brighten the few remaining dark corners of Planet Earth

My Creators:
Rosalind, the Centaur, John the Lion
My Protectors:
John the Gemini, and Eleanor the Libra
and My Comrades:
Mark the Water-Bearer, Simon the Twins
and David the Archer

Churita and Le Bang Bang for their company and timely reminders to take
walks, stretch and seek out treats, during the writing of this book

and Margaret Cahill for birthing my baby

And to YOU...

Aries, for reminding me that it's okay to fly solo

Taurus for showing me that though the seasons change,
the things that matter don't

Gemini, that without Thought we cannot Do, and that with too much
thinking we cannot Be

To the Cancers who helped me build nests and the ones who kicked me
out so that I may find my wings

To Leo who taught me that we define ourselves by the Light we share or
the Shadow we cast when we don't

Virgo, who knows that the Devil's in the details, but that God's there too

Libra, that every sunset painted, experienced and enjoyed is better
when shared

Scorpio, for killing me off so that I could be reborn bigger,
stronger and better than ever

Sagittarius, for journeys shared and for encouraging me to find out
for myself

Capricorn for showing me that just as you're never too young to be
wise, you're never too wise to be young

Aquarius, for reminding me we're all aliens amongst stars

Pisces, for waking me up to the reality that it's all just a dream...

Preface

My life truly became magical after astrology found me.

It would come as no surprise that I was first introduced to astrology by a Sagittarius: the Seeker and Keeper of the keys to knowledge, truth and wisdom, and no surprise again to discover that I myself was born under a Sagittarius Moon, an imprint suggesting an overwhelming soul-need to know.

As a teenager I was given the gift of a small print-out of my astrology chart which sat around my bedroom for quite some time. What led me one day to pick up that strange piece of paper with the weird symbols on? Curiosity? Destiny? I think it was skepticism. What could a circle with symbols know about my life?

What I read stopped me in my tracks – from my enigmatic relationship with my father, to my personal and secret insecurities and doubts, to my musical talents to a deep interest in magic and mystery ... and, allegedly, a residue of astrological knowledge from who knows when.

The Pisces Fish I am, was hooked.

I still remember my early days of astrology with fondness. Hitching a ride with my Sagittarius mother on her antique-hunting adventures to car boot sales in Newcastle upon Tyne, England in the early hours of the morning (flea markets to my American readers). I was committed to seeking old, not new, books that had any mention of astrology. I searched for scraps of insight, tidbits of truth. I was hungry for knowledge. The mystical feel of ancient information; the smell of wisdom within their yellowed pages. New books didn't hold the same promise. Old texts were my comfort, my teachers and my home. Each find fed and fueled my hunger for more.

In the days, months, weeks and years that followed I amassed all I could on the subject. I learned how to draw my own charts for family, friends, strangers and celebrities. I compared the charts with the people and the people with the charts. In true movie-symbolism fashion, my family weren't as keen on my personal quest and hero's journey, claiming I would end up in an asylum! I spent hours in my own world, comparing notes, texts, opinions and studies to find the one common thread that ran through it all.

And from where I stand now I believe that truth hides in many places, sometimes between two lies, but within everything hides a sparkle of eternal truth and if you seek, you shall indeed find. As in the world religions, our human mind likes to fragment and overcomplicate the simplest of philosophies and ideologies, but if you look closely enough and widely enough you'll soon discover that there is one simple thread that unites it all. I discarded the discrepancies and held fast to that thread which has led me on such a weird, wacky, and wonderful astrological adventure.

And that's when Linda Goodman found me. Not personally but in another and perhaps more magical and meaningful way. Linda was the first astrologer to put astrology on the *New York Times* bestseller list (1968), opening up the minds of millions to the accuracy and practical application of the field. Mysteriously and miraculously, her books found me – in order – in various locations. I still remember one of her later books putting itself in my path. At one particular car boot sale I passed a table with just three items for sale, a glass vase, a plate and there it was – *Linda Goodman's Star Signs.*

Years later I would find myself at a used bookstore (of course) in Dupont Circle in Washington DC where I would stumble upon Linda's last work, *Gooberz,* which I carried with me while exploring the States on Greyhound buses and trains. I would not discover until a year or so later whilst surfing the net that Linda had passed and I was unable to meet my astrological idol. I did find, however, that her works lived on and new unpublished material was being safeguarded by the folk at the then active website Lindagoodman.net who just happened to be running a poetry contest.

Of course I entered. Not least of all because of my curious connection to Linda but also because of the prize – a gift voucher to spend on recorded tapes by Linda herself, magic purple plates and more. How could I resist?

I won the competition. And that led me to chatting via email to Crystal Bush, Linda's friend who had been entrusted Linda's name and works just weeks before her passing. When Crystal said that my writing reminded her of Linda's, I was speechless. We conversed for a time and then, as so often happens, life stepped in and we each went our separate ways.

A year or so later, destiny would boldly alter the landscape of my life. I received a letter that there was an opening for a Resident Astrologer at Lindagoodman.net. I would end up leaving the concrete and heat of DC's city and flying out to the cool breezes and enchanted cliff tops of Santa Monica, California, amidst sun, sea, sand and palm trees.

My time there was enchanting. I was a writer on Linda Goodman's *Star Notes,* a newsletter sent out to her fans across Planet Earth, with new and exciting articles on astrological patterns, world news and some of Linda's unpublished secrets. It was my Dream Job. I would one day find myself living not far from the Roosevelt Hotel, on Hollywood Boulevard, where in the top floor penthouse suite Linda would sit nightly at her typewriter writing her epic *Love Signs.* I would end up following in Linda's footsteps metaphorically and then physically, stumbling upon the "small white cross planted on the far hill behind Grauman's Chinese Theatre", mystically mentioned in Linda's writings.

I would sit each day, the scent of the ocean blowing through the offices, under a portrait of Linda herself who watched over me as I drew and interpreted the charts for clients from all walks of life. I was a Pisces Fish in the deep end of the astrological ocean but I am ever thankful, for I learned to swim fast and discover a natural rhythm to the ancient tides of wisdom that seemed to move through me during each consultation. On some days, we swore Linda was around. Strange scents and synchronistic sensations.

One night, I had one of those dreams that is so vivid and lucid you would swear you'd entered another dimension. Linda came to me, materializing out of thin air from across the room. The air became crisp and tight. She was silent, carrying only two things: a cuckoo clock and a wooden owl. She never spoke a word but she seemed to have a message for me.

In the dream, I told Crystal's daughter Kelly-Anne who was part of the Linda team what had happened and she was stunned. "You're kidding me..." she began, as she revealed just why the dream was so important. When I returned to the offices the next morning, I told Kelly-Anne the tale of my dream that night. She was stunned. Her mouth dropped open and she turned pale. "You're kidding me..." she began. Deja-vu descended upon us as she reacted in exactly the same way she had the night before.

Kelly-Anne had been visited by owls regularly (and tells me years later she is still visited by them) and they were a sign of great change to come. Perhaps Linda came bearing a message that everyone would understand. That her cuckoo clock was a reminder that time weaves its own Saturn magic and, as the book in your hands will show, cycles change and our lives change accordingly. When Saturn entered Cycle 10 of the company's astrology chart (which you'll soon discover is the Rise or Fall moment for many of our Dreams) I knew we'd all come to the end of one particular adventure. Not long after, Lindagoodman.net closed its doors forever ... yet the magic lives on.

Since then, I still receive letters from Linda's fans across the world who have questions for her or want to let me know how important Linda was in their own astrological adventure. Linda never got to see the internet or the vast network of people who are still, to this day, touched by her work. But although she may no longer be with us physically I believe she still peeks in to see what I am up to, at times whispering metaphysical material into my ear and weaving her magic from behind the scenes, leading people to discovering their own inner truths through the works she left us.

From my humble beginnings studying in England, where I attended psychic fairs alone in Bournemouth (as my fellow students had no interest in metaphysics) to cosmic connections with those working at The White House in Washington DC, to reading for actors, singers, musicians and socialite parties in Hollywood, California, my journey now brings me synchronistically full circle. My family's prediction of ending up in an asylum didn't come true, although looking back my journey has been pretty crazy. Back in the UK, my family would end up resenting my targeted astro-analysis yet come to me for astro-advice. And twelve years after leaving England (12 being a powerfully magical number; the day I was born, not to mention the 12 signs of the zodiac and the number of cycles this book is compromised of), this book finally finds its way home over 5000 miles east of the mystical mountains of San Bernardino, California, to The Wessex Astrologer, nestled up on the cliff tops of the English Channel, back in Bournemouth, England.

That Sagittarius Moon I was born under now has a new yearning: to pass on and teach some of what I have learned on my own travels. With Saturn, the karmic taskmaster and wise instructor in my 9th house of seeking and learning, I am still a skeptic in many ways, cursed and blessed with the desire to find out for myself. So what you'll discover here is tried and true, a piece of the grand cosmic design as I have glimpsed it and delivered from direct experience, perhaps the greatest teacher of all.

Wherever your journey takes you, I hope you open your own mind long enough to let the magic slip in so that you too can witness the bigger picture and feel part of the great cosmic adventure we are all on.

The greatest gift astrology has ever given me and can give us all, is a simple one:

> to use the wisdom of the planets,
> to have a better life on Earth.

To the journey!

Your astrologer, Neil D. Paris

You can reach Neil at his website

www.NewWorldAstrology.com

This Crazy Little Thing Called 'Life'

How often have you looked around and wondered:

"Where am I going?"
"Will this ever end?"
"Am I doing something wrong?"
"What *should* I do?"
or
"What the heck is going on?"

Well, you're not alone! With life seemingly picking up the pace, it's easy to lose sight of the bigger picture. Sudden events (or a nebulous feeling of confusion) leave us wondering where we're going and what is really going on behind the apparent chaos and madness we see around us each day. We've become masters at overcomplicating things. But what if you had a tool to take a peak behind the scenes, to discover the real meaning hidden within seemingly unrelated events – wouldn't you use it?

Now you can. It's time to get back to basics, and use some of the most ancient tried-and-true methods of making life more manageable by bringing some understanding and natural magick back to our chaotic day-to-day lives.

That wisdom is found in the simplicity and profound practicality of Astrology's Solar Cycles.

This book will help you locate yourself in the illusion we call 'time': In a year in your life. **Every year, in fact, for the rest of your life!** To reveal to you, *your* Cycles, the ones that you alone travel through at varying times in the space of 12 months each year. This book will help you uncover the patterns that you alone move through *each and every year of your life* – like clockwork – and to help you discover ways in which to work with each of these special and significant Cycles to create the life you desire as you go along, thereby enjoying the ride.

And isn't that the real reason for undertaking any journey?

There are 12 such Cycles. They can be also called Initiations, in that if you pass one, you progress to the next level and things improve. If you don't, you get held back a bit (life is a lot like school, in that way), until you get them right. And you get to play with them every year. They all present key people, special challenges and specific situations that come along, as you knew they would (from a soul perspective), to test you, help you, hinder you – all with a view to poking and prodding you into evolving. Growth always comes with some form of resistance before the final push to the light, akin to the seed pushing through the earth to finally blossom.

Maybe every February 12th, you enter a period of 30 days when you notice you feel like redecorating, getting comfy, looking into moving, or something pops up to be dealt with on the domestic front? Maybe every December you have 22 days that are your best time for meeting people? Every August perhaps you lose stuff and every January your business skyrockets with just a little extra effort.

In some years, you'll feel the best of these Cycles (whose themes vary slightly or strongly every year you're alive, as the Game of Your Life progresses). These are the years when you'll feel on top of them, in control of them and loving them. In other years, you'll feel dragged through them, under the force of them or at the mercy of them. You'll want to tear your hair out or wonder why you ever signed up for this adventure.

Hang in there! The beauty about these Cycles is that they always change eventually. This book will clear up the timing on this too so you can save your sanity … and your hair.

Some Cycles are *up*, some are *down*. In some you soar; in others you crash – it's the nature of life; but the more conscious you are of what's going on at any moment in your life, the more you have a choice to either ride with the wind at your back or force yourself down roads you would have done better to ignore. Pushing against life's traffic is a headache when all you need do is turn up your radio and wait for the nearest exit.

That is why I wrote this book. We've somehow become a little disconnected from Nature. From times when people actually went to bed when the sun sank below the horizon and rose when dawn approached. When the seasons of the year meant something else besides which present to buy or which costume to wear.

But since we can turn on the TV or a light at any time and shop 24 hours a day, our natural rhythms of nature have been ignored, repressed or simply forgotten.

But they still exist.

And it's in following these natural rhythms that we can get ourselves back on track where we've slightly veered off. We can find a way ahead to again make sense of the madness, and find a simple workable magick and joy in living. Wouldn't you like to regain your childlike sense of wonder? Things change, and though we as humans may sometimes fight this tendency to remain open and innocent, it becomes our greatest ally, especially during difficult times.

This guidebook will aid you in your journey through a year in your life. Not just one year but every year for the rest of your life. Keep it handy. If your friend asks for a copy, tell them to get their own! You'll need it. You can use it to dive in to see what you should or could be (or what life is asking you to be) focusing on this month and where you're at *now* with a view to planning and mapping out where you're going.

You can look *back* to where you've been, to understand something that happened, as well as look *ahead* to where your changes are likely to be, but more importantly and more effectively you can locate yourself in the present, with the full potential to take today and do something useful with it; instead of continuing to react to what is manifesting before you or what stands behind you.

Message to Astrology Beginners

All you need to know to use this book is your Sun Sign, the one most people talk about when asked. It's the sign the Sun was shining in when you were born. You're a Gemini, a Sagittarius and so forth. If you don't know yours, you can find that out below. Forget cusps, there's no such thing. Check below to determine which sign you are, and if you're close to the changeover dates, consult an astrologer to determine which sun sign you are for sure (since the changeover dates can shift from year to year), or try the handy online calculator located at my website **www.SurfingYourSolarCycles.com**.

		Sun Sign Months
♈	Aries	March 21 to April 19
♉	Taurus	April 20 to May 20
♊	Gemini	May 21 to June 21
♋	Cancer	June 22 to July 22
♌	Leo	July 23 to August 22
♍	Virgo	August 23 to September 22
♎	Libra	September 23 to October 23
♏	Scorpio	October 24 to November 22
♐	Sagittarius	November 23 to December 21
♑	Capricorn	December 22 to January 19
♒	Aquarius	January 20 to February 18
♓	Pisces	February 19 to March 20

Once you know your sign, you can discover which of the twelve Cycles you're currently moving through. Every sign goes through their Cycle 1 when it's their season (when we enter Gemini, all Geminis are in Cycle 1. A month later, all Geminis are in Cycle 2 and so forth). This is called our **SOLAR SUN SIGN CYCLE**.

Once it has begun, everything is on a timer – a series of Cycles. This book will help you locate these Cycles and put them to use, to work for you. And if nothing else, give you something different to do other than sit around being bored or stuck, wallowing or whining about your lot in life!

If you get hold of your birth chart, you can go deeper in the final chapter of the book, to uncover the Cycles you'll be playing with your entire life by locating the exact day and time the Sun moves into a new House/Cycle. Then this book becomes your ultimate weapon and tool of transformation as you can prepare ahead and get the full benefit of its information. You can get a free copy of your chart at **www.SurfingYourSolarCycles.com**.

Message to Astrologers

This book is based on the Sun's journey around the astrological birth chart. Though they may seem simplistic, Solar transits are actually overlooked as one of the most basic and direct ways to tap in to any chart at any given moment in time. The Sun is the *spotlight* giving light to various facets of our nature so we can live well-rounded lives. We can't always be alone and we can't always be in a relationship. This is a world of polarity where balance is part of the game, even if we try to fight it. Ignoring the Sun's messages knocks off our reading of the rest of the chart and you're left … literally… in the dark.

Without the Sun, you're at the mercy of the other astrological bogey-men sent after you. And what's the use of Uranus/Neptune/Pluto transits, if not to ultimately affect your sense of self (Sun) by enlivening you/softening you/ forcing you into evolving?

I've found in all my years of astrological study and practice – from my humble beginnings drawing charts for family and friends, to my time as the resident astrologer responsible for continuing Linda Goodman's astrological work, to my current practice as a celebrity astrologer speaking to people from all over the world in all walks of life – that the simple stuff is eternally the best.

Without a simple and solid foundation, nothing else stands up.

PART ONE:
Your Personal Wheel of Fortune

Today's Date Your Sign:	Jan 20-Feb 18	Feb 19-Mar 20	Mar 21-Apr 19	Apr 20-May 20	May 21-June 20	Jun 21-July 22	Jul 23-Aug 22	Aug 23-Sep 22	Sep 23-Oct 22	Oct 23-Nov 21	Nov 22-Dec-21	Dec 22-Jan 19
Aries	11	12	1	2	3	4	5	6	7	8	9	10
Taurus	10	11	12	1	2	3	4	5	6	7	8	9
Gemini	9	10	11	12	1	2	3	4	5	6	7	8
Cancer	8	9	10	11	12	1	2	3	4	5	6	7
Leo	7	8	9	10	11	12	1	2	3	4	5	6
Virgo	6	7	8	9	10	11	12	1	2	3	4	5
Libra	5	6	7	8	9	10	11	12	1	2	3	4
Scorpio	4	5	6	7	8	9	10	11	12	1	2	3
Sagittarius	3	4	5	6	7	8	9	10	11	12	1	2
Capricorn	2	3	4	5	6	7	8	9	10	11	12	1
Aquarius	1	2	3	4	5	6	7	8	9	10	11	12
Pisces	12	1	2	3	4	5	6	7	8	9	10	11

EASY AS 1-2-3!

1. Find your sign and today's date
2. The number is the Cycle you're in right now!
3. Read the relevant chapter

Page Numbers:

YOUR SOLAR CYCLES

The theme/initiation within each Cycle is always the same for that Cycle. How it manifests, however, is subject to change.

Each year, the central theme will remain, and you'll begin to spot it. The lesson/initiation will introduce you to a new facet of this subject and most importantly, how you approach this topic, your unique brand of action/thought/feeling around this subject and whether it's helping or hindering you on your journey. For example:

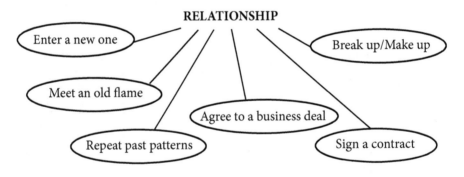

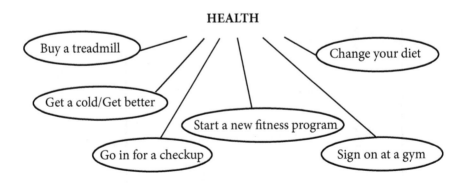

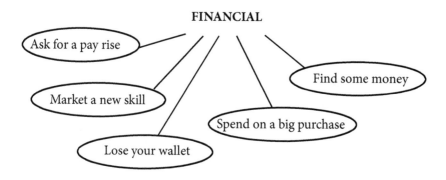

Look for helpers and hinderers along the way, *specific to the Cycle you're in*:

Helpers: cheer you on and provide aid and magical artifacts to help you on your way (money, tools, contact numbers, introduce you to other important helpers, give you a ride to a new destination, provide support for you to lean on, wise advice and so forth).

Hinderers: block you, throw up obstacles to throw you off course and see if you truly want to head in the direction you're currently heading in. They make life difficult for you, tell you you're wrong to want what it is that you desire, try to stop you or show you evidence of why you'll fail (using fear tactics). Some may even take things from you that you thought you needed (to see if you can find another way ahead).

Helpers always are welcomed, hinderers provide as much help as the helpers, but it's veiled and disguised as an 'obstacle'. It's during the tough times that we really get to shine and see what we're made of.

Treat your life like a movie and you'll begin to see the magic unfold before your very eyes.

Remember, these are all Initiations. Pass one and the next time it comes around you'll be stronger and wiser on the relevant subject matter, and you'll be bestowed the gifts you'll use during the next Cycle. Like a computer game, each new level introduces new 'goodies and baddies', new challenges, new opportunities to do better, sculpt your personality and go for the Big Prize.

PART TWO:
How to Use this Book

After you've discovered your Current Surf Cycle (using the table in the last section), you're ready to explore what each of these Cycles means for you.
Each Chapter is divided into:

Current Surf Cycle
At a glance you can find your current Cycle and learn the basic themes you'll encounter during this time of year.

People in the Spotlight
These are the people who will mirror back to you the themes outlined above. They'll play out the Cycle for you, as well as watch you go through the Cycle yourself. You get to teach as well as learn about the topics outlined and grow. Notice the symbolism they bring to you.

What you'll need
A tongue-in-cheek look at the tools in your personality kit that you'll symbolically (perhaps literally!) need, on your journey through the Cycle.

The Cycle
Outlined in full for you, divided into sections with key themes you'll face/experience/witness in this Cycle. Each year it varies, but the underlying energies and lessons remain the same. Get smart on these and you'll pass with flying colors! Either way you'll come out richer and wiser for having had the experience.

Action Plan
A quick-fire, sure-fire way to make the best of your Cycle and take advantage of its opportunities.

Up Cycle/Down Cycle
In some years the Cycle is easy – things fall into place and bingo! – you get through it without a scratch, with perhaps even some rewards in the process. In other years, it seems the whole universe is conspiring to cause you stress. How do you avoid winding up on the flip side of these Cycles, you ask? Simple. The flip side is not necessarily bad. Everything teaches you something. The dark stuff often defines the brighter stuff. These times give us perspective, make us more appreciative and help us determine what it is that we *do* want to experience.

If you find yourself in a flip Cycle then perhaps you took a detour, maybe you forgot your goal, maybe you gave your power away or maybe you just ran into a patch of what would seem to be 'bad luck'. No matter – the Cycle's ultimate goal is to teach you something about yourself. 'Good' and 'Bad' are only labels we put on things. Often curses turn out to be blessings, when all is said and done. And there is always more going on than meets the eye.

You get one major piece of freewill magic to use throughout any Cycle you're currently experiencing – you can choose how to respond.

Cycle Lesson
A final reminder on what this Cycle is really trying to show you.

Celebrity Spotlight
Here you'll see some examples of famous celebrities or moments in history that fell under your current Surf Cycle.

Tips to Navigating your Cycle Initiation
A list you can dip into for ideas on things to try during your current Cycle, to get you started, give you some pointers and give you a flavor of things to come, during this time of your year.

So, without further ado, let's reveal your personal Cycles and Initiations.

Your 12 Annual Solar Cycles

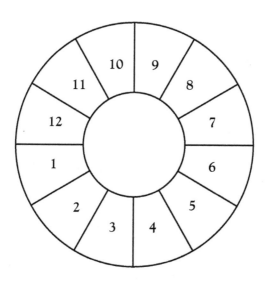

∾ Surf Cycle 11 ∾

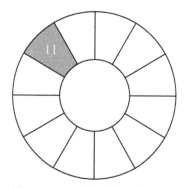

Time to Envision Your Future
Design your Dream
Plug in to Social Central
Renew Friendships and Foster Freedom

Liberating Liaisons with:

Old/new friends
Good friends/'fair-weather' friends
Strangers bearing gifts
Progressive movements
Social causes/organizations
Humanitarian groups
Marches/rallies
Strikers/picketers
Chapters/franchises/collectives
Fraternities/sororities
Rebels and utopian visionaries
Troublemakers/anarchists
Independent souls
Society's movers and shakers

Status quo/paradigm busters
Liberators, freedom fighters
Fringe dwellers or trendsetters
Technicians and techno wizs
Scientists/inventors
Mentally disturbed/challenged
Aquarius people
Psychics, astrologers
Outcasts, exiled or dropouts
Eccentric, offbeat, unusual folk
New Age followers
Electrical people/electricians
The wild and wacky

What you'll need:

An old rule book to burn
A totally new idea
Friends in all places
Clothes neither in nor out of style
A human disguise

Why not begin with Cycle 1? We'll get to that shortly. Firstly, let's discuss how you're likely to feel right now, during this your Cycle 11. You're itchy (not an embarrassing personal problem you picked up back in Cycle 8, we hope) for change, ready to offload the workload you've been carrying of late, and you feel like you need to break free of all restriction, limitation and control.

Right? Well this is it…

CYCLE 11 IS WHERE YOU GET TO PLANT YOUR VISION, SET YOUR MARKER, DESIGN YOUR FUTURE and DOWNLOAD YOUR NEWLY DESIRED DESTINY.

Intrigued? You will be. Let's dive in…

᮫᮫᮫

BID FOR FREEDOM
So why don't we begin this book with Cycle 1 (great question)? Experience has shown me that it's Cycle 11 that is really the beginning of all the Cycles in that it presents you with a unique opportunity to ring the changes in your life, break out of any ruts you somehow have become entrenched within, and redress and redesign your living conditions to something more befitting the free spirit you truly are.

How can you start something new unless you first decide what that is? Everything that manifests in our world comes first from an Idea. Cycle 11 is all about the mental thought energy level of existence. Things brewing there, long enough, are sure to manifest in the flesh.

We came into this life experience as spiritual beings seeking a physical experience. And that comes with the biggest desire of all – Freedom. Without it, how can we design our life as we want it?

So often when this Cycle comes around, you get to see exactly where you feel trapped, blocked, stuck, squeezed, and perhaps not living with as much liberation as you'd like. It's quite an eye opener. Even those of us who feel we're truly unique may have given in to peer pressure, bill paying, social conditioning or other external or internal issues. It matters not. That is why Cycle 11 exists. To remind you that no matter what has gone on before now, you can do it differently, you can awaken out of your slumber and you can move into a life you really deserve and desire.

First you have to make some choices on what it is you want to create.
Cycle 11 is your springboard.

So expect, somewhere, to be presented with many facets of your life that have become commonplace, usual, boring perhaps, or just plain routine. Then begins the fun process – Cycle 11's exciting time dedicated to helping you live 'outside of the box' – by breaking a few of the rules you've imposed on yourself of late (especially during Cycle 10 when you were up against all sorts of barriers, blocks and barricades). If energy is stuck, it's time to find a new, more dynamic way ahead. This is where it all starts for you:

Where you get to design your future. It's your time to think about:

WHERE you want to be (by this time next year perhaps?),
WHO you want to be,
WHAT you want to try, and
WHY it's time to shake things up.

You get to taste it all, first in your mind, by designing how it's all going to look, taste, smell, and feel.

Who the hell made any progress in society by doing what everyone else did? Booooooring! Cycle 11 doesn't want that for you. If everyone else is doing it, it's probably a sign you won't want to, during this time. You find yourself by standing apart.

Ask yourself: Are you letting yourself be unique? Are you a one-of-a-kind? Does your dress style (or lack thereof) reflect your total refusal to follow the crowd or have you become another media success – a corporate clone who looks, talks, acts and likes what everyone else has also been programmed to like (and buy). Or are you rebelling so much, that you're falling victim to dressing and acting like one of society's subcultures, with its own locked-in dress codes? Another prison. Oh dear.

Too much time spent in the other 11 Cycles has led you here. And in good timing too. Your life was just about to become pretty embarrassingly 'commonplace' or yet a parody of true individuality. Okay, maybe that's a bit harsh, but chances are you could do with having your cage rattled and your life shaken up a bit in some healthy and fun ways.

This is your Universal Wake Up Call!

ELECTRIFIED WITH ECCENTRICITY
How does Cycle 11 zap you out of any potential rut you were just about to furnish by denying yourself true freedom for the sake of 'security and comfort'?

Surprises!

That's what this phase is all about. Things that take you by surprise. 180 degree direction shifts. Sudden news. Events with no precedence. Change. Get used to it. It's how life gets you to sit up and take notice and laugh at how wild things can be by being turned upside down. Packing up and shipping off to New

Zealand (who cares if you haven't secured a job or home yet) would be a sign you're in the throes of your Cycle 11 vibe. It's the Cycle when you wake up to your true sexuality and stop conforming for the sake of social acceptance. Or you stop drinking coffee. Or sign onto a band. Or give up all social groups. Or join new ones. You quit a job (or get cast out from a company or position that no longer is available or working for you). Or decide it's time to stop doing This and start doing That. What's out is 'in'. What's odd is normal. What's bizarre is *so* attractive.

Basically, it's not about right or wrong – there are no rules except the rule that you must live free or die. Totally 100% pure individuality. In other words 'being yourself'. Someone comes out the closet. Someone shocks everyone by running naked down the road. Or chaining themselves to a tree in protest over the new road being built that would destroy the locally owned businesses – and is arrested (or appears on TV or a *Youtube* video clip online). Is it you? Who cares – as long as you're spotting the trend that life right now is about *throwing caution to the wind and risking rejection* by one of the most important people in your life – Humanity! Okay, it's a group of people but still it's a relationship between you and 'them'.

And this Cycle brings you into contact with a lot of oddballs that make up society. And you get to choose just which team you're a part of – or if you want to be a gang of One.

Don't think it has to be drastic stuff in Cycle 11. You could just decide you're done with a certain job since it leaves no room for growth. Who wants a title in a position they find truly boring? Maybe you decide you'll become vegetarian – or begin eating meat again. You name it, it's up for review right here, right now.

Now change is not usually a comfortable thing for most humans (we're creatures of habit). So when a friendship suddenly changes or someone ups and leaves your life or your job is turned upside down and suddenly you have to move, we see it as less of an opportunity and adventure and more of an upset. How could this happen? What is the meaning of this? What did I do wrong? Now what?

Try to see all surprises, reversals and changes in this Cycle of all the Cycles, as Perfect. They are each designed to give you the jolt you need to get you out of something stale. If it's a big shock and shift, it's in direct proportion to how much you needed re-awakening. How much you needed jump-starting to bring yourself back to yourself again. Small changes are reflecting the small nudges you need. Major electrifying shocks to the system are again just reflecting how much you may have got a little lost.

When you get that cold-water-in-the-face you know you're in the throes of 11-Cycle changes. And if you work with them you'll find that they become the most rejuvenating periods of your life, even if it feels like a lot of holy hell was flying around you and you'd never feel comfy again.

Change gets us to the new place we already exist in. We get stuck in the past and the comfortable and the habitual. We forget that we've changed. We look to old things to feed the new person we have become. Cycle 11 resets everything and allows us to catch up with ourselves. Wherever you're not free you'll discover it now and be able to make changes to rectify it.

SOCIAL SHOCKS

Some of the most important people you'll come across now are friends – old ones, new ones, the ones you fell out with, the ones you lost touch with (expect to stumble across one online, in the supermarket or while travelling, or bump into them in weird corners of the cosmos) and also strangers who are just potential friends-in-the-making. Everyone is a brother or sister now so keep an open mind and open arms; you'll need these to welcome and greet all the faces that pass your way.

Hermits take note – hiding is hard during this Cycle, unless you're hiding away in a laboratory or inventing the next amazing discovery. Life wants you to at least be open to socializing, to build a group of people who can aid you in the furthering of your Dream – the one you're conjuring up during Cycle 11 with your thoughts and the dialogues you have with others or even the things you mull over in your mind. Why bother hiding just yet? (There's plenty of time for that in the solitude and sequestering away you'll be seeking in Cycle 12 coming up next.)

Right now you need to see the world, the world needs to see you.

You'll be aided in this quest by at least one Aquarius person who'll show you the ropes but with no strings attached! You'll see firsthand what it means to be zany, wild and unpredictable, and just how important friends are in the grand scheme of your life on Earth. And how erratic energy can cause more trouble if it's not grounded in something useful to everyone.

The networks you make have a strong effect on you now, and the social web we all live in is affected for better or worse by who you team up with and what you do together. So do keep an eye out for the Aquarians (and other free spirits that pass your way), you're sure to want to ride with them for a time. They won't stick around forever, or if they do you'll see them every now and then when your life could use shaking up once more with a bit of liberty and a major breathe of fresh air.

People who make up 'society' at large factor in now – so you may find yourself a politician of sorts when you look around and say "why is the world being polluted by … annoying people /rudeness/corrupt politicians?" (When has it never?). Why is there a lack of recycling bins in your street? So fill in the gap. Changing yourself, your life, your community and what you offer the world is number one on your list.

Don't be surprised if some friendships don't last past this Cycle. Some people will fall by the wayside when you realize that the friendship has changed. Its terms and conditions and its needs and meaning in your life has become outdated. Maybe you're not letting your friends be themselves. Maybe they are hampering your free-spiritedness. It can be the saddest thing when close companions have to be released. Cycle 11 will help you unhook your claws from anyone you've become too attached to or too dependent on and anyone who is trying to control, define or use you.

True liberation is the name of the game. Anyone who can appreciate you for who you are will stick around. Anyone who has defined you, has limited you (or you've let them), won't. And you'll find the agreement, the contract, the relationship and friendship, will begin to show signs of loosening, dissolving or at the very least, changing to be re-formulated to work better for both of you. And if there can be no agreement you will part ways so that you get what you came into this Cycle/Initiation for – freedom to be You, without apology.

DESIGN YOUR DESTINY

Looking to the future becomes a major theme at this point in time – perhaps you're wondering where you should venture now (take your career to a new place or make more effort or move on to something else perhaps?) Whether you're set for a pay-rise or not, what new things would you like to tick off your life list and where will you be in a week, month, year from now? Perhaps you're just curious whether all the effort of last month is going to pay off?

Brainstorming is easy in 11-Cycles, fresh information pours in and you'll be surprised by the ideas and answers you get – they won't be anything like the ones you've come up with (or been given) before. Make sure you give yourself enough space and free time (at least mentally) to download some of these amazingly inspired ideas. Or to adjust to the sudden news that life is set to change completely in the days and weeks ahead. The possibilities you embrace and entertain now could just land you a Nobel Prize, or at the minimum sustain you with new hopes and dreams during the next annual Cycle.

Having a Vision becomes *essential*. Like-minded souls come into focus or friendships that aren't right for you begin to fade from view. You may reconnect with old friends or make some entirely new ones. Stoke the ones you have that warm you, guide you and nurture you, and do get out and socialize – it's worth getting out of your comfort zones to mix it up as much as possible – who knows who you could meet?

The people who can help make your Dream a reality, *are out there right now*. It's just a matter of connecting with them. That makes it a little easier and a lot more exciting. Can you believe that's possible now?

Put passion on the backburner, and don't be so touchy about everything. Detach – get some air and breathe, become more objective and scientific and rational about things. Perspective is everything. Chew on new notions. Exciting new horizons. Fresh approaches. Possibilities.

Breaking free of convention is perfect – I'm sure you've already seen or heard of some quirky new stories of rebels, inventions, scientific progress and some oddball stories that seem to inundate you during a Cycle 11 phase. Look around you. Something is in the air. The winds of change are blowing. Ignore them and a full scale hurricane will soon come in and shift your life for you. You can't avoid the inevitable.

The status quo gets a slap now – after all, how can we evolve unless we leave 'tradition' behind?

Some will try and keep you in your prison/box, others will do anything to help you free yourself and rebel.

CYCLE 11 PRIORITY NUMBER ONE: YOUR VISION BOARD

Grab some paper or open up a blank document on your computer. Don't wait, do it now. Write a quick list of all the things you want to experience, want to have, want to create and want to be this year and especially *by this time next year*. And the people you'd like to experience. And the situations. And the feelings.

Keep that somewhere safe. It's a tool you'll need again during this year. Why not print it out and keep it in this book as a bookmark. Just keep it somewhere you can retrieve it again.

This is a hugely important facet of your 11 Cycle. Before you moan and groan that you've heard this all before, or that you don't have the time to do this, humor me. It is the foundation of this entire book. Whether you choose to or not, you're already dreaming up your new goals right now.

> **Throughout your 11-Cycle periods of your annual journeys,**
> **life collects the frequency you send out,**
> **ready to beam it all back to you**
> **throughout the entire year.**

If you commit to chaotic and mixed messages, you'll wind up stumbling over creating for the year ahead. You can still make it, but it'll be trickier.

If you use Cycle 11 to get crystal clear about what you want in the year ahead, it'll beam it back to you with laser precision.

So it's worth the time you invest in this.

It's not just about putting it down on paper, (though this will give you something to refer to when you feel lost at certain periods through the year ahead), it's about the feelings and thoughts you're choosing, and the things you dwell on, that form the basis of the electrical connection you make with the 'You Right Now' and 'Your Future Self'.

Just think, in a parallel universe, there's a 'You' who is already at the place you want to be. They have what you want. They are enjoying the life you want to enjoy. You simply have to download the pieces of that energy program.

It all starts here, right where you are.

PHOTO ALBUMS, VISION BOARDS, MANIFESTATION MUGS

Search online for pictures of things that represent the places you want to be, the things you want to own, the relationships you'd like, the friends you'd love to know, the clothes you want to wear, the jobs you want to accomplish, the challenges you want to overcome.

Buy an empty picture frame and fill it with these images and hang it somewhere that you'll see it every day. By your computer. On the wall by your door. At the office. In your car. In your wallet (on a small card, perhaps).

Create a scrapbook you aim to review every morning and night.

Some coffee shops now offer mugs that contain an empty sleeve inside, which you can use to create your own photo collage. Another great idea.

Just find a way to a) Seek out pictures of things you want to enjoy/be/have/experience in the following year, and b) Find a way to store these in an easy place to review regularly. Enjoy the process! Review it regularly. Feel it. See it. Enjoy it.

I saw a friend do this and it was amazing to look back at all the things that had come to fruition in his life. He didn't even realize until one day he looked at his mug (containing a sleeve of personally collected photos) and gasped. From items he wanted, to jobs he wanted to try, to places he wanted to visit. I have experienced that too, even down to a photo of a balcony with two chairs overlooking a beautiful view. It was my special breakfast spot. And I wound up in a place that you would swear was the exact same spot, a year or so after that manifestation board was created. I still have the photo and I took a picture of the view and chairs on that balcony with my phone to remind myself of what manifested for me.

Try it. You'll be amazed.

PLANETARY SIGNATURE: URANUS

In the planetary family, Uranus is the drive within us to be free to be fully ourselves. Use this force during this Cycle to uncover your unique way of doing things and special way of being that no one else can mimic. So often we compare ourselves to the images we see on TV or in magazines, and feel we're falling short of the mark. But there *is* no mark. There are only individuals. Being one now is the best way to use this Cycle. Uranus will aid you in this process by showing you where you may be stuck in a box so you can then set about breaking out of it. Any sudden shock event in your life is perfect:

it's another gift to help you to start over, or re-work things better for you. Welcome it. Change – no matter or how big or small – is your ally.

BE-FRIEND AND BE A FRIEND

That's right. Be a friend – to everyone. Brother and sisterhood is the key theme – if it's not good for everyone, forget it. Okay, so you may have to be a party of one if the group doesn't agree with you, but in general a unified consensus is something to shoot for first, and failing that, go off on your own. By all means destroy the mainstream's notions of what is 'right'. Do it *your* way, a new more progressive way, but don't go too far – you have to make it useful and helpful to the planet as a whole, (remember everything is connected, pollute your world and it affects everyone else) – or you're likely to be kicked back to square one.

BREAKING FREE

Detachment and distancing ourselves from our bad habits and attachment to the past will help us break away from the destructive behaviors that are holding us back. Now's the time to experience *true* freedom, when you turn your back on your own past and say "Thanks for the lessons, it's time to make headway and go conjure up a new reality to live in".

Anyone who tries to label you, force you to do their bidding, or try and mold you into something that makes *them* more comfortable, is sure to be rejected outright, when you find you can no longer toe the party line or play the game everyone else is playing or wants you to play. You have no choice now but to be authentic, and if that means deserting others or being deserted because you're being trapped, then so be it. Freedom is freedom, and it often does come with a price.

Which is more important to you, social acceptance or self-acceptance?

Expect a feeling to arise somewhere in your life that says you need to break out, break away and break free. Maybe your job is boring. Check. Maybe you achieved something you always wanted to and now you need a new goal to keep things interesting. Check. Maybe your relationship has become dull, commonplace and lacks a feeling of forward momentum. All stagnant areas are reflecting back to you that *you're not letting yourself live as free as you know you came here to be.* Check.

So accept and acknowledge this inner discomfort. It will serve you and give you the impetus and fuel you'll need to shift things. Sitting, complaining is no longer an option. Something isn't working and it needs a radical alteration. Boredom can be fixed by breaking away from the old and trying a new approach or direction.

Throw in some liberating new ideas. Do it differently. Take your relationship to a new place. Spend time with new friends or old friends and

9

away from your relationship. Perhaps open it up so you can see other people. Try going new places together. Try being more like friends and less romantic suction-cups to each other. Clinging to the familiar is not what Cycle 11 is about. Even if you have a solid contract or commitment with someone, you need to *update it*, under Cycle 11. Your last Initiation (Cycle 10) was about solid and serious rules, restrictions and obligations, but that commitment is now over and you need to give yourself fresh inspiration. Everything needs to be upgraded and you feel it.

Don't take it all too seriously though, and don't fight needlessly for something you could just walk around. Is it that important? Why rebel? Is it an inner need to prove your independence? If so, maybe you don't truly believe you're free already. Exercise your innate birthright to be free without having to proclaim it the world. Just being yourself is enough.

And enjoy the fresh air of this crazy, quirky, funny, topsy-turvy Cycle 11.

TECHNO-TIME: WEIRD AND WIRED
Whether you wind up rewiring your home for cable, installing a computer, getting a digital camera, fiddling around with wires and circuits or designing the latest gizmo (or just find bulbs pop around you and electrical items begin to act up), you'll notice an increasing urge to tap into technology (and perhaps in some years, a desire to run away from all the buzzing/humming/vibrating waves). Maybe it's electricity you hunger for (notice hours swallowed up now with online surfing), or that you can do a hell of a lot at such lightning-fast speed with a bit of technological wizardry. It's all about knowledge and instantaneous revelation too, so you'll love the new gadgets wheeled out for you under this Cycle.

Maybe you're a mad inventor yourself, preparing to market a most amazing discovery? Or website? Or an idea? Maybe you're just playing computer games till 4am.

Since you're so *wired* these days, notice that strange pattern with computers or watches or other electrical items (or bulbs) that act funny around you. Could it be a sign you're over-amped yourself and your nervous system is a little over-taxed?

Drink more water, try some soothing chamomile tea, and try and unplug yourself from the sockets from time to time. The universal grid is an energetic one, and you don't always need to be tapped into the actual electric one. A bath or shower is a good way to clear off all that static you've accumulated.

Look for more interaction on the internet, the super information highway. How can you not want to plug in when there's so much to be had, weird people to meet, and it's where it's all buzzing. Ideas are flowing and you can be truly you, with no one getting at you for it?! (The flip side of course is that you become detached and hide behind a screen faking your name so you can express your 'freedom' - but that's not what Cycle 11 is about; that's the weaker manifestation, so be aware when you're slipping into a fake version of your true path, this Cycle).

DON'T SKIMP - MAKE YOUR WISH!

Wherever you are, whatever you may be doing, take a moment to close your eyes, light a candle, take some quiet time (in whichever way you choose), and focus on *what you wish to manifest during the year ahead* (or even into next year). If you bypassed the earlier section on writing it down then do this now. Ideas that exist purely in the mind's eye are only the first step. Putting pen to paper seems to solidify ideas in our unconscious and forms a great daily reminder to stick on the refrigerator of what you're trying to accomplish this year so you're not sidetracked.

This is where all the magic starts, on a mental level, the blueprint-creating level, where you craft just the *Vision*, and let the rest of your year bring you the tools, energy, passion and people who can help build it.

In Cycle 11 we can touch our future selves and 'download' this information into the present. So some meditation, chill-out, zone-out, quiet time is essential. Take those headphones out of your ears for a moment.

Where do you want to be next week, next month, next year?

Ask for it now. If you're not sure, then ask for guidance. Or for a path that'll do the greatest good for yourself and others. Make your future, present. You're missing a major astrological trick if you sail through this period and don't give some thought to what you actually *do* want in your life in the next year. Whether you know it or not, you could be unwittingly creating your wish list by what you sit and complain about repetitively.

Cycle 11 is about listening to the signal you're broadcasting. Are you fixated on the past, on the habits you've become entrenched in, or are you thinking about where you want to be? Whatever you dwell upon seems to stick with you for a large portion of your Cycles ahead. So do what you can to make it worthwhile.

Start your Manifestation Board or Picture Frame if you haven't already (this is your last chance!) of the images of things you desire to own, experience or feel, and hang it somewhere you get to dwell upon each day. Try an internet search for photos. It's quick. In five minutes you could have a whole page of photos of things that excite you. It's not just theory. Remember my friend who did this and looked back in awe when he saw a yoga symbol (he became a yoga instructor that year). I still have my board and things are still finding their way to me.

Begin each morning with some form of prayer/ritual/wishing process. Act as though you already have the things you want, even if it feels weird. Get used to pretending you have it all (it's your practice for the real thing). Stop talking about what you don't want/like and start going on and on and on about the things you *do* like and want. Do you get a funny reaction to that? Let's repeat it:

Start going on and on and on about the things you DO like and DO want.

The future is really a myth – a great 'con' for those of us who aren't happy where we are in the present. Everything you say, do, think, desire, don't say, don't do and don't desire is forming your future – right this minute! You're literally pulling it all to you. Think about it – whatever is going on in your life *right now* (today, this week, this past month or year) is all because of thoughts entertained, choices made, actions taken and so forth, from a moment way back when.

Your present is creating what will soon become your future.

Of course on a higher level there is no such thing as past, present and future. Everything is happening right here, right now, but space creates the distance necessary to give the feeling of progress as we move from where we are towards that which we want. Such is the game of life. What we want is already here with us. We're just not seeing it because we're seemingly separated by the illusions of space and therefore time (the distance it takes to travel to what we want or for it to travel to us).

Tack six months onto your present date and write it in your diary:

In six months time the date will be:

———————————————————

Or if you're not near a pen, at least sit here and say it out loud or in your head. Work out the date six months into the future.

Okay, so six months from now – where will you be, what will you be doing, how much will you be earning? Will you be happy? Ecstatic? Full of joy or pissed off at yet another person or situation and yet another issue that pops up? Will you be stronger? More resilient in dealing with change? Will your relationship be even more amazing or will you decide to go solo? How about your job situation? Will you retire happily, cruise the world, take a job abroad or be promoted? Well why not start thinking about that as a *real* possibility.

Be greedy. Be real. Be honest. Be genuine.

Give yourself what you want *right now* in Cycle 11 – don't wait for it. And the universe may just conspire to bring you those things to match you, and the energy you're putting out, during the Cycles ahead. Own it inside, to finally have it on the outside.

Cycle 11 is your 'advance' – your spiritual bank account that has an infinite overdraft capability. Keep cashing in, and you'll receive the goods *somewhere* in one of the other Cycles – if you stick it out and keep the Dream alive whilst working on each of these Cycles in turn. A stronger financial situation? Stay tuned for Cycle 2 (though it may arrive sooner). A relationship? Keep your eyes open at Cycle 7 (again, don't ditch those who appear earlier). The trick seems to be – if you don't receive it by its proper Cycle, and you receive it early, it's a practice run for bigger things *or* you're receiving an early gift as a thumbs-up. And if you don't receive it, it means there's something better coming along for you and you don't want to get bogged down with it at the moment. Or you're being so negative you're blocking the good stuff from finding you. You already know which it is. And you can always *change* it.

Reframing the picture of your life begins with a change of perspective.

ELECTRIFY YOUR EXISTENCE: EXPERIMENT WITH ECCENTRICITY

Celebrating your uniqueness. Look for people around you who have the audacity to show off their zany hair or crazy clothes; those who don't give a fig what others think of them. They all are showing up to remind you that it's *innovation time*, when you get to try on something new and truly be yourself, whoever that is (it's subject to change and experimentation under 11-Cycles). No one else can be you, even if they studied you for an entire lifetime. Only you get to play your own role this lifetime. Get with the program then – Your program!

Making wishes during Cycle 11 time (yes, as many as you want) is always guaranteed to shift energy in the direction of your desires with a view to manifesting something in line with them. Try it. This month, outline your future Vision, and bring it into the present. It's as simple as that.

> *Our goals define us,*
> *our hopes guide us*
> *and our dreams are our future selves finding us in the present.*

Align all three during this time of your year. Free yourself from whatever is currently going on. It's already old news! Whatever is manifest in the physical world, is old. Don't forget to keep creating your future by focusing on where you want to be.

Download a new dream, a new direction and a new desire. All it takes is the energy of attention.

It'll never fly,
if you don't try.

Dare to be different and dare to dream!

BOXED IN? BREAK OUT!

Cycle 11 presents you with an exciting time to commit to living 'outside of the box' – by breaking a few of the rules you've imposed on yourself of late. If energy is stuck, it's time to find a new, dynamic way ahead.

The easiest way to do this of course is to try a radically alternative approach. You've probably heard it said numerous times that the definition of insanity is doing the same thing over and over again and expecting a different result. Change your input to change your life's output. It works for computers; it works for your diet. It's simple. Your life, then, could do with a new approach, new people, new experiences, new clothes, new attitudes, new hopes, new goals, new vibrations, new feelings, new thoughts, new focuses, new directions, new dreams. Try an alternative option. If you don't know what that is, explore. Seek it out. Ask people. Look online. Be open.

If it's different, it's time to try it. How can you say it's 'not for you' unless you really try, so you know?

One thing that's fun this Cycle is calling up a friend (one who is open and free preferably) and asking them to go with you while you try on different clothes, hats and things you'd never normally wear. Who cares if you buy it, it's the experimenting that counts. Remember, you're shooting for a change of perspective now, and the best way to get that is to try looking in a new direction, from a new vantage point.

Brainstorming is easy in Cycle 11 –
life can't resist shoving fresh information under your nose.

AIR CYCLE 11

Since Air relates to the mind, communication and the flow of ideas, keep in mind that that freedom to move, discuss, theorize and share will help you enormously in feeling good during this Cycle and aiding your growth. Air needs to be wild, it needs to roam, to blow where it chooses. It can power huge generators like wind farms. It can turn into hurricanes, knock down trees or it can be used to blow gentle bubbles. In Cycle 11, air needs to find new direction. It does so by trying new things, going new places and blowing away from its usual course. Expect a weather change in your life, keep lines of communication open and listen to the winds of change through the whispers of others as well as your own intellect talking to you through innovative inventions, sudden hunches and nudges towards new possibilities.

GANGS AND GROUPS

Some years you may find yourself sitting in a yoga class surrounded by a group dedicated to the well-being of their mind, body and spirit. In some 11-years you may wind up fronting or being involved in a chess tournament or dance class, heading a cheerleading team, or marching for human or animal rights; while in other years you may find yourself stuck with a gang of deadbeats, marching with others who are fighting for some social cause. Or you feel socially isolated or undesiring of wanting to be part of *any* group – in which case your life and your Cycle 11 will be defined by the lack of a common group.

Or you may find that friendships have begun to change and you're left out of the loop and thinking about making new friends. Freedom, then, comes from being on your own, without anyone to enforce any rules upon you. Even a sense of social belonging can become too much of a structure for some of us during certain 11-Cycle phases. Whatever the case, your participation (voluntary, forced or withdrawn) marks the theme and therefore your experience of Cycle 11.

Invitations from friends (or strangers open to getting to know you) are sure to be forthcoming whether you choose to hide or accept them. Parties, social functions, events, cheesy-nibbles at a local art opening, a gallery exhibit, something going on at Town Hall, local church, school fair and so forth. How about a local concert? A dance class? Wherever groups of people hang out is where you're sure to find yourself pulled by someone or something during this Cycle.

Giving something back to the community is another way to look at the phase you now stand in. Whether it's helping to clean up or searching for ways and means to recycle your household rubbish instead of throwing it in the bin needlessly, or joining a local rally to bring attention to the plight of a certain section of your community (or a bunch of people on the other side of the planet who are suffering), or giving time to a charity to help the aged/ abandoned pets/sick children and so forth – working out what you could be doing to help out around this old Planet is a good way to spend part of your 11th Cycle time.

DRASTIC DEVIATIONS AND UNHELPFUL UNPREDICTABILITY
Shocks to the system are there for the asking, or in the making in Cycle 11. If you're stuck, you're dangerous. Simple as that. Everything can become a prison bar you want to twist, bend, or blow apart. This is when you become the rebel *without* a cause instead of with one, and cause trouble, create drama, fight people and turn your own life upside down because you're bored.

So change can become unhealthy when you keep jacking things in, cutting people off and abruptly shifting direction, because you feel you need to remain unfettered by any commitment or the entrapment of emotional connection. You can't be free if you don't have *some* limitations. Those with a lot of time on their hands never seem to get stuff done. Those with less free time use it wisely. That's a prime example. Your need for freedom could lead you to be reckless, and cause wreckage if you run roughshod over your life and those in it, in your bid to thrash around until you find some sanity.

15

So watch it; are you ditching things for the sake of 'progress' when you're not really intent on improving anything? Changes of scenery are great but you may just be replacing city names or people's names for new faces and places in order to continue the same dramas or run from things you haven't quite resolved. No one is out to get you, though you may not hear that this Cycle.

Those who are internally free give off a vibe. Those who aren't free fight most things externally so it is a very revealing time to see how free, unique and independent you really are, from even your own point of view.

CYCLE 11 ACTION PLAN
* Change something about your life – shake things up!
* Review your friendships – do they support you and your goals? Do you support them?
* Create your Vision List – the key to all other Cycles!
* Collect images of things you like. Program your reality.
* Go out on a limb. Take a risk. Break the pattern and mold.

In a dazzling year:
The prison bars explode and you're free. Better still, you didn't even have to tunnel out under the ground or hide in a laundry hamper to escape. You 'out' yourself as a weirdo and everyone loves it. You're the newest 'in' thing, but you don't really care what they say anyway. In fact, the more odd and truly independent you behave, the more other people seem to wake up and suddenly take notice of your existence. You turn them on by tuning out. Indifferent idiots from the past turn into fantastic friends. Strangers become people you wished you'd met months ago. And even those who still have a grudge against you can't deny that there's this 'thing' about you that just 'works'.

Whether it's the eclectic clothes, the new hairstyle, there's something wild and untamed about your aura. You're liberated. Your own person. You answer to no one but yourself and everyone embraces it. How can they not? You make changes in the community around you by refusing to accept the excuses that have been dished out for too long. You're a force of change, a catalyst to all who meet you. You're neither leader, nor follower. You treat others with fairness and equality and in return they give you the space to come and go as you please. Going north while all others are headed south is your way, and it's the right way and the only way as far as you're concerned.

New friends appear from nowhere who somehow know the right people to put you in touch with, to help you along your way. Your idea gains momentum and soon you find your Dream is fast becoming reality and in ways you couldn't have even conceived of. Life is alive. And so are you.

In a frazzling year:

Things explode around you. Your temper, your computer. Your friends have it in for you – that's if they even bother to call you back or *have* your back, during tough times. Fair weather friends indeed. Perhaps you're accused of not being there for someone who needs you. Either way, separations are common and rifts develop as someone changes or withdraws and becomes cold, logical and detached.

Pow! You're headed in one direction when life suddenly pushes you onto an entirely different path and all your best laid plans change in the blink of an eye. Your goals seem either too far away or too odd to ever get backing. How can you change the world when you can't even change what's not working in your own back yard? In down Cycles such as these, you're rebelling against ridiculous things like a new rule that says 'you can't take the shopping cart past the red line'. If it says Keep Out, you'll climb in.

Why? Who knows, maybe it's a secret death wish, or more likely you're so bored that you want to shock whoever is watching into realizing that you have nothing to lose and truly don't care who thinks what about you. It's interesting that you'd go to such lengths to prove how free you are. I wonder why..? Feeling a little 'unfree' are we? Very revealing. Some years you'll be exiled, thrown out, rejected, booed and laughed off stage or out of your own family, city, state or country. Maybe the space shuttle won't even take you. Earth is alien territory but that's nothing to how you feel even in your own life. Will the circus embrace you? If only you could juggle.

Cycle Lesson

Change is inevitable. The more we hold to having things a certain way, we risk stagnation, and we risk experiencing sudden shocks to our status quo in proportion to how much we need 'awakening'. Without change, we'd have no progress. No innovations. Individuality breeds creativity and variety. By not fitting in, some people have become some of the greatest thinkers, artists, performers and scientists. In all fields, those who stand apart, have brought us even closer together. By risking the rejection of the many, they ultimately serve the many. Our goals change in time. And as these shift, so do our social networks and connections, to reflect our new desires.

Celebrate differences and keep a focus on where you'd like to end up. Just don't be surprised at a few surprise detours along the way that make the trip even more amazing in the end.

Celebrity Spotlight

- ◎ The social networking website *Facebook* was launched on February 4, 2004 under Aquarius and Cycle 11.
- ◎ The light bulb was patented in the US on January 27, 1880, also under Aquarius and Cycle 11.

Tips to Navigating your Cycle 11 Liberation:

- Connect with friends.
- Find a group in line with your goals.
- Dare to be different.
- Decide what you want to achieve in society.
- Focus on a new hope or dream.
- Congratulate yourself on successes to date and be prepared to move into more fertile fields.
- Go out on a limb and do something daring, innovative, unusual.
- Change one thing about society you feel should be changed.
- Accept it's time to shift gears.
- Surprise yourself!
- Get moving – life, as well as our body, needs circulation.
- Drum up a new brilliant idea.
- Refuse to be labeled, confined, repressed.
- Breathe more – oxygen is our life force.
- Be futuristic.
- Keep a clear mind – aligned solely with your goals.
- Give up caring what others think.
- Instead of reacting emotionally, stand back and detach for perspective.
- Enjoy the company of free spirits.
- Unleash your uniqueness.
- Unlock your inner freak.
- Prepare for a revolution.
- Join somewhere – be a 'member' for once.
- Hang out with the gang or posse.
- Wear something weird.
- Stand up for a cause you truly support.
- Expect surprises.
- Break a rule – is it really necessary?
- Shift your status quo.
- Say "So What?!"
- Electrify your existence with a brave, bold move ahead.
- Give others space to be themselves.
- Try something totally bizarre.
- Go your own way.
- Realize greatest leaps in life come when we go against the grain.

‿ Surf Cycle 12 ⁀

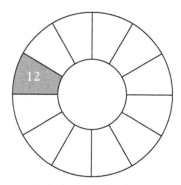

Time to Rest and Retreat, Rejuvenate and Recharge
Power Up at a Pit Stop
and Release Resistance

Cosmic Connections with:

Dreamers, actors and filmmakers
Creators and artists/magicians
Drinkers/bartenders/alcoholics and
    addicts
Self-help groups or members
Musicians and dancers, writers and
    poets
Energy vampires/fantasy-feeders
Nurses, healers and helpers
Escape artists or con artists
Victims/social outcasts/underdogs
Aunts/uncles
Psychics/astrologers/ Tarot
    card readers

Soup kitchen/shelter staff
Quantum physicists
Your local pharmacist
Pisces people/mystics or phonies
Divers/swimmers/surfers/boat folk
Therapists, psychiatrists and shrinks
Hospice/hospital staff
Charity workers/rescue teams
Photographers/dream interpreters
The confined/saints and sinners
Recluses, monks or meditators
People who sleep too much/
    not enough
People you have 'unfinished business'
    with

What you'll need:

A secret hideout
A fountain/flotation tank/jacuzzi
Music, incense and candlelight
A deck of Tarot cards or dream journal
A 'Do Not Disturb' sign

Inhale...

...and exhale...

Funny, how life can simply be condensed down to these two simple actions. It was author Paul Williams who said life is simply about emptying yourself ready to be filled again, and then emptying yourself once more. Like breathing. Without letting go of the in-breath, we can't take in new air. Without letting go, we shall die. And that's the theme of Cycle 12: to exhale, to let it all go – all the struggling and planning and trying – as we're asked to sigh, to experience the sensation of being empty... awaiting 'full-fill-ment', being filled full again, in Cycle 1, when new energy comes our way.

What is an exhalation phase like? You tell me – you're in it right now. I can do my best to sail you across its changing waters but Cycle 12 is kind of like surfing and swimming, not riding a bike. You have no pedals, no gears to shift neatly and systematically, nothing solid to support you – it's about flowing, a 'vibe', feeling your way ahead with only trust to guide you, faith to carry you through and the hope, belief or knowing that there is something bigger out there that has your best interests at heart.

For most, that's a tall order.

こうこう

Picture it – a river flowing to the sea. A man gets in too deep and struggles, thrashing around. He goes under, and can't stay afloat. He panics, kicks and screams and pulled down in the currents, drowns.

And then, that same man, upon giving up the thrashing around, his lifeless body rises to the top, to float downstream. Exactly what he was trying to do, wanting to do all along.

By giving up the struggle... he floats.

No, I'm not trying to depress you and convince you that you're drowning. You may feel it in some 12-Cycle years, it's true, but the idea here goes deeper. Water is a metaphor for emotions when it shows up in dreams (another theme we'll go into) and in our daily lives. Allowing the current to carry you is more important (and wiser now) than fighting against the tide. How many times have you heard during these Cycles that they are just that – Cycles! Your life will not stay as it is now – and it hasn't stayed the same – even if you've lived in the same place for twenty years in the same marriage or experiencing the same isolation. The world is never the same from moment to moment. All is in flux; all is part of a Cycle within a Cycle within greater cosmic Cycles.

Are you still exhaling? Good.

Letting go is a freaky thing for many, but it's a job you have to do, and do well, in Cycle 12. It doesn't mean letting it go all to pot and opting out. That's called quitting. Fine – quitting a job that's no good for you or an abusive relationship is a great thing but eventually you need some sort of direction, and then once again you trust the tides to move you closer to that new shore you'd rather be living on.

You've experienced Cycle 12 many times. Every year since birth in fact. Every year the Sun passes through your 12th house so you're no stranger to this phase. Even when you're not in your Cycle 12, you've experienced the feeling of Cycle 12 many times. When you're fired or lose a fantastic job and suddenly don't know how you'll pay your rent. Or when you hear a song that moves you to tears. Or when you're sitting in the cinema and the lights go down and you prepare to leave this world behind for a couple of hours. Or when you light a candle and sit in silence. It's a mystical feeling. Dreamy. You feel like you're floating. You may not always feel safe. But you're sort of insulated, maybe a little numb and things are just surreal and slightly muted.

Some of us have only experienced Cycle 12 feelings through alcohol or drugs that soften the edges and raise our emotional sensitivities.

We feel 'high'.

That feeling, that connectedness, that smoothing over of the sharp points of daily life is what we're reaching for this Cycle, and we'll find it by whatever means seems available to us at this time.

DARKNESS BEFORE THE DAWN

As the final stop around the astrological wheel (although only the 2nd part of our Dream incubation that we began in Cycle 11) Cycle 12 is like the 'clearing out the clutter' phase of your journey. Taking out the trash. Digging up the weeds that threaten to choke your newly planted wish seeds (that you just made in that previous and all-important 11-Cycle). If you've just joined us and didn't get a chance to enact your Cycle 11 Vision, don't worry, just stick with the material in this chapter and you'll help yourself along in the best possible way.

As far as 'wish-planting' goes you've just come from designing your wishes (whether you knew you were or not) and now they sit germinating in the darkness. Whether they were conscious (you sat and wrote down what you wanted) or by default (you were focused on things that weren't working), or you were designing your destiny by feeding energy into things that weren't as you wanted them... (what we focus on, grows) *seeds ARE growing in your life.* Cycle 12 is a strange time. We've planted seeds but what do we see? No shoot; no sprouts. No signs of life. For all intents and purposes they died before they began to grow or had a chance to.

Remember as a child when you planted your first seedling? You used to run back excitedly every day to check... and wondered if they were duds when you saw nothing. But things are happening, bubbling beneath the surface. Where it all matters. Where it all begins, like mushrooms growing in the darkness. So the fear of failure is often very strong now and it's completely natural. Your crop may fail. Something may be faulty. Maybe you didn't do enough or maybe you did something wrong or you could have done more.

Cycle 12 brings up life's 'what ifs' and 'maybes'.

But then, even during the darkest moments, when you sit wondering if anything is ever going to improve or work out in your favor ... one day you check and something is poking above the surface. Usually that comes for you in Cycle 1 (but you may be lucky enough to see it breaking through sometime during your current Cycle). You see signs of what you've planted beginning to sprout then, most often. (And you can decide if it's what you want to grow or not and you can change your patterns so that you'll grow something more in line with it what it is that you *do* want.)

Time is on your side.

For now, you're at that phase where you don't know, you're lost, confused, questioning, and at the mercy of the 'dark night of the soul'. Where all mystery and all potential lies. Everything and Nothing, all in one.

Maybe this year you'll see someone else going through this. By allowing them to, you help along the theme of releasing resistance (something you may be frustrated at their *not* doing).

We either play out the Cycles ourselves or others around us do it for us, often both.

WHAT LIES BENEATH
So, let's face this first off – 'stuff' is going to come up. Maybe it'll be through vomiting, maybe you'll be coughing up phlegm, maybe some tears are shed, maybe you'll be plagued with anxiety-ridden dreams where you're chased by your ex lover, a parent who's somehow your lover, a dreaded unpaid bill or some other monster that hasn't quite let up on you, still lurking in your subconscious. Cycle 12 is, as you'll see, a 'water Cycle' and is kind of like the other water Cycles in your year – Cycle 4 (your emotional past) and Cycle 8 (your emotional rebirth) – in that yes, it deals again with emotions. However, Cycle 12 is where we stash all those feelings we really don't want to deal with – we can't let go of them (Cycle 8) or leave them in the past (4). Or others around us can't. Maybe by holding onto us, they keep us chained to something we've already released (if we allow them).

Emotional repression is the Cycle 12's main target. The stuff you've tucked away inside your unconscious. And emotional transmutation is the goal. Resolving or relieving by simply accepting life 'as is'.

So what could possibly threaten to choke your wish seeds at this point? Anything, really. Fear is the biggie. It comes in many forms – worry, anxiety, stress, illness, feeling you're going crazy, panic, depression. Sometimes it manifests as addiction, as feelings of being powerless are given over to something that restores some sense of emotional harmony for the moment. but which ultimately creates the desire for yet more escape.

What a weird phase you're in. Words can't really do it justice. In this Cycle you could be witness to friends or strangers drowning themselves in drink or drugs (if you've managed to avoid that path yourself), old friends with unfinished business returning to ask for forgiveness, seek retribution (less likely, but possible) or to make amends for things they feel they, themselves, need to release. Your forgiveness may play a part in not only their release but also in your releasing the connection to this part of your past. Remember, what hasn't been freed up in your psyche and soul gets its chance now.

Maybe it's time to give yourself a break by seeking redemption for yourself?

Sometimes you may see others who refuse to let go of something, refuse to ask forgiveness or say sorry, and refuse to release something you did – maybe even you, yourself. The main thing to ask yourself now is: Have you released, have you forgiven and have you wrapped up one major theme, issue, situation, problem or chapter?

Get clear on this, to clear the way ahead.

PAST LIFE, PRESENT PATH?

Which leads us to the question of the soul, past lives, a history that spans before this current lifetime. Steven Forrest's *Yesterday's Sky* maps out our astrological soul's past in great detail for those interested in venturing into their spiritual history. Whether it's from childhood (who hasn't got some baggage from the family or from things that happened back then?) or from lifetimes ago, there is a strong possibility that something you repressed, ignored, denied or stuffed away into your 'forgetting box' deep in your soul where it's now 'safe', will pop open and leap out when you least expect it, or something will trigger you into revealing just what your sensitive spot is.

You thought you were over it? Think again.

Often, people appear now who pull you back to a specific period in your past. It could be anyone, but it takes you back to this whole business of *unfinished* business. Maybe they believe it's unfinished when it actually is (to you). Maybe you actually did clear it up. Really, they return to test you to see just how resolved you are.

Do you turn back or keep moving ahead? Are you really done or are you just claiming you are, lying to yourself or convincing yourself? Could the reappearance of a certain someone or situation be the signal that it's still active somewhere in you?

Buried treasure – that's the magic beneath all the layers of crap on your subconscious seabed. But what treasure was ever found without excavating, detonating a mountain, scratching through muck or a freak landslide that brought everything down? Your quest needn't be so Indian Jones-esque, but it will involve some form of 'emotional loosening' I'd call it – where you'll have to feel your way through what's happening or not happening, what's not working and what you think is really going on. (Though 'thinking' will only get you so far. In Cycle 12, it's all about feelings. You can't hide from them forever.)

All is not as is seems to appear during Cycle 12 and a major failure could be the great 'save' you had from something else. Don't roll your eyes – you have no way of knowing. Neither do I.

We can say that nothing great happens until you grope around in the darkness first – that goes for a newly sprouting seedling ... and a soul reaching for illumination.

> Our light is often marked by our darkness, or shadow.

FINDING THE FORGOTTEN

What have you forgotten, or claim to forget? What have you wanted to do but given up on, reluctantly? Who do you have something unresolved with? Which parts of yourself lay dormant and undeveloped? You'll find them in Cycle 12. Or they'll find you. It's always the same thing, when all chips are counted. So if you are suddenly faced with someone or something or some feeling from your past that rises out of nowhere, don't run. Face it. Feel it. The time has come to free yourself from something that has so far chained you, without your conscious awareness.

Are you repressing something? How can you know? Because you keep trying to come back to it, and don't even know it. Those repressing anger, somehow attract angry people. What we hide from (or hide from ourselves) seems to show up and finds us, time and time again. It's often what we unconsciously repress and thus need to consciously integrate into our personality.

We activate the Law of 'like attracts like' under Cycle 12, so you know what you have in your metaphorical basement (your psychic closet), because someone shows up in your life who wants to buy it, or engage you in it. Somehow they just *know* you have it. They've been magnetically drawn to you. Now you can turn them away and claim you really don't know what they're talking about, or you can say "Hmm, why did I draw this person in, what's in my psychic cellar, my celestial closet that could have attracted them?"

People sniff you out, in Cycle 12.

That's when you begin fishing around in all your personal junk to decipher what's going on and what you may have packed up and forgotten that you were carrying with you. Maybe you're still mad about something that happened to you? Maybe you feel guilt over something? You haven't forgiven someone for something? Or yourself? You pretend something doesn't bother you? You claim to have been healed when you're still hurting? Perhaps someone returns with something they feel that you left unresolved. Any object unreturned? An apology never offered? Seeking answers to these questions, probing your very depths, and rooting out your deepest issues and problems is where your true liberation now lies.

'Seek the truth and it shall set you free ...'

For some, that process comes through therapy. For others, it's a grief or loss or longing that opens the floodgates and blows the hinges off the padlock into the basement. A breakdown often precedes a break*through* and it's common for people to reach some sense of spirituality after a physical-world meltdown. Madness could be a first step in showing us there's something wrong. Something in our wiring goes 'off'. Our façade begins to crack. We may hit rock bottom and begin questioning. Deep emotional discontent shows us that something isn't working for us, that we may be off track with our real needs. Whatever it is, we suddenly become so open, so transparent, so fragile and so vulnerable.

That's the sign we're ready for a deeper initiation into Cycle 12.

RELEASE AND RELIEF

What do all of these experiences have in common – sneezing, getting drunk, sinking into the bath, getting lost in a sunset, dancing in the rain, running along waves lapping the sand, smoking pot, listening to an amazing piece of music, crying, laughing, sleeping, an orgasm, and sighing? They all contain a loss of the self, momentarily, a total surrender and submission to something – a moment, a feeling, an experience. You have to *be* during them, you can't control it. If you're to experience it fully, you just have to allow it.

So, Cycle 12 is about ***allowing***. Not accepting everything you think is crummy about life, human existence, your daily dramas, but just watching it all unfold and not feeding yet more emotional poop back into this time of your life. Judgment has no place in Cycle 12. Experiencing does. Deciding what you like/want/enjoy is the knowledge you take with you as you move into Cycle 1 (the Cycle all about Yourself). Cycle 12 is the rinse cycle on your washer, when all the dirt gets cleansed out. You can try and stop it but your clothes will be a heck of a lot nicer if you let it do its thing.

Does that mean you should stand by and watch yourself sinking down a black hole of emotional nothingness? Not really. There's a difference between allowing yourself to just *be* while sitting in a yoga position listening to music than from lying on a railway track waiting for impact. Could one be letting go and one be entitled 'quitting'? Maybe. Who am I to judge? One seems pretty damn final to me, and where would you get to enjoy your rebirth day (guaranteed ahead for you, scheduled specially during your Cycle 1!)? That's worth sticking around for; trust me. Nothing lasts forever. Nighttime always leads to daylight once more.

Cycle 12 is a lot like a suicide mission for the ego. Some of you may freak out when you read this but bear with me. Part of you basically wants so badly to return to that state when everything was connected, before the 'big bang' of life happened and you had to crawl out of a womb (or cave) and make something happen. Ouch! Imagine if a child looked around right after birth and said, "Oh wow! I came back?!" Maybe that's why babies cry during their first moments on the planet. Or are they tears of joy at a new chance to experience the physical world and all its tastes, sights, sounds and smells? It all depends on how you view life, the whole experience and what you hope to get out of it. If we stayed a child it'd be easy, right? Someone feeds you, clothes you, burps you instead of telling you to hold it in because it's 'rude'.

If you see life as a game or adventure, the fun is in the playing and living of it. Perspective is everything and it's this perception that creates your experience.

How are you viewing your life right now and how do you want to view it?

ISOLATION, FLOTATION AND COMPLETION

With such strikingly strong sensitivity, many people go 'off the radar' during Cycle 12. Vanishing is a great idea as long as you leave a phone number, a trail of breadcrumbs or tell someone where you're going (or at least that they can expect you back in time for supper).

Withdrawing from the hurly-burly seems inevitable at some point during Cycle 12. You can't be bothered with the noise of society, friends or even your own drama. You don't much care for mixing (unless it's another martini). You seek relief – from your own head, even. Many times you'll find you prefer being alone, or with someone you care about and not talking, or else relaxing and watching a stack of movies, or sticking headphones on while you're outside, ignoring the world.

That's what inspires some people to immerse themselves in certain 12th Cycle activities such as smoking pot, overdosing on sugar, playing computer games, watching movies, popping pills of any kind, having lots of sex, oversleeping and generally doing whatever they can to sink into a world of fantasy, emotion and soft-muted blurry relaxation.

You *need* to withdraw, to find a time out, to switch off, tune out. You're like a satellite dish tuning into the worlds beyond.

If it takes you away from here, your soul screams "Sign me up!" Remember though, whatever 'high' you seek, you'll have to experience and accept the 'low' coming down from it, especially if it's an unnaturally induced one.

I wound up on a submarine voyage in Cycle 12, and it wasn't until afterward that I realized the connection to the Cycle I was swimming through. It was beautiful. I felt I could live under the ocean all the time. Water, being submerged in it, paddling in it, drinking it or being soaked with it are all facets of the 12th you may discover yourself. I bought a gift certificate for a friend for a flotation tank experience, and didn't realize until later that they were going through their 12th Cycle.

Now, back in my own 12th Cycle, I wish I had bought one for myself (though it did rain a lot one Cycle 12 year which was awesome). And there have been numerous times when I felt drawn to taking a walk at the beach at night during this Cycle. Getting away from it all comes in many forms, and as water is the symbol of the collective unconscious, so too Cycle 12 may wind up plunging you in the deep end. From oceans, lakes and swimming pools to your bath or liquor cabinet or a '1000 oceans' of tears and love songs (listen to Tori Amos' single of this name for the ultimate in Cycle 12 messages), you're likely to take the plunge or get yourself wet somewhere, with a view to softening the edges of life and escaping.

If we don't accept or pursue this state of isolation, we may wind up facing confinement so that the initiation is experienced: prison, hospital, asylum, laid up in bed with the flu, anywhere and any way we are forced to take time out. Those who experience inspiration or transcendence usually experience this in a state of aloneness (meditation, yoga, the monk on the mountaintop). Many retreats are a form of isolation. By restricting yourself within certain boundaries you can connect to your oneness without distraction. Cycle 12 takes boundaries away, but often enforces them too if it will serve the same purpose – helping you to reconnect to your soul and see that all is connected – like being thrown in prison or landed in hospital. So for the best-case scenario now, pursue your peace.

As Joseph Campbell said,

"Follow Your Bliss."

How many great ideas have come to artists when they were taking a bath or going for a walk, or sleeping? Look up some great names such as Edgar Cayce (the Sleeping Prophet) or research how Einstein came up with his equations. (Interestingly enough they were both born under Pisces, the 12th sign of the zodiac and thus the ones whose lives represent the themes of this 12th Cycle). You'll swim upon at least one Pisces in the Cycle who'll show you the ins and outs of all this feeling business (when it gets too much and you risk becoming a victim or martyr, or when you can cash in on it by creating something really artistically awesome, or else compassionately helping out the underdog).

You'll find a consistent motif: switch off, zone out and you're suddenly tuned to a much higher level of intelligence and insight. Cosmic awareness. You're tapped in, and connected to everything.

With access to all you'll ever need.

PLANETARY SIGNATURE: NEPTUNE

Astrologically, Neptune corresponds to that energy within us that seeks to space out, tune out and tune into the voice within – that hunch, feeling, intuition or sense that gives us information above and beyond pure logic. Using the energy of Neptune will help you tap into the quiet you need to be still and surrender and trust that everything is working out for the best and as it should. Be careful, as with all planetary energies you have to watch for the flip side of each. Neptune can casts spells, cloud your vision, and lure you off the path with the promise of something enchanting, mystical, but utterly disappointing and illusionary.

Do what you can to find quiet time and down time, but keep your destination in mind. Another way ahead may present itself when you least expect it, when you're taking time to smell the roses. Then that voice inside becomes stronger and clearer and you'll know just what needs to be done, by what feels right.

MYSTICAL, MAGICAL – Turn Off, Tune Out, Tune In ...

If it's mystical, magical, fantasy-oriented and gives you that 'oooh' and 'aaah' feeling, you'll be drawn to it in this Cycle. Like fairy lights at Christmas time. Or fireworks lighting up the night sky; their explosions vibrating throughout your entire body. You need a soul-refreshment, a psychic pit stop. If you don't cash in now, you'll miss out for the rest of the year (and look for escapism in all the wrong places at all the wrong times), so use this month period as the time-out from all you've been doing, trying to be, striving for or hoping/wishing for.

Surely that soothes you; a pressure valve eases and your shoulders drop, right? That's because you're probably still trying to push ahead doing stuff when what you really should be doing is withdrawing, recuperating, and formulating new feelings (and processing old ones) based on where you'd like to go next. Letting your life catch up with you.

So rest. Relax. Take it easy. Go with the flow. Sigh a bit more. Drop your shoulders. Breathe ... Give yourself credit for all you've done. Be gentle. Let yourself feel sensitive. Go easy on yourself. Take a nap. Float on your feelings a while ...

Just 'be'. Whatever that means to you. (Stop thinking, analyzing, doing stuff etc.) Just allow your feelings, in all their myriad of changeable, kaleidoscopic glory. The full package in other words – and first you'll have to display that full package to yourself in private before you feel ready to expose it outwardly – as you will do in Cycle 1, next month.

What will you do with your time away? Many people fight the tide, twiddle their thumbs and feel as though life has forgotten them. They feel ignored, isolated, abandoned, worthless, overlooked. If you're a control freak, it's going to be tough – when the lands beneath your feet turn to quicksand and you're feeling emotionally out to sea. If you have any sense you'll create a little slice of downtime before life forces you into taking it, by landing you in bed, hospital, prison, or some other situation that separates you from the world.

Since most people find 'spiritual' moments of bliss in more generic ways, you could find this is the period when all your unhealthy addictions rise to the surface. Somehow, you feel nothing takes the edge off things quite like your favorite cocktail, stiff scotch, dry vodka, blended martini, or chocolate liqueur. Or a vat of ice-cream. Or the same feeling in a pill form, or something that pumps you up and helps you stay up all night cracked out and on a high. Or watching a hundred reruns of your favorite movie. Or sleeping eighteen hours a day. Or gorging yourself on fatty, sugary, oh-my-god-this-is-so-good junk food. Or chasing people's genitals. Addiction comes in many forms but the facts are the same – it's a replacement, an easy way out for wanting to lose yourself because there's too much of yourself – too much mental worry, physical fatigue, emotional pain etc. It means you're taking the physical dimension and all its illusions way too seriously or mistaking them for all there is!

If you can alleviate the stress sooner rather than later (by taking as much relaxation time as you can now) you won't be hungering for the ultimate escape or having to pay the price for coming down from that temporary high. Each escape or addiction is always followed by a crash as intense as the high you experienced. Without fail. Coming off is never as easy as getting on.

Take a break, switch off and tune out for a time. You deserve it.

CHARITY AND COMPASSION

Everybody hurts.

Thanks, R.E.M. The ones who hurt the most often try and hurt others. And that's when they need love and compassion the most. And that's often when we reject them the most. A never-ending Cycle of pain and recrimination. Compassion seeks to dissolve barriers, seeing the best and highest in everyone we meet. The potential that even they may reach a more evolved state of being, and if they don't, it's fine. Not everyone can do that alone. Some people need counselors, therapists, specialized individuals (astrologers fall into this category) or groups such as 12 step programs. (12 is the number of saving or suffering ... in that sometimes our personal pain is so great that nothing will fully heal and transform it – but seeing the universality of it, and thus seeking to help others with their pain in turn eases our own).

Remember the concept of trying to get away from ourselves because there's too much of ourselves? Sometimes the best way to alleviate the pain is to consciously turn the focus *away from ourselves* (instead of running away), deflecting it onto another, and helping them. Not to play the denial game, but to help another who is in pain or lost and thus gaining a momentary respite from the fullness of ourselves. Perspective. When we turn back to ourselves we often find that the problem or pain has magically lifted, resolved or healed all on its own. There's often nothing better or easier than helping another through what we have been, or are currently, going through. We understand, we empathize and we are well placed to alleviate suffering.

Often the ones who seek to help others the most, do so out of a knowing that they have too much of themselves or they can get lost in themselves too much. And by helping, they help themselves also in the process. To help ourselves, we just have to help another. Lifting the suffering of another aids our own recovery as long as it is done with pure intention and not as a way to run away from our own problems and seek to control others by 'fixing' what we personally perceive is wrong with them. Everyone is fine 'as is'.

SOUL SURVIVAL: SAVE OR SUFFER

So remember that this is the time when we ourselves may be forced to either save or suffer – save our sanity by releasing a fierce attachment to something or someone or some way of life or being, or suffer the eternal torment of being chained to something that isn't right for us (even a heavy, negative feeling). Perhaps we 'save' (or at least help, it has a less martyr-like ring to it) by starting a support group for people going through what we have or are going through ourselves. Healing then, is mutual. Or perhaps you'll visit rehab. Check in, or consciousness-wise, totally check *out*. But to hold the possibility of growth in someone affords us the same rights. Through your own pain and suffering, you can help another. Compassion comes when we learn what it feels like, and thus can relate to and understand others and their own journey.

If you were in their shoes right now you'd do the same thing. Why? Because you'd be them making the same choices. You disagree? Well you'll never know. Look at your life and you'll see you've made all the choices you've made because of you, your history, your feelings. Anyone else would have done the same in your shoes because they'd be you. I wonder, if we really did go back in time to relive feelings and emotions, what would be the chance of redoing the same things (because in that moment we'd be experiencing it

30

for the first time and thus act accordingly). That's more than this book can ponder. No doubt we'd do the same things in exactly the same way because it's how we felt at the time.

We can change the past, from what I have seen in astrology, by changing our relationship to it, and thus affecting our present state of mind and emotional nature. Thus we are free to live in the now, and not the 'then'.

When all is said and done, it doesn't matter. This is Cycle 12. Your closing chapter on a way of life. It's not about you anymore. Not in Cycle 12. It's about how we're all connected, how you're the same person as the guy walking across the road. You are all of us sharing the same air on the planet. We drink the same water (ultimately) and eat much the same food from the same earth. We are so close to each other, we pick up on each other's vibes. We all mourn together (September 11th, Princess Di's death, along with JFK's, and the Space Moon Landing, are all ways the world joined together and felt something). That's Cycle 12. We are no longer individual, we're not even cultural, but a bunch of 'I's who are part of one big I – beyond humanity, like cells in a human body, all necessary, all helping the whole and part of something greater. We're just all in this together and we *feel* it, it's no longer a nice idea or theory. It surpasses friendship. You feel the pain the other feels. You hurt them, you, yourself bleed.

This is the compassion so inevitably learned in Cycle 12, and if it's shut out, we end up pained within ourselves. The beauty of Cycle 12's gift is that no matter what happens you get to care for 'them' because *they are you*. Cycle 12 is when we really truly learn that what we put out comes back at us through our feelings. Everything offers us self-knowledge just as a tiny piece of skin holds our entire DNA or a piece of a leaf holds the blueprint for the entire tree. We know deep down that life is a game, that everything out there is mirroring us back to ourselves. This Game of Life is set up to show us that. Pain comes from believing we are disconnected and separate (and acting from this place). Once we re-connect with the whole, we feel our pain ease.

THE ART OF FALLING TO PISCES-PIECES
Pisces is the last sign and stage of the zodiac process and can help you understand this Cycle. Pisceans themselves swim through its waters on a daily basis. They understand. Nothing surprises them. Been there; done that. They'll remind you that in 12-Cycles, the more you hold on, the more you face crumbling and dissolving and it begins to hurt. The more you can go with the current flow and be compassionate (to yourself as well as everyone you meet), then the easier it will be. There's no need to pride yourself – pride being ego – on being someone who cares for others but who can't or who doesn't turn the same kindness back to the self. Also refrain from indulging destructive victims (or becoming one yourself) by no longer feeding the fire. Accepting,

without trying to force a solution is the best course of action this Cycle, and the less disturbing dissolution you'll face and the more spiritual peace you'll embrace and experience and enjoy.

In Cycle 12, the dissolving you experience is in direct proportion to how much you've let your false self or ego run the show (being too 'full of yourself', in other words too *full of the Self*) and bought into the physical world and its many temptations or illusions.

Do you remember Susan Boyle? She was launched to fame when she sang for *Britain's Got Talent*, shocking the judges and audiences alike that a 56-year-old of plain appearance would give such an outstanding performance. Her standing ovation led to such international media and internet attention that the pressure of fame and constant paparazzi presence in her life led to a meltdown – she was seen with cameras flashing inches from her face as she tried to shield herself, screaming, as she was passing through her own 12-Cycle. This led to much debate and compassion (a Cycle 12 theme) as the plight of a humble small-town woman revealed the lack of privacy inherent in today's celebrity-driven culture.

Cycle 12 demands that we find privacy and downtime.

It's a tricky time, when you're faced with swirling masses of confusing energy that threaten to consume you, dissolve all you knew about yourself and your life. The more you allow yourself to be carried, and to stay present through your feelings, the more magical the ride will turn out to be.

Every meltdown will show you something about your fears and your deepest emotional needs so embrace them. They're part and parcel of your annual voyage and have much to reveal to you.

I'M MELTING!

As things disassemble, disperse, dissolve and depart (take a look around at your life for real-time actual evidence of all of this); you get to detox to free yourself from things that lurk, people who drain, things that annoy, feelings and habits that corrupt, namely anything that doesn't really help you in your life. Gone. Bye bye! If it's not healthy and helpful for you, you'll likely go through these distinct phases:

* Denial of any problem in what you're doing (you're functioning, you can 'keep it together', it's not bothering you, "it's okay").

* A breakdown of things showing you there *is* a problem (work, health, relationship breakdowns ... signs that something is unstable/shifting/breaking down).

* Refusal or inability to release the cause of the problem (you seek to use the same methods of escape in order to run away from the

current situation, repetitive complaining, the same patterns show themselves or you deny it's causing you pain).

* An enforced release or further breakdown (you hit rock bottom, something or someone leaves you). Emotions erupt.

* Breaking away from it (you seek healing, you ask for help, you share your burden – rehab, group meetings, therapy ... you say goodbye to the cause of the problem).

* A final test to see if you're addicted still or really free (life becomes challenging and you're faced with the choice of 'checking out' as you did before ... an old pattern returns to test you).

* And finally, detox complete (you maintain 'sobriety'... you leave well enough alone, you know better, you no longer need/attract/fixate on the problem or reach for solutions that don't work). You have faith, trust and surrender.

It's hard to let go of anything, especially the things that aren't *really* that bad but which aren't that great either, such as unhappy relationships or dead end jobs. We can accommodate many things that aren't good for us (we're very adaptable creatures), except those we become comfortable handling ("better the devil you know that the devil you don't", as the saying goes).

Have you ever witnessed those animals who, after years of being confined in a small cage, are finally freed and can only step forward or backwards a few steps since they've become so used to that being their only range of movement? It's a really sad thing to witness. We're not unlike those same animals when faced with the possibility of being freed from our prisons. Many criminals re-offend just so they can return to prison because of the disorienting effect of being released from their 'safe' life, confined in a cell.

Cycle 12 helps us by not really removing things, so much as **dissolving our bonds or shackles to them**. We're not as bothered anymore or we're just too tired to deal with it all (or not feeling well enough to) or put up with it anymore and it has no choice but to fade away from importance in our life.

Look around you for evidence of this dissolving process. Someone leaves you. You're fired. Your relationship ends. A friend tells you they are moving away. You decide it's time to go. Someone splits. You find out you have a medical issue. Your dog runs away. It needn't be major, or even negative. Just notice areas of your life where things are wrapping up, completing, resolving, loosening, unraveling, and beginning to show signs that a new beginning is at hand. Because it is. Cycle 1 will show you this.

There's "beauty in the breakdown", sings Imogen Heap. As things wind down, there is a sort of sad beauty to it all. You don't feel the need to control it. Live and let live. Let it be. Somehow, everything is perfect as it is, in its current state of being. We just get to choose whether to interact with it or leave it alone.

PSYCHIC AND SPIRITUAL SUBTERFUGE

Expecting everything to be out in the open during this time is tricky. For starters, most stuff that's happening now is unconscious, behind the scenes, internal, beneath the ground, behind closed doors, secret, in private, and often even unbeknown to you. You're likely to be hiding things from others at this time or even yourself, escaping from the necessity of dealing with it.

Maybe you're just working on something that isn't yet ready to be revealed (a book perhaps, or a paper, project, or presentation). Most creations need that Cycle 12 period, when most work is going on away from prying eyes (in studios, in coffee shops, in dark rooms, back rooms, underground or away from the glare of the public or the press). Maybe you just need to keep it a secret while it brews. Cycle 11 is our brainstorming period when ideas whirl around, then we move into Cycle 12 when we put it all into the pot and see what becomes of it. Some of it won't pan out in Cycle 1, some of it may evaporate and yet some of it may congeal and start to form something solid. You'll see soon enough.

For you now get to have a 'feeling' about it. Don't so much seek results as instincts and hunches. We'll edit things by Cycle 1, but for now we see what starts to materialize from the swirling possibilities and we get a sense of a picture forming and which pieces will play their role and which are superfluous.

Expect then, when Cycle 1 hits (your next phase ahead), you'll get to deal with things in a more direct, frank, upfront manner. But you should get a sense now that something isn't settled, definite or certain. Maybe you're scared to 'out' yourself or tell someone the awful truth (in your perception). Maybe you don't realize how trapped you are within a certain thing (relationship, job, addiction etc). Often it takes being forcibly 'outed' by others (revealed, exposed, confronted, rejected) to help us see our way to clearing up stuff that's going on beneath our conscious awareness. (Interventions would fall under this Cycle for instance).

Running away is never a good idea, as it leaves things behind that someone has to clean up. And as you may know by now, you can never truly outrun yourself (after all when you slow down to catch your breath, there you still are).

So a root around in your unconscious basement, cellar, psyche, closet and cupboards may give you the answers you seek. What you can do right now is mostly just practice acceptance and allowance. Bringing it to light. Sharing with others. Being gentle. Helping. Looking after yourself as you would a newborn babe. Then in Cycle 1, you can act on new ways to fill the void of unleashing and the leaving behind of the things in Cycle 12 that were hindering you. If you don't work on this during 12-Cycles, things left hidden could lead to:

DESTROYING SELF-SABOTAGE

The things you forget, repress, deny or hide inevitably come back to trip you up, often when you least expect it (or at the worst possible time). 12-Cycles are great to show you where you're resisting the flow of life and hurting yourself in the process. Look at where your most intense negative emotion is and you'll find the place where you're holding on, pushing the flow, controlling or living in a state of fear.

Addiction seems to bubble out of control. All you may want to do is seek spiritual oblivion (through lots of sex, drugs, chocolate cake, sleep, TV). Usually an overabundance of something in order to blot out whatever your problem is.

If you seek a major release (you're craving that 'high') when you read this, it's a sign that you probably need a time-out to let things catch up with you. Maybe you've been trying too hard. Or worrying too much. You're beginning to get 'full of yourself' as we've discovered, and thus you're seeking ways to empty yourself.

Good. You're on track. By all means chase whatever rainbow you desire or crave but know that it's only an illusion and it won't bring permanent relief. Meditating, sleeping, resting, relaxing would serve you far better (and actually help you to release that resistance you've built up).

Unconscious monsters raise their multiple heads to trip us up or others see them and point them out to us. Something we do gets found out and we are faced with finally facing up to ourselves.

If you're exposed, be thankful. Life is reminding you of something you've been keeping hidden in the dark out of fear, shame, embarrassment or guilt. Why hide any facet of yourself unless you, yourself, have a judgment of it (and that can only attract someone who will reflect that self-judgment back at you)? If you were truly at peace with yourself, you'd attract only peace, or be untouched by others' energies towards you. Peace is peace. It can only trip you up when you are not living as a whole complete being. 12-Cycles remind you of the parts you'd rather ignore so that you can begin the journey back to self-acceptance.

Cycle 1 will ask you to stand in the light again and celebrate this process, so look forward to it. That process begins now. Most Cycles are really about preparation for the final revelation and result of your work *in the following Cycle(s)*. You'll have new clothes next Cycle but what you really want is a new sense of self, a new love for yourself and your Dream and a new confidence to pursue it, without the need to constantly self-check or look back over your shoulder at things you've been doing in secret or things you're doing that are harming you.

Cycle 12 reveals you in your full glory, warts and all, so befriend these undiscovered, undisclosed or unacknowledged parts of yourself and don't be afraid to 'out' yourself first, and revel in the glory of fully accepting yourself as a multi-talented and multi-dimensional being.

THE REAPPEARANCE OF REPRESSION

Whatever you stuff away into your unconscious always finds you in this Cycle. Like the horror movie characters that run from the monster (or shadow aspect of their psyche they are trying to avoid or deny), you wind up running straight back into it, time and time again. The bogeymen just don't seem to die. You can't hide. They find you. You can't move town. Somehow, they know your address even before you do. We're always connected to our repressions and they always magnetize back to us again, at some time. And usually that time is during Cycle 12.

Repressing something never works. It's a short-term fix. So you may feel it's karma that's haunting you. That you're being punished by some unseen hand for things you did before, to screw everything up just when (you thought) it was going so fabulously well. Don't kid yourself. The stuff in the shadows of our psyches runs the show mostly – those hidden areas of our lives, the deepest desires, the dark dwellings, the hidden, ignored, abandoned, repressed, forgotten, unwanted and denied parts of ourselves. The things we like to project onto other people and call them Monsters, Perverted, Evil or Bad.

Let's face it, we're all human and we all have access to the multidimensional facets of being human. Being happy. Sad. Depressed. Excited. Suicidal. Revengeful. Psychotic. Cold. Cruel. The list goes on. Those aspects of human nature you like to condemn, seem to somehow be rooted in you. Cycle 12 reveals often that the labels you put on others only reflect the issues you battle inside yourself. It's tricky to get a handle on sometimes, but the fact is that during 12-Cycles, what you repress will find you in the outside world by an outside agent – be it a person, obstacle, life event or feeling that will pull you back to facing it once and for all (in order to accept or acknowledge it, even if you don't fully understand it).

Turning and facing the shadow/monster/evil/addiction/problem in your life is the best way to defeat and overcome it. Watch any horror movie and the same formula reminds us of this. That's why this genre is so popular. You have to stop running and hiding to face your fear, head on. *Feel the Fear and Do it Anyway* is a popular book you may like to check out during this Cycle, as it gives you ways to embrace your fear and keep moving. Fear serves many purposes but mostly is connected to the possibility of *what might happen in the future*. You might die, but you may just live through it, and never be haunted again.

What an amazing time, then. Your denials won't be denied. The things you're stopping yourself from doing by blocking them will find you through the actions of others. If you catch yourself saying "How could you?!" then it's probably life reflecting back to you someone else who did what you have been priding yourself on *not* doing. You judge only what you are, or more accurately, what you don't want to allow yourself to be.

"Express yourself; don't repress yourself". Madonna is a 12th Cycle soul (her Sun is in the 12th house so she is continually working this 12th Cycle process). Her lyrics reflect the ultimate initiation for Cycle 12.

Notice the imagery Madonna uses in her work – sacrifice, good and bad, dark and light. Surrender. Release. Submission. If you express it, give it a voice, act it out (whether through therapy or through fantasy and imagination or guided creative visualization), you get to exorcise your inner demons and banish them to the light.

Things can only fester when they are kept hidden in the darkness of your psyche. Bring it all to conscious awareness. Cycle 1 will shine the light on it all, your job now in Cycle 12 is to let it all bubble up, ready for that time.

THE BEAUTY OF THE MYSTERY

Something else is going on behind the current events in your life. You probably won't ever get to see it, but you'll feel it and sense it in those quiet moments when you're not running from the caving-in that's going on, when you're insecure or nervous and sitting in the darkness wondering when you'll be airlifted to safety or when Mom is going to coddle you and make it all better.

Something sits in those quiet moments hinting at the possibility that it's 'all for a reason', that you can't see behind the scenes and what is being set up down the road. That whatever pain you're feeling is for a reason, and that it's all connected. You're part of a bigger story. Others are going through the exact same thing, however much they may hide it. Your journey is not just yours. It's all of ours. We know what it's like to feel and be where you are. Maybe not exactly the same, but the feelings behind it, we do. Or will do. We'll learn in time. And you can show us by sharing where you're at right now too.

Call it spirituality, call it coincidence or synchronicity, call it God, or the Universe or the Law of Attraction or Love, it's all tied up together. Something else is part of the story, part of the equation. The part science keeps getting stuck at.

You are a drop in a bigger ocean and what you're going through is part of your initiation training in Cycle 12, to ready yourself for a new life in Cycle 1. So don't get all bent out of shape about it.

ACCEPTANCE: ALL IS WELL

Just allowing works wonders now. Whatever comes your way, can you just accept it? A strange idea but one you'll come back to, no doubt, as perhaps your only solution during Cycle 12. After all what's your other option – to fight to resist it (Cycle 2), criticize it (Cycle 6), control it (Cycle 10)? That's all great stuff to do during the Earth Cycles, but Cycle 12 is a Water Cycle. You get further with feelings. You could try what you'd try during all of the other eleven Cycles but somehow it won't fit here. Nothing fits here. It all fits, yet nothing does. It makes sense, but it doesn't. So when something happens during Cycle 12, your magic wand is *to first totally accept it*. You don't have to like it, but you have to accept it, as the first step to moving on ahead and perhaps seeing a change in your circumstances surrounding it. Don't react. Just let it sit there for a bit. Sometimes you'll notice it all rights itself on its own, without your input or help. 'Being' more, and 'doing' less is the way to go. You'll see.

Treat Chapter 12 of your story as a chance for everything you set in motion before to catch up with you. You don't need to *do* anything, just sit and let all the molecules settle around you.

You may find in some years a total desire for illusion, glamour, anything that makes life shiny and glitzy. A beer or five. A pill. Sleep. Something to take that stressful edge off. We've said it before but it's important to remember this when you wonder whether you're losing your marbles.

If you're a movie star that's great (the glamour and illusion – not the losing your marbles, though just look at how many celebrities get caught up in glamour and wind up in rehab), but when you have a job in customer service and you're faced with yet another irritable member of the public, what then? You quite literally, 'check out' in a whole different way. Notice the best cashiers and public workers keep a light, breezy, detached energy around them, that takes nothing personally. They do the best they can, are polite and cheerful and let those who are miserable enjoy their right to be so. Allowing. Acceptance.

This acceptance (not taking things too personally – if you do, you're responding from your ego) may see others doing the same with you, and leaving you alone to figure things out; or they have so much on their own plate that they're just trying to let things be. Embrace this; it's all a great use of your 12-Cycle. Being left alone, abandoned, or rejected in Cycle 12 (or desiring to do this to others) may be the cosmos' way of stepping in to help you step outside of yourself. By being alone (all-one) with yourself. Sometimes there simply is no other way that works.

The chess pieces aren't so much moved as they are realigned, in preparation for a new game. Everything is about to reset back to a new default, and all faults cleansed, cleaned and cleared up.

If you let them.

Can you forgive yourself and others?

SWIMMING IN SYMBOLISM

Nothing is real in Cycle 12, and nothing is therefore set in stone. No matter what emotion is attached to it. It may feel real (that's the point) but it's all part of an elaborate illusion to help you play something out one last time, see if you can continue on despite not knowing stuff, or being in the dark and facing the shadows of fear and doubt. And, to give yourself a well-earned rest from all the other Cycles! Since when did we get *carte blanche* to schedule a vacation for ourselves and have the universe's approval? That time is now.

It all plays out this month from Cycles previous. Life catches up with you. That's why you can't catch your breath in some years and want to shut it all out. You need escape or rather to not act until you let the dust settle. Cycle 1 is about action, Cycle 12, where you're at now, is about incubation. You need to chill out. To let things happen. To accept all actions and outcomes. Call it karmic. Call it clearing house. Call it dissolving your attachment. Call it your payoff. Call it a moment when the light goes out, when you have to wing it on pure faith.

You have no evidence, no proof. You could be crazy, or high or just lost and confused. Fine. Be 'out of it', anything to keep yourself from plugging into the illusion of what is happening before your very eyes. It's a stage show, a magician's final act, a rabbit out of a hat and a smokescreen. Can you believe that? Don't. Don't believe any of it. Close your eyes and go inside. That's where the real truth is. Trust that. Follow what you *feel* and trust that as your guide, not on any other sense that may be faulty now.

I read a funny story in one of those silly glossy magazines while working on this chapter, and it described how one celebrity couldn't stand walking through the cheese aisle at the supermarket. She was pregnant and her senses were naturally heightened to such a degree that she couldn't bear all the nasty strong smells. Cycle 12 is like that. You start picking up a lot on things around you, especially things you can't see but that are hinted at, implied, sensed and felt.

Seeking out spiritual disciplines would help if you're feeling a little too lost. Signing up for a yoga class can remind you of the connection between body (Cycle 6) and Spirit (Cycle 12). Meditation, in whatever form, is also a great idea. Five minutes every day during Cycle 12 would be amazing. You can meditate (being mindful) whilst doing the dishes if you remain present and don't allow yourself to drift back to what happened last week or last year, or yesterday. (Notice how many times you've done that lately?) Sometimes just sitting, closing your eyes and dreaming is good enough for this Cycle.

Visualize. See how things could be. See how you could actually have things a little different/better/more suitable for your needs and desires. Play with this; see what happens when you unplug, step back, withdraw, tune out and tune into you.

I found myself getting back to my artwork at night, during this Cycle one year. I was completing a series of Tarot card drawings. The creative process was soothing, and I enjoyed the play of symbolism also. See what you can do to access that creative side of yourself again, where you get 'in the zone', and lose yourself for however long, just riding a cosmic wave of creativity. There's nothing better.

SERVICE WITHOUT A PRICE

Cycle 6 offers you the chance to perfect your skills, and get paid for it. Sometimes you may donate your time and energy to causes without anything in return, and that's more in line with Cycle 12. Here, you get to give with no thought of receiving, because you receive enough purely in the act of giving to another. Like the feeling of watching someone light up over a gift, or a hug or kind word that makes a stranger suddenly forget his or her troubles. Even if they don't smile or offer something up to make you feel acknowledged or good inside, you know you offered something to brighten or lighten someone's path for a moment and that knowledge is gift enough.

Intangibles, that's what this period is all about! The stuff you can't see, can't touch, can't smell, can only sense. You have no solid evidence that anything is really happening ... unless you follow the clues and signs that are laid out for you. Snatches of overheard conversations. A book dropping from a shelf. Something someone says as you turn on the TV. You're in one of the most synchronistic times (when things come together with deeper meaning, beyond coincidence). You always have been, but Cycle 12 removes the veil clouding your eyes, making it easier to see (if you can get your head out of the clouds of your own creation ... the doubt, fear, inner chatter etc).

That is why disengaging is the best way to get in the right gear. It affords you a moment to reset your antenna and begin tuning into something more important than the small problems and situations you may find yourself in during your lifetime's Cycle 12s.

Like a radio, you decide what signals you want to pick up, what you're focusing in on and tuning into. That's a major part of shifting your reality. Don't like it? Change the channel – or switch off altogether!

DISSOLVING ATTACHMENTS

Cycle 4 asks you to understand your past, celebrate it, and then release it and let go in your second water Cycle (Cycle 8). Cycle 12, the third and last water Cycle, is about dissolving attachments to all of it. Perhaps this is gained through forgiveness, perhaps through compassion; understanding that others are just doing the best they can in difficult circumstances. To err is human.

In the process of creating – weaving the Vision of Cycle 11 that then becomes the Dream of Cycle 12 (a dream because nothing yet is visible on which to hang our hopes, except faith in the darkness before the dawn) – one thing that is often forgotten is the process of letting go of attachment. The Law of Attraction talks of this as one important step to manifesting a desire, and here in the astrological Cycle it is Cycle 12 that specifically embraces it.

If everything is connected (see *The Divine Matrix* by Gregg Braden for some great information on this) then our Dream and Vision is already with us and only needs to find us on the slower physical plane. To let go shows faith and confidence that we are already and always connected to our Dream Vision. All we need to do is allow it unfold in its own time. Not our time. And time doesn't exist in Cycle 12.

MINUTES BEFORE DAWN

It may be dark. Let's accept that. You don't know the truth. Are you being lied to? Lying to yourself? Worried, anxious? Ready to give up? Confused? Lost? Drifting?

The darkest point has been reached. All fears surround you. Dawn approaches and in Cycle 1 (next up) you'll burst forth into the sun, but for now you have some quiet time in the dark. To mull things over. To get out the way of yourself. To let things gestate. You have no proof that anything will work out or be resolved. You have to take your hands off the steering wheel and have faith in a higher power (God, the universe, faith, magic, angels, whatever works for you). How else can you get through this period? Meditation, prayer, creative visualization, all these tools helps. Dream analysis, daydreaming up a better reality – all these things take pressure off the feeling of sinking into despondency that is so common in Cycle 12s.

UNDOING YOURSELF

If Cycle 6 – the polar opposite to this current 12th Cycle – is about fixing, improving and *doing* (actively seeking ways to make things better), then Cycle 12 is about the absolute acceptance of things 'as they are'. It's the time of *un-doing*. Of *not* doing. Unraveling (sometimes a scary thought), or untying the fierce knots we tie with our contradictory actions, thoughts, beliefs and desires.

At Cycle 12 we get to rinse off everything from the previous 11 Cycles. The rinse cycle on our astrological washer, as it were. When we rid ourselves *of* ourselves, of the soapy, muddy waters of the stuff we're carrying, amassed from so much activity. Now we just get to 'be'. Which means you may find during some 12-Cycles that your energy takes a dive, and you wind up sleeping a lot more, resting, taking it easy, indulging in movies, or crying a bit more, finding your sensitivity increasing, and looking back over things you had to let go of, things you lost, people who left you, and how life has left you where you currently stand. And there is a sort of aloneness in that. No one can truly be there with you now.

It's a moment between you, and the universe.

LOSING IT?

You may bear witness to someone 'losing it' in this Cycle, as we've mentioned. Their sanity. Their hold on reality. Their lives seem to come apart at the seams. The very fabric of their world is unhinged. Maybe they can't hold a job, maybe their bad habits are finally taking their toll and they're not making any sense. Maybe it's time for rehab – for yourself or another. Maybe you know that something is just seriously wrong in your life. Whatever the case, you'll see during 12-Cycles just how fragile 'reality' is (and how bendable) and just how much one person's idea of what constitutes reality is a far cry from someone else's. Are we harming ourselves? Or is it just harmless fun in the Grand Madness that is life on Planet Earth? We'll have to get clear where we're going, amidst the fog, if we're to avoid driving off the cliff edge.

Creating your own world and reality is nice, but gravity is inescapable.

Work out the difference between wishful thinking, creative visualization and the rules of the road in the physical dimension, to navigate safely through this magical yet precarious time of year.

THE MAGIC OF 12

12 serves as a completion point. It's technically the last house and sign of the zodiac wheel (although not the last Cycle by any means). Cycles run in circles and spirals.

As an astrologer I love the fact that I just so happened to be born on the 12th day of March and therefore under Pisces, the 12th Sign (and for the numerologists amongst you that was at 11.19pm – 1+1+1+9 = 12!).

Furthermore, the basic units of time (60 seconds, 60 minutes, 24 hours) can all perfectly divide by twelve.

12 is a magical number.

12 step programs are an interesting concept worth mentioning here, during Cycle 12. I'm no expert on them but I do know a number of close friends who passed through these programs and from my research they appear to hold a valid step-by-step method to break free from addictions of all sorts (drugs, alcohol, sex, love, TV, shopping, eating, gambling ... you name it there's a 12-step way to break it). Some people swear by them, others claim the group becomes the new addiction, an external support that can easily become the new 'crutch', blocking people from finding their own connection to their innate spiritual self.

Of course anything can become an addiction and I think that goes for any self-help program if it becomes a crutch. Everything is useful if it helps us reconnect with ourselves, but if that connection is only found through an agent or middle-man, the chances for a skewing of the truth becomes that much more possible.

So bear that in mind. I do recommend looking into the various methods of healing and recovery that are out there: Acupuncture, Therapy, Reiki Healing, Aromatherapy, Massage, Astrology, Tarot, Hypnosis, Psychotherapy, Hypnotherapy, Scream Therapy, Shamanic Journeys, Sweat Lodges, Energy and Body work (such as Rolfing), Counseling – research some online for yourself; there are so many out there.

12 STEP SOLUTIONS

12 steps make up the basis for improving our lives, it seems. Like the main chapters in this book, the 12 steps are for breaking free from any problem/addiction.

In our *astrological* 12th Step, we release, surrender, and connect to the very same Higher Power, whatever that may be for us. Prayer is one way to do that (it takes the pressure off us, and our egos). It's a form of asking for help, knowing we don't know everything and that we need some support. Others who have 'been there', can come forward then to assist us. But we need to be ready to move aside and let them. Again, another form of surrender. We don't have the right answer or even the methods that seem to work anymore.

Cycle 12 is a beautiful time for moving away from all the things that no longer work or serve us. We need spiritual answers for our physical real-world difficulties. It's the time we spiritually flow back to the great ocean of consciousness and connect to our soul once more. When everything is back in alignment – or rather *we* are back in alignment with everything, since it's always our alignment with it all that can be problematic – everything is fine. It always was fine, is right now, and always will be. Breathe that in, and trust it. That is Cycle 12 in action and all it takes is allowing that back in.

Can you let yourself flow?

The only viable solution to any dilemma or stressful situation is a spiritual one. Go back to your soul, your emotional center and whatever that power within you is, or whatever name you give it. That is the solution. Anything external to you, although helpful and an aid to your achieving inner connection once more (or tempting you to lose yourself further by using it as a crutch), is simply a means to an end. From a group meeting to antidepressants, from a slice of chocolate cake to a full-bodied orgasm. External seeking doesn't ultimately fulfil our inner need to feel whole, connected and complete.

In the darkness, in the silence, in the world inside, is the pathway. Through meditation, quiet, the release of emotions, acceptance, compassion, loss or solitude ... there are many roads Home. And all you need to do is find a moment to Listen.

CYCLE 12 ACTION PLAN
* Breathe. Flow. Relax. Drop your shoulders. Sign. Let go.
* Let life catch up with you. Resist less, flow more.
* Face the darkness – of doubt, fear, anxiety, not knowing.
* Use fantasy, creative visualization, avoid addictive escapism.
* Take a time out to take stock of things.
* Listen to your dreams. Meditate and see what your intuition says.
* Watch for synchronistic signs foreshadowing changes ahead.

In uplifting years:
You're on cruise control. Nothing bothers you. Anything can happen and you're a cosmic surfer, taking on any tide. Somehow it all seems perfect, no matter how bizarre things may be. You're chill, cool, Zen'd-out. Who says life needs to be any way in particular? Mistakes turn out to be glorious escape clauses (from things that would have been undesirable as it turns out, after all!) People triumph over the worst disaster because behind it all is the spirit that makes it all possible. Doors close on things that drained your energies; you begin to switch off to external distractions and move your focus inward to the peaceful vibe inside.

Whether you wind up composing (a song, novel, poem, collage), taking up art or swimming or just sitting and meditating, you'll find you'll pass endless hours that slip by in a matter of moments, as time stretches and you're lost in moments of ecstasy (the real kind, not the pill version). You feel connected to it all – everyone seems like a fragment of a bigger picture and it all makes sense and makes no sense at the same time, yet you understand. Your gut feeling is right – you can read people's minds, thoughts, and feelings. You could start a new advice hotline but at the same time you don't want to be inundated with people's problems 24/7. You're still hypersensitive but maybe this is part of your gift right now – being 100% aware, awake and in tune with the slightest variation in the air around you.

Somehow, you're inspired – you let go of the past and face a moment of darkness – where you have no real proof, no real answer to anything, you're left in the dark but it's a peaceful feeling and you're not lost, you're just without a map. Different thing. You're not aimless, you're happy right here, right where you are. Exactly where you should be.

In drifting years:

The tide pulls you and you're torn in different directions, but somehow still feeling as though you're being sucked down a whirlpool into the sewers, and you're flailing around half drunk, drugged up, or as though you just got up (reluctantly) from two hours sleep – the most you've had in weeks. Maybe that's because you are (drunk or drugged) or just totally out to lunch, but it doesn't make for an easy time of it when bills need paying and you actually have to show up for work sober and on the ball. You seem lethargic and what's the point of all the hard work anyway when things seem to be ending around you and nothing seems to be working out?

Some years you're totally lost. Others, you try your best and things dissolve, fall apart, break or just vanish. Keys, people you once knew, all that you hoped for or worked for. Poof! In a cloud of smoke. Crash and burn. Or just burnout. (Are you being prepared to be beamed up off the planet?) You wish that would solve all your problems, yet all you can think of doing is finding a way out of your head and body using any drug available to escape. Remember, this is just a Cycle, not your whole life. Don't judge the whole thing by one of its chapters (there are 11 other Cycles to go). Self-destructiveness may attract you at the time but then you have to clean up all the mess afterward. The drifting years are ones in which you get to take a time out so you can hit the bottom and then get back up when you've had enough wallowing in your own filth. So embrace the chaos. Whatever goes, let it. You don't need it. It probably was a real pain anyway, if you really look at it without those rose-colored glasses. Quit denying. Take a time out. Let things slide for a time. That's a great thing. Enjoy it. Wallow in it. Just don't give up just yet.

If you can stick around until Cycle 1 next month you'll see the sun again, but right now, the dark is at its deepest – there may seem no hope, no purpose and no point in *anything*.

But you'd be just seeing 1/12th of the bigger picture. Cycles change! Morning always arrives to follow night, gain always follows loss, life blossoms from death, so if you don't stick around and stay sober enough you may feel too groggy to make use of the great stuff coming. This venture into darkness is for a reason – to witness your own worst self, the one who sabotages the good stuff you had and have coming to you – so you can re-write the script by changing how you handle whatever comes your way. Now is the time to face the darkness and keep walking, even if there's no hope or faith you'll find a light switch.

For now, you may have worked it out already, that it's all your darkest repressed stuff bursting out, your biggest phobia, fear and worry.

And depending on how large your fears are, they will determine your experience in this Cycle, and how despairing you may feel or how dire it may seem to be. You have the ultimate control over that, in this, the most seemingly out-of-control phase you're likely to find yourself in, during the course of each annual voyage.

Hang in there!

Cycle Lesson

Releasing resistance plays a central role in every activity we currently engage in. In yoga, we tense and tighten the muscles in the body and at the end of every practice lie still in a posture called *Savasana*, a *resting period* where we let go. Some call it 'corpse pose'; a relaxing posture intended to rejuvenate body, mind and spirit and metaphysically a practice for the last resting position of our body when our spirits finally depart from their flesh and bone temples. Forgiveness, a major facet of Cycle 12, involves a letting go and allowing. Accepting how things are and letting go of how we wanted things to be. We live life 'as is'. Releasing judgment is also a central aspect of your current Cycle. Nothing is inherently 'good' or 'bad'. It just is. Release any labeling and know there's more going on than meets the eye, and what seems like a hinderer is actually a helper in disguise.

In life, energy is either moving or it is obstructed and blocked. That is when we begin to manifest disease (dis-ease, a lack of ease) in our lives, psyches and finally our bodies. Like congested traffic, things back up and soon we're enmeshed in even more stress. It's a 'Catch 22'. This Cycle reminds us that it's best to act like water, the element of this Cycle itself and the sign of Cycle 12 – Pisces, the Fish. Like the fish and the water it swims in, when we embrace the problem or obstacle and accept it, we can flow around and over it, or erode it with gentle and consistent patience and acceptance of our true nature. Everything changes through time. And even the hardest rock is worn down. Every obstacle will be lifted, eventually.

Just breathe.

Celebrity Spotlight

- ◉ Martha Stewart goes to jail for five months, for lying to investigators about a stock sale.
- ◉ Steven King spends 21 days in hospital after being hit by a car.
- ◉ Whitney Houston is found unconscious in her hotel bathtub (water symbolism) after taking medication (Neptune theme).

Tips to successfully navigating your Twelfth House Resolution

- ◉ Take time off – from whatever you've been obsessing over.
- ◉ Go swimming.
- ◉ Stretch and yawn.

- Turn off the phone and other electrical devices.
- Take the pressure off.
- Meditate, rest more, and catch up on some deep sleep.
- Stop resisting.
- Have a cocktail; unwind.
- Go to a meeting (if you're sober).
- Vigorously scratch your head to discharge static build-up.
- Start a dream diary.
- Begin journaling.
- Give up your secret addiction – for at least thirty days.
- Quit fighting what you don't like/want.
- Sit and gaze at the stars.
- Go for a walk by water.
- Buy a fountain.
- Light candles.
- Compose or listen to music.
- Write a screenplay, novel, poem.
- Dance.
- Cry and let it all out.
- Try yoga.
- Study reflexology or have a foot massage.
- Soak in a bubble bath or shower more often.
- Let it go, and go with the flow.
- Practice compassion when faced with others' troubles.
- Trust it'll all work out.
- Drink more water.
- String up fairy lights.
- Chill out at your local coffee shop.
- Know it's happening as its meant to.
- Let life catch up with you.
- Sleep on it.
- Prepare to wind down.
- Sigh often.
- Take up Kabbalah, Meditation, Buddhism, Zen.
- Listen to Pandora's Spa Station (pandora.com)
- Research your past lives (check out the Personal Reports at my website).

~ Surf Cycle 1 ~

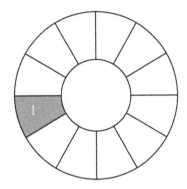

Time to Forge Ahead
Unveil your New, True Self
and Start Something New

Liberating Liaisons with:

Photographers/camera-operators
Cheerleaders/self-help gurus
Beauticians/makeover artists
Military personnel
The angry
Yoga instructors
Your brother or sister's friends
Personal promoters/PR reps
People who push/encourage/
    cajole you
Hairdressers/salon staff
Your grandma/granddad
Your friend's neighbor or sibling

Plastic surgeons/personal trainers
Aries types/aggressive people
People who look like or
remind you of you
Those who enhance your 'look'
The fashion conscious
Athletes/martial arts instructors
The self-employed
Psychologists
Friends of neighbors
Pioneers/entrepreneurs
Anger-management promoters and
    those in need of it

What you'll need:

An iron-clad ego
Chalk to draw some personal boundaries
Someone to interview you
A suit of armor and weapon of choice
Enough matches to light your fuse
An energy cocktail

Welcome to Cycle One. 'Numero Uno'. The actual *physical* beginning; when the curtains open on a brand new stage production of Your Life and a new series of potentials and possibilities.

Cue lights and:

Happy Re-Birth Day!

Yes, the first moment you enter this Cycle is your unofficial birthday or 'rebirth-day' as I like to call it. The day the Sun moves out of the secretive swamps of your 12th Cycle and into the very first Cycle of your new annual journey.

Here you get to focus on **yours truly** for a while – you, you, you, you and you! When you get to say *"Enough about me, what do YOU think of me?"* It's *all* about you. It's all about *you*. Which may sound great, but in Cycle 1 that becomes your number one hurdle and challenge – *you become your own conquest*.

It's so often daunting to locate yourself right now because after the last Cycle (the confusing Cycle 12) you often have lost track of yourself in the whirling emotions of what was leaving your life and you don't know who you are anymore because you've shed so much (or had to lose it reluctantly) and were so busy dodging your own bullets that you haven't stopped to think "what new things do I want to create now and who do I want to be?" Often you were so lost in stuff belonging to others that your identity began to slide.

That was then; this is now – The present moment. Now's the time. You can't put off this thing called Your Life, any longer.

FIRST IMPRESSIONS COUNT

This month, and this Cycle, is about how you see yourself and how people see you (the latter is less important, but you do want to create the right impression for what you want to achieve, right?); what you wear, what you do, how you act, how you *want* to act, how you want to be perceived by people (casting the right light, creating the right illusion/impression) and which new things you want to begin.

In short: How you want to recreate yourself and your world.

No small feat, but great things begin with a seed of an idea or, as Neil Armstrong would have said, "one small step". You've planted an idea in Cycle 11 (knowingly or unwittingly) and now it begins to grow towards the light. It's actually happening, and no longer just pure potential or a possibility (which it was, while it was germinating in the darkness of your 12th Cycle). This current Cycle is your burst of new energy like a shoot in spring. You've planted your seeds, sat and wondered if everything would fail or if you made a giant boo-boo in your choice, and now here you are when the sun is shining or just about to shine on a new possibility, a new life, and a brand spanking new You.

Who cares if it's winter outside and everyone else is huddled up around the fire in your corner of the world when this Cycle comes around? Who cares if no one else seems to have their act together, or know what's what? This month and this 1-Cycle is *your* springtime to leap into action, be first and foremost, noticed and heard – so get moving and stop dwelling on all the old things that never panned out or that you never got, last month or last year.

FACE FORWARD, SHOULDERS BACK, STEP OFF AND MOVE ON

So firstly – right here and right now as you read this (or at least by the end of today) – get over what happened last month. And last year. Do it. What's gone is gone (or should be) so stop talking about it, feeding it, trying to salvage it or bring it back to life. If it's meant to stay with you, it'll join you down the line, (and by then you may not want or need it). And you may be better equipped to handle it, if you want it. Right now though, it's important you stay on course and fulfill your duty in Cycle 1, to the person you'll have to truck around with for the rest of your life: **You.**

Trust me, *the rest can wait for now ... this is important.*

It's time to move on into your new chapter. Yes it's scary but yes it's also exciting when you stop to think that only great things happen with a risky bounding into the unknown, a leap of faith, and a change of direction or outlook.

Let's look at that – are you playing old stories and replaying old tales about yourself and your life? (If not, a medal to you, seriously). It's so easy to replay old tales, and get caught up listening to the same old story from the people around you. For example, do you remind everyone in earshot that you're 'this way' because of what happened when you were five? Or perhaps that your physical scar is from that fight when this guy did this thing to you? And what a tale it is too. Worth telling, right? But how many times have you told it already? Or made excuses that you're so impatient and that's that. It's 'how you are and it won't change, so get over it'?

Well, that's no longer true. It's time, whether you know it or not, like it or not (you know you do, secretly) to turn a page and go somewhere new, to change the story and the script and write new parts for yourself and **pit yourself against yourself**, to compete, to start a new record for yourself – if only, I repeat *if only* – so you'll have more pictures to add to your online profile and more things to look back on and say "wow I was pretty wild; that's awesome!"

Your past is being re-written here today. Your life is far from over. And to move ahead now in your annual game, it's time to take risks, and try something totally new.

From here on in, it all changes.

ALONE = ALL FOR ONE

Take a look around you now and chances are you've already started noticing one of two things:

... people leaving you alone by not calling back, not being available, not being helpful, breaking up with you, not in town, not well, not as reachable as before...

or ...

... people hounding you, life bombarding you with new possibilities, old questions and quandaries, people who can't stop chasing you or asking for something from you, forcing you to break up with them, separate, scream and reject them in some way in your bid to *find some space to be on your own to figure things out.*

Both are two sides of the same coin that push you to do one thing: decide what *you* want and urge you to take control of where you're steering your life. You may have to confront some people on why they are no longer as available to you as they used to be (if they're a good friend, or someone you care deeply about, for example) but you'd still do well to enjoy and welcome a break and a change to get back to yourself for a while; at least for a good portion of this Cycle. No matter what others are doing, you'll no doubt get the same end result: time alone to focus purely and simply on yourself, to get your act together. Yes this is a prime month in your annual journey to get a handle on this thing called 'You' which pretty much runs your life.

Who the hell *are* you?!

You're on your own now, to figure that out.

Perfect. Embrace the aloneness. It's when you're by yourself that you get to untangle from all the old ways and from old people. When you're **alone**, you're '**ALL ONE**'. Whole. Complete. You can now disengage from the old stories, the old people and places and the same old stuff/stories/scenarios/situations. And you get to change how *you* are, and how you want your life to be run, without your familiar crew and clan complaining about it because it upsets them that you're growing and evolving. Sometimes our nearest and dearest don't like that, it scares them that they'll get stuck where they are, without you. Gasp!

If you can, be conscious now and try to avoid creating scenes just to get your way because you're so out of sync with your Cycle 1 that you feel hemmed in and not dominating enough space. Slowly goes it. Number 1 Cycles are notoriously laden with arguments from people screaming "Back off!" to those who are coming a little too close and thus, fencing them in, manipulating or controlling them or not giving them enough space to be themselves. If you're beginning to feel this, do yourself a favor and *tell them you need time to yourself*, and go off and do something, or turn off your phone and go shopping for new clothes or just to catch up with some movies at home, alone. At least, stop feeding the old image of yourself and allowing others to indulge the old you. Help them break free by breaking free yourself.

In this Cycle, it always, always comes down to you, *what* you want, and *how* you want to be.

KNOW THYSELF

Everyone going through a 1-Cycle becomes a 'force' – some end up confused, unsure what it is they 'should' be doing. Some get muddled and mixed up as to who they are, now that some sort of change has been thrust upon them or consciously chosen. Others vanish from the radar, disappear from the usual places, and start re-styling themselves. You may fall into any of these categories depending on what sort of year you're having.

It's scary to be asked "who are you?" in a world teeming with images of others' creation (haircuts of the rich and famous, styles on the red carpet, TV fashion and media 'looks', 'what's hot and what's not'). In today's modern world, it's hard to know how *you* want to be or what you want to *try*.

Maybe that's the best place to start then, in your Cycle 1, by *trying* something new. Trial and error. Nothing ventured, nothing gained. A new pair of shoes, perhaps in a color you'd never normally wear. Try visiting a few new stores and browsing styles that you'd never have been seen dead in before. Do you like the clothes in your wardrobe? If not, what color is 'you' now? Ditch the old; bring in the new. Never wear hats normally? How about it? Shades during the night? More casual clothes, or how about switching it to business-style if you're always dressed down? Revamp, renew, refresh. These are your keywords.

There are plenty of options and plenty of new things to try, in Cycle 1. All it takes is the willingness to begin a quest and a journey to see what's out there. Want to go ballooning? Look it up online. Fencing? Find a local class. How about signing up for a new physical program – kickboxing, squash, pilates, running, rowing, cycling?

Basically, have a look around at what is out there under a number of different headings: Physical Fitness, Clothing Styles, Hairstyles, Local Events, Places to Go, New Places to Eat, New Parts of Town etc.

Maybe you'll figure out who you are this Cycle by firstly seeing who you're *not*. I call it the **Pinball Approach** and it's the way many of us actually live our lives. We say "that's not me", "I don't want that", until finally one day we realize we were taught and trained via these very same experiences (bumping into things we don't care for), to uncover what we *do* want and who we *really* are. To accomplish this in Cycle 1, know that you'll have to play the numbers game, butt a few heads or walls and have a few fights or friction-inducing situations that inspire you to stand up and say "*This* is me – either accept it or move on. Thank you and Goodnight!"

At least you'll know. You may feel a bit bruised, but bruises heal and you'll have stronger and thicker skin for it. And a stronger sense of self – the ultimate, eternal gift of a Cycle 1 well spent. But you can't do all of this by sitting repeating the same stuff from the previous Cycles, which is where *space, time and freedom* come in – to liberate you, in order that the potential growth of this phase isn't missed.

Use this Cycle before it uses you.

DUST OFF YOUR CYCLE 11 VISION

If you're coming to this chapter having already read Cycle 11, you should have your Vision List already completed. Wherever you left it (on your hard drive, on a piece of paper somewhere, in a desk drawer, hidden beneath a pile of clothes ... wherever) dig it out and read over it once more. It's time to *bring your Cycle 11 Visions and ideas to Cycle-1 awareness*. Remind yourself of what you wanted back then. See if it matches with what you want now.

For some of your Vision seeds, you may find you need to add something to tweak them to be more direct, more specific, more 'you'. For example, the Vision List sentence "I'm enjoying my well-paid job enormously" now becomes "I'm enjoying my well-paid job enormously along with the traveling, and paid vacations I get to take". Simple but succinct. Some Visions you listed may not seem to pull you or interest you in the same way they did when you first wrote them. Fine. Don't scrap them just yet, see if you can re-envision them, and craft them to work better for you. And if you can't, or they don't seem to fit anymore, then feel free to delete them. Words are words; it's the attention and focus you put on your list that is the important factor.

Look at your list. Has anything already happened or been achieved/gained/ experienced since you drew up your list? Awesome! Congratulate yourself and *tick it off*. You did it, you manifested! Remind yourself of that fact.

Now, is there anything you forgot about on the list that you need to keep in mind to maintain your focus? Beautiful. Post a note somewhere that you can see every day. Maybe you need to keep working on your book or presentation. Maybe you vow to go for a 30-minute walk every day.

Try re-arranging the list in order of **Priority** or **Biggest Desire**. You may find in some years that things are already aligning themselves to fit the picture of your life that you crafted in Cycle 11. Magic? I prefer to call it 'How Reality

Works'. Visions come first; then the blueprint and then the actions, people and motivations that create the situations that facilitate the creating … and finally the manifestation of the original Vision.

It's how everything gets done in the physical realm and what this book is really all about.

Your list is your road map, your tool, your blueprint and reminder of your plan. Bring it back to conscious awareness in Cycle 1 and remind yourself who it is that you're trying to become.

LOOK AT YOUR LOOK

You'll spend an awful lot of time in front of a mirror at some point in Cycle 1. Probably talking to it, or at least thinking to yourself about how A is bigger, B is smaller, C is lousy, D needs work done on it, E is boring and F needs rejuvenating. Maybe A is your hair, D is your smile, and F is your demeanor. It's all interchangeable. Hopefully you like a lot of it already. Maybe it's just the twinkle in your eyes that seems to have left, and you notice it. Maybe someone comments on how you look. Maybe it's time to shave your head, grow your hair out, start sporting a beard, try a new hair color, hit the gym – whatever it is, it's a sign you're changing how you see yourself, and how you want to see yourself and ultimately how you want others to see you.

In some years, you may find yourself in front of a camera too, dressing up in different styles, trying on different hats, costumes, styles and looks. Same theme.

You're different now. You're constantly evolving. What worked then may not work (or feel good) now. You're not the same person you were last year at this time. Let the world see that and let yourself see it too. It's so freeing to be who you are today, not who others have *grown accustomed* to you being. You have a right to change, you *have* changed so it's time to let yourself catch up with yourself. And you can do this as slowly or as quickly as you like this Cycle. It's your right and it's really your time.

Isn't astrology awesome?!

Reality hits in Cycle 1 that *the person in the mirror may not be the person you feel on the inside.* So it's time to bring the inside out, and make the outside more fitting with who you now are and how you feel within.

OUT WITH THE OLD, IN WITH THE NEW

Which leads us to this question – did you work through your inner-rumblings in Cycle 12? Those stirrings inside of things that bother you? If so, you're well placed now to bring out the best and banish the rest. And if you're still asking what 'inner-rumblings' are, I mean those things that happened in your last Cycle that bubbled up from within – the troubling, niggling, doubting energies that cramped your life and style and brought up all sorts of anxieties and stress. If you didn't work through them fully, you may find yourself looking as lousy as you feel, or finding your body is still trying to expel toxins from the previous Cycle in the form of boils, acne, spots, puss and a million other ways for your face and body to show you're in a detox mode still, or *something* doesn't want to be inside you.

Do *you* want to be inside you?

If your body is a temple, you get to move in during Cycle 1. Or move *back* in. You get to sign a new lease, turf out the squatters (negativity, pessimism, ill-health, doubt, depression) that may have taken up residence in your absence, and you get permission to paint, to rebuild (yoga stretching, weight lifting, dieting, exercising), to stick up a new door, tidy the porch and put a welcome mat out, or thorny spiky protection bushes to keep people at bay.

You may even find you get a chance or a craving to do the very same with your actual front door, or exterior to your home. It's all symbolic of changing your first contact with the world – and its first contact with you. Even changing the color of your shoes says a lot about your interaction with the world (according to color psychologists red shoes show an aggressive, direct approach, green shoes a more laid back one etc), since they are our direct physical contact with the planet and reveal that initial approach we take to the outside world.

PLANETARY SIGNATURE: MARS

Mars is Fire and was traditionally the Lord of War. He inspires us to be way more direct, definitely more aggressive and certainly confrontational in Cycle 1, and to push ourselves forward to get things moving and get things done! And we need it – to help us march ahead in this important initiation. Fire is action, and that is the key to success in this Cycle – to make those decisions, to make things happen, and to make a move in a new direction and not fear aggression and confrontation (otherwise situations may arrive to plunge you into a violent, pushy or heated situation). Do what you can, then, to find a worthwhile channel for your emotional/physical/intellectual/enthusiastic energy, to avoid being pulled into the ruts, pit-stops, whirlpools, draining black holes and other assorted time-wastes, during this important Cycle. It's about you – so keep yourself happy, and focus on your own business (even if it means telling everyone else you're unavailable for the time being).

ARE YOU REALLY IN CYCLE 1 YET?

Detoxing may continue if you've yet to release stuff from Cycle 12, so Cycle 1 becomes about a forced face-off with reality and the parts of your life that simply aren't working anymore. Have you released anxiety and worry yet? By all means let it out, it's part of the slipping off the old mask to create a new, more real, more authentic You that the world needs you to be. Cycle 1 kicks off your new beginning any way it can.

For example: if a relationship breaks down in Cycle 12 (the Cycle where things dissolve, fall apart or begin to fade and phase out) and you haven't accepted this fact, then Cycle 1 becomes less about embracing the new-you flying solo on to your next grand adventure, and more about fighting the tide and trying to paddle backwards to reconnect with someone who's floated away – which only further forces the much needed separation that was scheduled so you could develop yourself first and foremost away from a significant other (the true reason for this Cycle).

If you're in a relationship don't panic, you won't suddenly break up, now you're in Cycle 1. What you *will* need is acceptance that you'll have to 'go solo' for a time; whether that means sitting in separate rooms or taking separate vacations, whether that means informing your partner that you need time to yourself to figure stuff out, or whether they start getting irritated that you're always around and they need their time off from *you*! Being together while still maintaining yourself as a separate individual is the key theme. Finding new parts of yourself to share and keep your relationship alive and well and continuously growing.

In some Cycle 1 years you may indeed find that events seem to conspire to break you up from a connection you have, be it a romantic liaison, a professional partnership, a merger or some other agreement or contract. Whether they leave you, or you decide to move on from them, focus more on what you want out of things, how you want life to be and give it to yourself, rather than sit and sulk or point the finger or wonder what they are doing. Cycle 1 is about you. And you'll be reminded of this time and time again each and every year you move through it.

Making yourself happy becomes a number one priority.

FROM INNER RIFTS TO OUTER SHIFTS

We're taught that life should not be about surface or superficial things, but how many times do we reach to change the outer world and our looks, in order to feel better? We understand that at some level, working at the surface *does* affect the inside. And working on the inside is always reflected on the surface. Happy inside; happy eyes outside. An amazing haircut; a beaming feel-good factor inside. So number 1 – stop beating yourself up for obsessing over what's going on, on the outside of your world, your body and everything else. Cycle 12 was all about your innards and it's time to come out of the shadows of the basement and stand at your front door and stick a flag in the ground and claim your territory.

STAND YOUR GROUND: BOUNDARIES AND DEFENSES

Defense mechanisms are bound to be sprung when you're trying to claim your rightful place. Who will you chase off your personal lawn, this Cycle? If you find yourself having to do just that, remember it's all so you can claim or reclaim You. So, everyone's doing you a favor, really. Whether it looks that way or not. Helping you to find your confidence to just say "No". Boundaries are crafted in Cycle 1s, based on this new you. People can't get too close or you'll bark at them, but if they leave you alone too long, you'll feel their lack of attention also. Draw your boundaries and defenses but remember *only the insecure really need to defend themselves*, because it's up to us, whom we let upset us.

Defend your right to be you, but avoid becoming defensive in the process.

PLAYING YOUR NEW ROLE

Some Cycle 1s bring about a change of title – either you switch jobs, or you move, you're now single (no longer married or defined by a union or relationship you were involved in) or something leads you to wind up getting new business promotional material, a name on a door, or qualifications after your name. It doesn't even need to be dramatic. Look around and you'll find on some level a desire to recreate yourself and your outer form. You're no longer 'Sally the Cleaner' or 'Doug the Waiter'. You no longer play the same role. Or play by the same rules. It's time for *Your way*. You get to change the mask, change the costume and exit one stage and enter another.

Fancy changing your name? You can. Allegedly, you can call yourself anything you want. 15 names if you so desire. At the time of writing, the longest recorded name in America belongs to a German immigrant to Philadelphia, Pennsylvania. His first and middle names consist of one name for each letter of the alphabet plus his surname: '*Adolph Blaine Charles David Earl Frederick Gerald Hubert Irvin John Kenneth Lloyd Martin Nero Oliver Paul Quincy Randolph Sherman Thomas Uncas Victor William Xerxes Yancy Zeus*'. I wonder how many Christmas cards he doesn't get? I'm not surprised he was commonly known simply as Mr. Hubert Wolfe.

Who are you this year? It's a good question to ask yourself. Maybe you'll find yourself doodling a new signature or autograph, and why not? We spend so long doing the same things in the same way, it's Cycle 1s that get us cracking out of the 'code' that we've created and shaking it all up.

True, this can get confusing – after all, if you're no longer the person you were during last year's run around the Cycles, and you're not yet the new person you *will* be in the Cycles ahead, who the hell *are* you right here, right now, today?

It's time for a new name tag, a new mask and a new role to play. If you were always 'the shy wallflower' it's time to shift out of it and try something else. If you were always 'the lazy one' you can shock others now by becoming busier and more on the ball.

It's like being a clown stripped of makeup, an actor without lines, or a dancer without music. You have to figure it out yourself, find your own way and create an original path. Maybe one won't appear. Maybe there'll be no fanfare saying *"This is who you are now!"* or *"Go here, do that, drink this"*. Alice was lucky in Wonderland; you may not be. What you eat, or don't eat, drink or don't imbibe is entirely up to you. But you'd have it no other way now, trust me.

Are you ready and willing to wing it?

Does freedom scare you? Well deal with it, because it's what we all want and end up screaming over when it lands in our laps. It's the human polarity – never happy, and the 'damned if you do and damned if you don't' syndrome that comes with part of being in a human package on planet Earth.

Starting from *somewhere* is the place to begin in Cycle 1. Logical but we often get lost in the 'How' part of the equation. Somewhere means anywhere. Right from where you are. Look around you. Grab a pen. Write a list. Make a small plan. Decide what feels good, what things you've always wanted to try, and begin today. After you read this chapter or do it right now. There's no better time. Cycle 1 is about Action.

1-chapters don't always mean bursting on the scene with trumpets blazing. Maybe the season you're currently in (your Cycle 1) falls in the sign of Scorpio, in which case every year during this time (October 23-November 22) you'll feel a desire to withdraw from the scene (that's the Scorpio energy) work on what you want to discard in your life and yourself and generally skulk around the shadows or stay up late at night.

If you have Leo here, you'll probably start some new creative venture, begin dating or just amp up your fun levels hitting the nightlife or painting the town red (or your bedroom) or finding fun in other ways. That's the Leo vibe. You'll learn a lot about your rising sign or ascendant during Cycle 1 – that is, if you know your birth chart and decide to investigate. If this makes no sense to you, just stick to your Sun Sign (the one you know yourself as). You enter your Cycle 1 every year when you enter the season of your sign: Aries in springtime, Pisces from February 19-March 20 etc. **You can find out more about which sign you have active during your Cycle 1 by drawing your Birth Chart for free at www.SurfingYourSolarCycles.com**

So this is *your* time and *your* personal style and you get to explore it, by noticing what you're drawn to this year, and what you want, desire, hunger for, are curious about, and feel excited about trying.

Sample. Cycle 1 offers an abundance of possibilities.

THE INITIATION OF INITIATING

Cycle 1 asks you to start something. What is it that you're beginning? Moving house? Seeking a new home? Starting a new job? Trying to expand into a new field or strengthen your position? Seeking employment? Taking on a new project? Becoming a parent? A new workout program? A new diet? Living in the country for the first time? Moving to another continent?

Whatever it is, you either have to discover the new rules for the new path you're on, or you're making them up as you go. Step-by-step. Maybe you're still working on something from last year, in which case you get to give it new wings, breathe new life into it, change its shape, form, color or feel, or present it to the world in a new way. Old ideas in a new package. That's everything – there's nothing new under the sun – but we dress it up with fancy new garb and call it fresh, unique, original. What it really is, is clever – like musicians who take all of 12 notes and compose new pieces of music with endless variations. Or writers who take 26 letters of the alphabet and keep repeating and rearranging them in different codes and combinations to make us cry, shout, laugh, cringe, jump and feel.

Your first initiation into Cycle 1 could very well be the way you handle new starts, fresh beginnings, your ability to get the ball rolling, your way of carving a new path, of going off on your own.

Don't fight being alone, which has to become a prominent theme at some point. Either you can't help it or you just feel it. Time alone affords you the chance to stop playing the same roles with people around you, as we've said, and interferes with the process of them continuing to view you in a certain light. The light goes off and you're in the dark until you turn on the light in your own time, to reveal the 'new you'.

> *What you do with your time alone now*
> *is a big marker for how this year will pan out.*

If you're working on yourself, all will come to amazing fruition. If you chase people because you don't want to spend time sitting, thinking over your own life, you'll slow down the process of evolution and growth and wind up feeling left behind, or else not in charge of your own life.

And secretly, being in charge of you, is what you really want.

ANGER, AGGRESSION, ASSERTIVENESS AND ATTACK

Challenges always crop up in Cycle 1 that either test your bravery and courage, your anger and aggression levels and ways of channeling frustration, your method of attack and its appropriateness and effectiveness, or your ability to be spontaneous and act without word, warning or wondering.

Life suddenly says 'Catch!' or 'Go-Go-Go!!' All you can do is dive in, step on the gas and roll with it. Life gives so many clues now, and the ones that feel dynamic and interesting are the ones you're urged to pursue.

It's worth pointing out that Cycle 1 is also a great time to work on physical activity – to discharge tension, anger, and a whole host of other stress-related causes and symptoms. Cycle 12 shook up the dust and loosened the debris, Cycle 1 is about doing something with all that energy released and now at your disposal. Clearing stuff out is a good start. *Doing something* is a sure fire way to get the blood pumping, the energy moving and you feeling *out* of the rut you were sinking into. You simply don't have time to sit and dawdle or dwindle or dwell on things. And sitting stagnating just isn't an option anymore, either.

Yes, you'll no doubt get angry during this Cycle. Maybe at yourself, maybe at another. Perhaps you'll be the one who calls someone on something they are (or are not) doing? Someone had to say it, right?! It could get nasty, but as long as you are direct, blunt, to the point and honest, you can't really go wrong.

Your courage can really get people to sit up and take notice and shift them out of any stagnating rut they themselves are lingering in. So do them a favor by being yourself. You don't have any time for victims, you're out to be a warrior, and you'll defend and fight only for those who are trying. The lazy had better move aside.

CONQUERING CHALLENGES

Your 1-Cycle is also all about challenge, war and fighting, but there is no reason to waste Cycle 1 energy on such silly things or even getting into pointless squabbles. In the eyes of reincarnation we are all connected. 1-Chapters say channel your energy into a battle, yes. It's good for the soul. Conquer something! The gym for example, like the 'Abs, Buns and Guns' class that I took during the writing of this chapter (talk about an energy burn!) How about an old project that needs new life? Beat a wall down. Run a marathon. Sure, go to a shooting range. Shout, buy a punch bag and let your anger out. Face off with someone who did you wrong – whether in person, or just in thought; simply, directly, honestly ... then move on. We don't need a physical presence before us to effect massive change.

Cycle 1 is *pure energy* – and there are so many ways to use it, depending on what your 'default' is. Maybe you feel sluggish and not in the mood one year during your 1-Cycle to affect any big change, but you can do so by not acting physically but channeling *mental* energy on new ideas instead of dwelling on old stuff. No matter what your style, you get to affect *some* change in the form of your choosing. Brain or brawl. We need only think of someone, bring them to mind, and they are 'in our space'. So, if you need to get upset with someone, do it in this safe and secure energy-space.

It will create a change, guaranteed, if it comes from the heart. They too shall feel it. And some form of release will be afforded you in exchange.

Cycle 1 is all about setting yourself new challenges, choosing your battles and deciding how to conquer them.

Some battles lead to something created.
Some battles lead to something destroyed.

In the simple act of choosing creation, we choose destruction. The two really go hand in hand. We're going here for the battles that end up with something to show at the tail end; something that we can be proud of. The only thing we destroy is the void, the waiting, and the nothingness that was there before. Our product has been birthed by the energies of our 'personal spring' called Cycle 1 – be it a poem, a new home, a relationship, a baby, a novel, a painting, a portfolio, a presentation or a driving test.

SELF LOVE AND YOUR NEW TEST OF CONFIDENCE

How are you treating yourself? How are you letting others treat you? Self-confidence, often shaken in Cycle 12s, comes back with a vengeance now, or it should do, and you should try whatever you can to bolster your own and allow it to grow once more. After all, self-love and self-confidence are the backbone of everything you'll attempt in life. Self-worth will be the challenge and adventure in Cycle 2, but firstly you have to sculpt your personality and hone it to be strong no matter what happens.

Confidence is your goal in Cycle 1 and you'll no doubt face many opportunities to get it right, stand up for yourself and be the warrior you were meant to be (be it a spiritual warrior, yoga warrior, business warrior, relationship warrior, creative warrior, family warrior. You name it). Secure your armor, find your shield and withdraw long enough to work on these two key concepts: **Find reasons to adore You and find ways to put yourself to the test** (auditions, interviews, blind dates, regular dates, knocking on business doors, attempting new stuff) to *Build Your Self-Confidence*.

Then you'll be unshakable and unflappable by the time Cycle 2 rolls around. It's called smart planning and enjoying yourself can only bring great stuff.

YOUR PHYSICAL VEHICLE: BETTERING YOUR BODY, HARNESSING YOUR HEALTH AND ELABORATING YOUR ENERGY LEVELS

From so much time spent leaving the body in Cycle 12 (daydreaming, meditating, intense emotions, escaping, worrying, dealing with depleted energy or seeking a high to run away *from* the prison of the body), Cycle 1 now pulls you right back down into your life/body/present moment for various reasons as you emerge into the bright morning of dawn and you wake up to ask yourself: **How strong is my vitality? How much am I able or willing to shine?**

Your energy dictates your personal health and daily drive. How confident are you to get started on your new path? To be the warrior you need to be in Cycle 1, to have the push and drive to go for it that you need in Cycle 1, you'll need physical health, stamina and strength.

So 1-Cycles are great for launching new fitness programs, or strengthening your body. Build your immune system with vitamins, exercise, fresh air, water, fresh food and enough rest. Even if you need extra sleep, you have to *actively* pursue it now. Cycle 12 is about allowing, but Cycle 1 now is about acting. 'Doing' creates the strength to do more.

Look to areas of the body related to your sign. You may find some weak links in your chain here during Cycle 1, and a cold or other physical problem may be your reset button. Are you strong, energetic, or are you in need of an energy upgrade? Strengthen what you have; work on the weaker parts. Competitive sports or trying to 'up' your record is a great way to burn off energy, and often during 1-Cycles *doing more gives you the energy to do more!*

To recap: no matter what's going on around you, this month marks your *starting* point, where you get to truly enter the spirit of spring no matter what weather you're currently experiencing in your corner of the cosmos.

Somehow, somewhere, life is offering you a fresh start. A new beginning. A clean slate.

When you woke up on the morning this Cycle began, something inside had shifted. Did you feel it? Maybe it was just a new desire, a new bravery, the energy to get up, stand up and change something, or look at something anew or else turn a page (and a corner) with new determination. And if not, then it'll surely come, as surely as the seasons change and day follows night. Count on it. Expect it. Don't sit and wait for your bright moment. Turn the page, turn the other cheek and march on.

Start what you want, desire and dream of. This is the *do it now* stage of your astrological calendar.

ALL ABOUT YOU

You *have* to be selfish in Cycle 1. It comes round once a year and it all starts here as far as making something happen. What you set in motion in Cycle 11, will start needing a push forward now. You're the farmer but you're also the seed. Your Dream won't magically happen unless you take it forward and *do* something with it. So, make a move towards your Dream or whatever it is that you want. Make a call, write a letter, talk to someone, try your hand, make the effort, get the presentation together; initiate the steps towards some goal.

You'll be aided in this quest by at least one Aries person who arrives to show you firsthand what it means to put *yourself* first by doing so for themselves or aiding you in throwing off the shackles of caution and the past and blazing a few new trails with you (not to lead you but more as a sidekick, ally and comrade-in-arms).

Like the fireworks that go off worldwide for the New Year, this is a time when you explode onto the scene no matter which month Cycle 1 finds you in, each year. Which scene? The one you chose. Don't have one? Find one! Choose your scene and storm it. Invade. Push your way to the front. Blaze a new trail if there isn't one. If you want something, don't look for a way ahead that's been done before. Make your mark *your* way. Don't be boring. Impress yourself onto others and your environment as though you intended to leave a mark. As though you want your footprints behind to leave a trail showing you were there, like the ones at Graumman's Chinese Theatre in Hollywood where you can stand in the very same spot as Marilyn Monroe and a host of other celebrities (...did you see how tiny her feet were?!)

Take up space. Say *This* is me, World, this is what I want and you'd better get used to it. It's time to show you're proud to be yourself. You're here for a reason. Sitting here, reading this and in the flesh. And that the game – your game – is not over yet.

This is *your* time.

Pumped up enough? Good. I'm your personal pep-talk machine in Cycle 1. You You You. You rock! You are amazing! You're powerful, the best! What about *you*? Forget the others. Forget them. If they don't like it, they're not your people. Obviously, we're not saying that anyone against you is your enemy, and that you should selfishly ignore or trample over them, but if they're rebelling against the harmless new approach you're trying, then perhaps it's only a mere test to see if you'll give up due to outside pressure. Listen to advice (always a good idea) but in the end, make it *your* decision.

Be careful, however, that you don't wind up pushing others away by your unnecessarily selfish attitudes at this time of year. Maybe you'll be reminded by someone close to you (or even a stranger) that you're being too self-absorbed at the expense of others, too pushy, too gung-ho, too devil-may-care, too cavalier and too downright mean or nasty. Listen to the messages of others at this time, but don't lose your identity to how others feel you should be appearing or behaving. Use feedback to moderate your approach then continue on ahead.

FLUFFERS AND BUFFERS

Be honest, share with others and don't hurt them by being overly aggressive or pushy (be firm but fair; you'll get further) and your people will stick around after Cycle 1 and chances are they are pretty good people who may last your entire year.

If they choose to leave, then they were 'buffers' (those who arrive in your life to help you shift your life into a new gear, whether through ease or discomfort). Expect to meet plenty of those in your year ahead – those who remind you of your talents and thereby raise your self-value **(Cycle 2)**, ones who offer new possibilities and viewpoints **(Cycle 3)**, help ground you **(Cycle 4)**, show you a good time **(Cycle 5)**, help you out **(Cycle 6)**, partner up with you to teach you balance **(Cycle 7)**, lead you into the darkness to discover your secret powers **(Cycle 8)**, remind you that the life is a journey and the world is vast **(Cycle 9)**, help you up the ladder **(Cycle 10)**, shake you out of a rut by attaching jumper cables to your privates to electrify you into a more uniquely free existence **(Cycle 11)**, and remind you that there's more to this life than meets the eye **(Cycle 12)**.

Yes, your year is about to be filled with 'buffers' who come with one (or possibly more) reason in mind, and a job to do, and a message to relay to you. And get this – they *all* help you! Even the ones who seem to cause you no end of trouble, block you, upset you and generally get in your way or make you want to tear your hair out, are helpful. They aid you in defining what is right for *you*. So, give a small thanks for their big annoyances. Even the ones who seem to cause you stress are also your buffers. Soul mates come in many forms, especially ones that push our buttons, irritate and hurt us so we can grow, heal and evolve – and ultimately become stronger within ourselves.

Keep an eye out for them, then. They all lead you further back into yourself, to work out who you are, what you want, what you can achieve. And to help test you or prod you in new directions in order to do this – even if that's *away* from them, when all is said and done. Buffers are those people who (through aiding you or blocking you) inspire new growth within you. You don't have to like them (but mostly you will) you just have to accept the gift they give you – a reason and a chance to change, grow and evolve.

You've got to be excited now. If not and you're in need of a boost, you may bump into a series of 'fluffers' – those who fluff you up and puff you up by reminding you of your strengths, giving you a boost and upping your confidence with some well-deserved and much-needed ego strokes. We all need a good fluff now and again, and if you don't do it for yourself, you may just find yourself fluffed by others.

Just think: A whole new year filled with magical surprises; untold possibilities. This could truly be *Your Year*. Or at least an amazing one you'll never forget. Where will you go, what will you do, and who will you wind up bumping into?

MACHO: THE ME IN *MEN*

It's a very masculine time so traditionally 'male' issues are major now – just watch the news. Cycle 1 relates to war in various forms, so fights (and therefore fighters) are well starred. The army will love this period. So will athletes, firemen, cops and anyone who has to show a test of courage and strength. But wait, women too aren't immune to this, of course – symbolic testosterone hits them, and we'll see the posse of aggressive women hit the screen again. Just watch. Women get to test out their masculine or yang side, to be more politically correct. And they also get to work out how to be assertive without needing to resort to copying or modeling themselves after men. No one has ownership on the energy of assertiveness.

Everyone has a Cycle 1 – so the person who suddenly seems irate, irritable or more fiery than usual, could well be going through theirs.

Gender can get mixed up now and well it should. It's a new era. Roles are out. Masculine and Feminine are mere ideas. Individuals are 'in' (courtesy of the Age of Aquarius). People-kind as opposed to Mankind. Assertiveness helps us all, aggression when not channeled into useful activities, does not. No matter what your sign or gender.

WYSIWYG (what you see is what you get)

Isn't it funny to think we spend so much of our time perfecting an image and a face that we only get to see in the few moments we stare into a mirror, or catch our reflection in a passing store window or shiny surface?! Think about it, we only get to really see our faces (unless we're celebrities) in passing reflections during our day, maybe an hour or two hours maximum depending on if you wear makeup or just love yourself!

It's crazy to think of how much time goes into looking good when you look to how much time we get to actually enjoy it ourselves. If you boil it down, you're doing so much work for other people – after all, they are the ones getting to enjoy you the way you look, most of the time, right? Well it's true, but we really must understand that it does reflect on us and our self-judgments and self-opinions and helps us feel good with who we are. And who can't forget that we can change how we feel by changing the outside. Self-help gurus say "it's what's *inside* that counts" and "looks don't matter" but dig a little deeper and you'll discover that some of these are the ones layered in makeup or spend hours debating what to wear for their TV show appearance or latest book signing. *This is the physical dimension and looks DO count.* It's our first impression (this month will be all about that) and our first contact with the outside world.

Bees are drawn to the brightest flowers with the promise of the tastiest nectar. It's not such a side-step into the human world from there.

First impressions count this month, or at the very least are hard to shift once someone has formed an opinion. So ask yourself what foot you want to put forward and how you want others to view (and thus remember) you. Try entering every room with a smile in Cycle 1. See what reception you get.

Are you a 'what you see is what you get' kind of person? Or do you look as though you hide a lot? Are you mysterious? Sexy? Defensive? Annoying? Bratty? Calm?

For those comfy in their skin, the greatest gift is being themselves anywhere and everywhere. That's a freedom and luxury few get to experience without a lot of effort (effort being just the thing that goes *against* being yourself in the first place!)

Okay, so this Cycle you get to change or adapt or polish up your presentation skills. You always *do* create a first impression; the question is how do you want to do that, and what message do you want to send out? Changing your clothes will do this pretty fast. Your hair says a lot too. Your face and eyes are facets of your expressive toolkit. Play with eye-wear: contacts, glasses, makeup, false lashes or just let people see you more, give eye contact, look around instead of looking down.

Remember the color-psychology of shoes that we mentioned earlier? These studies continue to show that your color choice can affect what interviewers make of you. Wear turquoise and you come across as more communicative – people want to get chatty with you. Red shows you're assertive, direct and not to be messed with. You could take that to your local bar too and give it a whirl. Research *Color Therapy* and *Color Psychology* in your 1-Cycle as another tool to re-craft your personal presentation package.

Find out what makes you tick, and your body clock will happily keep on tocking.

THE SHADOW:
(met in yourself or others)

Frustration inevitably leads to anger or depression (often the same thing) in Cycle 1 because you feel the need to surge ahead but you don't yet know where and you don't know how. You feel stuck, yet irritable and itchy for growth and change. So you take your frustration out (as opposed to keeping it in) on others by getting into scraps and scrapes. What a waste of energy and fuel. Let frustration take you someplace new in your 1-Cycle, by putting it into anything, *anything* but wasting time snapping at people or barking at yourself.

You may be faced with angry people or end up just expressing it yourself. Or both. Banging your head against the cupboard or door, or burning yourself or cutting yourself is a strong possibility. Cycle 1 is aggressive and feisty and you can often end up injuring yourself or someone else hurts you because you're bringing in impetuous and inpatient and impulsive vibes towards yourself.

Get a regime and routine and program of energy-expenditure, then, to burn off this aggressive and direct energy and to keep it in check. Anything works. Walking the dog, going for a walk, a jog, push ups, working on a physical project, weeding, home improvement, aerobics.

Remember also what we mentioned earlier about the flip side of the selfish theme of this Cycle and don't become so me-me-me oriented that others ditch you and leave you alone (which is fine when it's to help you out but less helpful when it's to reject you because they can't be bothered making all the effort or dealing with your one-sided and selfish ways).

Tips: Go somewhere alone, do something you've always loved (or wanted) to do, that involves no one else but you. Or arrange something and take someone else along, but you get to decide what/where and when. How about helping someone else feel good about themselves, by being an ally in times of need. Help someone to help themselves. Boost their own self-image and confidence.

YOUR ACTUAL BIRTHDAY

The phrase 'many happy returns' they like to use in England to say 'happy birthday' is another way of honoring these Cycles. The Sun returns to where it was when you were born. Astrologers call it the **Solar Return** and a reading of this kind details the twelve months ahead till your next birthday, the theme of *this* year's chapter.

All of us can use this period to come back to ourselves. To return to our center, our source. To reignite our passion, our joy for living, our childlike innocence, our curiosity, our sense of possibility and hope. And to just have fun.

Making a wish is symbolic of this new energy. The new, improved you. You get to focus on something you want. Use the day of your birthday as an entire 24 hours to do what you like, wear what you like, eat what you like, meet who you want to, go where you desire, act how you want to, and really be yourself. There's no better time. Don't beat yourself up. Put criticism of anything or anyone, on hold. Make it a celebration of Yourself. Be selfish. Cater to your own needs. It's one day out of an entire year.

YOUR DREAM FINDS ITS STAGE

Remember the darkness of last month and your last Cycle? The tiredness, the questions, the confusion? Maybe it was quite a great time but you didn't know what was becoming of your 11th Cycle Vision, whether it had been swallowed up, died before it had a chance to flourish or whether it was the right one for you anyway.

Your aspiration *has* erupted from the dark ground from where it was planted. The seed *has* sprouted. All the other Cycles are now about tending to this vulnerable seedling. You'll begin to see signs and hear things people say that will relate to it. Others who are on the same page as you, find you, as if pulled by an invisible magnet. You have to watch your Vision and Dream, though, and feed it, nurture it, talk to it.

Your Dream needs you. It needs constant energy, not of the depleting kind (where you feel exhausted focusing on it – feeding a Dream is empowering and should feel good) but it needs continued stoking like a well-tended fire. I learned that process when I moved into a new home with a wood-burning stove. You have to keep an eye on it so it doesn't burn out or burn too hot too fast and literally burn itself out. It's the same with your Dream – you want it to burn steady and bright, to warm you for a long while instead of a fast burn.

Carry your Dream Vision with you into all you do and in how you are (or are becoming). You begin to embody your Dream in Cycle 1 crafting it in your very actions and choices (later into your mind in Cycle 3) because now you embody it and you are truly becoming it. By Cycle 10 it'll burst forth and receive public acclaim and then you'll prepare to plant new seeds for a new venture in Cycle 11 or take your success on to a whole new level.

So, your first Cycle is about seeing the first signs that you're manifesting what you set out in your 11th Cycle intentions. You're the one carrying your child, as it were. The new life you're going to live. The thing you want to make, build, create, experience. Whatever it is. You're going to birth it in the Cycles ahead. All Cycle 1s give you physical evidence and signs of your Dream in bloom. Look for them. You'll see them. They are there. So make sure you keep that in mind. Enjoy the process. Keep moving now, and keep directing yourself towards what you want. Just aim in the right direction and use confidence and your ego to blaze a trail.

That's it. Cycle 1 in a nutshell.

CYCLE 1 ACTION PLAN
* Move forward and give up looking back.
* Decide how you want to look and act now.
* Grab your Vision 11 list and reacquaint yourself with it,
re-inventing it where necessary.
* Be confident, assertively drawing new boundaries for yourself without
going off half-cocked.
* Try new things.

In a sunny year:
You're the bomb. Life thrust you into the front, to call the shots. You're looking good, and whether it's a makeover, a new outfit, or just time spent in front of the mirror or camera, no one can deny you're Hot! Your name is in print; people are talking about you. You're encouraged to have your say and people seem to not only respect you (even when they disagree) but also give you what you want. You're Mission Unstoppable.

This month you may be spending more time alone but that's fine by you, since you're driven by a new plan and a new direction and you need some space to work out what you want, anyway. You can be single even in a relationship – how can you help others if you're not sure what *you* want?! Independence or rather inter-dependence has never felt so good. You boost peoples' confidence, giving them the power to one-up their lives, and in return they offer to power you up also. Win-Win. With each new lead, opportunity, event, meeting and anything else you get into, you soon realize that starting from the beginning is best – a check in and quality time with your favorite person: you!

How are you looking, how are you feeling? Pretty damn good, it's true. You have that certain style, that certain 'something' but there's room for improvement. Others will help you out in working out whether that shirt fits, that dress flatters you. They'll fight you of course, but it's all part of the fun. With your own ego running the show you're bound to lock horns at times, but you'd rather they said it to your face than whine about you later behind your back. You respect directness now and will have to be that way yourself.

You wind up having to lead something or someone – to push something ahead that you've had an idea on now for a few months. A new project. Pursuing a new person. A new look. An original idea, a fresh possibility. Do it. Get it started *now*. You have the firepower, energy and confidence to have people take notice of what you're doing. Don't wait for others to get moving or you'll miss out. It's all up to you now.

Why? Because it's all *about* you and everyone is quite happy to comply. People come to you to ask you to deliver – to create this special new 'thing', head a project or product, be the one in the spotlight and the one to get the ball rolling. You're the front-man or front-woman. Whether you get the glory or not depends on if you stay around long enough to claim and enjoy it, but chances are you'll be asked to be somewhere else soon enough and once more, you're off – shooting yourself in a new direction with new dreams and new desires.

You're amped up and powered with something that can only be called 'cosmic', for you seem unstoppable. Especially during those times when you seem to have nothing to show for your effort. You know everything you do is a step in the right direction. *Your* direction. Destiny is something you create as you go. There's no path other than the one you're creating for yourself right here today with every decision, thought and action. No matter how small, each day you add another rung to your ladder. You're already on the ascent.

In sunny years people comment on your hair, your smile, your eyes, your look – you just look fantastic, full of the sun. You're courageous, nothing can stop you and you are free of the weight of the past, carrying an innocence about that you that can only be called refreshing or beguiling, alluring and simply irresistible. Stellar.

Basically you win just by being you. There is your star power. And again, in case you somehow missed it the first three times ... you look fabulous.

In a crummy year:
If you're on the flip side of this Cycle then you have got some lessons to learn and challenges and hurdles to overcome in order to pass the Initiation of Cycle 1. It's all about You, but you wish it wasn't.

Maybe you really don't look your best. Maybe it's a bad hair month. Or it's all about everyone else *but* you. No style seems to fit, and not only is your hair salon appointment a catastrophe but you're either in the spotlight when you'd rather hide or you're ill-prepared and under constant pressure to take the lead when you'd rather just follow (or hide). People just won't get off your back, and you won't even give yourself a break.

And don't even mention the countless people who are annoying you, blocking you (or maybe you're the one throwing a fit?) Whatever the case, you're to blame. Sorry but that's the lesson in this Cycle – you are the one living your life so you can't blame others when they don't give you what you want. No one owes you a damn thing so it can be rotten when life doesn't take off or you're handed thorns instead of roses.

If you're in a grimy month, pick yourself up and do some of the things suggested at the end of this chapter to perk up your own appetite for life. *Getting moving* beats sitting at home sobbing into your Cycle 1 sleeve. If you have no energy, weirdly enough when you start something or get up off the couch or bed, you'll find you do have more energy, suddenly. You won't know until you go.

Chances are too that you need a fight – so you're spoiling for someone and if no one is handy you'll beat yourself up. Why all the trapped frustration and aggression? Work out what is bugging you and fuel yourself with it to make some necessary changes. Something new is needed in your life. Can you spot what it is? Watch it though – you could be headed for a bashing of another kind if you carry around an aura that says "Start something with me please, I'm itching for release!" What a waste of good firepower! Take it to the gym, at least you'll wind up with better defined muscles at the end of it.

Anger and aggression could be issues you have, along with selfishness. So be vigilant to irritation and anxiety. If you're giving too much, you'll feel ripped off. If you take too much, others will desert you or call you selfish. Neither side is nice so you may have to draw some lines and let others defend their own space. If your confidence is low right now, you'll feel irritable and start taking it out on others. Find the nearest hill and go hiking... immediately.

Cycle Lesson

Without a new perspective, and the confidence to draw personal boundaries on who we now are (as opposed to *who we used to be*) it's difficult to assert ourselves in the right directions for what we desire and who we now have become. Establishing self-trust, self-love and self-motivation, enables us to then blaze new trails, free of baggage, and light enough to embark on a new quest, invest in a new Vision and explore new possibilities. We're free now to be whomever we choose, but that involves a major leap into the unknown. Fear plays a role but not the starring one. Taking a risk does.

Celebrity Spotlight

- Jackie Onassis was in her Cycle-1 (in the final degree of Scorpio no less) when her husband JFK was assassinated beside her.
- Oprah Winfrey was broadcast nationally in her first episode of *The Oprah Winfrey Show* in 1986 and Ellen Degeneres came out as a lesbian on the same show in 1997, both during their 1-Cycles.

Tips to successfully navigate your Cycle 1 Initiation

- Do it *now*; stop procrastinating.
- Find out what is bothering you and confront it.
- Be first – in the line, in the game, in the project.
- Keep moving forward; keep up to be kept up.
- Bang something – anything, except someone else, or your own head on a wall.
- Avoid bruises, cuts, burns and fights by re-channeling energy and slowing down when necessary.
- Get the ball rolling.
- Play some sports or hit the gym.
- Find a new look – define yourself in new ways.
- Have a haircut, tweeze hairs. Wear hats, for hiding, coverage, mystery.
- Launch a new product.
- DIY (Do it Yourself)
- Be courageous – no more pussyfooting around.
- Change your name or title.
- Stand up and be counted.
- Be active and assertive, not passive/passive-aggressive and annoying.
- Stop complaining and start acting.
- Be impulsive.

- Give slow people lots of extra leg-room.
- Save yourself a headache by moving *around* obstacles fast.
- Buy a groovy pair of glasses (cosmetic or just for fun), shades, or spectacles, or how about a monocle for the heck of it?
- Take up marital arts, self-defense or some T'ai-chi energy related discipline.
- Ask yourself how *you* want to do it.
- Go play squash, tennis, anything where you can compete and thrash a ball around.
- Go wrestling, boxing – anything where you can compete and thrash someone around.
- Get rid of your old plates, glasses – anything you can enjoy smashing to pieces.
- Run instead of walking (but watch red lights if speeding!)
- Be selfish – eat the whole box of chocolates or do it just for you.
- Wear red – it gets you noticed, raises your blood pressure, burns off extra energy/calories and gives you the attention you need (and the confidence).
- Lead others. Don't wait – if you want it done, do it before anyone else even mentions it.
- Go for some bodywork or treatment – spa, orthodontist, chiropractor, masseur.
- Ask someone to pull your hair or give you a scalp massage.
- Buy yourself new shampoo, makeup, skin crème, beauty products.
- Shoes!
- Don't wait for someone else to offer, ask for it or give it to yourself!
- Start a new project or idea each day – you can finish it another time.
- Eat more red foods for energy – tomatoes, strawberries etc.

~ Surf Cycle 2 ~

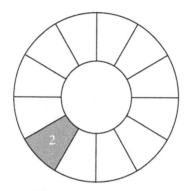

Time to Use your Tools,
Satisfy your Senses
and Appreciate Your Value

Cashing in on Connections with:

Bank staff/financial experts
People you owe/people who owe you
Big spenders/cheapskates
Chefs
The Indulgent
Farmers/builders
Hair stylists/beauty therapists
Your Mom's friends
Self-esteem life coaches
The Generous/the greedy
The Wealthy
Musicians
Designers

Appreciators
Gardeners/landscapers
Abundance coaches
Salespeople/collectors
Singers/dancers
Those close to the land
Taurus people
Sexual sirens and studs
Stubborn folk
Huggers/sensual folk
Massage therapists
Connoisseurs/gourmets
Sculptors/painters/artists

What you'll need:

A taste for quality
A comfy place to wallow in wonder
Music, food, sex, scents, fabrics, hugs
Money tucked away somewhere
A piece of land to grow, nurture, enjoy

Sitting comfortably?

If you're not then do so and come back. Nothing will make sense or help you right now until you're in a place of more comfort. So do what you need to do (eat, drink, dance, sleep etc) and then come back and we'll continue…

All good? Great. So, last month you had to fly solo and rework yourself, agreed? You were urged to re-ignite your own fires, start something over anew and were forced to focus on yourself, with time away, time apart and time to yourself in order to do so. It was 're-invention' time once more in your Life Story. So far; so good.

Now, it's time to do something with the New You that you are discovering.

In short, it's time to **get your priorities in order**.

What do you value? What's it worth? Really. With everything you are going through, putting yourself through, or being forced to go through, stop and ask yourself this minute:

"What is it worth?"

Is it 'worth it' to you and what are you worth in the situation? What are you worth? Ever asked yourself that lately? Now you'll have to. So we'll repeat that:

Is it 'worth it' to you and
what are you worth in the situation?
<u>What are YOU worth??</u>

Why underline this? Because it will become the sticking point that will either elevate you to a new height during this time or force you down until you 'get it'. You'll get back what you feel you're worth in this Cycle, whether you care for it or not. And you may get a lot of stuff that seems unfair, so you'll get very clear on what you do feel you're worth. Oh boy. Stick around – at least you'll get to see where you're at in this new Cycle of growth and to see if there's room for improvement (which is basically the intention of all 12 Initiations in this book).

Can you put a price tag on yourself, your offerings or your services? Do you have skills up your sleeve which can't be sold but which truly are worth a fortune (like understanding, knowledge, wisdom, caring etc?) If you sold stocks in Glorious You, what would be your value? Why would we want a piece of you and what you have to offer or have to own? Can you work out your net worth; your bottom line? How much are you worth or *could* be worth? How much do you even have right now? How much do you need? Do you have too much outflow and not enough inflow? Are you overspending without keeping any back-up for yourself? Or are you hoarding what you have out of fear of loss? Are you stuck too much in materialism or can you sell yourself for more assets?

If you're confused with all of this so far, then hang tight. "**What do you value?**" may be a tricky question for some of us. Let's make it easy, then – Take a look at what you spent most time doing today, this week, this month, this year. Is it up to your satisfaction?

What do you value?

If you're still not exactly sure, then simply look at what you:

* **Spend money on**
* **Spend most of your chosen time doing**
* **Get deeply involved in**
* **Do to earn money**
* **Surround yourself with**
* **Find yourself drawn to, repeatedly**
* **Do with no compensation because you adore doing it**
* **Like having, enjoying, being**

These things show us (whether we agree with them or not) what we actually *value*. After all you're making an investment each time you give it your attention. If you value drama, you'll pursue plenty of it, this Cycle. If you value money, you'll make *that* your god and worship the dollar, pound, or whatever currency you're currently hungering for. (Funnily enough, wealth is relative – a million dollars in the States is only 500,000 pounds in England, at the time of writing).

The point is, there's always someone poorer and richer than you materially or emotionally, depending on your viewpoint.

So these things you're pursuing now, *are* important to you, whether you know it or not. And yes, they can be out of synch with what we 'claim' to value in life. If you value peace and you're constantly seeking or provoking drama, then something is out of alignment. If you value respect and are constantly disrespecting people, you're a walking contradiction. If you love the country and spend more of your time in the city, then you're sending out mixed messages to yourself and the world.

Your world.

Cycle 2 *gives us ample evidence and advice on what we actually do value and whether or not our values are aligned with our soul-value – what we madly, truly, deeply want, to feel satisfied while on Planet Earth (and surprise,*

surprise, a lot of it may not be as healthy as you'd like to think). Contradictions cause blockages in the flow of what we create and manifest in our lives. Mixed signals result in chaotic and confused creations.

So, we're going to look at your desires in Cycle 2. Can you fight your addiction to gorge on things that are not healthy for you? How do you know if they are not healthy? They make you feel lousy. Simple. It's all very simple – or can be, during this special Second Cycle.

〜〜〜

CASHING IN ON CYCLE 2

The easiest place to start (or an area most of you will find yourself facing at the onset of your 2-Cycle) is in the whole arena of your money, possessions and survival. Where are you at materially? Is having 'little' freeing you to pursue more spiritual goals? Is being spiritual synonymous with going without financially? Is money 'evil' or just another form of energy? Can you be rich spiritually and *still* have a comfy bank balance?

What do you owe? Are you being honest or manipulating people out of their possessions? Are you truly earning your way? Or stealing and cutting corners? Are you worth every penny? How are you cashing in on your mad skills? Are you using your money to further your comfort, the beauty quota in your life and the comfort of others? Are you investing enough in yourself? What do you need to get by? Are you 'surviving' or 'thriving' and which would you rather be?

You may find yourself on the phone with your bank for some reason – to transfer funds, ask about various accounts, to order a new debit or credit card or to query some strange charge or activity on your account. That also goes for any company that receives your money. From online purchase tracking and paying your bills to comparison-shopping for the best deals. Your attention will find itself firmly planted on your money during this Cycle.

Hashing out a plan to make you more money is a great way to spend some time during Cycle 2. Sit in a coffee shop, have a comfy warm drink (or a cooling lemonade or whatever else it is that will give you that good feeling) and craft a step-by-step plan to improve your situation.

Trust me, Cycle 2 gives you the practical power to get it done.

THE PRICE IS RIGHT NOW: Money, Cash, Wealth AND Abundance

So firstly, your Cycle 2 is about *your* money, but it goes deeper than that. It's about your self-worth. The amount of comfort in your life *right now* is in direct proportion to how much comfort you feel able to handle. Weird, right? Or put another way – you can only handle the amount of money you're allowing into your life. This is your current comfort level.

Look around. You can handle whatever you have, and can't handle what you don't have. If you could, you'd have it. Maybe you don't want it, true. Why not? Maybe you're happier without it? Maybe you're learning some much needed lessons, and that's admirable. But times change and you can change your mind. Who said you need to learn your lesson in poverty? (If your astrology chart seems to suggest your soul chose this, then you can still work your way out of it, by first embracing your starting point.)

Some lessons are easier learned in barren wastelands, but if you're getting bored maybe it's time to rethink your setting and continue your learning whilst feeling a bit better about yourself. It can't hurt.

Maybe the things that bother you are in place (by you) to keep you from being too apathetic ("if I have to struggle to survive, I can't be lazy..."). It's worth a thought. But you know what? It's also worth giving thought to anything *other* than that which you don't have or isn't working. Don't get caught in the spiritual trap of dreaming up reasons why things aren't how you want them. If you want them, it's likely they're on your road map for this lifetime and are things worth obtaining. If you switch your brain mode and focus not on justifying your misery but on *fueling your discomfort in order to reshape your life situation*, you'll find yourself on course to gaining what you desire. If you want it, you can do it.

You're pretty great when you need to be...

So where do you fall on this scale right now? (It may shift around, but you'll notice your outside situation mostly reflects your inner feelings and thinking, before long). Tricky eh? Can you believe you can change the outside by changing your inner feelings (can you feel rich and beautiful drenched after a downpour, crying, walking down the shadiest part of town after just being robbed and knowing you can't pay your rent next month, for instance)? Well can you?! Maybe not right then and there, but there comes a time when you'll have to. Because if not, you're letting the outside situation affect how you feel inside, and legend has it that your inside creates the outside. Catch 22? Maybe, maybe not, but:

> *it's best to feel and live as if you were wealthy this month than chip on about how poor you may claim to be.*

Even though the above example is a little drastic and dramatic, it reminds us how as humans we do let what happens outside affect how we feel inside. Try to avoid letting yourself feel a victim, or at the mercy of others, or lacking something, lacking *anything* in Cycle 2. If you don't have it, **give up focusing on lack, get clear about wanting it, and know you are worth it**. Those are the golden keys to gaining what you desire.

Begin today to make room for these new things.

LIGHTS, CAMERA AND ACTION-PLAN

It's Cycle 2 – Practical pro-action, in other words. Get something moving. Make something work for you. Your looks, your skills, your magic. Your 'thing' whatever it is. Get practical. You have the idea, you've seen what *isn't* working, and you now have the energy at your disposal to *affect a change in your life circumstances*.

Remember your key steps: for everything you're experiencing that you no longer want (or any feeling of something you do not desire), flip it over to what you *do* desire. Write it down. Give it a date to be achieved by (don't be too stringent, it's not about meeting deadlines here, merely setting intentions). Give it a body instead of letting it just be 'another great idea'. Putting pen to paper gives something a physical life. So does talking about it. Telling others. Telling yourself. Getting it out there. Be pro-active in *any* form to start achieving more of what you want. If you make steps towards your destination you have to get there eventually.

Then, ask yourself where you currently fall most of the time from the choices below:

Prosperity Consciousness: is happy with what it has, enjoys quality, knows that price tags don't mean a thing but will happily spend fully on what feels good. People who have prosperity consciousness know that the universe is limitless and that as fruit trees continue to shed apples, money going out will return, because they are using it to create and enjoy beauty and aren't withholding – from themselves *or* others. They know they deserve it and they're allowed to enjoy what they want. Desire is a friend and ally pointing them in the right direction.

Money is another form of energy – like hugs, or kisses. It's enjoyed, created to be enjoyed, allowed to come in and spent on continuing the Cycle. A psychic friend of mine (a Taurus, a sign connected to Cycle 2 and one you'll no doubt bump into this Cycle) once told me she doesn't worry about holding on too tightly to money, she lets it "evaporate, so she'll get soaked in its inevitable downpour". It's not always about money though – it's just a sense of feeling rich no matter what, and money is a reflection of this. These people are happy with whatever they have. They are full. They always are.

Poverty Consciousness: feels there is a limited supply so must hold on, save, scrimp and be 'practical'. Luxuries are a waste of money. Things have to be worked hard for. At any moment there may suddenly, once again, be a shortage. Survival instincts kick in; energy restricts, attracting more reason to be fearful. Others have more so in order to gain more, people with poverty consciousness have to withhold and protect what they have and give out little, in order to save it and make it grow. They worry it's all going to come to an end and they'll become homeless, or food-less, so they live with the fear and therefore the need to safeguard and never *fully* enjoy what they have – as it may leave at any time. They feel lighter and cleaner having less, even though they may claim to want more. Experience has proven thus. And so the fear continues. And so does the creation of experiences proving the rule of lack (Cycle 9 will reveal more about self-fulfilling prophesies). Discomfort becomes a comfort zone.

So...

...which one are you living in tune with, most of the time? Since this forms the basis for most of your interaction with the material of this earth plane (and this phase of your annual adventure) it's time to get back in tune with what feels good to you. Try the free abundance meditation under Cycle 2 at **www.SurfingYourSolarCycles.com.**

Liking yourself is the bedrock of all you can create and 2-Cycles are a great time of year for you to launch your own 'getting to like who you are' campaign. If you don't feel you're worth it, who else can?

It's hard sometimes – what do we do when faced with something we don't like? Ask yourself why you're interacting and dealing with it. What do you have to gain or learn? This Cycle is about *gain* more than loss. (If loss teaches you the lesson of worth and value then yes, you'll lose stuff, but it doesn't have to be this way).

It's not really about endings or losing something – that comes later in Cycle 8 in various forms, when you've used up the value in it and it needs recycling. For now, you're working on *finding* and *building* a value. So if you're stuck with something you don't like in Cycle 2 you must value it, logic would say. At least be honest enough. If you value it, you care. If you care, you want it and more of it, and if you want more of it it's because you *are* it.

TRY THIS: 'WRITE A NEW REALITY' CHECK
Try this simple game to shift you to a Prosperity Consciousness. I first came across this in the book *Ask And It Is Given*, by Jerry and Ester Hicks. Take your checkbook and write checks out for things you'd love to have but that are expensive beyond your wildest dreams – anything! Write it, date it, sign it. No limit. See how it feels to be dealing in these sums of money – sums that, for most, are ordinarily beyond our means.

Play with this! Go window-shopping and add things to your shopping-list when you get home. Write the check! Another great process is to tear items out of a catalogue that you want, regardless of price tag. Act like you have the money or the means and you can have whatever you like – and as much of it as you like! Begin collecting photos of the items you're shopping for. Enjoy how it feels (I know you'll like it).

By doing this, you re-write your reality, and re-program your consciousness with prosperity. Science has shown that the brain knows no difference between a thought and what's actually happening. When an athlete visualizes running a marathon, the same muscles fire up and the brain activates as though the body was running! So when you write a check for bigger sums than you're used to, you're 'trying on' a different lifestyle. Getting a feel for it. Making it seem commonplace and normal. That's the way to reprogram your unconscious. Create a healthy habit. And keep it up.

This game will help you re-align with the idea of prosperity, the feeling of bounty, the appreciation for desire and the acceptance of good things into your life experience. Basically you're writing checks as if you had the money. You'll see a shift immediately and it's a fun way to spend your time, instead of dwelling on lack.

Why do things only because you have the money? Enjoy the feeling of richness now, today. This goes for attributes in others you like – appreciate those aspects of other people you value, compliment them on it, gift them for bringing that quality into your life, and in exchange you'll activate that part within you, and also send a message out to the universe that you value these things. And you'll get more of that sent your way. Not bad, eh?

EARTH TO YOU: WHAT DO YOU WANT???

We seek ourselves in life, to know ourselves, to understand ourselves. We feed on bad stuff because we have become attached to the bad stuff. The dramas. The discord. The 'dis-ease' (which often manifests during the next physical Cycle – Cycle 6) if we don't catch it now. We may even feel it's all we're worth. Abusive relationships we're stuck in, for example, or jobs we dislike with a passion. And it stops us from building something stronger, better.

So try this: name your addiction. Admit that something isn't working for you. Name your hunger. Accept it.

That's step 1 on the infamous 12-step program (kind of like the astrological 12 step guide you are currently holding).

Secondly, notice what you *do* want. Move there. Build there. Make a plan there. Think there. Focus there. Dream there. Dwell there. Do you want the cake or want to get healthy? If you want the cake, keep eating it until you either get sick, bored, explode or no longer want it. Non-judgment. Cycle 2 says **gorge**, find the value in it or get so sick of it you can move on and focus on something else.

Most people suffering anything they didn't like got so fed up with it that change was inevitable.

But what if it becomes all-consuming? What if you get lost in the feeding of your unhealthy nature? You won't. You will in Cycle 8 when you reach fever pitch, but don't sit around waiting for change to make a decision for you.

What you focus on in Cycle 2 keeps going until you shift the focus.

So thirdly, find something else to do. Anything. Take a bath. Watch a TV show and come back to your situation, issue or problem. Your life will change when you make small and simple changes. Guaranteed. Practical ones like focusing elsewhere and then seeing where you're at.

We don't need to keep pursuing things we don't like even though we feel attached to them. If it's a relationship dynamic, you clearly feel the need to interact (or you wouldn't be), so look at what it is that feeds you during the not-so-pleasant connection you may have now with another. Guilt? Fear of loneliness? Sex? The attention, the fight, the drama, the pain? If so, then now do you know you don't want that?

If you don't want it, what can you do to get *more* of that which you *do* want – more peace, comfort?

Be that way: be peaceful, be comfortable. If the other wants to join you, great!

If they want to fight still, then they'll do that, but not with you. Your world can be peaceful if you choose it. It starts with you, in Cycle 2, and you are your own gardener choosing which seeds you value and therefore want to enhance and grow. It simply begins with a practical and lasting grounded plan of what you want to *build and grow* in your own version of Eden.

Decide today how you want your world to be. How does it feel? What is there to eat? What colors make it feel good? We will visit your garden and see what flowers or weeds grow. We'll give you more of the same. People will find you in Cycle 2 and know what your garden houses and what seeds you plant, and will offer you the rest to blend in with what you already are planting and growing.

You'll be aided in this quest by at least one Taurus person who arrives to show you the pitfalls and potentials of the whole sphere of physical life, how being materialistic is a boon or a bore, how to enjoy the physical world and how to handle money, how to enjoy *yourself* more and offer some great advice (and bad examples) to help you make your own mind up on what's right for you and what you value and hold dear.

If you don't want it in your life experience don't stand for it. Don't *fight* it (and risk becoming it) but do stand away and stand down and stand aside; this alone shows you don't desire it. By not engaging in something, you show you don't want it! Do that. Be active in showing the world what you **do** want, if need be by showing what you **don't** want.

Interaction is everything. What you touch, smell, taste, point to, talk about, sit next to, embrace. It all says a lot about you. Want beauty? Then be around it. Or better yet: Be it.

HOW DOES YOUR GARDEN GROW?
So a reminder for you in this, your Cycle 2, because you're growing something here this month whether you know it or not: You're growing your self-esteem and self-worth by what you will and will not tolerate and accept and embrace.

You're telling yourself what you are available for in this annual Cycle, what you want (in the form of the currency called attention). Someone can shout at you (attention) or give you a hug or money (attention).

Whatever you focus on; grows. Whatever feeds you; you'll seek to feed yourself with. Is your diet nurturing you (and we're talking about what you do with your time and energy, not just food). You may be shocked at what standards you're setting or *allowing* for yourself.

Just how much have you 'settled' in Cycle 2?

If you're on track you'll find things only get better – you get more money sometimes, or you receive things that feed your spirit or help you enormously, you buy nice things for yourself or you are landed gifts and opportunities to reflect back to you what you *really* value and want.

After a period of a difficult and turbulent home situation, I was offered the keys to an apartment for a week. My friend was heading out of town, and I had the place to myself, to be alone and peaceful, to watch movies and cook for myself. It was bigger than my place at the time and was quieter and had more gadgets. It was in a better area. It felt amazing, I realized and remembered just what I valued – a quiet, peaceful and respectful home with a place to dream, and just 'be'. Now I can take that out into the world and re-assemble and enforce *my* way over what I want to experience. I have control over this.

Remind yourself that you do too, in your Second Cycle.

As a small extra note here, gardening becomes one possible outlet, and you'd be wise to get a potted plant or hanging basket to bring inside. You'll find more contact with nature is essential – sitting in the sun, eating your lunch outside instead of behind a desk, having your socks off in the grass, feeling your hands in the dirt, being in or around water more. You name it. Get back to basics and bring more of the natural world into your possibly overly technological or sterile existence.

CHOOSING COMFY

This month, during your personal 2-Cycle, invest in things that make you feel comfy and cared for. It's essential to your peace of mind. Your comfort level (or lack thereof) will dictate how great this Cycle shapes up to be. So do what you can to make your surroundings warmer/cooler/cozier/cleaner – whatever you need to feel good. That's really what you're ultimately going for right now – the 'feel good factor'. Like the pair of fuzzy socks I ended up buying under one Cycle 2 winter. Unbelievably comfy and unbelievably cheap (double score!) Good vibes bring more of the same to you. It's magical yet it's also pure common sense (something else you're loaded with this Cycle – notice how you have no time or patience for flimsiness, phoniness or waste).

No excuses, no cop-outs. **Make yourself feel good**. Seeds grow in the strangest of places so don't worry on the 'everything is not yet in place so how can I move ahead or feel secure?' mode of thought. Just plant some new seeds this season. Keep it simple, keep it real and give your time and energy only to things you think are *worthwhile*. Leave the rest and move on.

This is your fastest and most direct and practical way of crafting your path to prosperity and success during Cycle 2.

Handouts are common in some years so don't look a gift horse in the mouth (assuming there is no value attached to it, *attach* a value to it, by appreciating it and being thankful for it!) Maybe it's not wrapped exactly how you'd like it to be, but the universe wants to bring you wealth during this Cycle of this year, not take it away (unless that will give you the necessary prod once more to show you what you don't desire! You're really doing it to yourself ultimately). And the universe seems to know better than you do what you want (you can't kid yourself, and the universe is the ultimate mirror reflecting back to you where you're at with yourself).

It's worth being *specific*, in case you get what you asked for but it wasn't exactly what you had in mind. Oops! Again, be *as specific as you can*.

If you're not focusing on growing, you may find yourself focusing on lack. It seems inevitable. But look, this thing you're being offered is worth taking if it increases your value, comfort and practical support. Nothing lasts forever, nothing remains the same, but in Cycle 2 focus and invest your time, energy and money on *securing and maintaining something that will at least get you through the rest of this month with some stability.*

That's important. You need to not be rushing around wasting your time and energy by scattering. That's for Cycle 3 when you're meant to get out and move about. But secure something in Cycle 2 and it'll support and secure you through the other Cycles. So if anything, get back to practical basics instead of floundering over five attractive options. Limit your scope at some point and knuckle down to actually getting settled for the time being, so you can start putting down some form of roots.

Don't worry about stagnation – if you're already stuck, you'll feel it and Cycle 2 will ask you to get sensible and move out of a situation. You're working slowly towards Cycle 4 when you finally come home to yourself and find some sort of real safety. But it must first be built.

For now, however, land, ground, dig a trench, do something to secure a plot of land, a little space dug out the earth where you can put a few symbolic seeds, a nest egg, something for later, and something to help you stay put so that you can begin tending to the garden of You. At least you now have a focus, instead of drifting aimlessly.

Cycle 2 is about what you need, how to get it, asking others for help, and deciding what is best to focus on, to grow it. Choose your plot, think about your crop and plant the right seeds, or at least nurture the ones already planted by watering them and tending to them. Stop doing and investing in things that detract from your goal. (Pull out the Vision List you created in Cycle 11 and review it). Stay 'in the field' as it were, and stay committed in all areas, to your own growth, to furthering your own security.

The better you feel, the more allowing you are. The more allowing you are the more the good stuff will find you. Resistance keeps it away and at bay. It all starts with feeling good.

Decide what vibration/energy is dominant within you. On the subject of money; when someone mentions the word 'relationship'; when you talk about your city, your family, your social circle.

Get comfy, reach for the best feeling thought, do what you can do to enjoy yourself where you stand, with a view to moving towards an even better place (because, ultimately, you are...)

Get comfy – and, for the time being, tell everything else to get lost!

GETTING COMFORTABLE WITH DISCOMFORT?

Cycle 2 is an interesting one to experience because we sometimes get to witness just how comfortable we have become with *discomfort*. Maybe we settle for second best. Perhaps we're not altogether happy but we just accept it by giving up or remaining rooted in negative thoughts/feelings/patterns. Possibly the treatment we receive from others reflects our own distaste with ourselves (if you don't like you, then why should anyone else give you a big slice of the good stuff either?) It can be a harsh life lesson and a major period of awakening.

Are you in a rut? Are you feeling stuck? Are you wallowing or indulging in destructive emotions, patterns or activities? Are you just accepting things as they are so much so that you're no longer trying to improve your circumstances?

Yes, it can seem overwhelming but starting today make some small steps to simplifying and making your world more beautiful. Clean up. Organize a little. Light a candle. Lie on the bed and listen to music for a bit. Try drawing. Sing in the shower. Laze in a warm bath. Go for a massage. Or give one to yourself, or a friend. Be mutual. Hug yourself. Start simple. Getting comfortable sometimes starts when you look around and say, "This is not right and now I want to experience more how I really want to feel".

Your next step then, is about making things more comfortable by abandoning your own attachments to the old stuff. Old habits die hard but in Cycle 2 you can truly relinquish them, so long as you find new improved ones to take their place.

HEY, BIG SPENDER!
It stands to reason that it's mostly during Cycle 2 that you'll do some of your major spending, with big purchase items. Sometimes it's out of necessity – something expensive breaks down or needs replacing.

Sometimes a bill comes in that has to be taken care of (from that medical procedure you'd almost forgotten about, or the mounting subscriptions you've amassed throughout the past year, or the website renewal notice that arrives out of nowhere). Sometimes we get to splurge on something frivolous or glamorous, or perhaps on an experience (a season pass to a theme park, or a stay at a stellar hotel or a meal at a fancy restaurant).

You may find that it's during this time of your year that you spend a lot on others. It doesn't always have to be about you (that was Cycle 1). So you may splash out and shower others with gifts if you're in a position to. And they don't need to be expensive. Cooking for another, sharing a meal or just giving a massage or sharing your company is gift enough. Cycle 2 relates to the energy of Venus (see further below) and it's all about 'nice things'.

So whether you have enough to spend on what you need (or just desire) or whether you're scrimping and trying to save, robbing Peter to pay Paul (let's hope not literally), you'll find that now is the time when Big Numbers come into play and the whole area of expenditure and shopping (comparison, window, online or in-store) happens in a major way.

PLANETARY SIGNATURE: VENUS
Venus in Cycle 2 is earthy – reminding us of the pleasure (Venus) within the physical (Earth) realm. That means nice sounds, scents and so forth. That's why we spend more now. Or want more now. Comfiness. Quality. Quantity. Great sex. A cuddly hug. Amazing food. A nice sleep-in (and of course a cozy bed). A bubble bath. Venus casts her spell over us in this Cycle to enjoy more. To beautify ourselves and our space (make your bed, clear clutter, put up artwork, play music, light a scented candle, burn incense or oil, get new pillows and so forth).

Through appreciation of what we have, and the desire to further our enjoyment, we begin to share our generosity, thereby securing more of the same energy moving towards us. Like a universal bank, we receive constant funds of abundance, to enjoy. Our appreciation and enjoyment touches, and is felt by others, who in turn gain from it.

GIVE THANKS; GET MORE
You have a *lot* to be thankful for. Surprised? Your eyes for one, if you're reading this. You'd miss them if you lost them tomorrow. Did you eat today? Great. Did someone cut you off on the road while out driving? Nice, you have a car! Did you drop a call because of the signal? Wonderful, you have a phone.

Did you turn on the heater or open the window or flip on the air conditioning to cool down? Lovely. It's all a gift. Not a paycheck but a real gift. Well-being. The freedom to choose. The documentary *God Grew Tired of Us* follows the amazing adventure of refugees from Sudan visiting the Western World for the first time and discovering the 'miracles' of refrigerators and donuts! You'll marvel at how much we take for granted.

Giving thanks and being thankful for the good you already have (working lungs, eyesight, the ability to walk, your friend who bails you out, a smile from a stranger on the street today, a comedy show that cheered you up last night etc) opens the door for the universe to fill your shopping list. It understands what you like and therefore what you value and Cycle 2 piles on more of what that is – but – you have to set the bar, raise the standard and maintain it *by showing thanks for what you already have.*

GOOD VIBES, GOOD TIMES, GOOD STUFF

The good times have only just begun! No matter where you are currently at (during some Cycle 2s you'll already be in a pretty luxurious place, whilst other years in Cycle 2 you'll read this and wonder where your luck ran out) keep your eye on the prize, *your* prize, and keep a smile on your face knowing it's all unfolding as it should. The more you focus on the great stuff, the more is attracted your way. Do yourself a favor then as you read this, and ditch focusing on/obsessing over/dwelling on whatever it is that feels bad to you, or stuck.

You may have heard it before and roll your eyes in doubt, but how much are you putting it into practice? On a continual basis? If not, isn't it *worth* it to you, to at least try?

Ask yourself if you're weeding out those strangling weeds from your garden called doubt, futility and impatience. Weeds grow faster than anything, when left untended. That's why we have gardeners; but how many of us do our own personality weeding?

That's Cycle 2.

Fill your life with things that make you feel good. Simple. And the rewards will become evident instantaneously.

You can't continue ahead now unless you keep the soil clear so things can grow. Your life can't do with choking drama and idle hands. Your dreams *need* you to make them possible. And if you don't have a dream, start with a desire. To lose weight, to gain weight, to meet someone, to take your car in to get fixed, to build a business, to raise your income, to launch a project, to get out of a bad situation. *Your causes are all worthy causes right now.* Worth. Worthy. Worthiness. All good keywords for this cycle.

Regardless of whatever else is going on, maintain the good vibes and they'll continue to find you. Let money find you, know it's on its way, know you're worth it, and picture everyone handing you money because they quite simply *want* to. Play this game at the store: when the cashier hands you money, you receive it and say thanks, and mean it. With eye contact if possible, as though it's a gift. It is, energetically. When you hand them money to pay, say to yourself you're feeding yourself with something you desire and the money will return to replace it.

It's all a game, you're not playing with a set amount, it can come back in larger amounts, so tell yourself it'll come back in larger sums and mean it. People want to hand you money, they want to pay you, give you things and help you out! How happy have you been to pay for something you really admired, wanted, desired and craved? If you don't believe it, then fine, great – but they won't either.

The universe wants you to be right this Cycle, it wants to *prove you're right, to prove to you the accuracy of your own golden rules.* If you say something is a certain way, Cycle 2 will provide the practical real-life evidence to show you this. So you can say "See, I'm right!"

Can you believe that people want to invest in you because you want to invest in you? The universe works through people (they are your angels, this Cycle) so be available and open to taking what is offered. Enjoy it. Welcome it. And receive it. Like I did with the key to a peaceful home, not *my* home but since I wanted a peaceful home this Cycle, I got it. In that moment it was mine. And a couple of years or so after experiencing that, I now have a much bigger and quieter home than I ever dreamed possible back then. And I am so blessed and so thankful.

Eat, drink, laugh, dance, sing – and be merry. The universe loves a party, so host one in your heart today ... and more generous guests will be sent your way.

LET'S GET PHYSICAL

Food. Sex. Sensuality. Scents. Sights. Sounds. Manifest materialism. You claim you're not materialistic? Well, this chapter of your year is all about that, and for a very good reason. Cycle 2 will show us how we're doing with this physical life – do we have enough money, the right bank account, are we saving enough, are our spending habits messing up our lives creating debt or destruction, or is poverty consciousness causing ripples (we believe we don't deserve it; we fear money or feel it's evil, or fear we'll never have enough)?

Are we enjoying the physical body we've landed this lifetime? Are we enjoying nature? If not, then it may be time to do some of that weeding of your garden before you plant seeds. You do need good soil conditions even if it's not perfect. But you may as well begin this Cycle, in the first week of it, by tending to your earth. Improving it. Making it a quality that you deserve *and* desire.

Are we comfy in our bodies, in our jobs, in our homes, our beds, in our sex lives, in our gym routine, in our eating habits? Do we have enough sensuality – are we in touch with ourselves as a physical being? When was the last time you treated yourself to a gentle hug/massage in the shower? Are you expecting others to nurture you physically while going without giving it to yourself? Get busy today – you are your number one lover! Give yourself to yourself in Cycle 2. Go on!

Taking off socks and shoes and walking barefoot is a 2-Cycle experience, so is sitting under a tree. Getting back to nature. Being natural. Home cooking as opposed to take-away meals. Slowing down and smelling the roses as opposed to rushing against the clock. Long lazy sumptuous bubble baths just for the heck of it, or a longer-than-normal shower. New soaps, colognes, scented candles, new foods, aromas, textures.

SATIATE YOUR SENSES

Life is full of simple pleasures we often take for granted. Whilst living in Los Angeles one 2-Cycle, I ended up mapping out local hiking trails because my soul was screaming for more trees, more greenery, more parks and more grounding. I took more baths. It helped me sleep better. I wanted to get more comfy, earthy and chose filling foods. You'll feel the same.

What will it be for you? More hugs, rubs and cuddles? I think I'm already tapping into this greater need on the collective front – touch is so important to me (I have a 2nd house Moon in my birth chart, and thus my needs – Moon – are eternally in a sort of 2-Cycle). I think people underestimate the power of touch sometimes. When was the last time you were touched or gave someone a bear hug? What will you do to give yourself more grounding this Cycle (cut out caffeine or sugar perhaps, or drink more tea or cool lemonade on the patio, more time in the sun or at the park)? You'd be amazed how little we touch or are touched, and a lack of affection can lead to obsessions and a desperate need for affection which turns into sexual compulsion or overeating (or sexual repression and anorexia). Miss out on this now, in Cycle 2, and in six months it may reappear as a distorted form of physical gratification in Cycle 8 where our desires can become fixations on unmet needs. Then we may get to experience many symptoms of the same basic human need – we are tangible beings in this realm and we need a physical experience.

Tangible physical experience, then, is a major focus of your Cycle 2.

Nature is a place to recharge and find serenity so try and seek it out where you can. It's hard to be at war with yourself or anyone else when you're in a place of beauty – in a forest, by the beach, sitting in a sunny spot (even in your own living room with the window open), a park with your back against a tree, lying in the grass or walking barefoot. Nature plugs us back into our eternal source of power. Isn't it time for a revisit?

In 2-Cycles you'll notice that your senses are hungry:

Your **ears** need special melodies and music now; have you noticed? Your soul makes you reach for some soundtrack to sooth you and uplift your spirits or otherwise fit the mood you're in, alleviate suffering or reflect your reflectiveness. Is it time to get a new pair of headphones, a personal music player, a new CD collection? Or perhaps to spend more time listening to the simple soothing sounds of nature?

Your **mouth** waters for certain foods, from comfort snacks to 4am donuts, to green salads with that special dressing you can only find at that special shop, from that delectable wine to the cheap bubbly you can get two-for-the-price-of-one from the local store, from heavy meals to multiple snacks, you'll notice a hungering for specific foods as your appetite increases and your aura screams *feed me!* By all means indulge but try to go for balance where you can, to avoid overdoing it in only one food group. Your body will soon tell you when you're off balance.

Be careful if you're not feeling especially hungry as you could be feeding yourself in less healthy ways – getting high on *not* eating (studies show it can affect you in this way, making you highly wired), filling on sugars, being so busy you're not nurturing yourself properly. *You need food*, so fuel yourself sensibly or at least regularly if you find yourself indulging in special treats. Yes this is a gorging month so feel free to satiate your senses (like the huge box of chocolates I bought myself while working on this chapter during my own Cycle 2).

Your **nose** hunts out special scents – notice your purchasing of gingerbread candles, peppermint cologne, chocolate flavored lip balm, vanilla incense, luxurious shampoo and conditioner, special tobacco, unique perfumes, memorable hairspray, and any or every other possibly product you can buy that has a special smell you are drawn to. You choose. You'll notice and point out scents a lot more – from sexy body pheromones, to pungent nasties when you pass rubbish bins. Maybe you'll find yourself filling your lungs with the warmth of your fresh, clean laundry. What feeds your inner bloodhound?

Your **hands/feet/body** are hungry for certain fabrics. Like the feeling of fresh clean sheets on the bed. From comfy sweaters made of cashmere, silk, velour to rough textures that make you feel safe, strong and sturdy. You need beautiful stuff around you, and the concept of beauty is different for everyone. What's your personal style? One woman's gold chiffon scarf is another woman's gaudy nightmare. One guy's tight jeans are another guy's social embarrassment. Whatever feels good is what you'll go for, so notice a desire to buy new items that feel good to your touch, and generally give you that good vibe.

I found myself buying one of those screensavers of a live roaring fireplace during one particular Cycle 2, since I had no actual hearth at my home. It was soothing and magical to have the burning crackling fire in the background. Cozy. Comfy. And it felt so good. Though I prefer natural things, this helped a lot to generate the feeling of ease and comfort. It's not so much the actual thing but the feeling it engenders that you're truly going for this Cycle. A faux fur throw to cuddle up with on the sofa is cheaper than a real one (and more animal-friendly). And it feels just as soft.

You're all about quality and (where you can get it) quantity. Problems come when you start wanting more of one to the exclusion of the other. Why weigh heavily on either end?

So again to remind you (you need reminders in Cycle 2): Where are our values? What is most important to us now and long term? What do we care about, and what deep down do we *really* need? Back to basics. Can we have it? Can we allow it? What are your basics requirements? Can you live with purely these things for this month, or more importantly perhaps can you even try? Are you willing?

Are you willing to give up A to get B? Can we even *feel* the possibility of having what we want? Well, can you? That's a really important key and the next step in appreciating and enjoying the full extend and benefits of your own personal Cycle 2. This is *your* Cycle, your own. (Important words in Cycle 2, what is yours, all yours and no one else's. And do you let yourself enjoy it?)

IF YOU HOLD IT, IT'S YOURS!

Even if you rent, the place you're currently at is *yours*. No one else lives there. It's your home. Sure you may not own it literally, but it's yours during this time and place. Do you like it as it is? Or do you live as though everything you have is borrowed, worthless, used or second hand? Not that's there's anything wrong with something that has been passed down, or had a previous owner. But the key here is just that – ownership. Cycle 2 wants you to *have* something to call your own. If you have it here and now, today, it is yours. Tomorrow maybe not, but here it is. In this moment. No one else can be holding it, if you are.

Enjoy it!

Say repeatedly this month:
I want this.
I deserve it.
I am entitled to this.
This is Mine.
I have earned it.

Earning something feels good – it means you did what you felt you should do to get what you wanted. It didn't mean you needed to kill yourself overworking (unless you believe you need to work hard to have something). You just have to *feel good about what you've done and thus allow yourself to enjoy the benefits of the effort you've made.* You gave something and are receiving something in return. It's a contract of sorts. An energy exchange (which is all money/barter/trade really is). You were worth it.

How about doing this, during your Cycle 2: Do something good for yourself or another and then reward yourself. Pay yourself. Is it surprising to hear that? *Pay yourself!* Stop saving *just* for rent or for essentials, don't over-squander but *do* give back to yourself to prove you are worthy of the investment. Stop thinking "I don't know if I should – what if I need this money for something else?" Live like that and you'll always find that there's 'something else' and you'll be in even greater need of more for yourself because you're depleting yourself, overlooking yourself, cutting yourself out of the rich rewards of the cash flow in your life. Try to move beyond thinking you need more money and always for 'something else'.

You need it now for this thing you're thinking over. As long as it can improve your life right now in a practical way, either emotional comfort (something that's not so overpriced it causes more stress) or a practical item that will be an investment (in yourself, your work and your ability to support and improve your life; a gift that keeps giving back to you) then it's worth putting a little more money into it.

Money will come around to replace the stuff you spent. It can't if there's no room for it to come in. It needs to keep recycling, to show you need it because you're using it! The universe watches you, it truly does. It sees your real needs and motivations. The universe will react, to replace the funds you spent on a worthy cause – You are your worthy cause. Yes?!

Yes.

Buy yourself something. Give yourself a pat on the back, a rub, a sexy glance in the mirror, a more comfy bed. Laughing yet? At least crack a smile and try it. You'll be amazed, trust me, in what transpires this month when you *feel like your life is worth something*.

It really is.

You can't sit and demand things if you're not working on yourself, though. There's no energy exchange and that's what Cycle 2 is about. Effort put in = the results that come out. Garbage in = garbage out. The universe doesn't like us using spiritual laws to cash in and do nothing. Actually, let's re-phrase that. The universe has no bias, it doesn't care if you're lazy, but what we put out is what we get back. That in itself is reason enough to inspire us to make some effort. Neither does the universe care about the 'whys' of your motivation or intention.

You just need to *make something* and *make something happen* to show that at least you're making an effort. Once more: *make an effort.* That is Cycle 2, if nothing else. Who cares about results, it's not harvest time – you need to get out in the soil and *scatter seeds*. It works in nature so where do you get to be exempt from natural law?

Life follows nature, so follow nature and your life will follow your plans like clockwork. Everything has a season...

EXERTING EFFORT THE EFFORTLESS WAY

You can't be lazy in Cycle 2 and expect to grow (except around the waist ... if you didn't already put a little on in Cycle 1) unless you've already worked hard and you're now earning a return. In which case, congratulations; enjoy it but be careful you don't wallow in it or forget you need to keep moving forward. But for now, indulge, it's Cycle 2 and it's about feeding your belly, your bank balance and your enjoyment of life. It's your turn on the wheel so buy the car, go on the cruise, invest in the luxury carpet. Whatever you want, it's yours if you can afford it. And if you can't and you decide to max out your credit card, just know in Cycle 8 you'll have to take care of it six months from now, or at least you'll have to start making those payments big time.

Everything in Cycle 2 *must* be paid for somehow. Financially or energetically.

Don't forget it, everything has a price in Cycle 2 and everything is a give and take transaction. Don't take what you're not willing to pay for or pay *back* for, in full or in kind. We're not only talking money. Everything has a value in Cycle 2, you just have to work out what it is for others and what it is for you and if you can afford it. So before you continue, find out the price and work out what it's going to cost you short-term and for the long haul.

Will you make an effort to ask for what you want and need, or go after it, even if it means doing some footwork on your own and putting your skills to the test (writing, speaking, people, business etc)? It can be simple; it can be effortless. But it still needs to have effort involved (even the word effortless houses the word 'effort'!).

Are you uncomfortable and if so why are you tolerating that? What's the payoff for pain and suffering? Are you 'settling'? Are you being greedy or lazy? What can you do to make simple changes to all of this *today*? What are you 'available' for? This is your signal to the universe for what you are open to receiving.

Put up with crumbs (or continue to dwell and focus on them) and you're wearing a neon sign saying 'Available for Little'. Simple.

Only accept the best (or "Expect a Miracle!", as astrologer Linda Goodman promoted) and you're wearing a sign saying "'The best' please find me, because I want and deserve you".

You're not hoping or wishing, you're expecting. Forget about the ones who said, "expectations cause pain". Be available for the best, and the best must find you eventually. It is Law.

In Cycle 2, what you truly want in the healthiest way possible, wants you back! Your desire is a perfect match to you. To give you something, teach you something, offer you a new way of enjoying yourself. You're allowed to want what you want. Once you get it, you're then faced with what to do with it and if you want it any longer. But we'll cross that bridge down the line. Forget 'thinking', that's Cycle 3, for now it's about building something. Planning it. Can you share the wealth you already have and be grateful for the riches already present in your life?

There is one way to get what you want without burning yourself out. By appreciating what you have, being clear and firm on what you do want. By moving step-by-step towards it, moment by moment, feeling by feeling, thought by thought, action by action, belief by belief, expectation by expectation, visualization by visualization. Small, easy baby steps. That's all it takes. Continued effort. Apply yourself; a little every day. It'll soon mount up. And you'll get there in the end.

SELF-ESTEEM AND SATISFACTION: DO YOU THINK YOU'RE WORTH IT?

An aspect of Cycle 2 that many of us forget, but which we're bombarded with during 2-Cycles, is the aspect of self-worth. Do you feel you're worth being treated well? Are you worth loving? Are you worth being given nice things, having nice things? Are you worth a great job? Are you worth being respected? And do you feel others are worth it too?

Self-worth is your starting point in Cycle 2 to get in alignment with the good stuff around you. Maybe you've quit taking care of yourself because things have been hard. Maybe you're feeling sorry for yourself. Ask yourself when faced with a problem or obstacle or challenge, "Do I feel I'm worth it?" "Do I feel you're worth it?" and "Do I feel it's worth it?"

If you do, you can only attract more of the good stuff to you, to prove this rule.

Try saying, "**I'm worth it**" this Cycle and really meaning it. Try it now (if you're in public try it later, but also begin saying it inside to yourself), then mention it to others in conversation. It may feel awkward, selfish, unnatural at first – a good sign that you truly need this therapeutic process! – but finally you'll begin to hear yourself saying it out loud. It's empowering. You'll feel a sense of a release and relief; that you are actually allowed to feel good, to experience joy and satisfaction. And as we've mentioned many times over, Cycle 2 will bring more of this to you.

Feed it and it will feed you.

TOOLS OF YOUR TRADE

What resources do you have in your possession that you could cash in on? Are you good with people? Knowledgeable on a special subject? Psychic abilities? Emotional caring? The ability to fix things? A great organizer? Handy with a hammer? Green fingers? Someone who can see the bigger picture? Tell someone is lying? Perk people up? Skills and talents are uncovered now, in your 2-Cycle; they are extra tools in your kit. You can use them to secure more for yourself (cash, security, prosperity, well being, self-worth) or you might complain about the lack of these things simply because you're not aware or tapping into them! (Did you know there are websites out there where you can be paid a fiver for... well, just about anything!)

Lack, in Cycle 2, is just a sign of a well that you can fill up easily. And things happen now to push you to develop those 'lacking' areas of your life. Cash in on your inbuilt talents.

Note: You find others remind you of your talents by tapping into the exact same ones within themselves. Or someone receives a gift of something you truly want to remind you of your ultimate value, and perhaps it is one of your major goals and strongest desires right now. Use your opening awareness to see what is around you. If it's showing up, it must mean it's close to you vibrationally/energetically, and you could be the next stop if you keep yourself in alignment with it.

BEEF UP YOUR BOUNDARIES

Cycle 2s need us to get practical, get moving in the direction of our desires (outlined in our 11 Cycle Visions – revisit that list that you designed in Cycle 11) and then to draw some boundaries so we don't waste time needlessly pursuing things that aren't part of our dream. You may have to draw the line with certain people, projects, or pastimes, but it's worth it. Is it helping you enjoy your life, find more appreciation, or work you towards your dream? If not, rethink it. You're setting up your boundaries and availability for the future in this cycle.

PICKING YOUR PRIORITIES

Due to its desire to get you practical and using your resources wisely, Cycle 2 is the best time to start getting a list of things to do day by day (or the night before). It's simple – make a list and check stuff off when you're done. Each day you'll get more done than you used to.

Simple. Effective. Try it.

Priorities are likely to shift. From casual sex to serious relationship needs; hoarding money to enjoying the moment more. From worrying about today to planning for a stronger future; from focusing on work to reconnecting with your kids. It's up to you to find out what is important now.

Now *focus on that*.

NOT JUST STUFF, YOUR STUFF: TREASURE OR TRASH?

Whether you have to move and therefore pick up and touch every single object you own, or have to price things to sell them, or you're buying things for yourself; you get to focus on your stuff and the things you surround yourself with. I helped a friend of mine move during his 2-Cycle and he had to go through every item, individually wrap it, and he kept finding things he forgot he owned tucked away at the back of the closet. I heard him say, "Do I want this anymore?" I don't know how many times. Stuff accumulates. A year goes by and we've amassed new things, whether from gifts or things we just can't let go of.

Ask yourself the same thing: of everything! Do you want it anymore? And if not, why is it still in your life? By the time you get to Cycle 8, roughly six months from now, you may be faced with the ultimate test of letting it go or having it leave your life. And it may be even harder then.

So whatever stuff you're looking at, focusing on or arguing over (maybe it's the old things you've carried with you all your life or new things you have to buy to replace the old), you'll see what you have and you may be surprised to find they don't mean the same to you anymore. They don't hold the same feeling or meaning or value as they once did. Great. It's time to upgrade. Let go of stuff that's bogging you down. Cycle 1 helped you find the new you, Cycle 2 helps you surround yourself with objects that reflect that. And that could mean fewer things, as you clear them away or give them away, or it could mean a different brand or quality of stuff.

Let your surroundings reflect you by choosing things that inspire you on your new path.

Your things are important now. The stuff you don't share. The things that are personal to you. Stuff no one else has any rights to. You earned them. Whether it's a gift or something you paid for, or found, if it's in your possession and wasn't stolen or borrowed it is truly *yours*. Congratulations! And it's worth saying – if you do cheat, steal or otherwise manipulate people out of things in Cycle 2, it'll come back and bite you in the future somewhere and you'll lower your own appreciation of things and devalue yourself in the process. What you put out comes back, so somewhere you'll end up being disrespected and unappreciated – if only by yourself.

And that's so against the principle of Cycle 2, because it's simply *not worth it*.

So ... look at your belongings. Your items. Your objects. Your possessions. Your junk. Your storage unit. Your boxes under the bed. Your things. Your special trinkets. Your one-of-a-kinds.

2-Cycles are virtually guaranteed to see you buying some special things you truly want to possess. Nice things. Things that will last. Or things that are quality but last only for the moment you're enjoying them (a 90-minute massage, a gourmet box of chocolates, a cocktail, great sex).

HAVE IT TO GET IT

Ditch hope. Hope is always for something out of reach. It may arrive. It may happen. It may get better. May. Might. It's a potential, solely a possibility. *Knowing* on the other hand means it's a given. A strong, stable, solid fact. You don't need evidence or proof, because you just know. Like your name. Ever checked your birth certificate to verify it? No. You know. Even if you're unsure, you have to *know* somewhere in Cycle 2, or at least act as though it's a given.

The Law of Attraction states that we can only attract that which we are (or that which we vibrate to energetically... what we're in-tune with). To be rich we have to be rich (or at least have convinced our unconscious we already are by reveling in the bounty we already have). Rich is a feeling, not a state of being. We get more of what we are. What we focus on becomes us, we become it. We become that which we desire.

See how most of us have been walking around waiting, wishing and hoping for something that often never materializes? Why would you want something if you already have it? It's how it works energetically. It's magnetism. Like the single folk who laugh when they meet someone and suddenly everyone else seems interested in them. By having a relationship, we relax our urgent need for it, and thus it comes to us. We attract that which we are, and are vibrating to. Act as if you have it, and it's yours. If you want wealth, you have to carry a wealth signature, a vibration that is wealthy. It's not about what you have in the bank, its about what you have inside. Cash in on your internal incentives.

'Getting something' of course doesn't mean our lives are then complete, fixed or eternally content. For many of us, the climb to getting this object of desire is worth more than the actual attainment. Children get bored with their toys eventually (the build-up to Christmas morning is much more energetic... the *expectation* and *anticipation*). Adults get bored with their cars. We get the shiny red one and we're still stressed. We get back to full health then begin eating unwisely again. The quest and the conquest it seems are more important.

Why?

Because the objects themselves that we pursue aren't the things that give us anything. The feelings are inspired and created from within. *We want the feeling, not so much the object we pursue.* We believe external things will make us feel a certain way (when I get 'A' or 'B' I'll finally feel happy); but it never works that way.

We want the feeling, not the thing. And feelings can be generated anytime anywhere without any prior experience of them. Impossible? Give it a shot. Give yourself one minute to think, act, and feel like a billionaire. You can do anything. Go anywhere. Be anything. Buy anything. Right now, as you're reading this! Look around. Want it? It's yours! All financial stress of unpaid bills and debt and survival has gone. Wow!

Do it. See it. Feel it. Really indulge. Enjoy it! Then read on...

How did you get on? Feel relief? Excitement? Wonderment? Did you see through new eyes? What shifted? You may not be a billionaire this moment, but you know the feelings you want to experience: Relief. Excitement. Calmness. Possibilities. You became it. You knew emotions. Use them as your fuel coupled with your desire for 'things'.

Ever heard of the phrase, 'fake it till you make it'?

It works along the same lines, although holding the thought that you are pretending can be defeatist, but it's a starting point. The principle is that by acting confidently for example, eventually we'll become confident. How can you not? The emotions we choose to fill up our inner space draw others of like vibration to us; bad days bring bad stuff. You've seen it time and time again.

So if you want it, act as though you already have it. *Feel* it first and foremost. Focus on it still, with passion, desire, attention. Not as though it's far from you, out or reach, but here with you, at this moment. You already own it; possess it. It's in your hands, your life, your experience. It's not foreign. It's known. It's *yours*. Act as though you don't need it; you just want it. Cycle 2 is less about needs, remember, and more about Desire.

Then give thanks for having it!

'Have' it, and you're more likely to get it.

And don't forget the key ingredient in this potion – know you can have it, because ...

You're worth it.

CYCLE 2 ACTION PLAN

* Write down how much money you *have* right now. To the penny.
* Write down how much you *need* for all the necessities (rent, phone, car, food etc).
* Review your budget – can anything be cut, improved or tightened up?
* Write down how much you *want* (monthly or yearly).
* Enjoy simple pleasure – baths, walks, nature, food, hugs.
* Know you're worth it. Set your value. Name your price.
* Invest in yourself!! Remind yourself that you are entitled to the good life.
* Prioritize what you truly want, value and need, and be pro-active:
* Begin moving towards it, today.
* Write some checks for things you desire. Enjoy window-shopping for new things you'd normally feel were beyond your reach.
Begin feeling the possibility.
* Relax ... patience ...

In a sunny year:
People pick up your tab. They offer you dessert. You get taken to the fair or to great restaurants, you get to sleep in comfy cushy beds with no scheduled wake-up time, you get to wear silk pajamas and laze about, you don't need to lift a finger or pay a dime. A major gift lands in your lap and it's exquisite. Wow! You can pay all your bills and have money leftover for boxes of chocolates, your drink of choice, a new pair of shoes or comfy sweater, sexy shirt, or make-up or whatever else you consider a quality item you really desired (or a gift for someone you love). Or in those random years when you have very little, little is all you need, want, crave or desire. You just get by, or people give you things, or cash comes in when you need it most. You're content. Rich even, with simple pleasures (the best things in life are free or can't be touched or seen etc).

In materially wealthy years – the ones where you get to actually see and *hold* the items of your fabulous 'ch-ching!' wealth, luxury is around every corner from gifts given to you that blow your mind, to sensual hugs and massages offered free or for trade – you still really get to remember that the best things in life are truly free (and why do you need to pay for anything when there's enough goodwill to go around?) But you can buy the things you want anyway, so what the heck! You want to share your good fortune with others, who in turn bring you more of the same. You have no need or desire to be cheap or stingey! There's enough food, comfort, cash, drink and good vibes to go around. By giving, your own supply is replenished. How can you gain more unless you empty first? Holding on creates stagnation, and energy likes to move freely! You can enjoy, receive and give because: You feel 'safe'. Or in reality, feeling safe brings these good things to you.

Some years you'll hit it big – with a lottery win, a payout you never expected, a settlement, a windfall, or a new job that offers more. Other years you'll have little but feel like you have it all. The same feeling is felt – you feel 'full', you feel 'wealthy', you're surrounded by nice things (yours or others' it doesn't matter it's still being drawn to you). You can't be in the presence of anything you're not intended for very long in this world of attracting-molecules, you can only end up *really* close to what you are, and if you stay around it long enough you really become it.

You feel you have all bases covered and everything you could ever wish for. It's a feeling not based on material goods (though you may be surrounded with them, it won't matter). You're handed gifts, and even if you're not wealthy in the bank people give you things that are so useful, and really help you out when you need it. Someone is watching over you. Providing for you.

The great money years will see you buying some of the best stuff, and not worrying about the cost. You get to satiate your senses. What a treat. In other years you may find things given to you that you never even paid for – you're just as wealthy but it was offered to you on a plate. Eat up! It's your turn for the good stuff, so enjoy. The more you accept, the more is given. The more you share and enjoy, the more is given. It's a repeating Cycle of abundance. Good feelings magnify. It feels as though you're banqueting with the Ghost of Christmas Present.

In a crummy year:
The Ghost of Christmas Past is pestering you with unfulfilled obligations, bills, pending payments and broken promises, and the Ghost of Christmas Future haunts you with visions of being on the streets, unemployed or stuck; and it worries you and drains you like a bad tax audit. In these years, you're scratching under the sofa for the last two coins that'll allow you that second load of laundry. You get paid 100 and a bill comes in for 120. Rent goes up or it's the 30th of the month and rent is due tomorrow and you only have a quarter of it. The website you created last year now needs you to renew it for a fee and since it generates work you'll have to. You're eating crackers instead of crème-filled cookies, having a night in the bath instead of the local bar even though your friends are throwing a party but you can't buy any drinks and you're too proud to let anyone else pay for you. How demeaning.

You're wearing socks two days running or longer because you never found that last coin for the laundry. Tofu lunches, rice dinners and soup suppers are your staples. Someone makes you feel bad and you keep beating yourself up about it and it's no surprise it gets worse because you're feeling lousy anyway and in some way, they're right. Look at you. What a loser. Something breaks and you have to fix it and you're struggling and fighting to claw your way back to zero (status quo) without any gain. All that effort lost or wasted, or you have none and you're stuck, squandering time and squandering the little you have to wallow or indulge. You have no plan, or the one you had you can't let go of, and it's failing.

So it got bad. Accept it. Stop resisting. You're a stick-in-the-mud (or stuck in a rut), and you know what your biggest problem is? The complaining you're doing! Do you want to change it? If so, you need a plan, something concrete to stick to. Otherwise you'll drift. Start where you are. Stop complaining about what you *don't* have and stick-stick-stick to what you *do want*. With tenacity. With firm determination. With 100% of your being. That is plan enough, right now. And do things relating to it. Simple. Have that plan and eventually you can't go wrong, and you'll suddenly find you're going right.

Cycle Lesson

Self worth is the basis of everything you set out to do and life now helps you confront how much you value or devalue yourself. We focus on what we value and feed the things we desire. Without a strong sense of entitlement, we can't accept and create the goods we want (nor enjoy the things we already have). Finding our inner resource and our inner richness gives us a platform and a tool that will aid us in furthering our dream, otherwise we're spinning our wheels avoiding what we say we want by finding proof we don't deserve it. Life is trying to show you that as you decree, so it is.

Celebrity Spotlight

- ⊚ Cher (a Cycle 2 Taurus) puts her 1.7 acre plush (and self-designed) Malibu estate – which includes six bedrooms, seven bathrooms, a theatre, gym, tennis courts, several verandas and reflecting pool – on the market for $43 million, during her Cycle 2.
- ⊚ Viv Nicholson – born with Venus (money, beauty, expenditure) in Taurus (Cycle 2) – wins a whopping £152,319 on the Littlewoods Pools in England in 1961 and says she will "Spend Spend Spend!" – a catchphrase that remained with her when she was finally left with nothing.

Tips to successfully navigating your Cycle 2 Evaluation

- ⊚ Put your priorities in order – what's important to you?
- ⊚ Open a new bank account that saves you money or earns you credit.
- ⊚ Sign up for a credit/debit card that gives you cash each time you use it.
- ⊚ Ask for a pay rise or adjust your rates to reflect what you deserve.
- ⊚ Go for quality not quantity. Say "I'm worth it" often.
- ⊚ Invest in something useful – stocks, bonds, a savings account or personal tip jar.

- Stick money to your wall or bathe in a mountain of bills.
- Buy the brand spanking new car, house, outfit, computer, ring, watch, sun glasses, _____ etc. (Fill in blank with your choice of luxury).
- Learn about Abundance and the Law of Attraction.
- Carry more cash and less cards – see, feel, smell the sensuality of money.
- Look for loose change under your sofa or bed, in a pocket/or laundry.
- Replace old or worn out objects, you deserve better.
- Light candles; buy incense or a new perfume/cologne, soap scent or body wash.
- Start growing your own vegetables.
- Buy a pendant, scarf or something for your neck.
- Go for a massage – you'll wonder why it's been so long.
- Sit under a tree or in the park with your socks off.
- Give yourself a hug (and anyone willing).
- Find music that reflects your mood.
- Give yourself a break and be lazy.
- Go camping, hiking, for a walk in the park, to the beach, rock climbing, have a food or mud fight (Cycle 2 hungers for nature).
- Sing - Cycle 2 connects you to your throat chakra and thyroid.
- Bring more color and earthiness into your life.
- Value everything you do – after all, it's an extension of you.
- Eat well – cook a gourmet meal, bake bread, a cake, make muffins, make it a *feast*!
- Get more fresh air.

～ Surf Cycle 3 ～

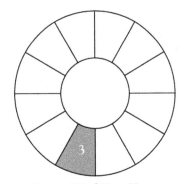

Time to Find Your Voice
Seek and Share New Ideas
and Let Curiosity Connect you to New Possibilities

Memorable Messages from:

People who want to talk to you
People you don't want to talk to
Writers and public speakers
Authors and editors/librarians
Interviewers and messengers
Bus drivers, cabbies and truckers
Those texting calling/emailing you
Your phone company/carrier
Your cashier
Gemini people
Spokespeople
People who are 'busy'
Parking attendants/valet parking staff
Your driver/car rental or sales staff
Your brother or sister
Karaoke staff

Train station attendees
The people waiting in line with you
Gossips/chatterboxes
Your neighbors – above, below, next
   door, across or down the street
   from you
Telemarketers and salespeople
Online chatters
Post Office staff/mail delivery agents
Your partner's relatives
Your friend's date/lover
The one you're sitting next to
Computer departments
The local reporter
Mail delivery staff /people at the
post office

What you'll need:

A notebook and working pen(s)
A hungry mind
A crystal clear phone/microphone/pager/computer
A reliable ride
Your tongue in the right way

Look around you. Take a closer look. What do you see?

Things a bit dull, boring, monotonous, the 'same old same old'? It happens. It's not long before the fresh loses its sparkle, you get tired of being so practical in Cycle 2 battering your budget or balancing your bankbook in order to get what you want (or work out if you can afford it) going without or possibly over-indulging (lucky you) ... and now, you have to start something else off, go on a new quest of discovery. Need some space? Time for a change, you think?

Well, breathe a sigh of relief (breathing is something you'll be doing a lot of this Cycle, and you'll need it) because Cycle 3 is here. I like to call this one the 'What's New Pussycat?' Cycle because you're invited to ask questions, get curious, sample, try out and talk and think to your heart's content.

In short, it's time once more to get moving.

In your 3-Cycle, you'll get to explore your world, seeing familiar places from a new perspective and discovering others that you never even knew existed. Now is also the time to experiment with other modes of transport – catch a bus, roller-skate, walk, or maybe trade in your car for a different model.

Whatever the case, you get to not only change how you *see, explore and get through* your day and world, but you get to change *what you do within it*.

What you're looking at gets to change as does *how you're looking at it*.

One change affects the other.

Like the day you decide to sit in the library, find a book you never expected, chat to someone who becomes a new friend and invites you out and you wind up meeting the next person who has something you really need, to continue on to the next level of your life. Change happens and it's here, this month. Ready to stop planning, get up and start plodding on? Good.

This is a get up and go time, and it'll be fun.

IT ALL STARTS WITH A THOUGHT

The first thing you'll probably notice, if you haven't already, is the millions of ideas you have. You have to decide how you'll use your brainpower right off the bat. I decided to dedicate fifteen minutes each morning for meditation at the onset of this Cycle, one year. Calming your mind is a great thing to do, to ready it for the multitude of options ready to pour forth.

You're likely to have an itch and you're not sure what will scratch it. A trip? Getting out certainly helps. But where? Anywhere! What about throwing a dart in your local map?

Visit your local Information kiosk or tour guide facility immediately. Grab a free paper for your area, to see what events, shows, or openings are happening today, tomorrow, this week and this month. There will be something that grabs your attention, guaranteed. Life wants to help you now, but you have to at least make the effort to *look*. If you up and get going, a new location could be just the thing to help you rediscover a lost (or more likely forgotten) part of yourself.

Cycle 3 was the time of year I found myself in Tujunga, California – a place I knew nothing about and had never visited before and discovered the 'E.T. House' was just down the road, the place where they filmed the actual movie; tucked away in the quiet valley outside of Los Angeles.

Chances are you'll notice pretty quickly that you're having to visit a new part of town. Maybe an invitation, a new job lead or a friend has moved (or you, yourself, are planning it) but you'll wind up driving down new streets, visiting new vendors or stores or businesses or apartment complexes on new streets in new neighborhoods. Bingo! – you're already being initiated into Cycle 3 and all its benefits.

Your job? Just to stay alert and stay curious. An ***open mind and open eyes and ears bring you all you need now***. New Stuff. Freshness.

And those great visions and ideas flying around – are you writing them down, making a list, keeping a file on your computer or personal organiser, or scratching it down on a notepad, or telling whoever is nearby at the time? (Yes, suddenly you and everyone around you is chattier than normal.)

If you don't ask and you don't explore, you don't get. You can't sit at home and expect Cycle 3 to deliver people through the mail. True, the universe does have a way of finding you, even in hiding (and you may just wind up with an all-important missive reaching you in the most far-out of places) but no matter where you are when you're reading this during *your* Cycle 3, you may find the mail holds some clue, or your computer does – via an email or website you stumble across. But you still need to make the effort. Didn't Cycle 2 teach you that?

THEN COMES YOUR SAY

Yes, someone wants to hear from you. Or you want to have your say. You'll have to answer an important question, answer a serious email, make an important phone call, get your ideas down on paper or in some tangible form, or at least get your tongue in straight and your brain in gear. Someone suddenly slaps a microphone on you and asks you to speak up. Or you feel it's so important to spit it out and straighten someone out by telling them where you stand. Or maybe they're about to do the same to you. Or they want your signature on a document. It happens without fail when your 3-Cycle clicks in. Just you watch. You may have to choose your words carefully, or someone is picking over what you've already said or going over it with a fine-toothed comb, judging, critiquing or editing what you had to say, and why you said it.

You may even be marked now by the absence of words, and the things you choose not to say (or forget to).

What do you want to say – what is your ultimate aim? Find that and keep it in mind when you open your mouth. Try not to stray from what you're seeking and what you want to say. Words sometimes get us lost, unless we know where we're trying to get to. Keep your mental destination in mind and it'll be easier. Then you won't get sidetracked by the strong verbal tactics of others, or get caught up in silly games – arguments, debates and hot-air time drains.

Expect then, a lot of sharing on the communication front. Like the bus driver who somehow couldn't resist getting into a verbal duel with a lady who somehow upset him when she got on the bus, for about ten city blocks – during one of my Cycle 3 trips around town. The whole bus was host to a showdown of biting criticism, religious spiel and venomous attacks, that (by the end of the ten-block stretch) actually seemed funny. People just have to vent and there's plenty to say during Cycle 3 – whether it's you, or those around you at this time.

And it needn't be anything of substance, if you get caught up in pointless verbal venting.

MESSENGERS ON THE WAY

During your 3-Cycle, the universe may use your brothers and sisters, neighbors or other strangers on the street or anywhere else, to grab your attention, or deliver a timely message or clue to you. Random pieces of paper, books falling off shelves, someone handing you something. And so on and so forth. You can help the process along, therefore, by actively seeking new things and going new places. Even online classifieds. Newspaper ads. Chatting to someone about your proposals, views, ideas. You'd have to be asleep to not see the signs during Cycle 3. Something is crackling. Information is flowing. Things are adapting and changing. You're on the move, or soon will be.

Yes you're busy, but look – life is piecing together a puzzle for you. See it yet? Stay alert.

With so much mental mind-buzzing, you're sure to notice an *increase in communications*. We'll go into what kinds soon (stay glued to your mailbox, email inbox and voice mail for further details). The airwaves are alive. People are talking. If not with you, then *about* you. The air is magical. More emails and text messages I am sure get sent and received by people under Cycle 3s.

What about you?

Tapping away at the keyboard, replying to voice mails, trying to keep track of the 1001 things you have to do, people you have to see, things you need to take to the post office, forms you have to fill out, documents and paperwork you're stacking up or rifling through? Let's hope it's not a Mercury Retrograde for you or you're sure to be backtracking through a lot of what you've already begun, during Cycle 3.

You'll be aided in your communication quest by at least one Gemini person who arrives to remind you what it means to ask questions, and seek answers (whether or not you find them). Whether they frustrate you with their busyness, their little white lies (or huge black ones!), let you down by being overbooked or ditzy, or show you the best ways to communicate, or the new technology to use to get your message across (a new phone, computer, printer etc), you'll get a Communications lesson free of charge. Stay alert, go along for the ride, and make your own mind up when faced with the choices presented you. Gemini tour guides are a lot of fun, and a change of scenery is always a good thing.

MERCURY RETROGRADE?!

Mercury retrograde happens three times a year and without getting too complicated, it means that the planet that rules this Cycle, Mercury, appears to go backwards in the skies for about three weeks. You can imagine what that does to any attempt at communication. If it falls in your 3-Cycle then this year will be one you should keep an eye on to make sure you don't trip yourself up by overextending.

In these Mercury Retrograde Cycles, you'll hear from people you have unfinished business with, get to clear up your paperwork and computer hard drive, you may delete names and numbers from your phone, decide you need to stop talking like this or stop harping on about that, or you find you're cut off from one person or you decide to draw an end to communication with another. Or you get to see just how you've been using your time and brainpower and change it. Not to mention the old writing you can retrieve and revamp and rework.

Re-writing, revisiting, re-minding and re-wiring your world is all part of the Mercury Retrograde period, especially when it falls during your 3-Cycle. Go back, see if you missed anything, then decide how you'll proceed. Inject newness into the old, wrap it up and decide if it's worth carrying with you into your present and future.

Expect also some things to be re-scheduled. People to disappear. Things you buy to have to be returned. For people to not call you back. To not get the message. Or for you not to get an important one, yourself. For a voicemail to get wiped, or a computer file to get deleted. Or your phone or keys to vanish (or reappear if you'd previously lost them). I'm still waiting for mine to show up in this Cycle, as I lost them before I entered it. I'll no doubt stumble across them soon.

Whatever is begun/launched/initiated/bought under Retrograde Mercury (especially if it relates to Mercury stuff: meetings, phone calls, television/ radio/writing/speaking engagements, listening, computers, books, paperwork, commuting, scheduling, communication tools, neighbors, siblings, work procedures, ideas, etc) is likely to turn out differently that expected, if it pans out at all.

Mercury Retrograde periods reflect back to us how we're using our minds (that's Mercury stuff). Cycle 3 does the same, but under a retrograde period you get to see it in its full force. What you think about, dwell on, obsess over, hold pictures in your brain over, talk about, and chew on, is more likely to manifest, from the sheer force of attention you're giving it. Retrograde Mercury periods give you a chance to retrain your brain – to work better for you. To retrace your thoughts, and to decide to think differently. To focus on solutions, not problems. What you desire, not what you don't desire. To keep your destination in mind and not to fuss over the small details that are annoying and niggling you, and keeping you from your main destination.

So use this period – see how your brain is being used by what is showing up in your life experience. In the conversations around you. The themes, the events. The symbols.

Ride it out, be adaptable and realize that it may just work out better for you (and get you out of something that really wasn't right for you) if it does go belly-up during this oddball Cycle. If you don't like what you're looking at, look somewhere else.

CARS, COMMUTING AND CONVERSING: OR GET OUT AND SPIT IT OUT!

You may begin the Cycle on the very first day and find that one message you receive is very important indeed. Something someone says really hits you hard and makes you stand up and pay attention. Either way, somewhere in Cycle 3, what was said is sure to be a big deal indeed.

Prepare for some pretty big emails, telegrams, whispers, calls, letters and gossipy news.

More people hop in their cars and commute and more people hike up their phone bills in Cycle 3, because there's so much to say and just not enough time to say it.

You may wind up playing chauffeur during your own 3-Cycle at some point, like my friend who ended up irate over carpooling stresses when he worked for a local high school. The students were training for an upcoming parade but apparently no parents were available to help on that day. You may have to be the chauffeur or find a driver during this time just like he did, last minute. For some reason life needs you to get up, get going and get on the road (or get the show on the road). Keep your car in tip-top condition with fuel checks, oil changes etc. Be on the safe-and-sure side, so you're not left stuck at the roadside ten minutes before the game/movie/interview.

[If you can't afford a car yet, maybe it's time to get familiar with the local public transportation routes.]

Don't have your license yet? Maybe it's time to go for it. Cycle 3 is the best time to learn something new, especially driving. Or to renew an old license.

UPGRADE YOUR TOOLS

Speaking of renewing, how are your communication tools? Is it time for a new fax machine, laptop, music player, stereo? A new hard-drive or zip drive to back up your computer files just in case something happens. I began burning professional CDs of my astrology classes during one Cycle 3 and my laptop DC jack was broken so I had to buy an external battery charger to gain access to all my files again. Maybe it's time for a better phone plan? Enough minutes? Maybe a shared family/partner plan to save cash. A speakerphone, or headset while driving (and have you made a note of that car tune-up I already recommended or does something in the car need repairing?). Or maybe you need a backup in case the battery drops on an important call.

Maybe you never had a phone until this Cycle, like me – I held off having a mobile phone at all until I finally decided it was best to be connected in case of emergency somewhere, and it was in a Cycle 3 that I made the leap.

Sadly the local birds are feeling this – did you know that many have left the cities now due to an overabundance of mobile phone signals? Progress comes with a price it seems.

Buy a bus pass, carpool – make travel and traffic a lot easier (and cheaper) – or be prepared to make friends with your local city cabbies. Either way, you're going to have to find a way from A to B and chart the times, schedules, traffic flow and so forth as Cycle 3 wants you to find the best way to get from point A to point B, allowing for possible sidetracks or detours to point D first.

You may have to get on foot and walk quite a few blocks around town to get by, during some Cycle 3s. Again these times are designed as a pit stop in your annual quest to find new things. Otherwise you'd be repeating last year, and no one wants that. Each year is a new chapter in a grander story. Your story. So if you find yourself having to walk, keep an eye on the scenery, and the people who pass by on your way from who knows where to wherever you're going.

MR OR MRS COMMUTER ON THE MOVE

I'm sure you're reading this while on the go, or at least during busy days when you're commuting or between calls, conversations, thoughts, emails, projects or web sites.

It's a great time for:

- New publications (fancy writing for a local rag?)
- Advice columns (you could be the next great Agony Aunt/Uncle/ Bitchy Best Friend).
- Radio shows (call one up, be a guest or host your own online).
- Talk shows (join as an audience member or tell them about yourself and your work).
- The book/novel you've had sitting around on the shelf or in the back of your brain.
- Online blogs (written or visual).
- Journals (private or public).
- Jobs and projects in the communication fields.

This Cycle is a paparazzi party. And you're in a prime place to be involved – if you have the right thing to say, don't mind getting up out of any rut you may be currently sinking in, and don't mind telling it like it is.

How confident are you with your ideas, and how willing are you to have your say? Are you a good writer? Show us. Have a great voice? Get on radio, record a CD, read for the blind, do children's audio books. Go to karaoke, even. Get a voice-over contract. You have to start somewhere. How about learning a new language, or opening up a dictionary and learning a new word? It's a trivial pursuit month – keep an eye out for finding some piece of information and then someone needing you to pass it along not long after.

You're the networker this month, the phone switchboard operator; plugging people in, passing stuff along, getting people from A to B, D to K (maybe even Z to T) and generally staying busy with your octopus arms. You may decide to try what is a passing fancy, something fascinating while you're symbolically window-shopping and finding what is worthy of your time and attention.

Get used to juggling, and watch your caffeine intake, you're wired enough!

PLANETARY SIGNATURE: MERCURY

This Cycle is ruled by the planet Mercury – the messenger of the planetary family, and under the element of air, relates to circulation. Hence the need now to get out and circulate, to get the air moving in your life (hopefully not just hot air), to circulate about your world, moving here and there, zipping around, collecting the pollen of information like a bee in a beautiful garden. Freedom to change, adapt, shift, sample is essential if this process is to be successful and enjoyable.

With Mercury, we can collect information, label things and use our mental faculties to understand them. We sift through data, learn, and communicate our thoughts. Our findings are pooled into the vast energy-library out there (like the internet). We can discover what others have thought, and how we think about their own discoveries. Using the energy of Mercury now to look, seek, ask and see, we can do our part. That way, you'll be ready to create your bigger picture in the Cycle directly opposing this one (and thus strongly connected) – Cycle 9, the time of finding meaning in it all.

WORDs ARE YOUR sWORD

If you have a presentation or you want to put something down on paper or sell it, this is a great time – use the right chosen words at the right chosen time and you'll hit it big. It's your re-wiring month. Why bite your tongue – this is *the* Cycle of chitter-chatter! Be careful though (gossips or loose lips take note), you'd better be aware just how loose your lips are or how forked your tongue is, if you don't want to turn Cycle 3 into a monumental mess you'll later regret (in Cycle 4 a time when we have a habit of replaying the past).

Wherever you end up, whatever you think and whatever you are inclined to say during this Cycle, remember **Communication is everything**. So, if you can, keep talking – but *make sure to listen too*. We may get to hear a lot from those around us on "can you believe how they spoke to that person?" or "did you hear what they said?"

We judge others on what is said and accordingly are judged in Cycle 3 on what we say.

Sometimes stuff gets lost in translation in 3-Cycles, you think you're listening but you're really pulling apart what they said and putting together your own dialogue or waiting for a gap big enough to shove your big mouth in. Clarify. Question. Double check. Repeat if necessary but firstly make sure you really, truly heard what was said.

And ***don't assume!*** Assumptions are dangerous in Cycle 3, you need the facts. The cold, logical, when-you-bring-it-all-down-to-basics information so that you can make an informed decision. That's why you're a journalist in your own life this Cycle. Collect clues. Seek out info. Scope out the bottom line. Fish for facts. Nose out knowledge. You're in your own Trivial Pursuit Cycle where information is there for the asking and for the taking if you have an appetite.

Do yourself a favor: Be a clean slate, without prejudice or bias. Find out what was meant. Some people use words well in Cycle 3, while others may infuriate you because they "didn't mean it like that". Don't get clever or try to be smart, just keep following the thread of thought or line of conversation and you'll soon be taken to a new and better place.

What are you writing or could you write? A novel, screenplay, poetry, a blog, a speech, a letter of complaint, a postcard? Whatever it is, it's a big deal and should be. It's showing where you are right now. So keep working on it.

Or start it. And remember, it is *permanent* (unless a fire takes the paper out, or a computer crash erases a hard drive). It's eternal and we forget that fact. You could change an entire world with your story (*A Christmas Carol* by Charles Dickens is still read and played on TV every Christmas and the same holiday lyrics are sung every year from who knows when!?), or be unforgettable to those you hurt (like one cruel word, during an argument).

Words do matter, whether you slap them down on paper or across someone's face through the air or over the phone. You'll learn that, in Cycle 3. You have the power of a magic spell ('spelling', takes on a whole new meaning in this Cycle as you 'cast spells' with the words you choose). Watch your mouth, then. And the words that cross your lips, or sit on the tip of your tongue. They move mountains or build walls. Bring down barriers or best-friend bonds.

Think about the power of the words "It's over" or "You're fired". And then think about the power of the phrases "I'm sorry" or "I love you".

During Cycle 3 you have to be clear on:

What you are trying to say.
What you are actually saying.
How you are saying it.
Who you're saying it to.
What you're saying to yourself.
What you want someone to say to you.
What others are saying to you.
How they are saying it.

It's all the same thing. Whether it's you speaking or someone else. There is a theme at play and you'll get to see what your brain is doing by what themes are showing up for you. Are you headed in the right direction? If not, you'll see it by messages showing you (like street signs) that you're going in a direction other than the one you really want to go.

You may feel backed into a corner but if you can,

Say What You Mean, and
Mean What You Say.

READING BETWEEN THE LINES
Communication is not always verbal. Sometimes people speak purely with their eyes. Reading body language would be a great idea, this Cycle. What's not being said overtly?

Sometimes it's okay not to speak, not to share. We need breathing room. So much is going on inside, it's like we're in a constant dialogue within our own heads. A tennis match, a game of squash or ping-pong. We may find we're constantly chewing on something we heard, read, or something someone said – or didn't say. Often it's what we leave unsaid, that makes us stand up and pay attention in Cycle 3. Remember there are many languages, body language, online abbreviations (*BRB*: 'Be Right Back' etc), the choice of colors we wear that reveal a subtext, and how we phrase things (or how others do) is somehow much more important to us now at this time of year.

In those moments when you're on overload, is it best to let others know this, so they know where you stand? Yes. If you're upset, should you stay in touch or cut your losses and split? Careful – Cycle 3 can see you bouncing around as if in a pinball machine. We don't want to always over-communicate and then under-communicate and build resentment. You owe it to yourself to air your grievances and share your ideas. And we need to hear them. Then everyone can breathe and there's room again to stretch our arms (but not swing a cat, they don't like it).

CONTEXT IS EVERYTHING
How you speak often changes in relation to where you are and who you're with – so watch for issues with inflection, tone etc. On the internet for example, the rules are different to in-person conversation, a social chat, a business interview, a talk with your Mom, or recorded audio or TV presentations. Sarcasm is a luxury in some contexts, and you don't want to mess something up or miss something due to your lack of knowledge or acceptance of context.

Wherever you end up, chatting casually will make you friends, so long as you're not chatting to someone who needs your respect instead of a brother-sister banter with you.

RE-WIRING YOUR WORLD
If you notice phones breaking down, emails not getting through and other glitches, it's not because the gremlins are out in force, it's because for some reason your methods and means of communicating aren't working and are in need of an upgrade. Life will see to it that you'll do that this month. Whether that's forced by you or someone you know having to take their phone/computer in for an actual upgrade or if that's someone telling you that you're not communicating properly, it's really the same theme. Even cars have a habit of breaking down, and they are all symbolic in your life of how you get from A to B and how you process information.

Maybe the method you're using to relay information isn't working. Are you texting instead of having real person-to-person conversations? That's a big issue these days, it seems. Are you arguing online? Would a nice hand-written card feel warmer to receive than a clinical email? Can you hire a plane to write your message in the sky? Leave a trail of clues at home so your spouse can feel special. Small touches and new ways of sharing your thoughts go down as stellar ideas in this solar Cycle.

Look for ways to *re-wire your life*. From adding new electrical sockets or adapters, to hiding loose cables you're likely to trip over. From finding new ways to store paperwork and books, to keeping your place clear of clutter.

Watch what you do each time you think about something (is it a repetitive thought?) each time you get into a vehicle (are you starting your journey off in a negative frame of mind?) and how and what you're doing while holding a phone or speaking into a microphone. Observe. Any patterns? Are you on autopilot or truly speaking and listening? Are you saying something positive while worrying behind the scenes about the negatives?

In Cycle 3, I've been in a car with a deaf friend who nearly sideswiped a truck because she couldn't hear its horn and was too busy typing away on her text messenger – while driving! Cycle 3 will remind you time and time again, that although a lot may be going on (inside your head, outside in the world): You Must Pay Attention!

Cycle 3s are the Cycles where we get tickets from parking without thinking (or reading), where we speed for the same reason, or because we don't have both hands on the wheel. Use speakerphone to save yourself a heavy fine. A momentary lapse in focus could change your entire life (or someone else's). Remember the days when we were without mobile phones? I know, I know it's hard but you have plenty going on right now without over-stretching. And a moment of quiet would do you good.

You're like an electron in your own life passing down roads, like messages buzzing through a wire. How you do it, what you say, what you're thinking of before and after and during phone calls, emails, and while out driving are all important aspects of your current travels. *Keep your mind on your mind and tongue* and what you're doing with them both. Cycle 3 will teach you a lot about how you speak, how you think, how you come across, how you connect, how you dialogue with others, your self-talk (what you chew on mentally inside the space and privacy of your own mind) and so on. And whether it's helping or hindering you and your current life goals.

Another friend told me on the very first day of his 3 Cycle that "I can't believe what my friend just said to me online". A message was delivered with shock value and an important dialogue began. Sometimes what we've been holding in and holding back, *must* come forth under Cycle 3. Let it out.

SHIFT IN SURROUNDINGS

Since your mind is more active, invisibly casting its nets all over on the quest to fish out new information and make new connections with new folk, you're going to cause a few ripples around you. For a start, strangers take more notice of you. It's like you're suddenly wearing a sign saying "Talk to Me!" They begin chatting, asking you questions – about your dog, the jacket you're wearing, if you know where such-and-such is. The cashier asks where you work, then you find she's been wondering about the exact same job – or knows someone who knows someone who may be able to bring more work *your* way.

Just today at the local store during my own Cycle 3, the cashier asked about my new laptop, as I sat writing (trying a new drink the in-house coffee shop was offering). And I was asked the time, on the walk home. Strangers love to talk to you in Cycle 3. It's fun! You'll laugh when they do with you, too. Or will you be the one initiating contact? I dare you!

Being open-minded now could literally change your world, if you can get out of the rut of familiarity you may have sunken into – make eye contact, smile and show genuine interest. Let people in or at least closer, by adopting a friendly nature. Put yourself in social contexts, like the wine-and-cheese event I found myself in, randomly, while I was working on this book, during another Cycle 3 phase.

Play the 'who has the next piece of my jigsaw puzzle today?' game, each time you leave the house. Even the mean lady at the bank may have something else to say – some clue, message, however unappealing at the time, hidden behind the fluff she may be talking. Life can only 'find' us mainly through events involving other people – they are the universe's mouthpieces, and spokespersons. So look out for messages winging their way to you now through the "WWW" the Window to your Wonderful World: your surroundings.

KNOW YOUR NEIGHBOR(HOOD)S

Our local neighbors and neighborhoods become important to us in some fashion during Cycle 3, possibly because we're venturing out into them more, meeting the regulars in the area (or becoming one) and we're discovering new facets of it (as we find new parts of ourselves in the process). We get to see the new scenery – people and places that surround us. New neighbors move in, old ones move out. Someone pops up to introduce themselves. You get to say "Hi" to those around you more often. Maybe you'll just show up at the local Annual Art Walk.

In some 3-Cycles you may find you have to butt heads over an issue locally. We have to tell some of our neighbors to keep the noise down, or the nice ones upstairs to come down, for the party we're throwing! Neighbors always, always have something to tell us about ourselves. Especially right now. What are they up to? Whoever these people are, they're an important part of your journey so see what messages they're throwing your way. Do they mirror you, remind you of you, or oppose you? Whichever way, it's closely related *to* you. This is *your* journey, remember?

I moved house under a Cycle 3 and wound up taking my room-mate's dog for walks around the new neighborhood, which gave me a great reason to explore without looking lost or shady when I was loitering on corners at midnight. I even pinned up local maps on the wall in my home, a great idea for your own Cycle 3. Feeling free to explore and experience inspires our curiosity, which is just what this period of our year wants from us.

PICK A PERSPECTIVE

Enjoy getting lost where you can, if you have the time. Cycle 3 months get you into new territory, new surroundings and amongst new faces to help keep you fresh and youthful. Enjoy *not* knowing – where you are, what to do, who to talk to and how to get back home from here! (Going home is your next Cycle, so for this month get out and stay out where and when you can). When you hit Cycle 9 you'll go through this again on an even grander scale as travel takes you further afield, so test the waters now by being more social, curious and willing to adapt to new settings.

All of these changes in your neighborhood and local environment serve to offer you a new perspective; a fresh point of view and the tools, people and changes you'll experience now are necessary to bring this to you. New settings and new scenery help bring out new thoughts. Or you can change your scenery by changing how you look at it, and how you view it, label it, think about it and talk about it. Either way, a change of scenery is inevitable in this Cycle, whether it's internal or whether you physically find yourself in new locales and enlivened environs by choice or by the universe's perfect synchronicity.

I used this technique to pass exams while at University. Each time I studied a particular topic, I'd move to a new location and keep to those places. Then, each time I re-visited them, I'd access all the thoughts/ideas/information/memories I had *the last time I was there*, and the time before that. It was like my personal library. Location became the container for the information. New places help you access new information. New scenery inspires new thought. And new things to look at change your point of focus and point of attraction.

If you don't like what you're looking at, change your focus. Look somewhere else. If you don't like how you feel, change your mind and change what you're thinking about. Watch what happens when you begin doing this. You'll be amazed.

WORKING WITH YOUR HANDS

If you're not fidgety, you're waving your hands around when talking, or you're fiddling with a pen, coin, biting your nails or otherwise twitching. Our nervous system seems amped up in Cycle 3, and you may end up walking faster, talking faster (or in some Cycle 3s, having to slow it all down by force so we can understand you, or you're working on a speech impediment or communication block or issue). Maybe you buy a ring, a new watch or bracelet or gloves, nail polish or a new tattoo on your arm to emphasize this part of your body – something strangely connected to Cycle 3.

Using your hands is a good way to burn off energy: writing, typing, playing an instrument, origami or other paper art, painting, doing hand puppet shows, sketching, learning how to sculpt or cut hair, gardening, sewing, drawing, conducting or learning sign language.

Digits (both on your hand and in your phone) become important. Are you turning into *Dynasty*'s Alexis Carrington with a sudden desire to don a pair of elegant long-armed gloves? How about new jewelry for your wrists? How about learning to palm read? Cycle 3 somehow reminds us of what's in our hands or close to them. And the whole 'idle hands' thing of course.

Keep an eye out and you'll see.

BEING A BUSY BOOKWORM

What are you reading? Well, apart from this book (and may I say, what amazing taste you have, clearly ...) What you're reading says a lot about where you are this Cycle 3 and where you're headed. Is it foreshadowing, when you find yourself reading the travel magazine and perusing pictures of Australia? Or the new computer advertisements with the hopes of upgrading? What are you trying to find out about? What does it say about your current place and where you want to go? Are you on track? Or are you wasting time with possibilities with no road map? Are you reading autobiographies with a view to your own story that you're itching to write, or an article about something wild that happened to you?

I received a gift of a book I had wanted for so long, handed to me during Cycle 3 out of the blue.

> ***What we think about and focus on in Cycle 3***
> ***is practice – a form of foreshadowing.***

We're setting up our intentions and mental focus for the Cycles ahead.

Keep an eye out for what other people are chatting about and which books they are reading too. Listen in, politely of course. A couple came into a coffee shop when I was writing this chapter, sat down right opposite me in my booth, said "Hi, we're going to be your new neighbors" (a Cycle 3 symbol), and started chatting about a guy on the bus (Cycle 3 commuting) and the book he was reading (Cycle 3 information). Public transportation always seems to creep in during Cycle 3 somehow, whether because you're taking it, or someone you know is taking it, you're stuck behind it on the road, or someone has a funny story about public transport. For those who don't own a car, or whose cars break down during 3-Cycles, you'd be surprised what this opens up for you. Stop being a snob and get on a bus!

And if it's not books, you may find yourself having to learn heaps more on a certain topic, whether from online websites, magazines or from asking your friends their thoughts and opinions. From researching health problems and how to cure them, to how to tie a slip-knot to how to pass the written driving exam. Don't laugh; you'll be amazed at what you end up researching or reading about, this Cycle. You'll find you have to fill your head with new information; it's inevitable. True, some of it may be totally useless and irrelevant, but it's still fun. What you do with it could change your life for the better or help someone else out when they need it, so don't scoff: **Prepare to play Messenger.**

Knowledge is power so soak it up and be sure to deliver it to those who ask the right questions.

WHAT'S IN A NAME?

There's something about Cycle 3 that gets us playing with names. You may suddenly have the urge to change yours, fiddle with a new spelling or practice a new signature etc. Or you meet someone who's edited their name or changed it altogether. Or you start calling your dog by a shortened or more fun version of its original name. It's a labeling time of your year when you give things names to make it easier to classify them or have fun with them, to make them familiar.

You're often very verbal about someone being "an idiot" or someone being "clever" or this being "awesome" or that being "perfect". It's all a judgment of course – *your* judgment, and as long as you know that, you'll let others be as free to *label you* as you have been doing to them. Just be open to the fact that people may not look upon you as highly as you might have hoped. We all do it; we humans like to name things (even though we're all just vibrating molecules at the base level: rocks, trees, tables and your ex lover ...) Quite humbling isn't it when you look at it like that?

You could use this name-calling period to sign up for game shows, particularly ones using word-play since you're likely to be making new words up daily, or filling in crosswords, playing word-scrabble challenges, or desiring to leave your graffiti tag somewhere by carving your name into a tree or tattooing someone else's name on your arm or at least stumbling across words you've never heard or having to thumb through a Thesaurus.

When was the last time you looked into a dictionary? It's astounding how limited we can be in our vocabulary, and it's Cycle 3 that throws new words at you to open up your life and give you a little bit more in the way of 'labeling-ammo'. Watch how you spell things, and look for abbreviations and clever ways to cut time. Your wit level increases and your banter-ability is pretty impressive. Watch the chats you have with people, and you'll see the difference now.

Cycle 3 is your tool to understanding what *LOL, ROFL, TTYL* and *BRB* mean when you're in an online chat room (laughing out loud, rolling on the floor laughing, talk to you later and be right back, respectively) – just make sure multitasking and the subsequent delays don't upset those you're talking to who have less patience. Internet is the same as telephone communication and in-person communication when it comes to manners, etiquette and human respect (or *should* be). Just the forum is different (see previous section on *Context*). Simply because you're hidden behind the privacy of your own screen shouldn't mean common decency goes out the window.

Not everyone is as busy as you are, or as fired up right now. This is your Cycle 3, so be kind and courteous or keep yourself to yourself until you can be available to those who need you.

SIBLING CYCLE

Everything is symbolic. You'll see it the more we progress through your personal Cycles, this year. The theme you're moving through is repeated through people around us (whether they're doing a good job at negotiating each Initiation/Cycle or not, they still teach us something about it all).

This month it may be something your brother or sister is going through that parallels your own life, or you're in a prime place to hear them out and pass on some wisdom – or they have something you need to hear. A random phone call placed to them, or received out of the blue from them (not so out of the blue once you're armed with this book year after year and you'll spot the trends and patterns) that could make amends, build bridges and bring benefits. You never know. Chances are something is up with them, since the Sun is activating a Cycle that involves them indirectly, so it's worth investigating.

If you don't have siblings, you may find that other people are talking more about their own brothers or sisters. Or TV and media themes portray sibling stories with more frequency. Same theme; different delivery. You could get to play a surrogate big brother or younger sister to someone (or vice versa). Maybe your neighbor grabs your ears for some important point you should absorb (or learn to steer clear of). Again, chances are there's a message here just for you – so don't knock it; keep your ears open.

After many years I re-connected with my brother on *Skype* (the online/communication tool), and saw him visually and chatted about what was happening in both our lives (sharing ideas). The same Cycle, a good friend told me his brother had his car stolen and his house keys along with it, and his brother was coming to live with him (at the same time I was staying there). Again, two Cycle-3 symbols in one. Back to my brother: we discussed ideas and options. It cleared the air for us and gave us fresh insight into where we were both going.

Bingo! The key to all Cycle 3s, there in that moment simultaneously.

Ideas and options: to see more, experience more, and to breathe new air into tired lungs. Literally – by getting out, talking, moving about. I had to take in a new neighborhood as the Sun was entering Cycle 3 (sometimes the Cycles come faster so be alert). I bought a new headset for the computer. I messed up the remote control on the TV and had to fiddle to get the signal back. I watched cable TV for the first time in a while. I got to enjoy *Tivo* (a device that lets you record the programs of your choice and skim through the commercials). All these options!

3-Cycles are great for life's buffet choices.

FRIENDLY CONNECTIONS

This Cycle is pretty great for making friends, if you feel you need more interaction. You could hide behind a computer screen and chat to people now, or you could get out and go to your local coffee shop on a platonic date, just to spend time catching up or getting to know one another. Making friends is easier, as you're friendlier, more like a big brother/little sister. Be courteous, curious, ask questions and people will be drawn to you, and find you interesting in return.

BREATHE!

Get more oxygen in Cycle 3 – literally focus on your breathing. Do it right now. Let's do a breathe-check together. Don't worry it's okay if you've had a drink, this won't land you in jail.

Inhale. Very good. Now exhale. You may find like many people that you're not doing it correctly. When you inhaled did your upper chest inflate? You're doing it wrong then.

If you inhaled and your diaphragm/stomach areas inflated first, you're on the right track. Do you breathe through your nose? Great, it slows the breath down. Yoga is fantastic in this Cycle 3 period, as is anything that stills the mind and slows it down during a period of fast thinking and moving.

Smokers get their regular cigarette-break to coat their lungs in tar (a form of slowing-down by breathing during their inhalations that non-smokers don't get). So if you're not a smoker, take your own cigarette-free breaks. Don't miss out on getting outside for air time.

Or open a window. And if you do smoke, well enjoy your puff, or try some clear air in those lungs instead. Either way, getting air, slowing down and filling your body and mind with oxygen *helps enormously* in Cycle 3.

You need your brain this period but you also need it to be crisp, clear and free of shadows and cobwebs. Watch, therefore, for sugar crashes, caffeine highs and overloading your nervous system this month. Facial ticks, muscle spasms, hand cramps, mouth problems, skin rashes. Repetitive Strain Injuries. All symptoms of an over-strained nervous system and potential Cycle 3 burnout.

Try fifteen minutes of simply sitting and breathing. Clearing your head and mind. Picture a fresh breeze blowing through your mind, cleansing all heavy thoughts, or a crystal clear river running down through your head, washing away all worries. It works. And it's a good practice every year you find yourself in your 3-Cycle, to clear away the mental muck you've amassed.

So a reminder: keep a check on your breathing throughout the day. If you set up good habits now in Cycle 3, you'll carry them with you into all the other Cycles. Oxygen is good. And it's free. So please, breathe greedily ...

TALK TO STRANGERS
Since your environment is trying to get your attention and show where you can affect the most change in Cycle 3, people from your environment (from outside your four walls – the ones *inside* will figure in Cycle 4) start making important waves. Look around; people want your attention. People on the street you don't know. Since they stumbled into your neighborhood during this Cycle, they come under the umbrella of possibly important persons for you. And only you. It's *your* Cycle 3, but maybe it's theirs also! So stay alert to messengers (and they don't always say what you want to hear), through people around you, also through passing conversations, snatches of words on the breeze, a flyer flapping at your feet. Words are magical weapons, incantations, 'spell'-ings, that call to you during Cycle 3 – often from the lips of the nearest soul who can provide a channel.

And often you learn from what's not said during this time (defined by lack of words). Silence can say just as much. Other times you find what you need on a piece of paper, in a book, on a notice, or scrawled as graffiti somewhere. Some philosophy may emerge from just listening to your intuition.

MIND AND MENTAL MAPS
You can change your mind in Cycle 3. You will. You must. Many times, I'm sure. Cutting people *off* from further communication is another option. You'll likely reconnect though and have the same conversations. We are often on 'repeat' during this time of year, saying the same things till we get tired and change the record. We get to air our beefs (less for others and more so we get to hear and get clear ourselves about what's going on in the swampy lairs of our own minds). It helps us get clear, unless we're merely parroting the same garbage to anyone close enough to hear. We do so love an audience in our 3-Cycles; just make sure the content is fresh and interesting please (especially if we're stuck next to you in line). So, changing our minds is the same as

changing our mouths, and changing what we say, how we say it and who we say it to.

Let's face it, in Cycle 3, you need a *Change of Perspective*.

If you're an aggressive speaker you may find your audience is repelled and you need to tone it down. If you're passive-aggressive you may find you need to step up your game and be direct and blunt or face further problems. If you're a communication coward you'll probably have to face your fear and start learning how to speak, because in this world it's wonderful to get by with shy glances or mean standoffish-ness, but you only truly have your needs met when you can tell someone what you need and what you want.

On Earth, for the foreseeable future as a human,
communication is your make-or-break.

What is being said this month, to you, by you and by others to you? Listen. Is there a theme; a pattern? Can you learn something from it all, try something new and can this open up a new pathway for you?

I came across material relating to the Universal Laws, which is truly worth looking up online during your 3-Cycle. **How you're using or abusing your mind** is essential to come to grips with now, before you start reacting to what manifests in other Cycles, because of what you are thinking about and dwelling on in this Cycle 3 (and then in Cycle 4, a time of revisiting the past). Some day soon your Cycle 3 *will* be your past. So re-write it in a better direction now whilst you still can, by how you use your mind-power. This is your chance to clear the air and keep your head clear and focused in the right direction.

Co-creating your life experience is what Cycle 3 is about, by steering your mind rather than letting it carry you away like a pair of wild stallions on a rickety old stagecoach.

Why waste precious mind-magic on useless junk (like reacting to what is going on right now) instead of focusing on what is to come (because you're creating it). Look ahead, and keep walking. Channel your energy, discipline your brain-power, focus on what you want to experience, and let the loose ends fall by the wayside (idle hands and minds are dangerous in Cycle 3 ... you risk being sucked into dodgy drama, wasteful wanderings, superficial situations and people who are all talk today and hard to reach tomorrow).

Was it worth it?

DOUBLE DEALS AND DODGY DUPLICITOUS DOWNRIGHT DECEIT

Because Cycle 3 is a very changeable Cycle, you could end up juggling because option A and option B are both pretty lame and you need a third option. There is one, if you get out of the pinball-game or tennis-match being played in your head between two or more options. There's always a new choice and if not, there's *always a new way of perceiving things*, of changing how you see it in your own mind; how you play with it in your own brain. With so many things changing you may find you slip into double-speak, where you lie for the sake of keeping these options open longer so no one knows your motives.

Be careful, you're a step away from being a used-car salesperson trying to sell a lemon, when you slink into lying to people. And they know where to find you (from Google for example). The web you spin in Cycle 3 takes a lot of getting out of, unless you're really clever, but why waste so much magical brainpower on trying to keep track of it all?

By all means be flighty, flaky (you have to be, to keep yourself as free as the social butterfly you are now). So what if you don't say the thing someone wants to hear from you? This is about *your* say. They have theirs, but what do *you* think? And are you going to tell us?

Your job is to visit different flowers in your neighborhood field, to see what new seeds others have planted and are sprouting (from their own Cycle 1... maybe it's your job to connect them to people who can help *them* ahead with their dreams) and not get locked into definite options until you are ready to play the field. But lying to get your way will eventually trip you up; Cycle 3 may find you being clever with words, witty and fun, fresh and effervescent, but if you cause trouble with double-speak (like most politicians) you'll end up upsetting someone and it can only come back to bite you.

Where possible, be honest and if you can't deliver ... then simply say you're not available and keep moving on.

CYCLE 3 ACTION PLAN

* Decide what you want to discover, and begin asking questions.
* Get clear on what you want to say so you don't get led astray.
* Remain youthful and curious.
* Read, talk, discuss, share, trade.
* See which new tools you can use to get your message out.
* Freshen your perspective with a jaunt somewhere new.
* Check your local free paper for new events, places, classes, groups, and trips.

In a busy year:
You have the gift of the gab – you're witty and *on*, you say the right things to the right people and they say the right things back – like 'Yes' by email, or a

major Invite for you personally to tell everyone else what you think in public. You're *hot* – you're juggling a phone while signing a new business contract while thinking up what to buy at the grocery store for dinner, while petting your cat and waving to the neighbor passing by.

Cycle 3 is a multi-tasker's paradise or a slow coach's worst nightmare. Rush Rush Rush. Hit 'Escape'. Press 'Pause'. Hold that call. Rewind that tape. Catch that bus. Take the next exit. Close the deal. Sign the check. Be there by 5. Call me!

Driving in a new part of town you stumble across a new store that grabs your attention and whilst exiting from it you spot an ad on the wall for a job you've been thinking about. You call the number, land a new job and make a new friend in the same day.

And, the traffic home was beautiful.

Your writing comes along in leaps and bounds; you can juggle fifty things in one day. You are talking on the phone while ordering a meal, while taking a call on the other line, while texting, while noticing the color of the woman's dog across the road, while making a note of a line you can use in a poem later, while solving yesterday's crossword puzzle conundrum that you never quite forgot, while planning where you'll go for lunch tomorrow and what's on your shopping list for tonight.

All this and more your brain can handle.

From amazing emails to things arriving in the mail that you've been waiting for, you can't help but continue smiling at all the great possibilities pouring forth into your life. One clue leads to another, which takes you someplace new. It's all so fresh. There's no time to be bored or stagnate – how can there be? There's too much to do, and so much to try, explore, learn and experience. It's so good to be alive.

In a dizzy year:
You're all over the place – figuratively and literally. Mentally you're tied in a cobweb of engagements, contradictions, possibilities – but nothing really solid to show for it. It's all in the air, castles in the clouds, possible pie in the sky and potentially pointless. 'If' has become a way of life. They say they'll call. But it's been weeks now. You sent the email (did it get lost?). Or you decide to vanish for a week and give no word of your whereabouts, leaving others floundering.

On top of that, you have calls you have to return from those you'd rather not hear from. And emails piling up (mostly spam) and a new computer you need to buy … You have places to go and the car is at the mechanic's or about to be repossessed or you can't afford one.

People lie, promises are broken, and communication lines are straining or snapped. When you speak, you don't feel they're listening and if you shout they accuse you of being a bully. You hang up. They slam the phone down. No one is really listening; it's all point scoring or jibber-jabbering. Your pen snaps as you're taking down a number so you scratch it on the pad only to call it days later and find it's a digit out somewhere – and you deleted the email and voice mail.

You block an email and then unblock only to find they've blocked you! Or you don't have a phone book and the internet bill needs paying. Or your phone signal keeps disappearing during a conference call. Or you just miss the one train that would have got you there with five minutes to breathe.

Some years it's not as tedious, you're just fried from too much thinking, writing, speaking, and commuting. You say it, say it again, continue repeating it and you're suddenly repeating it all, for no purpose other than to get stuck in the present, by not finding the space or room to move on. You crave rest time – but wait, didn't you add to it with three cups of coffee, a sugary snack and no 'unplug' time? You're talking in your sleep; sleepwalking through real talk. Brain-overload. You need to make some decisions, in the clarity of space, peace and quiet.

Do yourself a favor and step out for air (rather than another cigarette/caffeine break).

Cycle Lesson

The mind is a powerful thing. It can hold an idea until it becomes a reality or it can repeat like a scratched record, replaying the same redundant material. Curiosity is the spark that drives us to seek out answers to the questions we're asking ourselves. And answers lead to more questions. We begin to collect the jigsaw puzzle pieces of something bigger. What, we don't yet know. But we don't need to. The process of collecting data is all that matters now – what we like, what we don't like. Our focus is a welcome sign bringing more of the same, to us. Communication bridges the gap between ourselves, the universe, and the others we share it with. By learning the language of human communication (and the unspoken dialogue, with animals, those unable to speak etc) we can give a voice to our thoughts, a name to our desire, and collect more information to help us in the creation of our Dream. Our only job is to keep the lines of communication open and clear.

Celebrity Spotlight

- *Google* acquires the video-sharing site *YouTube* for $1.65 billion in *Google* stock in Cycle 3.
- To promote the new electronic book-reader Kindle, Scorpio author Stephen King (born with the Sun in Cycle 3), made UR, his then new novella, available exclusively through the Kindle Store on October 22, 2009 – during his Solar Cycle 3.

Tips to successfully navigating your Cycle 3 Investigation

- Make the call.
- Spit it out.
- Say it like you mean it.
- Go for a stroll.
- Truly *hear* by actively listening.
- Get your head together first, before anything.
- Write the letter, email.
- Stick it in the mail.
- Re-connect.
- Upgrade your phone.
- Remind yourself of your purpose in each encounter and experience.
- Cover more ground.
- Give it a fresh spin (truthful where possible).
- Explore the neighborhood.
- Contact siblings; check what they have to say/what they think.
- Be curious and youthful.
- Sign up for a library card.
- Say 'hi' to the man walking the dog past you.
- Get clear.
- Sample.
- Get a car tune up.
- Buy a bicycle or other method of transportation.
- Ask questions.
- Make a new decision.
- Add one new word to your repertoire every day.
- Be on the move.
- Talk to strangers (yes this is actually a good Cycle for this!)
- Read a new book.
- If you can't say anything nice or honest, then keep quiet.
- Learn sign language.
- Ask advice.
- Don't get bored – get out!
- Be friendly, everyone is a brother or sister now.

∾ Surf Cycle 4 ∾

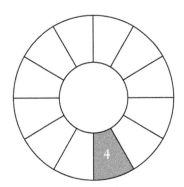

Time to Get Comfy
Safeguard Security
Re-establish/Replenish
and Replant Roots

Emotional Encounters with:

People from your past
Families/homemakers/homeowners
Apartment managers/landlords
Your mother (or someone else's)
Carers/huggers/the needy
Chefs/caterers
Real estate agents
Your partner's father
Your stepmother or dad's new wife
Your cousin
Antique dealers
Decorators and photographers
Diggers/archeologists/historians/
    patriots

Those who feed/house others
Painters and interior designers
Defenders, guards, bouncers
Feng-shui experts
Home furnishing store department
    staff
Women in general – busty blondes to
    maternal moms
Big chested/breasted men and women
Over or under-eaters
Cancer people
Undertakers, funeral directors
Time-share staff
Regression specialists

What you'll need:

A warm, cozy den to hide in
A teddy bear or human surrogate
An ever-refilling fridge or personal chef
A dragon in the moat

Cycle 4 begins, straight away, by asking you "Are you at home?"

That depends on where you are, and what a home is, firstly, – a room with four walls, a castle, a fence to keep people out, an invitation to let people in, a garden, a library, a party? Is it a feeling you take with you no matter where you go? Is it your aura space, your 'bubble'? Is it your family, your country, even your body?

It's all of these. And possibly more.

Everyone finds 'home' somewhere different. 'Wallflowers' prefer the safety of the corner, to watch and take it all in from, without the pressure of the spotlight or too much attention. Extroverts feel uncomfortable with too much isolation and prefer the middle of the room, or to move about, mingling with others in order to bounce ideas and feel alive in the heat of interaction. Introverts seek internal solace. Extroverts seek external validation. We each find our safety and security somewhere unique. Neither is better. Neither is less evolved. It's just our natural programming, or often our childhood training. It can change. But it's what we have to work with often instinctively, unconsciously. This Cycle is about finding out just what that conditioning may be, how it may be hindering you from being the person you are today, and where it's right for you to safeguard your own feelings of comfort in this all-important foundational Cycle.

What particular brand of 'home' is right for you *now*, in this Cycle?

You may just have to shift things around if you're not providing yourself with the right platform from which to launch yourself. So expect some discomfort on the way to being more comfortable. It stands to reason. Your crop (the Dream you're incubating and growing from Cycle 11) can only be as rich as the soil it's planted in. Cycle 4 lets you take a closer look at your soil, your base, your foundation, your roots; the ground beneath your feet is essential right now, to your continued growth.

So, expect to review what's going on beneath your feet, where you currently are. Literally (the foundations, groundwork etc) and symbolically (the emotional undercurrents, safety, security and comfort) as well as internally (are your feelings affecting where you're planting yourself?) You may even get to see this theme played out in those around you; for instance seeing someone having to move, relocate, renovate their home space, smoke out fleas, buy a new bed, rearrange furniture, or people going back home or dealing with their families and their past a lot more.

You are evolving and your personal space will evolve along the same lines – some years it may feel like teething troubles, growing pains, and it's really uncomfortable, whilst in other years it's a lot easier and you feel quite content.

Either way, you'll achieve the goal of *finding a new sense of home within yourself regardless of what's going on outside*.

FEELING YOUR FEELINGS

Easier said than done. Feelings are irrational things. No matter how much we try and use Cycle 3 intellect to analyze them, talk about them or rationalize them, we sometimes quite simply have to just *feel* them. Ideas are for thinking; feelings are for feeling! That is why we now move from the airy mental 3rd Cycle into the watery, sensitive feeling world of the 4th.

Yet how many of us run from our feelings? Condemn them when faced with them in another? How many of us let ourselves really be the feeling creatures we truly are?

Giving feelings a life – hearing them and voicing them – is a great idea now. Painting a picture. Writing a poem. Crying. Listening to sad music. Singing a song to show how joyful you are. Whatever the feeling, it's not a tangible 'real' thing (that we can hold, like the 'stuff' of Cycle 2), but it certainly feels real to us when we're in its grasp. Feelings do have a reality and if we don't honor and respect them, they're likely to start creating a reality of their own (and what was once a *feeling* of something has a higher chance of *becoming* that very thing embodied and made flesh: our worry becomes reality).

Expect in Cycle 4, that you're going to feel some strong emotions. Some may be lower vibrational (depression, anger, upset, fear) and some may be higher vibrational (joy, hope, optimism, gratitude, love). Enjoy them all. None are 'good' or 'bad'. To us they may feel that way, but they are simply an energy resonance. That helps us decide if we are on track with our inner soul compass.

You're a human and emotions are a gift. Emotions tell us where we are. They are our '**Pain GPS System**' and our '**Joy GPS System**'. (Pain showing us we took a turn down a path that we need to understand; Joy showing us we're heading towards a destination we desire).

How do you feel and what does it tell you about which way you are heading? Are you moving towards a solution, or focusing all of your energy on a problem? Are you bemoaning your past and present or looking ahead to make something new happen?

EMOTIONAL EVOCATION, ERUPTION, EDUCATION AND EVOLUTION

How comfortable are you with feelings (yours or others?) Do you let yourself cry? Can you let someone know you're angry and what do you do when faced with an eruption from someone else? Take it personally or understand it's their feeling and they have a right to feel how they feel?

Feelings pour forth in Cycle 4 across the board (as one after another is evoked through life events that inspire us to feel them): yours, your partner's, your ex lover's, friends', your current roommate's, your family's, your boss's, you name it. Everyone around you seems to arrive to remind you of *your* feelings, often by over-expressing their own. How many crybaby whiny souls will *you* meet this year in your Cycle 4?! Emotions erupt from seemingly out of the blue, but which usually can be traced to some form of repression from the past that has reached boiling point.

If it's few, then maybe you're the one who's playing that role? If so that's fine, but try and move from complaining to being pro-active in actually improving your situation. You can't sit and wallow forever. If you face a lot of over-emotional souls, maybe you're just repressing your own and they're playing it out for you in an exaggerated manner to get your attention. People reflect our inner deeper-most feelings back to us. Like does attract like. Repress a feeling and someone is sure to come along to play it out for you, to remind you that it still exists in your energy field, however much you've buried it.

Maybe it's to teach you how to help out where need be and give a little bit of that much-needed mothering energy we all need. The key is Nurturing not pandering to people's self-indulgent and self-pitying patterns. Herein lies the next phase of our emotional journey – when our feelings begin to *educate* us on what we need.

Either way, feelings, emotions and strong heartstring activity is scheduled for Cycle 4. How else can you be moved to move forward in life, unless you're pulled where it counts – in your feeling center? Therein lies the evolution of our lives, by the feelings that become our signposts of progress. Those who find it hard to uproot and move forward will be inundated with hard emotions and feel they are drowning. Those who seem to surf easier are those less likely to hold on during the tide change that's inevitable in Cycle 4.

Water gets us moving in Cycle 4, be it tears, or the natural stream of life. Everything is cyclic. And we rarely get anything done in life unless there's a feeling behind it, a strong one. So watch for those feelings now and you'll learn a lot about where you are.

It's all about comfort or finding a new comfort zone, so you'll find those around you playing out the theme for you some years during this phase of your yearly Cycle. Some people may move if you're not, and become stressed and insecure, needy or exhibiting more emotional change than you. Or maybe you both will be. Then you can help each other. But those who need you to play Mom will be only too happy to check in with you. And those who want you to grow up may cut emotional strings with you.

It happens a lot during Cycle 4. This is a Cycle of endings, so you'll find those who need to pass from your life emotionally will do so during this Cycle 4. Prepare to say goodbye a lot then in Cycle 4, and it may not always be a textbook or Hollywood goodbye, it may just be silent, swift, sad or excruciatingly painful. But you'd be best to wrap things up and move on.

If you're lucky though, Cycle 4 will see you shaking hands, saying "we did well" and then moving in different directions. You may even get to re-connect and re-establish roots with someone you lost touch with, reconnecting to see just how far you have both come, to celebrate the past, to resolve some issues left hanging and to gain perspective on your current self. No one shows up that doesn't have a message about who you are right now. No one comes into your experience without a reason and a gift. Reconnecting to celebrate the present and your growth is the ideal, but often we turn so crabby in Cycle 4 that our eternally hungry and needy inner child rears his or her head and ruins the show by being just what it's meant to be ... childish.

Feed, clothe, and house yourself first, before you try and be there for others. Don't offer what you can't provide first. You need your reserves full before you do the mothering thing for others, in Cycle 4.

Depending on your sign and chart you'll be facing different kinds of emotions at this time – intense ones you'll need to clear out (if this Cycle falls in Scorpio this month), practical ones to help you secure your life (if it falls in Taurus) and so forth.

THE EVER-PRESENT PAST

During Cycle 4 our needs come surging up from within us – including old needs based on the emotional diet we were force-fed as a child when we had no choice on how to react, or have a say in what was transpiring around us (childhood is our unconscious training-ground where we soak up the rhythms, rhymes and reasons of the adults in our lives). Suddenly, we're acting like we're ten again, or five. If we've become stuck at a certain age due to things that happened or things you never received (but needed), you're going to wind up repeating them or chasing them in Cycle 4, to **relive** old memories and **relieve** yourself of them.

Relive-relieve is your mantra and motto for Cycle 4.

So you may find yourself repeating some trauma you never fully understood or accepted. You may find that where you were abandoned in the past, and are still hurting, you'll wind up abandoning someone else or else being abandoned again. **Relive.**

If you move through this, find understanding and then see the truth of the situation, you get to experience the same situation, gain acceptance and move on. **Relieve**.

It doesn't always need to be anything upsetting. Reliving things is often a way of celebrating where we have come from, and how far we have come. The past is a way for us to mark progress on our paths. What you're going for is one last reliving (if possible) in order to relieve something unresolved. Getting stuck on replay too long is a danger we all face in Cycle 4, so ask yourself is your therapy really helping or are you simply using it as an excuse to keep yourself retelling (and thereby reliving) the same stories, energies and patterns from your past.

Is it time to resolve something left undone, perhaps? Cycle 4 is often known as the 'Chapter Closure, Cycle Change and End of a Matter' – because, quite simply, it no longer matters in your life, and your life will try and remind you of this by helping you/urging you/pushing you/nudging you/screaming at you (whichever is needed and most likely to get your attention and whatever you're not open to responding to ... in short *what it takes to get you motivated to changing*) to put the seal or stamp on it and send it on its way.

It's time to accept, and move on from, certain aspects of your past.

LOOKING BACK OR HOLDING BACK?

Trips down Memory Lane, then, are inevitable. Sifting through old photos yet? Checking in with family or contacting childhood friends? Is someone you knew from your schooldays coming to visit? Or are you stumbling across old things you lost or forgot about? After all you've done, your past catches up with you. You dwell. Something sticks in your mind or heart and you go over it, repeating it in your mind and soul to understand it; to *feel* it. For some reason, reliving it feeds you on some level.

To work out why, perhaps? Why this thing happened? I believe we often repeat and relive memories (usually difficult ones) because the emotional energy was so amped up at the time that we failed to truly live in the moment back then. And we review and repeat it (or act it out again and again) in order to understand it, gain something we missed from it, and to integrate it into our psyche so that we can finally move through it.

I read somewhere once that our bodies remember, even long after our minds and hearts seem to have forgotten. Often, during a traumatic or intense moment, we hold our breath. We don't fully breathe and release the feelings of the moment and in the moment. Our bodies store that tension in aching muscles or within our emotional muscles and we then run the risk of reliving those moments through our bodies in tension, physical trauma, accidents or illness. By breathing through each emotional moment, we get to free ourselves from the potential weight of carrying something unnecessary after the event.

Often we relive something in order to try and avoid making the same mistake again (understanding brings wisdom), or to relive a joyful moment we crave to feel once more. Are you reliving a better time at the expense of your current satisfaction and happiness? Or trying to free yourself from a bitter moment. Regret? Remorse? Guilt? Sadness? Peace?

Buried memories (involving any possible human emotion) are dug up now, to be freed so you can create anew by being lighter in Cycle 5: your season of joy. How can you have fun (Cycle 5's major theme!) if you're still carrying Cycle 4 baggage around?

So you get to that baggage now. What do your cells remember? Something has to go. Will you give it up or cling to your long-ago luggage, and become a needy, spoiled child, who licks wounds and manipulates and controls as you're forced to move on from something familiar, habitual, safe. Or will you outgrow the old moments you've become so attached to, and find new emotional connections to nurture, to see you through the next chapter of your life?

Don't get me wrong, Cycle 4 *is* about getting stable, getting settled and getting safe. You need it. It's your pit stop. Emotionally you get to sigh, to dig your feet in and lie down on a comfy bed and sleep. To give yourself the things that have always comforted you. Cookies baking in the kitchen and breakfast ready in the morning. A comfy cottage. Reading or listening to the tale of Bilbo Baggins in *The Hobbit* is a great way to spend Cycle 4. Its theme? Home, family, and the safety of the familiar; leaving it and returning with a renewed sense of self and inner strength; key themes you'll understand reflected within it, and within your life during your 4-Cycle.

Your own story will reflect the exact same themes in varying degrees. Where are you right now on your own Hobbit adventure?

FEED YOUR NEED

Needs are a funny thing – often when you eat the chocolate cake, you feel full for a while but then, a few hours later, you 'need' more. Are needs ever fully met or are they something we work towards slowly? Is our need a persistent hunger pointing at a deeper emotional issue, or is it a healthy way to say 'it's time to eat, it's time to get warm or time to rest'?

Sometimes, if it's not needed you'll find it ends, or is taken away in Cycle 4. You can read more on that in the *Chapter Closure* section, up ahead.

And what is really a 'need' anyway? No one 'needs' a cigarette. They hunger for one. No one 'needs' sex. We may believe we need them (I'll be irritable if I don't, I'll get sick, I'll lose my mind, I'll fall apart etc) yet:

> ***we need only these basics things for survival:***
> ***a safe place to live, healthy food to nourish us,***
> ***fresh water to sustain us, clean air to breathe.***

That's it. After that, we've entered the adult kingdom of desires and luxuries and the pursuit of pleasure and success. Of course, the need for these things is usually the thing that kickstarts the desire to fulfil them, make money, and so enter the adult world.

As children we need more simplicity, and it's that part of life we get to relive at its most basic, fundamental level during our 4-Cycles. What 'floats your boat', then, and keeps you buoyant?

That's Cycle 4 and its ultimate mission – giving you flotation devices, to keep you from sinking or drowning. Ask yourself:

> Do you need this right now?
> If not, then do you want it?
> If not, then why pursue it?
> And if so (and you do want it), then why don't you let yourself enjoy it?

Separating out what you *need* from what you're *used to* out of habit, ritual, childhood, your past and what you've been gorging on your whole life, is your current challenge and mission.

WHAT YOU'RE EATING AND WHAT'S EATING YOU

On a final note here, food does seem to become important during this Cycle. I received a few free gift cards for a grocery store as a beautiful token of goodwill from the universe during one particularly tough 4-Cycle. A friend of mine wound up house sitting (Cycle 4 Home), and in exchange for looking after two dogs and two birds and numerous house plants (Cycle 4 care-taking), he was invited to raid the cupboard and fridge for all the goodies they had there (Cycle 4 Food). Another friend had to take his pets to the vet and de-flea his house, changing the bedding, vacuuming and making the place more comfortable. And this was in my own 4th Cycle, so I got to partake in his 'getting comfortable' theme by helping him, providing a safe space for him while he cleaned out his place, and was there for him during a challenging time as he tried to look after his upset pets (two dogs, a cat and a snake).

You either get fed or feed others, cater to them or they cater to you. Or you need them or they need you. Maybe you're doing a bad job and your cupboards are bare. Food is another way we 'feed' ourselves. Problems with over or under-eating and dietary and digestion issues could be a signal you're not self-caring as much as you should be, to float happily.

Make sure you're eating well in Cycle 4, and if not, then how about trading meals for a massage or something else if you're tired of cooking or eating out? You need to eat.

MOMMY DEAREST

Needs produce two things in our lives – a child or a mother. The one in need and the one who can provide. One cries to have its need met. The other plays provider to that need. Maybe it's our own inner child, or maybe it's someone else around us acting needy, or maybe it's us who are crying and screaming for solace. Maybe we have to play both for ourselves (we're crabby and so we need to go and eat). Being a child means we'll wind up needing or seeking someone to pay the role of Mom – so our own *actual* mothers could figure strongly now (or your Dad if he played the nurturing role for you, or a grandparent or sibling) – as you fight her (or whomever it is) for what they didn't do for you, or seek them out to give you what they always *gave* you (apple pie, a stern talking to, money, a roof or something else).

You may find that someone else's mother figures strongly in your life now – as was the case when I moved during a Cycle 4 period and my partner's mother took us shopping for curtains so that we'd have a comfy nest and lots of privacy – something you'll crave during 4-Cycles.

If your main caretaker is not there, you may end up having to play Mom to yourself or you may expect or demand someone else play that role for you. Every child needs a mother of course, and you get to decide, hopefully, which side of the spectrum you'll play on during Cycle 4.

The healthiest way is to play both ourselves, but some years we don't get it so easy and we're tested out on our ability to do the caring thing for ourselves first. For every need, we need a mother who feeds it (if it's healthy and nurturing) or stifles it and helps us find a new outlet (if it's strangling us). The 'hand that feeds us' features strongly now, whether that's ours, or someone around us. Do we bite it, accept it or struggle against the co-dependency of it all?

Are we smother-mothering or being a true caretaker? Are you being your own best Mom? Because that's really the point. If you're not happy, quit complaining. Change it yourself. Look after yourself. Be good to you. Happiness is a choice.

Magically, the more you self-nurture, others will be more than prepared to get in on the game too and begin helping you, nurturing you, and comforting you, often without you needing to ask or even needing the help but which you'll appreciate all the same.

FAMILY BONDS, TIES AND APRON STRINGS

The original nurturers (or the ones who should have taken on that role) often return now in the form of family members, or people wrapped up to resemble them. Family issues re-ignite those parts of your psyche that never felt coddled, fed, looked after or loved. Guilt could re-ignite, along with resentment. Cycle 4 returns you to the scene of the crime with a visit 'back home' or else parents may come to visit or check in with you, to bring something back for you to deal with or use in your present. It's all symbolic and reflective, and helpful if you can see beyond the moods of the moment.

Family drama, trauma and memories often remain with us throughout the rest of our lives; it's classic psychology. Relationships with Mother are taken into female relationships and how we get on with Father can dictate the men we choose to get close to or rejected by. I think it's interchangeable – all relationships are holographic of each other and seem to all carry at least one common underlying and unifying major theme. If you were lucky enough to have a beautifully nurturing family past you get to enjoy this once more in your current setting, bringing the best of the past to the present and sharing it with others, perhaps in a caring capacity professionally, or just being more attentive to others' needs at this time.

If you were amongst those who suffered some emotional slight in the family lion's den, you get to work on it now by seeing how your emotional connections are with others and the common threads and themes of pain that may be making themselves felt once more, for you to relive and deal with. Maybe what you think about one thing is really the past wrapped up in a new disguise?

**You can't escape the past in 4-Cycles but you
can face it and befriend it
so it works for you and with you
and not against you.**

What did your family do or not do that is following you around like a bad smell? Is it leaking into your present and leeching on your close intimate relationships or inner emotional state of comfort or dis-ease?

Family is an outer representation of our *inner family*. Our various 'sides' all working together to function as a whole being. Who cares how caring your blood family were? Now it's up to you to continue looking after yourself or finding others who can show you and teach you how to care for yourself in healthier ways. It may sound harsh, but it's the way of the world. Everyone has to leave the nest, even if they remain physically within it their entire life. Time moves on and things change, and we have to be sure to keep up with our ever-evolving self.

If you want to feel better, then ask for help and see how others are doing it. Everyone's home life was different, now you get to pick and choose how you want yours to be *right now*. If you're still young or at home with family reading this and unable to create a new home life for yourself or do not wish to, you can at least take a note of what's happening and maybe write it down somewhere to reflect back on in another Cycle 4 year later down the line. Underline the emotions in the air and your involvement or lack of participation – these are themes you may end up repeating as you progress through life, but at least you can see what was yours and what was other people's so that you don't end up in a therapist's office years from now thinking you're a terrible person because Mom was unhappy and Dad was mad etc.

If you decided to live at home, you may notice that old age doesn't stop the age-old patterns from re-occurring, in which case you'll be wiser of the ways of the past and not get so caught up in them when you see an action replay. You may get to decide what your part will be this time and whether you'll feed old traumas or just enjoy the good stuff and move round the minefields instead.

And of course you may find that you get pushed out of the nest during this Cycle or feel the desire to get going yourself. It's all part of your Cycle 4 urge to get comfortable in a situation that feeds the new you.

You get to choose your emotion input and reactions and responses to all that happens to you, and by doing so you set the tone for your own inner home and sense of self-comfort. Keep that in mind this Cycle 4 when you're faced with things that don't feel good and you feel powerless to change. Your inner world is yours and yours alone.

HABIT HOGGING

Needs, when fed repetitively, can become habits and then addictions. During Cycle 4 you get to see what hungers or cravings you have that lead to overeating, overfeeding, and overdoing (or under-eating, underfeeding and under-doing) and have become (or risk becoming) fully fledged official 'addictions'. Stuffing yourself is the same as constant purging, when it comes to emotional extremes. Has the ritual and repetition lost its rhyme and reason? If so, it's serving a need, but has no purpose outside of that. Even helping others constantly can deplete us and become a habit. The need to be needed for example. Or having someone always pander to us when we're being a crybaby.

Cycle 4 shows us what we're expecting in the way of feeding. Expectations crush us and cause pain in adult life because we simply can't always expect others to do for us what we want. That's our job. And our initiation into the world outside the nest.

We eat to stay alive, but also because it's pleasurable. When we eat only to cram down an emotion inside, we've lost the plot and our bodies begin to rebel. Are you eating to live or living to eat? If we drink for the taste and the pleasure it brings, we're enjoying an experience. When we drink to avoid a feeling or situation, again we're in danger of creating an addiction.

The basis is the same – needs relate to feelings – if we have a feeling and use a repetitive act to escape from it, we set up a further need to satisfy the original need creating even more unmet needs that create more needs to escape the need! The Cycle goes on – but it doesn't have to. Cycle 4 encourages our needs to become overblown, so we get to see where we're in **dire need** of *nurturing* (that's all a need is and an addiction is – a sign of its lack). We need some form of feeding or nurturing (loving).

So, the unloved parts of ourselves reveal themselves during Cycle 4 but the weird moods, the illogical reactions to events or people, the passive aggressive ways of getting what we want, the manipulation of those around us to make *them* feel something (in order to have them do something for you or feel the way you feel) can all distract us from this one simple fact. Maybe we just feel unloved. Suddenly, it's as if the world is submerged in oceanic feelings you can't control. You can't. Feelings are feelings and its either sink, swim or float – the first two will eventually wear you out or kill you, the latter involves letting go and just 'being' and all else drops away and you're suddenly lighter.

SOUL SAFETY AND SURVIVAL

So – are you getting your needs met? What *are* your needs? Are they real to you *now* – or are you trying to feed old hungers, desires? Why aren't you caring about yourself? Is a need a necessity (food, clothing, shelter, warmth)? Anything outside of this isn't a need, it's a desire. A desire is a luxury then, as it can be pursued once these bases are covered. Love for example may keep us healthy and young and vibrant and make us feel good, but we don't 'need' it. Oxygen we need. A comfy bed we desire. Separate the two. Chances are you've been pining over, or fighting for or getting upset about, something that you're choosing, but don't actually need.

Once you've worked these out, you'll be well on your way to higher levels of Cycle 4 but it's worth spending some time watching which feelings comes up during this time. People are sure to arrive in your life to push buttons – if you have any that is. If you do – welcome it. Any feeling you have, any reaction you have, is sure to be something from the past, a childhood conditioning, an outdated or outworn method of survival to *keep you safe* (or what you perceive as safe, which could even mean 'not feeling' when it comes down to it).

FURNISHING YOUR RUT?

That's all Cycle 4 wants to do with you – keep you safe. But that gets old and becomes its own pattern or habit. And as soon as you go on autopilot, you've become a cliché – a repetitive ritual with no reason. You've become your own addiction, your life follows the path of an addict, doing the same thing over and over expecting it to change you or make you feel better and it doesn't, so you try harder and repeat it. Being 'safe' in Cycle 4 is nice for a time (a pit-stop to recuperate) but you have to get out of it (and you will) once you realize just how much of your soul you've been feeding and how much of your ego you've been trying to placate with goodies (or trying to hammer it by denying yourself the very same – still thereby making your ego the ultimate God in your life).

Phew! It all sounds so heavy. But it really isn't. It can really be quite simple.

Become a turtle: Get safe, get situated, get squishy-comfy, enjoy the things that have always made you feel good, protect yourself however you feel you need to and then be prepared to take those feelings on the road with you, or leave some behind while you expand your comfort zone as your journey continues.

HOME: REPOTTING YOURSELF IN NEW, MORE FERTILE SOIL

Spending such self-indulgent personal time in Cycle 4 nearly always creates some sort of energy shift in the home space – after all it's a reflection of your inner world, your private side, your personal sphere where you can Just Be. No one knows what goes on behind the private doors of humans worldwide. That's why there's such a big pull to create 'reality' shows where we get to spy on them. We like to pry; yet we hate our privacy invaded (unless we're doing it for sexual kicks in Cycle 5 or 8, more on that later!) So, when you're changing your insides, and reviewing your personal side, you may experience some shifts in the home.

Suddenly, something may need repairing or fixing or replacing. You need a new fridge (a sign you need a new way to 'stay fresh and keep cool' perhaps?), a new bed (a sign you need to find more downtime and rest perhaps?), or there's a leaky pipe somewhere reminding you that you're leaking energy (like tears) or that you need to seal something up and stop squandering/wasting or avoiding? Repairs are well worth it now as it's a sign of a psychic and emotional upgrade inside of yourself. *Treat your outside like your insides in 4-Cycles* – most people do anyway whether they realize it or not (that's why the famous art of feng-shui works so well).

You may even be faced with the headache I suffered one Cycle 4 year, that I'll never forget – a cross country move that landed me with a landlord who lied, a property that wasn't ready, and two days to find a new home after living out of cases and hotels, with all my belongings in a rental truck. Not nice. But all worked out.

So you may find you get to ask the all-important question: **Is it time to move?** Move where? Well, I mean move *on* – from an old location, a job, a person, a situation, a habit?

Surely it is. We can't stay forever even in our childhood home (which no matter how difficult, is our emotional comfort zone or default because it was our training). Even if we do live there for the rest of our lives, it changes. *We* change. Those around us change. There really *is* no comfort zone, only repetition and habit. Cycle 4s enable us now to shake out of our old habits and patterns and try new things. Yes, it comes with discomfort, but the new feeling of comfort that *will* come in the aftermath, after the awkwardness, is well worth it. Remember moving? The stress and strain? When you wished you could have just turned back and put it all back the way it was? And then remember how great life was after you were settled in to your new place?

Remember those feelings – they'll help you now when you're likely dealing with some of the same themes and issues.

Someone may move in or move out, changing the flow and dynamics of who you get to interact with in your personal space. It reflects an inner shift with the various parts of your personality. And that counts for the first people who 'trained' you in the human world– the family, again. Some years in Cycle 4 you'll get to deal with something your parents did, to bring you the knowledge of something you may have judged when they were going through it themselves. Fighting noisy neighbors could reflect the arguments your parents had. Surroundings mirror original emotions of the day. Maybe you actually have a reunion with a long lost relative, or you decide it's time to cut off your father because he's abusive. Something stops in Cycle 4, or you decide to reconnect and carry it on.

Whatever emotional baggage you decide to pick up again in Cycle 4 can stay with you, so work out if it's again *fulfilling* a need or *filling-full* some part of yourself where you feel a void and need extra nurturing. Do you feel you need your Mother (or mother-surrogate) to provide for you, or can you play Mom to yourself and let her be free to be herself?

In one Cycle 4 I moved just as this Cycle began, and then during the final days of the Cycle I ended up talking to someone else about moving into a space *they* had – bigger, more privacy, quiet. Everything I really needed.

Needs. 4th Cycle. Comfort. 4th Cycle. Moving to a better location for your current needs. 4th Cycle. The pain of uprooting (again?!) is always worth the comfort that lies in wait at the other end.

PLANETARY SIGNATURE: MOON

This Cycle is ruled by the astrological Moon and the element of Water – representing our emotional nature, forever changing but something that, if acknowledged and honored, can become the best tool we have for navigating life. It's an eternal anchor that lets us know which way our internal compass is pointing – towards the improvement of our conditions, or to the past where we're replaying old scenarios and thereby creating them anew in the present by our continued emotional investment in them. The best way to create a worthy future is to honor our current feelings and then get back to the business of injecting them into where we want to go next. Internal security creates outer security, and feelings are the way there.

FIND A NEW NEST, STEP OUT OF YOUR COMFORT ZONE

Whatever it is, it's time to bail out, jump ship, fly the nest – in search of a new place to call home.

Or it's time to renovate and clean up where we currently are and make it more comfy too.

Our body is our ultimate home on Planet Earth, our 'spacesuit' in 3-D. Being 'at home' with oneself is the greatest comfort one can possibly attain this side of the veil, and it's a worthy cause. With unshakable self-support, care and love, we can handle anything.

However, the familiar is a potential trap in Cycle 4. Eventually, what was comfy and safe threatens our very growth when we suddenly feel the need to stand and defend and protect our rights to keep things *exactly the same as they've always been.*

Even countries follow these Cycles. The United States, for example, is perpetually in a conflict of this sort: it's a Cancer country (born July 4), which is similar to living eternally in Cycle 4 in some way (Cancer is the 4th sign of the zodiac). The American Dream is to own your own home. "As American as Apple Pie" is a catchphrase, and of course none other than Mom's own will do. Tradition reigns supreme. Catchphrases like "Never Forget" are a testament to the Cancer Sun.

Yet with an Aquarius Moon (the Moon in astrology reflecting our needs) the US has a constant need for Cycle 11 (Aquarius is the 11th sign representing the throwing out of tradition to make radical alterations). A constant theme that runs through American comedy is the outsider (Cycle 11) within the family (Cycle 4), the overturning (Cycle 11) of family values (Cycle 4) and the conflict between closeness (Cycle 4) and space (Cycle 11) within the family circle!

You'll find at least one Cancer arriving to help you navigate the rapids of your emotional life in Cycle 4, and by their examples you'll learn how family can help or hinder us and how finding roots and settling into a comfy home space is essential to the rest of our path.

SAFEGUARDING YOUR SPACE

During Cycle 4 a dissatisfaction often grows within us about our own four walls, our garden, our plot of land, our bedroom, the safety of our locks; but we fight change, we resist – unless we don't feel safe, in which case we can't change things fast enough. And that's when we are suddenly kicked out of a nest, thrown out of our apartment, even rejected from our culture or community or even country (the homeland is Cycle 4).

Where do we belong? Comfort zones were made to be broken, in the bigger scheme of things. Nothing stays the same. Nor should it. That would get boring. If you find this happening to you, just pack up and find a new place to set up shop/camp and continue on, and if you stagnate then up and move again. Home was never meant to be a physical thing of immortality, a place that will *always* be there; you're lucky if you have that but even that changes (vines creep over the windows, the roof leaks, the nice neighbors move away, the area is renovated).

Nothing is stable, everything is transitory (which is the gift this book is bringing you hopefully, the faith that change is for the best if we work with it, instead of resisting its natural flow). So updating and upgrading our comfort zones enables us to stay present, stay current and take the best of the past with us – ourselves! We are our pasts, and that's enough. We are the best of our pasts, the prize of our present, and the jewel and reward of our futures. We need to hop out of what's comfy for the sake of growth and to keep learning and then continue on.

So, find something uncomfortable and do it! Sit in a coffee shop when you'd normally read at home. Call friends and hang out with them if you are normally always by yourself. Try working at home if you're at the office all the time. Try leaving to do work if you work from home usually. If you have never been swimming because it scares you, then go try it. Try new things. Go new places. You always have home to go back to. See how comfy you can get in places where you normally wouldn't be. Soon you'll find that comfort has more to do with *yourself,* and you'll find home anywhere in Cycle 4. The ultimate lesson and learning curve. You'll always create a new comfort zone out of habit.

Give yourself time to expand and stretch your current comfy place and you'll find it gets larger and you can handle, take on and be more.

YOUR TURNING POINT
You can't get away from it in Cycle 4 – family appears, based on how you act now (notice how you laugh like your mother, act like your sister, or shout like your father during Cycle 4, or even those who you have made *into* your family in Cycle 4 ... family surrogates) and you get a chance to untangle from 'their' ways and become real and authentic in your own right. My brother flew out to visit me from England during one Cycle 4. Your childhood roots and conditioning are back in your life or just more active, so you get to see if they are useful patterns or you're merely reacting to triggers of old energies.

The past *has* shaped you, but you can use your new knowledge in the present to reshape yourself and sculpt away some of the old ways and recreate yourself in a new image. What do you need now and what works? The rest is scrap and belongs in the scrapbook or on Memory Lane gathering memento-dust for a rainy day when you're bored or need to remember where you've been. The past can help us locate ourselves in the present, or suck us back into an endless spiral of playing and replaying a moment in time.

Celebrate how far you have come. At least once in Cycle 4. You deserve to. And then continue on. You may decide you've had enough of your current nest and fly, or seek a new home somewhere else – bigger, smaller, higher up, lower down, warmer, colder, in a new city, state, country or planet (depending on when you read this book). Which leads us to:

HIDE OUTS, TIME OUTS

Are you comfortable in your own skin? That's the ultimate home we all have, it's personal and unique to us. It has inside furniture (our thoughts, world views etc) and our own decorations (or prejudices and beliefs) and our own storehouse of nick-nacks, memories and trinkets collected and held onto from our past (stored in our unconscious in secret boxes).

A skin rash or irritation now could suggest a discomfort in your body, or something inside is trying to be released. Are you cooped up in a jail rather than a home? Can you make more space, open windows, get outside for some air now and then? Can you make your house more of a *home* (no matter where you may find yourself)? I'm always amazed how even the homeless here in Los Angeles seem intent on trucking around with shopping carts stacked (and I mean stacked!) with their belongings, to give them their own sense of a familiar home. Sometimes we just can't let go of our safety blankets and a need is a need, however obstructive, hindering or illogical it may be to others or even ourselves.

Cycle 4 is a great time to get comfy then, and you may find you wind up sinking into a sofa at this time (even luckier if it's in someone's arms too) or lying in a bubble bath or relaxing with your favorite movie. Shutting out the world temporarily is a great way to reinvent and enjoy your own world as you wish it to be, and to see where you're at with yourself. You can only do that with *your own space*, so think twice before offering it up to anyone else if you're not feeling it, to avoid unnecessary scenes when you're feeling boxed in and unable to just be yourself. Ask yourself, "How do I feel about this, and how do I want to feel?" Then proceed ahead.

Hiding out in the familiar is a great way to power up in Cycle 4. Give yourself this time. You may not leave the house for days but so be it. Settle in. A time out is essential at this point of your journey, when emotional foundations are built to support your new climb to a new place in your story. If you have to travel during Cycle 4, living out of suitcases, hotels or having a 'home on the road', you'll still be faced with the quest to be comfortable and make the best of where you're at, and make yourself at home.

Cycle 4 is decompression time from the past few Cycles and the effort you've had to expend to date.

Whatever the case, you have a chance to find a new place of comfort and security during your 4-Cycle, a new 'womb' to see you through the next leg of your life's journey.

See this month (or however long this Cycle lasts for you personally) as strengthening the bars on your car as you travel through life's safari. You don't want to get walled up inside forever, but you do want to keep yourself safe inside so you can enjoy the ride.

Getting comfy has never been more important. War decreases the more our inner selves are at ease. Inner comfort rarely ends in outer conflict.

CHAPTER CLOSURE

Cycle 4 ends a chapter of your life. What was launched in Cycle 1 needs planting or you may need to re-pot it. It may die. Sometimes our seeds do. Or wither on the vine. Cycle 4 often sees an ending, a chapter closure where you have to let go and not smother or over-stifle this thing you want to nurture or grow. You may have to let it go and say goodbye indefinitely, which is hard, as it pulls at your needs this month to try and maintain and safeguard yourself by keeping things the same. At other times you may get to say goodbye for a period of space before revisiting it again.

Chewing over the past is easy but also makes things hard. Nostalgia kicks in which is nice for a time. We reestablish ourselves in *this cycle* by going over the past. By seeing how what we used to do made us feel good (or not so good) and whether to repeat (or reject) it now. This time last year you probably did the same thing. But getting stuck there, as we'll discover many times in this chapter, is a surefire way to invite change to breeze through our world in a disruptive manner, in order to show us new things.

What a strange concept eh? You're trying to get rooted, get secure and find stability and a place of safety in the world ... but ... you're also trying to tear yourself up from the inside, because you need to grow and not get stuck. You're reviewing and preserving the past, yet you're finding new memories to create in the present.

Maybe then a compromise will serve the paradox, in that you can get settled and re-instated and more secure if you follow up on the process of doing the hurting thing of uprooting. There's a payoff and a price to everything (something we'll get more into in Cycle 5).

You'll notice – guaranteed – an emotional period this Cycle 4, when you visit old places, old people, old situations – all inspiring old feelings. Memories. Haunting pains. Longing. Yearning for yesterday or yesteryear. All to warm your little toes and keep your soul comfy. Enjoy it. Just know you're walking down Memory Lane on a tour, not moving back there. You can't. Time has moved on, yet you can *maintain and keep the best of the past and keep it with you here in the present*. That's the best use of a Cycle 4 – work out what you want to keep, as a matter of **essential security and soul space and peace**, and bring it with you. The rest you can do without now, and that's where you'll experience the 'Chapter Closure' part of Cycle 4.

**Wherever you're *not* at peace,
you're *not* at home.**

With any trouble you face – start there, and you'll soon be on the road back to a safer, comfier and more peaceful place.

THERAPY AND IN TUITION (INNER TUITION)

Entering into some form of inner-work is a great way to use your 4-Cycle. From a check-in with a therapist or spiritual adviser or close friend or family member, to a heart-to-heart with yourself, you can't avoid revisiting, rehashing and replaying parts of your past so you can understand where you presently stand. Dig it up if need be, to see what you're playing with. Put it all on the table. This clears the way to seeing clearer without hauling around excess stuff you no longer need. That goes for stuff at home, in your cupboards, under your bed, in the basement or attic. Still have packed boxes? Empty them. You need space. Bringing out what is within helps us to do just that.

So find a way that feels right for you – the best ways may not initially feel comfortable, but this part of your 4-Cycle process is about unhitching yourself from the hooks of things that aren't working for you, and it takes a little adjustment to do that.

Go slowly, be gentle and breathe easily. It's a process. Whatever Dream you set into motion in Cycle 11 now needs the right home and you are the incubator, and your life is the zone where it will manifest. Making yourself at home within it, allows the Vision to unfold in a safe environment also. You're a mother carrying her unborn child, and you need support in giving both of you the best environment in which to give birth in, in Cycle 5 – your next and upcoming initiation.

THE SANCTITY OF SOUL SPACE

The safety of the familiar, your favorite womb, the known, the creature-comfort sense of safety and 'family' we feel in Cycle 4 (and the flip side, when we lose the sense of these things) can bring us back to one aspect of the 4th Cycle that many forget: soul space. As stated earlier, the past often makes a reappearance by a *re-occurrence* of past life events in your soul's history. Maybe what is transpiring now is giving you a chance to replay, relive and revisit aspects of you and your life that you never fully accepted, embraced, experienced, felt, understood or acknowledged.

> **This time round,**
> **it's less about *what* is going on and**
> **more about *how you feel* about it.**

Keep that in mind if you sense you're repeating something, or it has a strangely familiar scent to it. The soul remembers, your body's cells remember. (Remember that theory we mentioned previously that suggests during times of traumas we don't breathe, we catch or hold our breath, and thus the cells in our body store this original trauma because it wasn't moved through, felt and released?). So your body may still remember some of these moments even if you consciously don't. Find the core theme, problem, issue, concern, feeling, as Cycle 4 becomes a quest to *uncover* the roots of issues presently felt. Therapy, family confrontations, emotional outbursts and the release of long-imprisoned emotions are par for the course during your 4-Cycle. Allow them. Embrace them. Feel them.

Maybe the problem you're really having is a build up of so many times you never allowed yourself to feel, were told you were wrong to feel how you felt or were laughed at or rejected or ridiculed because of how you felt. Do yourself a favor now and *honor your feelings*. Break the possible chain in your soul's ancestry. Then you can free yourself from the past, by giving the original emotion the attention it needed at the time, and finally move on.

Soul space is essential. Walling yourself up at home is guaranteed at some point in Cycle 4. You just don't feel like going out, you'd rather camp out on the couch, watch your favorite movies (what a way to replay favorite parts of your past in the best possible way!) or look through old photo albums. Turning off the phone or just having earlier nights is a sure way to refuel yourself and give yourself the *personal time* you need.

CYCLE 4 ACTION PLAN:
* Make home, wherever you are.
* Decide if it's time to repot or renew your current space.
* Check in with family or revisit the past – and clear it up.
* Be honest about your feeling: be vulnerable and open.
* Draw up a list of top needs and begin to satisfy each yourself (or ask for help if necessary).
* Be there for others in any nurturing way possible.

In a grounding year:
You just belong. Right where you are. Which could be anywhere. No matter. You feel connected, at peace; things just feel 'right'. Even if you're having a hard time paying bills or you have some other issue to deal with, you know you can handle it all and it doesn't cause even a nuance of insecurity (or not enough to make you lose any sleep over). You're grounded, like an anchor in stormy weather, and your own port in a storm. You're eating well, have enough food or others are giving you gifts to feed you. There's plenty, and even if some days you come up short, you feel good with what you have – it always seems enough.

You move to a grand new location – an apartment overlooking the ocean or forest or cityscape of your dreams, or you just land a cushy pad with low rent or an extra room or free parking space (or even just get to house-sit somewhere outstanding). Score! Your landlord or tenants are so caring, considerate, helpful and soothing. Family sends you a check in the mail that covers the new laptop you need or a new bed set. You get to repaint and find just the right shade. And a furniture sale is going on and you scoop the best couch and get free delivery. Internally, you feel comfy, you don't need to go out and you don't need to stay in, but somehow you feel at home wherever you go. And if you find in certain moments that you don't feel so great, you withdraw, regroup and get back out there. Someone gives you a key to their cozy cottage in the country, or a seaside beach house for the summer. Or you win a dream home. Or you find a group of people you really get on with and you spend time at each other's pads cooking and chatting, well into the night.

In a floundering year:
Emotionally it feels as if you've been evicted. Cast out, banished, abandoned. Maybe you were, are or will be or are just terrified of being homeless, without solid ground. Or you feel cut off, ripped off and unsafe and unstable. You can't get the apartment or house because you're not the right height, gender, sexuality or it's not ready, and the owner has ripped you off, or you don't have the paperwork. Your roommate becomes neurotic and you have to get out – yesterday! You're avoiding the landlord because your rent is late, again. Even if you do find a place to call home, you're just ill at ease, and somehow awkward in your body. Maybe you're stuck where you currently are. With seemingly no options. No matter the case, you feel unsupported, unloved, and every time you try and better yourself someone seems to get in the way or help someone else out and you're left to fend for yourself. Life is unfair! It's as though you were ditched to make your own way.

Where are the supportive people? Talk about the birth-experience all over again; rejected into a cold, cruel, uncaring world. Now what? You're awkward, hungry, cold, crabby. And (you hate to say but it's true) so needy! You can't get over what happened, the injustice, the things that didn't work. Oh, regret. It's awful. How could this have happened? You're starving, for food, hugs, affection, love? Whatever it is, you're without it, and it's stressful. Foundations are rocky, shaky, destroyed, crumbling or you're in quicksand with no safe space, no moment to breathe, or your safety and security is gone in an instant and you're left saying "where do I live, where do I go, where do I start from?" What do you let go of and what are you being forced to give up? It's like all these endings hit you at once, and you're left trying to maintain your safety, security and sanity!

Stand back. Detach for a moment. Realize that your current path affects one major area above and beyond all others: Your emotions. It all comes back to *how you feel right now*. If externals (your job situation, relationship picture, health, current circumstances) are affecting you, then you're allowing yourself to get knocked off balance by things that aren't you. Yes, you're caught up in it all but these things are transitory and not permanent. Nothing ever is, really.

Remind yourself that everything is temporary. Everything shifts. It's cyclic. If you're on the downside of a Cycle, it will change. It always does. It starts by one simple thing that *is* in your control (while everything else appears not to be): **How you choose to feel about it**. If you feel down, sad, angry, upset; then feel it. Allow it. Don't beat yourself up over it. Your next step is then to decide how you *want* to feel. You can do simple things like having a drink of water or eating something (even if you're not super hot on the idea because you're just not feeling it). Try it.

You need the basics covered. Simplify. Ask someone for a hug. Call someone and alleviate your upset by sharing it. Everyone goes through hard times. This may be yours, and others will understand. We've all been there, trust me. Ask for help where you can and where you feel you need it. Then get to a place of self-mothering. Do what you would do with a child who has been hurt. Look after yourself in simple ways. Warmth, affection, food. Emotions are fickle things, and then one day suddenly they change. The rain evaporates, the dark skies brighten and something happens to make you wonder what the fuss was all about. Comfort is coming, just face the discomfort now and commit to staying the course.

Cycle Lesson
We're only as strong as our foundations. Take care of the roots and the blossom will take care of itself. Every seedling eventually needs repotting in order to continue thriving. Yet as creatures of habit, we find change difficult. Especially emotional shifts that change the very landscape we have come to rely on – the familiarity that once nurtured us now strangles our growth and freedom. Testing the foundations is an essential part of building a strong home. So welcome the emotional ripples that test you at your core. Home isn't a physical thing, it's a feeling within. The ability to handle any emotional tide, the ability to bend in the wind, the ability to chart any sea no matter how stormy, is the test of real strength. Acknowledging and accepting our feelings is another. Without them, we lose our humanity. Getting back to basics, taking care of our needs, our inner and outer home, connects us once more with the heart of humanity.

Celebrity Spotlight
- ◎ OJ Simpson's chickens finally came home to roost when, in Cycle 4, his past caught up with him and he was sentenced to prison.
- ◎ *Mommie Dearest* was released on DVD, July 17, 2001 under Cancer, the 4th Cycle.

Tips to successfully navigate your Cycle 4 Foundation

⊙ Make yourself at home no matter where you find yourself.

⊙ Find out what you *really* need, and what you really *don't* need anymore.

⊙ Consider moving to a place better suited to your current needs.

⊙ Redesign your living space: re-paint, try feng-shui or move furniture.

⊙ Revisit the best home you had (in memory if not in person).

⊙ Seek emotional guidance – ask your intuition, then ask someone you consider 'family'.

⊙ Put your feelings into a painting, song, dance move, card, letter. Give it life!

⊙ Find your family – blood relatives or your chosen kin. New if not old.

⊙ Reconnect and re-establish close bonds with others.

⊙ Be sensitive – open your heart and soothe troubled waters with a smile or sympathetic ear.

⊙ Mother issues? Release your own, relish your own or become your own.

⊙ Nurture – feed yourself and others; be gentle.

⊙ Create a sacred space and respect the bubble of others.

⊙ Look after someone, something or yourself.

⊙ Ask yourself if it's a need or a desire – which is more important right now?

⊙ Buy something for your nest: new pillows or a comfy bedspread.

⊙ Take a bath before bed.

⊙ Cook for yourself or someone you know.

⊙ Drink more water, shower – slow down and sometimes … just sit.

⊙ Flip through photo albums, go to a history museum or do an archaeological dig through your own diary/psyche.

⊙ Try a new recipe or make your favorite treat.

⊙ Give hugs freely.

⊙ Give voice to your emotions.

⊙ Ask "What do I need right now?" Ask another what they need?

⊙ Enjoy a belly-rub.

⊙ Create a *new* comfort zone – be safe, comfy and yourself in new places.

∼ Surf Cycle 5 ∽

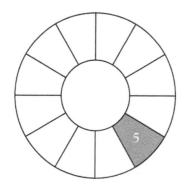

Time to Focus on Fun
Create!
and Make Love

Astrological Appearances by:

Performers/show-offs
Thespians and theatre-goers
Party planners and party animals
Actors, dancers, musicians
Drama queens and kings
Actual royalty/aristocracy
Children or those who work
with them
Childlike or child-ish people
Your kids or someone else's
Gamblers and high-rollers
Celebrities/the elite
Game-players/bossy boots
Your next date

Leo people
Confidence trainers/mascots
Your lover/bit on the side
Matchmakers and flirts
Your partner's friends
The arrogant
Artists and painters
Those who can work a room
People who run the show
The producer, director, writer or talent
Melodramatic people/spotlight seekers
Risk takers/sporty types
Competitive people

What you'll need:

Your name (and mirror) in lights
Your own stylist
Unwavering pride
A personal spotlight
The nerve/audacity/confidence/ego
Presence/charisma/'it'

You've started on a new path, looked at your options, sat at home picking over your past, dealt with family issues or domestic disputes, worked through some deeply personal stuff, decided what should stay and what should go, revisited past conflicts and tried to seek some relief and resolution ... it's been quite a busy time working out what makes you tick and where to replant yourself in a new more fertile soil, befitting the 'new you'.

Not anymore.

You just burst forth from your Hobbit hidey-hole into the bright light of **your 'It's Great to be Alive' Cycle 5!** Welcome to the stage (literally) of your annual journey that reminds you to Just Keep Loving It (All).

First off – don't look back. Dwelling is old hat. Old news. Part of your last Cycle, so leave it there. For now, stick to what Cycle 5 is all about, since that's where you're currently located, like it or not. (You'll like it. I know you will). You can't help but end up liking Cycle 5, because whether it's a great 5-Cycle or a low 5-Cycle, it's always big, it's always bold and it's always dramatic. And secretly, inside, that's what you desire right now. High or low, it'll go down in your history as a time of big possibilities and memorable moments.

Cycle 5 is usually the time in your year when you'll be encouraged, quite simply, to let your hair down and have a good time. You're urged to find your Joy again. This then, is your opportunity to remember the innocence of childhood, when you weren't yet burned by the hot flames of desire, pummeled by passion, and ripped off emotionally by those who let you open up and then 'loved' you by bruising your sensitive heart and trampling on your fragile ego.

And, if you didn't quite have one (a childhood that is, forget thinking you don't have an ego), this is the chance in your year to do just that – enjoy giggling, eating dessert first, playing in the muck or rain, dressing up or taking your clothes off!), throwing paint at something (or makeup on yourself) and finding and creating your own unique style (even if you don't have Mom around to stick your creation on the fridge and show the world your genius ... get the violins out, eh?). Well Cycle 5 is rather big, bold and dramatic as we said – so don't blame me if this gets a little chocolate-and-roses. Deal with it!

Astrologer Linda Goodman once said that giving is effortless and it's our true nature. The apple tree doesn't choose to whom it bestows its fruit; it simply must. Without giving, the tree would die.

In our lives, it often becomes a scorecard game of give and withdraw when we seek only to protect ourselves from hurt once inflicted or suffered (it's the same burn). However this Cycle 5 of yours asks you to continue giving birth to ideas, games and projects that feel good, no matter the consequences to your ego. You can do it, you've done it your whole life (picked yourself up when things didn't go totally according to your plan), but this month it's time to get conscious of *continuing to give of yourself – the thing that only you can give, and not to worry so much on what you get back for doing so.*

AUDIENCE APPRECIATION OR APATHY

The reception you receive this month may be really bad. You may give gifts, love others to the best of your ability, and they may still rain on your parade. It can happen, like an unexpected summer downpour. Anything is possible. But whether you let it affect your joy in life (your *joie de vivre*), or whether you let it dictate whether you'll shrivel up or close off your heart, is another matter. Therein lies your power this Cycle – so my advice: stop reacting to the reception you are or are not getting! Some will love you, some will hate you; some won't even care. Or maybe there's the worry you'll trip yourself up just as you're having your moment in the spotlight. The resulting fear is the same – possible shame, embarrassment and social humiliation.

Again, who cares? All that matters is how you continue on your own path, for Cycle 5 increases your creative light, if you don't let yourself darken like some of those who may stumble across or block your path. And all you're being challenged on, currently, is your ability to *play* the game, not on how well you do.

Let that relieve the butterfly anxieties fluttering in your stomach and heart.

PLAY AND PLEASURE

Playing is the ultimate act of creation – of getting up and doing it and simply having a go. It involves a major risk – the audience may boo, the lover may walk, the art be trashed by critics, the haircut receive laughs on the street, the gamble fail, the open heart be swallowed whole, the song flop, the film script bomb, the idea crash and burn ...

You want to be the world's greatest lover, or the next Van Gogh, the next Oscar actor, or just loved without feeling like you'll be dumped the moment something goes iffy. We're all presented with a stage, this Solar phase, and we're all given the choice to walk on, or hide in the wings watching more fearless souls take to the spotlight. (You're kidding yourself if you believe they're not nervous, they just have no other choice because it's shine or die under Cycle 5.) From my research, every top entertainer gets nervous before their performance without fail and it actually enhances their delivery.

Shining is the only way to keep the darkness at bay.

If you're swamped by the shadows now, worried about withering away, the only choice you have is to continue burning brightly with no other power source but your own right to be respected, your own need to create and your own vision of how something *could* be.

151

And the desire for a great life!

Desire is your fuel and passion; your road map. And while many cultures and religions see 'ego' as something to move beyond, to ignore, repress or destroy, it is your ally in Cycle 5. Befriend it. Enjoy it. And you can use it to steer your ship where you choose.

The singer Madonna is a Leo, and all Leos live in a perpetual Cycle 5 of sorts. Madonna stands out as a strong and clear example. "Express yourself, don't repress yourself" (*Human Nature*), "All the world is a stage" (*Take a Bow*). In her song *Die Another Day* she sings "I'm gonna destroy my ego". Since this is her own life path mission (she was born with her Sun in the 12th house of ego submission) this may be her message to the world. However, try telling that to most Leos whose Sun burns in the other 11 houses of the astrological wheel!

Ego, in Cycle 5, is your golden ticket. Don't snub it. Many think denying the ego is the way to en- 'lighten'-ment, but in Cycle 5 I'm here to tell you it is not.

PLANETARY SPOTLIGHT: SUN

The Sun in astrology relates to all things connected to this particular Initiation. It's the giver of life to Planet Earth. When it spotlights your 5-Cycle, you're urged to reach out like a sunflower seeking the Sun itself, to become the Sun and shine as only you can, to wear the actor's mask of your own creativity, to let your light shine and your lust for life ooze into everything you do and everything you touch. To stamp your life with your own exuberance. To live from the heart and love as only you can, no holds barred, in your own unique, inimitable way. Be like the Sun and refuse to darken or dampen yourself. Sometimes the Sun's job is to keep on shining no matter how dark the skies or how impenetrable the clouds. Burn off the darkness with your own brilliance.

EGGING ON YOUR EGO

Cycle 5 *needs* ego. It gets things moving, it's the juice in your car, the magic in your battery, it gets things done, and it's the impetus to change things for the better. Ego is the spark of spiritual light given a backbone and a reason for being and gives you a desire and gets you out of bed in the morning (after all what is the point of being a soul unless you're incarnated into the physical world to effect change and experience physicality?). Without ego, everything just remains a great idea with no impetus to be created: a painting without an artist, a blockbuster without a writer. Pure potential. It was ego that led most people to their great works (or did they attract their great works to them due to their desire?)

Even acts of compassion happened because someone *wanted* to make a difference, make a painting, spotlight an issue, help the sick, and couldn't *not*.

You're in charge of where you place
your energy and intention.

What in your life do you have *no* choice in doing because you must do it, because it *is* you?

That's your Cycle 5 phase in action. And your spiritual purpose in action! It's not about success or failure; it's about *playing the game.*

So one thing to bear in mind is not to take anything too seriously this Cycle. Not if it starts getting heavy. Not yourself. Not how you look or act. Not what you do. Now how it comes off. Not what you create.

Love yourself but get over yourself, in Cycle 5!

By all means find a new way to express yourself during this Cycle, and give it your all – you'll need a channel for all of your passionate, playful, creative energy. Find something to try and see if it's fun, let your ego shine and do what only you do best. What is that, you ask? You've probably been doing it your entire life.

If you're still wondering what that is, look to the **house and sign your Sun is placed in your astrology chart**. My website has some pointers and audio clips to work out what that is. Any astrologer will be able to tell you more. If we shine in the house of our charts where the Sun was placed at our birth, then only great things can happen because we are fulfilling our purpose on the planet. Simple ways to achieve big things.

The Sun plugs us back into Cosmic Central: the source of all our power. Cycle 5 is one way to do just that. What sign is the Sun currently traveling through as you're moving through your Cycle 5? Use the attributes of this sign to power yourself up. **You'll find a list of attributes for each of the 12 signs of the zodiac at www.SurfingYourSolarCycles.com.**

Power up and you'll have all the energy you need in life, by *simply being You*. The easiest thing in the world, if we get out the way of ourselves and let ourselves just be!

No one else can live your life – you're the Star of your own Story. Will it be a story worth telling to future generations?

Shine on!

THE PLEASURE PRINCIPLE
What feels good to you? Cycle 2 gives us a grounded approach to the pleasure principle (by revealing to us what *physically* feels good), but Cycle 5 asks us to step it up a notch and demand some form of ego-reinforcement by pursuing and getting the things we want – things that build us up and make us feel good inside.

For in pursuing Cycle 5 you get to power yourself up like never before. You get to *really* feel happy you're alive. That life is worth all the drama, the problems, the risk-taking and the darker days. For those moments when life is glorious, when you can't help but smile and life just 'works' – Cycle 5 is your direct route to uncovering these once more.

Pursuing pleasure is your way ahead now. Not money, just that good time feeling. Did you miss that with all the serious stuff happening?! There is no other Cycle so specifically designed and designated to *playing*, pure and simple. No deadline, no clock-watching, no work. Every creative person and every creative act has to allow this part of any project, their 'Cycle 5' when they simply thrash around in the mud or water, and see what they come up with.

How many great ideas came when people were taking a bath, eating dessert, going for a walk, a drive, or daydreaming? (Like Archimedes, who screamed "Eureka!" in the bathtub, and Einstein suddenly discovering his Theory of Relativity).

You don't need to wait for others to show you a good time this Cycle, the concept of self-pleasure is relevant now also – if no one is around offering you that magical feeling, create it yourself!

Allocate some time, then, to mindlessly sitting by a fountain, seeking inspiration, taking a bath, walking by the ocean, going for an ice cream, getting theater tickets to a swanky show. Treat yourself. Give yourself some inspiration time.

CHILDREN AT HEART

You can't play, have fun, let go and get a bit wild unless you allow yourself to be a child. Have you seen these youthful souls play? They don't care, there's no 'rules of engagement' – they may seek attention and approval with a "look Ma, no hands" cavalier attitude, but if they don't get it they'll soon find something else to do to entertain themselves. Take that as your key – **entertain yourself and sooner or later you'll wind up entertaining someone else**. And even make a career out of it perhaps (or have a rollickin' good month at any rate).

After all your hard work this year you need some simple fun time! Be around kids; work with them if you can in Cycle 5 (you may find them showing up anyway), or anything and anyone who simply has a good time, no reasons, no justifications and no excuses. And remember everyone's inner child – they show up in droves this Cycle. I love the quotation I once read that went along the lines of, "Adults are just big people with a backlog of unmet childhood needs". Somehow you trigger everyone else's inner child in Cycle 5.

How about your own, is he or she happy?

I've seen people attend fancy-dress parties, get auditions to join dance groups or opera performances under Cycle 5. Others suddenly get taken out on five dates a week (more on that below). Others are barely reachable because they're out at a different bar each night or always at some party or other, this Cycle. And others are just messing around and loving it. Trying on new looks, style and colors. On an easel, computer, notepad, dance floor. You name it, people are creating it, right now!

Are you joining the ranks of artists out there, committing to creating something, anything?

You'll be aided in this quest by at least one Leo person who arrives to remind you just how much fun being a child really is, and also how ugly it is when our inner child isn't allowed to play and the ego storms that are created because of this!

A DATE WITH ROMANCE

That's right, this is one of the best Cycles for getting out and dating. For lapping up attention. For being wooed, courted, romanced, adored, worshipped and made to feel special. And making others feel important too.

If you're currently with someone, how much romance is still alive in your relationship? Can you extend the honeymoon and make each other feel special again? You may have to give it to get it! Proving you're the world's greatest lover is something many get into this Cycle 5, or if not, just the fun of being taken out or taking someone else out is enough to light our inner fire and get back in the game. Romance is alive now, and if you're with someone it's a time to bring that back, no matter how long you've been together. Dating affords us the chance to put our best foot forward and enjoy others at their best before they show the things about themselves that *they* feel aren't working (and when they are pointing the finger at you for the same reasons).

Why do relationships go so well at the onset and usually lose their sparkle and break down as time goes by? At the beginning we are looking for things to like in the other. And they are doing the same with us. Without fail, we find what we are seeking. We elicit that response from the other. As time goes by, we expect less of the good stuff and so end up with less of the good stuff.

So ... can you start appreciating, liking, focusing on the good stuff and actively seeking it in someone in your life, in order to refresh your relationship and bring back the initial feel good factor? You can, if you give it a go. It's never too late. The person you met at the beginning is still there. Re-establish why you both met and you'll re-energize that initial spark and magic.

So everyone is happy in Cycle 5 during the dating season of your year. It's not about finding a lover forever, it may happen but its more about playing the odds, taking a chance, playing the numbers game if need be and celebrating the best and brightest in everyone else around you and letting them enjoy and spoil you also.

What a time!

Is it any surprise that **playful and frivolous sex** is part of Cycle 5? Yes, you may have more options to 'sow your wild oats' now. Or you may channel everything into your new painting or poem or work presentation. But people will notice you, people will praise you, flatter you (how can they not when you're wearing a neon sign that says you want that right now!?) and you may get noticed by someone involved (or you may be the one who already has someone) and be enticed into an affair of some sort to indulge your ego's insatiable need to feel like a god or goddess. As indeed you are.

If it's not about hurting anyone and you can be honest about it all, Cycle 5 is about finding and rediscovering yourself through the playful realization of **sexual conquest, experience and adventure**. Adrenalin pumps. It's the same anywhere you are taking a risk. Having to be the best or at least put on a good show.

Why do you think it's called sexual 'performance'?

On a last note in this section, matchmakers say (according to a detail-oriented Virgo I knew during 2009 when I was working on this chapter … since then who knows, it may have changed) that most people have to play the numbers game around 80 times before they find 'The One' (who they'll spend the next chunk of their life with, at any rate). As an astrologer, I think we meet people when we're ready for it, no matter how hard we search. So if this is true, brighten up and lighten up and get ready to be 'in it to win it', and allow for a few disappointments on the road to finding a suitable mate … or at least, to begin with, a suitable date!

We have many soul mates that pop up at various intervals in our lives, for specific purposes, so really it may just be out of our hands.

Enjoying life, then, becomes the biggest magnet for those worth being around who see *you* as someone worth being around.

Like attracts like.

Be light, be bright and they'll be drawn to you like moths to a flame. How could they resist?

Added note: It was during the editing of this section that, in another Cycle 5, I actually saw a moth drawn to a candle flame in my home and being ignited; its wings smoking as it continually flew into the flame itself, lured by its hypnotic bright mystery. Flames kill moths. I never really thought about it before. But they'll keep coming back – so be sure that what you're attracted to isn't harmful to you. Just because someone takes an interest in you, it doesn't mean they're right or healthy for you. And sometimes the brightest lights can become our biggest mistakes. Just a thought!

LOVE ME, DATE ME, ADORE ME, TAKE ME!

Cycle 5 tests you on *how much love you have to go around*, the quality of your love and your willingness to dish it out. And that means you have to be 'full of yourself' in some capacity, in order to give of yourself. You have a *lot* of love to give. Unlimited. Who gets a share of it? We'll discover this when you take us on a date or when you give us your creative skills. Date us! Love us! Flirt with us! How can you give love? In many ways. You have your own brand. Your unique style. So do I. So does your ex lover, and chances are it didn't really work for you.

Some give love through gifts, so you could try this (splash out and get something for someone for the sheer pleasure of saying "You're special"). You could give them your attention (calling them, checking in, showing up when you know they finish work to ask if they want to go for a drink). You could help them out (doing a favor is some people's way of showing love). Now Cycle 5 may reveal something interesting to you: that the style of love that you love others with is *how you yourself will recognize loving behavior*.

This can get tricky when others don't love you as you love them. Some people won't drive to you, if you live across town, even though you'll make the effort. Is that a lack of love? To you, yes it may just well be. Some people won't ask how you are, when you do. Same thing. One person's mode of loving is another person's idea of eating glass.

So, look during this Cycle at *how* you show love, and you'll be given major clues as to what you feel is loving behavior. And there begins a learning curve on what you can look for when you're out dating. You can compromise but that's more for Cycle 7 when you already *have* someone around. Cycle 5 is about finding the suitors, going on the dates, testing the waters and seeing what's on offer. It's window-shopping time when you get to try on the merchandise, touch the goods and see if it feels right for you.

LIGHTEN UP TO LAP THE LOVE UP

Don't take yourself seriously in this Cycle. Fives are about changing the scenery again, adding fire to your fuel and fuel to your fire. About getting crackly and excited and amped up and ready for action on some level. You need it – to take a risk. You need to maintain your bright, fun-loving side. If it stops being fun in Cycle 5, your ego is too involved and you'll need to step back and see if it's growing too large and consuming everything in its path with its needy demands and hunger for attention, or if you're truly not getting your love needs met.

We often show love in the manner we are accustomed to being loved (or at least desiring to be loved). It's the principle of giving gifts we'd like to accept. It all sounds a bit narcissistic and indeed it is, but we do get to see how we want to be loved by how we love others. So keep track of what you're giving out in the way of love vibes and what you're getting back, because there is a correlation if you spot it, and you may be surprised that your messages are more mixed than you may have first thought.

Can you love others as they want/need to be loved, whilst still being yourself? Maybe another feels loved when you fold their clothes, listen to their grievances, call them up sometime instead of always waiting for them to call. Maybe you do it differently, but can you love them as they need to be loved, and also let them know what you yourself need? Start by giving others what they need. That's a great way to express your Cycle 5, and you may even find that in return others will love you as you yearn to be adored.

Mutual back-scratches ... nothing better.

ROLE PLAY AND ROLLS IN THE HAY

If Cycle 5 is about shining your light then it must also be about finding what makes that light shine, finding the source of its power and uncovering your unique methods of plugging back into Cosmic Central, your very own personal connection back into the energy that keeps everything going and glowing.

For some, it's recharging their batteries by relaxing. For you, it may be being the life of the party; being around large crowds. Maybe it's reading in a quiet park, maybe it's having sex. Maybe it's doodling. Expect then, to spend some part of your 5-Cycle finding a way to power up in order to do this 'shining' business. (By the way look what happens to egos when they don't have fun and play ... like Jack Nicholson in the very appropriately named movie *The Shining*.) All work and no play could turn you into an axe-wielding psychopath – or at the very least, a miserable wreck that no one wants to be around. And *that* is the worst feeling during 5-Cycles.

Be warned. Egos get fragile in Cycle 5 so the best way to avoid mishaps and mountains out of molehills is to find your very own cord back into this universal grid of energy, without expecting others to fill you or fulfil you. You've got to do it yourself first, or show willingness to try, for Cycle 5 to open its wonders and make you feel like the star you are.

So, your role could be to be the top dog, the queen bee, with others orbiting around you like satellites; moths to that proverbial flame. Or you could be the one who charges yourself up by feeling powerful and important by being around others who are big and have the power (and audacity) to shine. You shine by proxy. You hope their light rubs off on you, or maybe it just makes you look good by being close to them or knowing them (Hollywood runs on this idea). And looking good may be your way to shine. You'll find your way, your 'thing'; your way of taking the stage and lighting it up with your very own soul-spotlight. Cycle 5 is all about this and is willing to give it to you in any way that you're open to it.

Somehow, somewhere, and in some way, this Cycle, your audience awaits ...

ENTRANCE STAGE LEFT: DRAMA KINGS AND QUEENS

In Cycle 5, emotions are always pretty obvious. Things get blown up to bigger proportions, which is part and parcel of that craving you have for attention and theatrics. It's natural so don't fight it.

Right now emotions are either out there in the open or else we're polluting rooms by withdrawing our light and becoming known for the dark clouds we bring in our wake.

Either way, our light is felt by its very presence or its lack. Again we're reminded that **'darkness' is just a lack of light.** And that there is never truly complete darkness in the world.

The Sun is always shining, somewhere.

That's what we should bear in mind during Cycle 5, when we're bursting with vitality that screams to be heard, or else shrouded in shadows.

If we don't receive the applause and respect our dramatic side needs then we risk sulking, withdrawing and sitting on it, becoming cold, calculated, devoid of love and dreadfully detached. (Shiver).

We're *all* prima donnas. Somehow, somewhere, in some way. For some of us, it's at home. We just have to dominate space, and control what goes where and what color which wall will be.

Some of us feel the need to lord over others at our place of work. We like to call the shots and delegate. Others love being the star of the relationship and others love being the king or queen bee in their social circles. We each want a bit of the glory. Cycle 5, though, seems to work well when we give our glory, and focus less on expecting to get glory back, because we surely will if we're genuine and authentic in the eyes of ourselves or the world or whoever else we want to applaud us or scratch our backs.

TV shows like *American Idol* or *Britain's Got Talent* showed us how big 'anyone can be a star' ideologies have become. Even if you're a wallflower, or you're just still reeling from a trying-and-tiring Cycle 4, no matter what, no matter where, no matter how, you *must* release your dramatic, creative, fun-loving freed-up side now. It's a *need*, a primal urge asking you to; to avoid the showdown of fireworks and foot stamping, which this portion of your annual journey could quickly lead to.

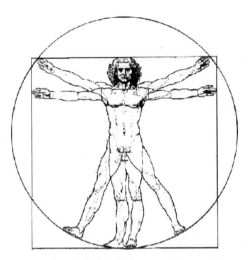

The Number 5 is symbolic of romance (Venus the planet of Love is connected to the Number 5 and if you stand with your feet apart and your arms outstretched, you become your own 5-pointed star). That's why 5-Cycles are about shining, dazzling and being your own creative powerhouse of love and all good things. You are the center of what you create; the giver of birth, the divine spark, god-like in your ability to give life and bring life to whatever you conceive.

CREATIVE CHECK-IN

So, take a look at your life at this point of your year. How do you want to give the gift of your big, bright and bold side to the world. Via your job? Your humor? Your ability to have a good time in general? Your smile, perhaps? Your wink? Your flattery? Your musical/artistic/leadership talents? The way you make people feel special? You're brimming full, even if you can't see, sniff or sense it right now, but trust me there are few things worse than sitting under Cycle 5 and temporarily losing (or forgetting, more like) your light. It's Cycle 5's job to help you reconnect to your inner light, and chances are you're already being invited or urged to let it out. To shine. That's it.

And the final point is this: to shine, to truly be a beacon and a Sun, sometimes our only job is to be ourselves, and not to try. Isn't one of the Sun's main jobs to brighten dark skies? By being itself? So don't get lost in the 'I'm not *doing* enough'. That defeats your purpose and dis-empowers you. *Just keep finding things you enjoy doing, and do them. Hunt them down.* Take a risk, a gamble; try your hand at something and try not to care about being good at it because:

Getting good at it comes in Cycle 6 and that's next month.

First you need to know what to perfect, yes?

Whatever shadows appear now, dispel them by turning up your own pride, your own self-respect, your own self-love. Your own inner king or queen. Cheerlead someone else to pick up your *own* confidence. It's amazing how this works. Pump up another and the part of you that knows you deserve the best will be pumped up in the process, even if you're not quite surrounded by it just yet. *Focus on good stuff, and good stuff focuses on you.* The part of you that wants quality five-star treatment wants to be heard. Give it attention. To receive all you desire, Cycle 5 dictates that we need to:

Give back. Empty your creative genius.
It's the only way to keep refilling.

MIRROR, MIRROR ON THE WALL
MIRROR MIRROR ON THE WALL

With all this showing off and shining and standing center-stage and celestial spotlighting, you could let it all go to your head. It's a good idea – big heads lead to big bright ideas and bold moves, beautiful and brilliant creations. We owe it to the artists in our world for the glory they bring to us. Or the sports stars. Or actors. The ones who entertain us on our dark days, or allow us to cry on the very same days. And the ones who cheered us up when we'd almost lost hope, or the ones who reminded us of our own human condition and the struggles in our own lives.

Shy people rarely command our attention. It takes 'balls' (and I mean this metaphorically of course) to be big, and make big things happen. To even let yourself *want* to be big, or do something big.

We need pride to accomplish, a little pizzazz and ego-power to withstand the possible failure or rejection or the letdown we've spent so long trying to avoid. Pride gets you there. It puts you in the game, on the map and in the thick of it. Lottery winners had to actually *buy* the ticket. Singers had to sing their first song. Actors had to audition. Pride gives you that certain 'it' factor. You're proud of yourself, your work, your looks, your accomplishments, or even just your efforts if nothing else is forthcoming.

But pride can balloon up and this brings us to the downside of Cycle 5. Your life suddenly takes on melodramatic overtones. You become a soap opera star where you're gasping and wailing "How dare they!?" and "Can you *believe* they did this to me!?" and "Don't they know who they're talking to?" Be forewarned, this Cycle is a mess if you're not getting the attention you crave, or giving yourself the right kind. You need big doses of whatever your brand of that feel-good factor is.

My advice: Buy a mirror and kiss it before it gets to this stage; but if all you do is stand staring into it wondering who is the fairest of them all, or worst yet, not even asking the question because no one else could possibly compare to you, then quickly turn your mirror over. True, maybe others aren't as dazzling, but that's a little too narcissistic and it's not helping you create in the ways you're meant to be. Enjoy a little vanity, please do. But then get back to the business of adding some personal special touches to your Dream or Vision created in Cycle 11. Become your own personal Public Relations person. Put a personal face to your dream. A name. And use your ego to push it under others' noses and back it up with confidence.

False Pride (masking insecurity) could ruin something good, especially after you built those cherished emotional bonds with people in Cycle 4. Don't lose it now by expecting others to throw rose petals at your feet or be more concerned that it was *you* who created something and less about the creation itself. By all means get credit but what happens when your name is misspelled or isn't as large as you'd like it or you're not mentioned fifteen times at the award ceremony?

Did you do your best? Do you feel proud? Yes? Great! Well the rest is a bonus and you'll lose the plot if you sit around wondering when the world is going to treat you like a celebrity. What's that – you already are one? Well, in which case Cycle 5 asks you to go one better with a new style or a new creation. If you're not famous (yet) or you don't care to be, then just feeling you did something special is enough.

GAMES AND GAMBLING

Prepare to play a game this month/Cycle. From the roulette tables in Vegas to a card game with friends; from a soccer match to the game of Truth or Dare; an audition or job interview to the revealing of your artwork or getting back into the dating game; appearing on an actual Game Show or having to wear a costume and play the game of acting, to wearing a suit for a black tie event.

Games involve some form of *rules*, some form of *payoff* or attention/glory and some form of possible *rejection* or failure. That's the fun and beauty and allure of the whole thing. Take sporting events for instance. Competing becomes part of the game. How else can you prove you're wonderful unless you come first, do it better or beat off some form of competition who were also vying for the same thing? How healthy is your ego? You'll find out in Cycle 5 because this month you'll no doubt be held up to someone else's standards (or your own) and judged accordingly.

Are you hot or are you not?

Let's look at the **rules**, firstly. Gambling and games involve knowing at least some of the rules going into it. Research your market, know your territory and market your target audience. Know what impression you want to create, what mark you want to leave behind and what memory you want to give as a parting farewell. Doing a good job is one way, looking your best is another; having manners may work for some of you, whilst for others it's being better yourself than anyone else. To win, you have to play by the rules laid out. Don't dive in unless you know the risks and the rules, because once the game has begun there's no turning back until the final whistle blows and the scores are tallied.

> **What are you being judged on?**
> **What are you judging yourself on?**
> **Focus on these areas for maximum effect.**

Then there comes the **payoff**. We only go into a game or a gamble because of the thing(s) we'll get out of it. What is it? Attention, applause, a medal, honors, respect or love perhaps? Maybe it's *all* love, when we get right down to it, in various guises? This Cycle is made of it. Everything comes back, somewhere, to attention – which equals love. And we're hungry for it. The payoff, depending on how large it is, will determine, in 5-Cycles, how big the investment we're willing to make is and how far we may fall, crushed when we don't attain it.

Take a beautiful face for example – what people have done in history to pursue their object of attraction ... the personality disorders we ignore to pursue The Beautiful Face. Or the great sex.

So secondly:

> **work out if the payoff is worth the investment.**

Chances are it is or you'd not even be contemplating playing the game. And if so, know that the bigger the payoff, the grander the fall and the more dramatic it will all feel.

And finally, the **rejection** aspect. The failure. The 'not getting what you want' part of the deal. Can you handle it? Does it make you get back up and try again? Or does it crush you, because you still doubt yourself or your worthiness (and didn't do your Cycle 2 homework on self-esteem ... go back and do some revision now).

Get this, though: We cannot truly lose anything!

> **Rejection is often a form of protection,**
> **because something doesn't (or will not down the line),**
> **resonate with us.**

Rejection, then, could be our ultimate warning sign. Even if we truly feel that the gaining of the object of our desire would fix or feed our entire life. So accept that possible loss is part and parcel of your current Cycle. Go for what you want with gusto, and jump up and down if you get it, and if not, know your effort does not go unrecognized and the universe will set something up much better and more in line with you, down the road.

And just think, you've added something to your life resume. Not bad, eh!

Gambling is about the thrill. A momentary feeling. The possible payoff. So is the seeking of any pleasure. From a bowl of ice cream to a romantic first date. The difference is in the feeling it engenders and how long the buzz lasts afterward. It's a moment of excitement, possibility, a feel good factor and a rush. You may come out the other end feeling sick or wish you'd never bothered, but for now you're playing the game, pursuing the chase, knowing the stakes and willing to risk it all for that infamous feel good payoff.

Congratulations, you're well into your 5th Cycle and the star of your own reality show!

FIRE CYCLE 5

Fire is Action (see the 'Cycles of Elements' in Chapter 13). So this Cycle is really about just giving it a shot. Igniting yourself and refueling your inner fire. Being stubborn and fixed in your attitudes, to stand firm in your resolve and to be confident enough to go for a piece of the pie, a slice of the gateau and a major part of the glory. Blaze with your own burning light. You deserve it. You're worth it. You're the source in your own story. You're the battery and the charger. You're the celebrity now.

VACATION, PARTIES

Many of us, stuck in jobs we don't like, seem to pursue our 5-Cycles by taking vacations, to really tap into that level of play where we won't answer a phone and we get to leave it all behind at home or at the office. Sometimes, as adults, it's the only way we get to be children again. We can skip the meal and have dessert. Maybe we lie on the beach the entire time, in weather and conditions that are far removed from the chore of our day-to-day life. Great. It's a shame we have to wait for vacations to be free enough to play, but sometimes we need to be forced to do so. 'Scheduling in' time to just enjoy life may sound like a contradiction, but it is essential to your journey so you don't want to miss out or you'll be complaining the entire year.

That's why Cycle 5 designs events and parties to get you to hang your work suit up and let your hair hang down (while looking fabulous of course). You're Rapunzel (or you were, in Cycle 4), trapped in your home tower, and now life wants you to get out, jump out, do whatever you can to get out of home and get to the party/ball/event/limelight.

How can we all enjoy you if you're not out here for us to see, meet or experience?!

JOY, PURE AND SIMPLE

When was the last time you laughed till you wept?

You know the feeling – when all is right with the world, when something is so funny, you just lose it and your stomach bounces and your lungs ache and you can do nothing but weep.

How can such a joyful feeling elicit a physical response so similar to grief?

Emotions are all connected, and oh-so similar. The release we experience with tears of happiness is the same as the release we feel through tears of sorrow, just the energy behind it is different. Cycle 5 is about *creating* – not always sitting in front of our TVs, not just listening to someone else's ideas, concepts or work. It's about being an actor in our own lives, and the director and the scriptwriter. It's about being the star of our own show. The giving of our gifts away to the world.

What are you consuming and what are you creating? What are you going to make? What are you going to draw/paint/sing?

When was the last time you did something simply for the *sheer pleasure* of it?

What makes **you** really happy? And why aren't you doing it? At this Cycle there is absolutely no excuse – no matter *what* is happening in your life – to not *salvage the moment and turn it into something you want it to be.* Even in a war-torn corner of the globe (and let's face it, which corner *isn't* war-torn if humans are currently living there?) we can look up to the skies and realize there's a bigger world, and we can bond with those around us, and find a space and a reason to see the insanity behind it all. Life's too short to succumb to the madness.

Someday this will all be over – and that fact should alone make us, no matter what, find a place to *enjoy this moment* with all its apparent pain, chaos, confusion, insanity, injustice and ridiculousness. Enjoy the cosmic joke!

Humans have been programmed by those above them (seemingly 'above' but no more evolved) to think life is about struggle – but it was never intended for that. It was a jewel, an opportunity to harvest riches of experience, in a 3-D world where we get to savor all we create. Imagine that – we get to not only bake the cake but eat it too! Try that when you're floating around without a body in another dimension. Somehow, we have forgotten this, in the race to blame others or ransack lands for gold, oil and other reserves.

We can take this power back, and remember our purpose. To laugh, to have fun, to enjoy every waking moment of this human life we lead. Isn't that a more noble and fulfilling way to exist? Look at your nearest pet for tips on enjoying life's simple pleasures.

In our personal Cycle 5, we are urged to become artists and co-creators once more (consciously, for we always are, even during the darker days) of our life experience.

And to remember that ultimately ... no matter what ... and no matter where:

Happiness is a choice.

CYCLE 5 ACTION PLAN:
* Take charge and create something.
* Remember your childlike innocence.
* Make everything an act of love and joy.
* Leave your unhealthy ego at the door.
* Have the nerve to just go for it.
* Show us what you can do.

In a shining year:
You blaze like the Sun. Dazzling wherever you go, you can't help but be noticed (or maybe you're doing it on purpose, you show off!) A trail of compliments and accomplishments follow in your wake. Somehow, you make everyone feel as though they are the most important person in the world, and in return they make you feel special too. You attract others like a moth to a flame, like planets around your strong gravitational pull. Good feelings abound. Life is a mutual fan club. You love it; it loves you. You seem to wind up attending amazing parties, meeting fun people and laughing more than you ever have done.

You take a risk and the girl/guy says yes and the next moment you're out on a date with the stunning beauty you never thought you'd be sitting across from in a million years. Sexual energy bubbles beneath your skin, and you've many options on whom to share it with. Your artwork takes off with flying colors, and your creative work is attracting all the right kind of attention. You're just *on*. You look hot. Even *you* think so. The mirror and camera love you. You find a new hobby or pastime that you wonder how you lived without – it's wild, fun, and you can lose yourself in it, and you don't give a fig how good you are at it; it gives you a thrill, a rush, a lasting buzz. My God, can life get any better?

In a whining year:
The clouds come in, the light bulb pops, and you're plunged into darkness. Whether it's a total eclipse of the heart or something equally as devastating, you seem to be at the butt of unpleasant vibes, which pull on you and make you feel less than the shining star you know you ought to be. The crowd boos, or walks out halfway. You give your best, and no one seems to care about it,

or merely just don't say "Thank You". Your performance anxiety reaches new levels, and in return others are nervous around you. In bed and out of bed, it seems like extra hard work, which it never used to be. Your pride is wounded and you simply can't understand why this is happening (the idea of being humbled probably hasn't even entered your mind yet…) Oh rejection. So cold. So callous. So cruel. How could this happen? And why you?

Creativity comes in fits and starts, that's if you're not suffering from some form of block, where you feel dried up and out of ideas or drive. You need plugging back into something but you don't know what (try your Sun sign and solar house to amp up your energy and vitality levels). Externally, you're reminded just how great you're *not*, and there's always another show-off proving they can do it better, or who are ready to trample on you in the bid for fame or glory. The creations you make seem to lack something – a spark, perhaps? Talent? Maybe you did a bad job at painting your bedroom and couldn't be bothered to change it. Maybe your art gets rejected. Maybe your writing is a complete waste of time (in your own less-than-humble opinion). Talk about a king or queen ousted off the throne. It's truly time to take out the violin … but even the players on the Titanic had a more interested audience than you do. Oh dear.

Cycle Lesson

Feeling depleted, down or dark is a sign you've turned away from your inner light. The act of creating reconnects us to this divine spark within. Creating something reminds us of our true birthright – as cosmic creators, gods experiencing temporary amnesia on the physical plane. Powerful manifestors. By shining a light on things that bring us joy, we continue to raise our own inner light and tap into that special muse, the thing that energizes us and gives us inspiration to continue creating – making babies, or artwork. Delivering something new into the world. Without this, we become starving artists devouring other peoples' concepts, creations and ideas, and we become lethargic and ornery.

We never fully grow up, nor should we. Tapping into that playful side reminds us of the cosmic joke that all is playful, life was meant to be played as a game, and we are always in control of our creative self-expression and how we feel, painting our world in dull or bright shades with the brush strokes of our own choosing.

Celebrity Spotlight

- ⊚ US President Bill Clinton (Leo the Lion – a Cycle 5 symbol) creates *Parents Day* in 1994, celebrated on the fourth Sunday of July, during the sign of Leo and Cycle 5.
- ⊚ '*True Love Forever*' day is celebrated every year on August 16, during this Cycle.

Tips to Successfully Navigating your Cycle 5 Creation

- Go dancing.
- Tell someone you absolutely adore them.
- Be seen and be heard.
- Show off!
- Take an acting class.
- Get colorful – in behavior and wardrobe.
- Sing, write, act.
- Be bold.
- Shine with all your might.
- Give yourself a beauty treatment; whatever makes you feel self-pampered.
- Take up painting or just throw a new color on your bedroom walls.
- Go on a date or take yourself on one.
- Visit the cinema or a theater show.
- Attend a film audition.
- Love whatever you're doing, wherever you are and whomever you find yourself with.
- Google your own name.
- Be vain and proud!
- Take new pictures of yourself.
- Be in love with everyone for an entire day.
- Flirt, flirt, flirt! Anytime, with anyone!
- Dish out compliments, spread joy.
- Tell others how amazing/cool/hot/nice/helpful/funny/sexy/kind/awesome they are.
- Make someone smile.
- Put someone on a pedestal.
- Enjoy being hoisted up yourself.
- Act like cameras are following you everywhere.
- Expect the best!
- * Go Five Star *
- Perform!
- Go get a fantastic haircut or new style.
- Dress to impress.
- Throw or attend a party.
- Work with kids.

～ Surf Cycle 6 ～

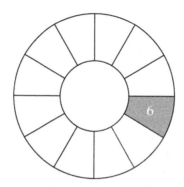

Time to Slim, Trim,
Simplify, Shape-up,
and Self-Improve

Helpful Happenings with:

Cleaners

Yoga instructors/fitness experts/
gym staff

Chiropractors/nutrition consultants

Your pet

Your aunt/uncle

Your stylist/spa staff

Assistants/secretaries

Your doctor or nurse

'The Help' (lucky you!)

Your coworkers

Writers/editors

Virgo people

Your employees/social workers/
co-workers

Perfectionists

Colonic specialists/diet and
detox gurus

Self-improvement promoters

Healers/helpers

Someone who does you a favor

The health-obsessed

Your mother's neighbors

People who nitpick/
organization specialists

Time management experts

Workaholics/slaves to the daily
grind

Job-fair staff/ non profit workers

Employment agents/the unemployed

What you'll need:

A scrubbing brush
Plenty of clean clothes
A daily planner
A big slice of humble pie (with no ice cream)
A membership to your local spa/gym/health center

The party may or may not be over, but someone has to start cleaning up the mess and guess what – yes, that person would be You. (Or in great years, you are suddenly surrounded by helpers who give you a handle tackling the job. Even better!)

Cleaning up is the theme of Cycle 6 – our acts, our apartments, our closets and our bodies. You name it – if an ounce of dirt has seeped into it and it's beginning to fester, or show signs of wear-and-tear, then this Cycle is about rooting it out and improving it with bleach/medicine/exercise/medicine/air/attention/focus. Suddenly everything that's 'wrong' or needs fixing in our minds, bodies, houses, jobs, schedules and daily routines, pops up like clockwork – and often seemingly at the most inopportune moments (although you may hate hearing this, but it's astrologically perfect timing).

Perfectionists love this Cycle since they have so much they can get on doing and improving, while those who prefer to leave well enough alone and laze on the couch can become fed up pretty damn quickly with the onslaught of issues that seem to demand attention this month.

It's time to banish bad habits from your life. And how do you do that exactly?

By replacing them with beneficial ones. Often when we 'quit', we stop something, but there remains a void. Diets are a prime example. We starve; then gorge. Switching one thing (unhealthy) for something else (more productive) we can finally overcome. Leave a gap and you risk trading off one life-force leech for another.

Are you ready to make life a little better for yourself and perhaps those around you in the process? Procrastination gets you nowhere now, so let's jump right in!

WHISTLING WHILE YOU WORK?

The universe (courtesy of your boss, your parent, an inner feeling of 'It's time!' or something else we can't really avoid or ignore) issues us a new assignment this Cycle – a new job lead, a new chore, a new plan and a new improvement program in a certain area of our lives, perhaps in multiple aspects.

For you, this year could be a sudden change at work or on the job, from moving offices, to new equipment, to having to deal with new staff members because your old coworkers, the ones you'd gotten used to, have suddenly quit, been fired, changed departments or simply moved away – like my friend who was offered the position of boss during his Cycle 6 because his current one was heading off to new horizons.

Bam! More work, more money, a different schedule.

Maybe out of the blue you can't work, due to a family or health issue (health we'll get to, so stay tuned). Suddenly there's fresh energy at work, for better or worse. A management shift could have a ripple effect and your job duties are changing along with it. Your boss needs to call a meeting to announce a new regime/protocol/company policy/scheduling structure.

If you're self-employed, the way you go about your daily work is up for review. Are you getting enough done, or wasting your time? Could you do things better or find new tools that will help you cut corners or perfect what you've already started? Maybe it's just time to clean up your home office space and wipe off your computer keyboard from a year of sticky fingers and muffin crumbs.

Cycle 6 says, *what we're doing on a day-to-day basis is set for re-evaluation* – and we get to ask ourselves "Is this useful?" "Can I do better?" and "Am I doing the best job I can do for myself and others?" Maybe your workload will increase; maybe you'll be putting your feet up for weeks without doing anything. In short, are you happy or at least content to bow your head, bend your knees and offer up your unique brand of service to a world or society in need of what it is that you do? You may have to scrub the floor a few times but when it shines you'll feel glad you did it, even if your arms are aching afterward.

When we're not doing what we're good at and what we enjoy, we start to bung up our systems and things start decaying. What you do and how well you do it are two key ingredients in the mix in this special brew you're concocting during your annual journey. This is the time in your year when you may want to jump ship and move to a new job, or to give the current one more of your time, energy, focus, discipline and commitment.

If you're not being of use in your own life or in the lives of those around you, then it's high time for a change. You may find that coworkers remind you of this and begin to show signs of strain or they come to you and ask for help. You can count on it. Or others will need your advice or support also; Cycle 6 is a time for being there for others with little or nothing in return.

And yes, you may even get to learn about all of this by suddenly becoming needy yourself through no choice of your own (such as a friend having to stop by with a care package because you're stuck in bed sick or a clinic/doctor/nurse/hospital helping you out because you've done yourself some damage).

CLEAN UP in AISLE 'U'

This is *the* month of your annual journey to get things cleaned up. You know you have to get things organized, ship-shape, and running smoother. Look around at the mess that's built up in certain corners of your life, and there's no way you can disagree that a clear out would be good.

We're talking about an interior clean – old thoughts, feelings, ideas (a physical or emotional colonic/enema would be a great idea) and an exterior clean – dusting, sweeping, wiping, sorting, clearing, filing, tossing and arranging.

I had an internal exam during Cycle 6, and ended up on antibiotics for three weeks, but was glad I had the check-up as I would have had no clue there was anything working at less-than-optimum capacity within me. Somewhere I was out of synch with myself and like clockwork Cycle 6 revealed this to me. And most importantly it gave me a chance to improve my physical condition. I'd recommend the same for you, no matter how you feel or how healthy you appear to be.

Get yourself checked out to stay on top of yourself. No one likes a doctor visit (or dentist) but you'll save yourself a lot of stress in the long run (and potential bills) if you do that now.

Life is upkeep. There are heaps of things that need continual fixing, repairing, replacing, adjusting – from your body to your mildewy shower curtain. This is your Cycle to kick-start that process, one thing at a time. Everyone should have at least one 'To do' list stuck up somewhere this Cycle with a string of things that need tackling, repairing or tossing out – like my friend who was systematically going through every drawer, box, cupboard and corner of his apartment clearing things out during his 6-Cycle. Furniture ended up on the street, closets emptied, all in one fell swoop. The results: his place felt and looked three times larger, and he had room to breathe. And in turn, his job and health showed signs of immediate improvement. One thing affects another in Cycle 6 – it's the domino effect in action. Ask a feng-shui expert (the art of arranging space). Space free of clutter, releases energy and everything begins to work better.

Life is **upgrade and upkeep**. From websites that house more information, to computer viruses, checkers and program patches. From telephone contracts and vehicle insurance to physical space to house growing families.

Upgrading involves bettering something, to take into account its new needs. Where can you upgrade now and are you willing to invest the energy (emotional, physical, mental, financial) in attaining it?

Get things straightened out to see an improvement in all Cycles to come. That's the payoff (above and beyond the gambling payoffs you tried in Cycle 5). The short-term irritations are worth the long-term result and rewards.

FENG-SHUI THE EASY WAY

It's amazing what a clear space can do for you, this Cycle. If you don't have one, I'd recommend doing that as soon as you can. Start with one area; one room. Make your bed each morning, perhaps. Clear up your desk and buy a trash can if you don't own one. Bag up your rubbish. Dust. Wipe down your computer keyboard and monitor. Clean fingerprints off your doors. Sweep. Wash the floor. Tidy up the pens or get new ones that actually work. Hang up your clothes, fold laundry instead of shoving it drawers or throwing it on the ground in a heap. Donate clothes you no longer wear or wish to wear. Chalk up a check-list each evening on what to tackle tomorrow and review what you achieved today, however small.

You'll feel so much better and can think straighter if you have a clear deck. So force yourself if you must, but try to have at least *one* area carved out in your life where things always have a place and you can sit and breathe without worrying about inhaling dust or sitting/stepping on something.

Following a schedule is perhaps the only way to truly navigate Cycle 6 and get the things done you need to without forgetting or having to go back over things a second time.

Remember the 6-Cycle motto: clean, safe, simple, effective and efficient.

YOUR TO-DO LIST

Here's a quick check-list of useful things to do in your own 6-Cycle (you'll come to like them in Cycle 6!):

Get healthy – Ten sit-ups is better than sitting doing nothing! If you're bed-bound, at least try gentle stretching; rotate your neck, wrists and ankles. Try the book 6-Minute Morning: Stretching by Faye Rowe. Simple. Gentle. Effective. Breathe deeply. Schedule check-ups. Try vitamins or find out what a balanced diet looks like. Check your body type. *Geri Body Yoga* (from Ginger Spice of the Spice Girls) is a great starting point for those wishing to try yoga, another activity that brings enormous benefit during this Cycle.

Get regular – from bathroom habits to sleep patterns. Becoming slightly more robotic/systematic will actually do you a lot of good. Look at the food you eat – can you lay off the sugar and caffeine for a bit? Eat more salads and fruit? Try home cooking so you know what goes into your food (grab a recipe book or have a quick look online, you'll be glad you did!) Any healthy shift in attitude and diet can only aid you this Cycle.

Get clean – have an extra shower or bath to cleanse your energy field. Soak longer. Scrub your tongue. Drink more water by always keeping a bottle handy. Make sure you're keeping up with regular hygiene habits. If not, implement new ones until they become automatic. Brush twice a day minimum. Floss. Wash your hands.

Get organized – craft a systematic approach to whatever it is you're trying to accomplish. Buy a storage container, bookshelf. File or throw away old or useless paperwork. Stick your bills on the fridge so you'll remember to pay them on time.

Get a diary – use your phone calendar to beep an hour before appointments. Have a morning and evening checklist of things to complete, and prepare your day the night before. How about a short meditation to begin each day on the right note? Clearing the deck before bed sets you up for success the next day.

Get tidy – a clean outside helps you keep a clean inside. Empty drawers, clear closets, unpack boxes, clear floor, shelf, table or desk space. Do the dishes in the evening. Throw away clutter!

Get a Plan – a simple routine or schedule made now can have a profound impact on your entire life and outlook. Try the same thing at the same time each day, for a week. Clearing a space for new stuff often opens the door for new things to arrive, like magic. Get a regime and stick to it for at least a month.

Get helping out – grant favors with no expectation of return. Accept favors. Giving and receiving helps both giver and receiver. Ask people "Can I help you with anything?" or "Is there anything you need?" And if you need help, ask others to help you out also. People love to be of service. It feels good and is as much a gift to them as it is to you.

Get focused on your job – want a new one, a side one or upgrade within your current one? Ask and go for it now. Talk to coworkers. See if you can expand in your current field or see if there are other jobs out there more to your liking. Get to know your coworkers. Seeking employment? This is your time. Scour ads, post classifieds, tell friends, browse online.

Keep busy – start a number of projects. Plant seeds. The best will sprout.

And above all while finding a way to do things better – **keep it simple**.

Re-read that:

Keep   It   Simple.

DAILY SCHEDULES

What do you do from the moment you wake up till the moment you lay back down again? If you sleep eight hours a night (lucky you) then that leaves just *sixteen hours a day* when you're awake and living. Weird when you think about it. Is it true that "there aren't enough hours in the day"? I guess it depends what you do with your time, and what you can leave for another day.

So sleeping eight hours leaves you sixteen hours to accomplish something; a piece of something larger. What do you do with your sixteen-hour shifts?

If you sleep less (most of us do), then you may have more hours, but it's cut into by the time you spend at work. What then? What do you do with your 'free time'? Can you spend some moments on the job, doing something purely for yourself? Meditate, relax, or visualize how amazing it feels to have your Dream Vision (from Cycle 11) coming to fruition.

How's your sleep pattern? Are you bored? Do you move like a robot from the bed to the shower to the car to the job? Or do you find yourself flailing around forgetting to brush your teeth, stumbling over last week's laundry and forgetting to eat? Simply put – is your schedule helping you and healing you –

or hindering you? Is it efficient? Do you get a lot done (and rest just as much) or are you overloaded or just picking at work and pretending?

Daily Schedules seem to come first in the order of clean-ups. Sometimes coworkers can't show up so you get the inevitable phone call asking you to climb out of bed earlier. Or you wind up with a second or new job that demands you become a tad more disciplined. Or you lose your job and need to scour the classifieds in your pajamas. Maybe you land a role on TV and need to shape up. Maybe your back starts acting up and you need to go in for chiropractic treatments twice a week. Maybe the doctor says rest for two weeks, maybe longer.

Whatever the case, your day-to-day life and the running of it is sure to change or become a major focus of your attention. You can no longer drift through your day on autopilot, under Cycle 6. If you do, that's when the 'problems' start surfacing in order to get you to have a change of mind on how you're running your own show.

Schedules are habits by any other name, really, so if you don't see yourself as the 'schedule' sort (you will, be the end of this Cycle) then see them as daily habits.

You'll be aided in all of this by at least one Virgo person who arrives to either help you out and show the beauty of having someone grant you favors, or they'll give you tips, clues and ideas on what is and is not healthy, based on how well they themselves seem to be doing in all these areas.

Prepare to implement a few new good habits, to replace those old outworn and unhelpful things you're doing on a daily basis that quite simply lead you nowhere useful.

HOW HEALTHY?

Yes, I don't blame you for glancing over this section and wanting to skip by; chances are you're already cringing because you fear the answer? No matter where you're at in your own health plan (or lack thereof) you could do with picking up some dandelion tea this Cycle; it's a great de-toxifier. And some fruit juice, or fruit itself. This is a good cycle to cut out any excess sugar, caffeine or junk foods to give your body a break from processing so much processed food.

Cycle 6 says: where possible, 'go natural'.

You don't need to spend your entire bank vault savings on organic food, nitpicking over labels (though you'd do well to at least check what you're consuming and the quantity of artificial stuff you're ingesting). You want to stay as clear as you can this Cycle, not least to purify yourself from past months fun and frolics – Cycle 5s were synonymous with the pleasure principle, need we say more? Giving your body a chance to catch up is also a great way to clear your mind. And after what you were up to last month you may want to think about it, just to get back on track.

The key to this whole Cycle is: ***Mind and body holistically working together as one***. Your mind regulates your body's health. Clear head; healthy body. And a calm, relaxed and well-maintained body creates a sense of peaceful well-being within the mind. It works both ways. Dwelling on worry and anxiety reinforces mental issues that manifest as physical and behavioral problems. It's not mathematics, it's not science, its just common sense. We're an energetic system, an amazing biological machine, a complete whole and anything that is felt anywhere in the body is reflected elsewhere holographically. (Our hands and feet are maps of our entire system, as we've discovered in the area of reflexology. Blockages in the body show up in specific areas in the hands and feet).

Key Note: Acupuncture, reflexology treatments, massage and other natural healing methods and remedies are worth investigating, such as: color therapy, chiropractic treatments, chakra meditations, yogic breathing techniques, natural detoxes and colonics.

Poor nutrition shows up now as sluggishness, and it's worth taking a look at that salt, sugar, caffeine intake or to work out if you may have an allergy. Try a chiropractor, go to a herbalist, visit your clinic, see a doctor, have a simple check up. And follow your intuition if something doesn't feel right to you. Your body is talking to you always. Listen to it.

And ... drink pure water. Lots of water. That, if nothing else, can kick-start your cleansing.

And it can't hurt.

WHY HEALTH PROBLEMS?

Stress. Imbalance. A wake up call from your body telling you that you're off track with yourself. When you're not working, or doing something you feel is useful, when you're not happy with the work you are doing, and when you're over-analyzing and letting the multiple anxieties of modern day living get to you, it seems to show up in specific areas of the body that correlate to specific areas of your life. Everything is energy and each part of your body has a job to do. One area of imbalance ultimately affects everything else.

A body, soccer team, corporate company and just about anything else is only as strong as its weakest link.

Patching up those soft spots makes the whole thing stronger and you want things to ultimately run better in 6-Cycles. That's what makes the nitpicking such a positive attribute, as long as it doesn't go too far and you wind up creating the opposite result. You can find a list of possible signs and symptoms of imbalance affecting you personally in your own Cycle 6 by visiting **www. SurfingYourSolarCycles.com**. Find the faults. Then get to work on improving them. Don't expect perfection. Leave that for the saints. Going looking for problems is a surefire way to create them (and thus find them).

Relax…

PLANETARY SIGNATURE: MERCURY

We used the energy of Mercury during Cycle 3 when it was airy – related to the area of communication. Now we use Mercury in its earthy form, to put our knowledge to practical use and to sort through what we have amassed so that it can be put to work for us. Is it useful, necessary, helpful? Facts are all that matter now, the rest can be left to the side. We squeeze the juice for the relevant details, getting to the core of the issue. That's how we diagnose, and that is how we heal. Then Mercury energy can flow once more, operating at its maximum potential. All it takes is the asking of the right question, and providing the correct solution.

WRITE YOUR WRONGS

People make lists and follow calendars during Cycle 6. Have you had to do that yet? Putting pen to paper is well starred for success in 6-Cycles – written work takes off, and editors will find this a productive time too. If you're in the service industry: waiters, hairstylists, designers, vets, counselors, customer service, anything where you're helping, aiding, and providing a service to someone or something, you're likely to find new work leads. Find new ways of doing things or revamping your current style of business and whatever it is you offer or perform: a new website, name, business cards, networking process, advertising procedure, welcoming sign, shop front, style of service or the actual services you offer. You name it, you'll find it a great time to adjust what you're doing or offering with a view to improving it all.

Gyms will fill up with new recruits passing through or those really looking to improve their biceps or metabolism (feeling the urge?), and likely you'll be one of the ones taking classes, getting an instructor, signing up for yoga, poking around pilates and so forth. Will we see you jogging past us tomorrow morning?

Plastic surgeons no doubt find more clients working their way to them during people's Cycle 6 – as will the teeth whiteners at the supermarket or the 'new' skin cream guaranteed to transform your face. Somehow, we simply can't resist making things 'better' during 6-Cycles.

Health problems can be tackled now too; taking care of something that's 'not quite right' or that long-awaited health check up. What's your doctor or dentist's name? Exactly. Maybe it's time…

Even the most scientific amongst us may turn to herbs or alternative healing methods when traditional means aren't enough. Cycle 6 will aid you along your path if you try new ways of healing old problems. Maybe it's not the symptom that is the problem, but the method of treatment?

Shape up, clean up, tighten up and smarten up.

Welcome to your Cycle of **SELF-IMPROVEMENT**.
Crack out the mop and bleach and start scrubbing.

CRITICAL EYE

You're so detailed in Cycle 6, or you're forced to be. The tiniest thing, you'll notice. The crooked picture on the wall, the small stain on someone's shirt (hopefully not your own, or you'll go nuts). The fact A isn't long enough, B isn't cool enough, C isn't fast enough. On and On. You become so exacting for a time, which is how it should be. How else can you make things better unless you can focus on the weak links in the chain – in your work projects, your living situation, your relationship, friendship and your career objectives? To do better, you have to be able to see where there is *room for improvement* and that means not shying away from the problems, issues, niggling doubts and annoying errors etc.

So ... be open to criticism, or you'll find Cycle 6 a tricky Cycle to navigate. There is *always* room for improvement no matter who you are or where you are.

Don't get *too* anal though – you could become a nit-picking perfectionist who controls everything and expects it all to run according to *your* plan. Plans do fall apart in Cycle 6 but that's to test you to see if they really are strong. And who has the right to say something is 'wrong' (sometimes the biggest 'mistakes' turned out to be major blessings in disguise). Even the best laid plans fall part. Don't stop trying, just stop trying to make things follow a set plan. Your plan. You have to allow room for things to work out better than even you could have dreamed. Imagine...

Oh, in case you forgot – is your To Do list up yet? On the fridge or wall or in your diary? If not then today, do that! Write a list of things you have to tackle, things that need fixing or repairing or throwing away. Things you could try and do better. A health program. A better schedule. Earlier mornings or sleeping in? Try a new pattern. At least for one day. A time frame and an alarm clock to keep you on track.

Without this, Cycle 6s are cranky, glitchy and irritating. So do yourself a favor and get that one knocked out early on. You'll be relieved as soon as you do. Guaranteed.

Cycle 6 is a great time to springboard yourself into a better-run life and a more appropriate lifestyle for what it is you want to accomplish. It's all perspective – *your choice of actions either supports the dreams you made up in Cycle 11, or they pull against it* and keep you chained to running in circles for another year.

Are your actions and your daily habits and choices supporting the dream you have and how you want to be?

If not, ditch them. Scrap anything in your day that gets in the way of furthering your dream and goal. Simple as that. At least try it for this Cycle. Some of you may have longer Cycle 6s but for most of us it's probably a minimum of a month (four weeks, if you break it down to more manageable chunks) to get this right (or at least better).

It's worth repeating that – **Manageable Chunks**. Break everything down into an easier unit. If you're dieting or working on a project, break it down into separate days – what will you do on Monday and Wednesday and what will you try and complete at the weekend? What will you do for five days a week? What about the other two? Break it down further perhaps (10-11am you can do push ups and 3-4pm is your free time etc). Whatever works for you (and you'll figure that out as you go).

You lose nothing by having a new go at old things. *The way to instill a new habit is to install one!* Doing it, repeatedly, reinforces the action and before long, you have yourself a new healthy habit. And all it took was the simple action of regularity.

Yes, bad habits are sure to pop up now. More than ever before. They'll become extreme. They'll fight you, and try and resist you changing them. They'll try to hang on. You may seem to be fighting a losing battle until you realize that fighting them is useless. You just have to try and make a conscious effort each day to keep a clear space and a clear mind and a clear piece of paper to make a list of what to try and manage and take care of. Try it. Starting simple is perhaps the only way *to* start.

So as long as you're doing this detailed work, breaking things down to smaller and more manageable chunks, your life becomes a method, a process, a building plan and you're no longer flailing around trying to fit all this stuff into a day or week and then getting stressed, burned out and running away from it all or complaining you're getting nowhere. Stick to the plan by at least designing it to have your needs met – some free time, some hard work time, some going without time and some indulging time.

How many of us really follow a great and easy plan like this? By all means skimp on fun for an hour if you must but balance it out with ultra-fun time ... *or* ... even better, make everything you do fun so that you'll enjoy doing it or at least enjoy yourself while doing something less than fun.

It's all in how you tackle the work, that determines the quality of the work you get done.

If you take two steps forward and three back for a while during this Cycle, don't beat yourself up about it. It's not about being perfect, it's about seeing what does and does not work for you. So annoyances are part of the path.

Welcome them, or at the very least, laugh them off.

And keep that clear space – every morning, or evening to try and clear up stuff. Take a look around you; how messy is your current situation and could a clear-up give you the peaceful space and feeling to clean up other areas of your life? Try it and see. At least then you can put this over-abundance of 'improvement energy' to work on something useful and worthwhile instead of fretting about what you're not getting done and what isn't working!

Nitpicking details are useful when it comes to noting the hours of the day you're taking your medicine, the meetings you have to attend and the days and deadlines and bills that need to be paid to avoid late arrivals and late fees. But keeping track of all of this comes down to your detail-attention abilities, which you'll hone now in Cycle 6.

FIX-IT

Try not to lose your mind when you find yourself faced with a multitude of annoying difficulties and challenges that crop up during some challenging and tiring 6-Cycle years. Take for instance the one Cycle 6 that I experienced during a sweltering heat wave in Los Angeles, California. After waiting a week for an air conditioner I ordered online, it arrived and didn't work properly. After gallivanting to a local store on foot and bus, I found another to the same specifications. It didn't fit. I had to take it back. All of this taking place in unbearably hot weather.

For some reason, 6-Cycles can seem as though life itself or someone 'up there' has decided to give you a hard time. But it's not that. Really, it's just about finding ways of doing things better, having things better; and the surest method is to have the things that aren't working for you blow themselves up to bigger proportions to get your attention. How many times have you been living a certain way, putting up with a certain thing or person, because it was familiar, routine and habit? And then, when it suddenly got painfully obvious or annoying, you saw it wasn't working and you really had to fix it.

Yes, 6-Cycles are about wising up. You may be faced with a continual barrage of things that fall apart, need fixing, improving, adjusting, re-doing, re-aligning, altering and so forth, but just think – when it finally gets done (which it will) things will be so much better than before.

Embrace everything hitting the fan (that's if your fan actually works to begin with) so that you know what to clean up. And when it's all done your life will sparkle with a new brilliance and you'll be well placed to attract even more good stuff.

And finally, next Cycle is all about having fun with others, so if you've been so work and detail-oriented just think that the pay off may be to hang around with someone stunning, sexy, peaceful, cool, fun and as awesome as you are. Now that is a pay off well worth working towards.

Get it ironed out now, so you can chill out after.

How did my air conditioning story end? I found other places outside the home to work – a friend's spa, with an amazing air conditioner; in coffee shops, which got me out and made me feel less isolated while keeping me cool (and I took more yoga classes which added to my Cycle 6 health benefits). And after continuing the search I found the perfect machine at the last place I looked. And it had a fancy remote control with it, compared to the piece of scrap metal I originally bought.

And now I get to enjoy cool air and things at home work better. Don't give in, when faced with problems at this time. Cycle 6 tests your ability to commit to tackling them with stamina, endurance, commitment and a sense of humor. And when things don't go 'according to plan' (your plan), find something else to do or make it work in your favor. Everything now can be turned around to benefit you. And maybe that's the point of your problems? To show you there's actually a better way for you than the one you seem intent upon. It's worth a thought.

SHARPEN YOUR SKILLS

So, you can play the piano. How well? You're a writer ... but how rich is your vocabulary? You can seal the deal, but can you improve your telephone manner? Are you giving a presentation? How interesting and accurate are the slides/percentages?

Everything can be done better. So leaving room to be *a little bit better than you are* in some area, is a great way to use Cycle 6.

If you need more skills, become an apprentice. Find someone in your area (check online, in the telephone book, post an ad or ask around) who does the same thing and who preferably does it better? Humble yourself. Ask for help! It's amazing what you can receive during Cycle 6 if you'd just ask for it.

Learn a new twist on an old talent. Can you play chess? Solve a Rubik's cube? Whatever you're good at (or even 'just okay' at) can be taken to a new level if you're willing to humble yourself and be open to the fact you *don't* know it all and you *can* improve. It'll only make the rest of your year that much greater if you take those extra steps during Cycle 6, to add new skills to the mix you already have. Allow yourself to slip down the ladder and take up a position lower down (or in the back room) to learn how to sharpen your skills, polish your performance and otherwise improve your insight and better your position so that later on in Cycle 10 everyone will get to see just what you're made of.

You have plenty of time. Cycle 6 affords you the time to slow down to get the pieces in place.

!HELP!

Applying for help may be one way that you experience some Cycle 6 years – you can't do certain things for yourself so you need to ask another (financial help due to unemployment or sickness, or as simple as asking for a ride to the airport, or for someone to cover you at work). You may be the one providing the favor in other years (picking up their groceries or prescription or helping pack up the moving truck). Whichever way the Cycle is experienced, lessons are learned and things are improved upon. Help is given, offered, shared and accepted. That's all that matters and it doesn't matter how. Everyone has their part to play.

Help could equally refer to 'the help' as it's so (affectionately?) called. Those people who clean your carpets, or come in and clean up your filth. Or polish your nails, or fix your fridge, cut your hair or clean out your colon. All those jobs you either don't want to do, would rather not get messy doing, or just can't do as well. Ah, aren't you glad there are trash collectors out there, and doctors, and those who don't mind unclogging your toilet, and peering into your mouth? Again, everyone has their part. No one is better or worse, but you may find yourself on the more humble side this Cycle (or being 'humiliated' to help you learn the lesson just as well).

SERVICE

What kind? To service something means to fix it, give it a check-up, overhaul or work on it. All key themes for Cycle 6. Service also refers to the things you offer other people. The quality of the work you give (customer service) and the type of service you offer or could offer, or the support/help/aid/favor you could be in a position to grant someone should you choose to do so. And let's face it, we all have something someone else could use or do with hearing/knowing/learning/having.

So let me remind you now in your Cycle 6 – you have something, be it a skill, personality trait, ability, object or connection, that someone else (or a whole bunch of someones) could really do with at this moment. Be prepared and be willing where possible to offer, share and deliver yourself with no holds barred. Offer what you have and others will be in a stronger position to offer what they have too. Win-win.

GET IT SORTED

Cycle 6 is another of those nuts-and-bolts earth Cycles (along with Cycles 2 and 10) where you have to get practical and physical ... about what? Not money (that's 2) and not your direction and public path (that's 10) but on improving your situation by gaining the tools you need to do a better job and make things easier for yourself and others. Depending on which sign the Sun is traveling through as you read this chapter, you'll find yourself coming into contact with or seeking certain tools you're in need of, and the reason you need them.

Earth signs during Cycle 6 bring more practical tools and methods. You need things that are essential, durable and of good quality, and also that perhaps make life more comfortable. Fire signs are more likely to seek tools and procedures that get things done, that help them speed up their lives or promote themselves or make things more fun, creative and dynamic. Air signs may invest in learning, communication tools, or sharpen their ways and means to connect to others with gadgets and gizmos. And Water Signs may find tools and processes that afford them more privacy, peace of mind, psychic and spiritual space and emotional comfort.

Look now to buy, borrow, barter or be given things that will aid in improving your life and making things better for yourself. Or so you're in a better position to better someone else's position in life. Each of these Cycles is about you, but also about your contribution. By improving your life, you aid in the improvement of others' lives, and the general happy vibe on the planet.

Look for a shift in tools, an improvement in circumstances. Maybe your company upgrades the computer systems. Maybe you get a new computer monitor and it's as simple as that. Maybe your new vacuum cleaner saves you from having to clean every other day. A new water filtration system saves you time and money after previously lugging bottles of water home from the store.

It can be really basic but it's all about improving your life flow, by cutting some corners, or getting a bit more practical and simplistic so that you get the job done with fewer bells and whistles.

PETS ARE GOOD FOR YOUR HEALTH

If you have a pet, you may find you need to take it to the vet for a check-up, or have to stock up on new food, a different kind of food, or you meet people who tell you about a new dog park, or your cat gets an attitude. Whatever pet you give home to (you could even end up volunteering at an animal clinic or hospital) you'll find you have to play caretaker in some form (which leads to our next section about human care).

Maybe you'll actually get a pet during this Cycle, or your furry family gets larger – it's a good time for it. Or you wind up pet-sitting for a friend (like the Cycle 6 I ended up surrounded by two cats, a kitten and a fish). Traditional astrologers called Cycle 6 the time of 'unequal relationships' which basically means the animal is at the mercy of you, as you're the hand that feeds it. Looking after something or someone less fortunate is a great way to spend your time. You may even find you earn money by moving into a job where you have to care. Volunteer services are often discovered in Cycle 12 rather than Cycle 6 but at least you'll find out now who or what needs that care.

And coming back to the whole 'unequal relationship' theme, animals actually give a lot back to you in case you didn't see this already; they soothe you when you're down. Cats' purrs have been proven to heal not only themselves but the humans in their presence; stroking an animal lowers our blood pressure and provides companionship, and a big welcome home when you walk through the door after a long day out there in the hectic world. A dog gets you out and gets you more social, when you walk them round the neighborhood. And if you're single, who knows who you could meet when you're out walking your furry friend!

BEING CAREFUL AND FULL OF CARE

Being sensible is just part of the Cycle you're in. Maybe you have to say to someone "sorry I can't come and play, I have chores to do". Maybe you have been overdoing the sweets and cake recently. How you care becomes a top priority, starting with yourself and working on outwards towards others. Doing favors now or receiving them usually comes from a need, or the fact that something isn't running according to full speed or capacity. A friend helps you out because you're sick in bed. Someone gives you a ride because you have a flat tire or you can't carry the bags. And so forth.

Mainly you get to be helped or help out. Simple.

Being helped also provides a service to others. The care involved spreads good vibes just when they are needed the most. Other people get to feel good about being there for you. You get to feel good from easing someone's stresses, strains or pains. It works both ways, so don't be afraid to reach out when you need a little hoist up life's ladder or a pick-me-up. Helping another is often what someone needs to take them out of the doldrums and complaining of their own life situation. Have you asked anyone if they need anything lately? Have you checked in to see how someone is doing or if they are improving? Make someone's day.

On the subject of care, don't forget about self-care, doing whatever you need to do to look after yourself. Cycle 4 was more about self-mothering emotional care, licking your wounds and if need be by putting band-aids on them; Cycle 6 is more about practical care: A better toothbrush, a homeopathic fragrance at home to relax your mind, better toothpaste (or dental check up), a faster computer, a new storage shelf, an In-tray for your bills, a calendar or schedule planner. Stuff that is useful, necessary, pro-active, helpful and beneficial to your body, mind and spirit, as a whole. That's the sort of care to go for.

CYCLE 6 ACTION PLAN
* Clean up your surroundings, your body and your health.
* Ask others if they need help with anything.
* Learn a new skill or a way to do things faster/easier/better.

* Decide if it's time for more suitable employment.
* Get to know your coworkers, spend more time with pets.
* Go for a checkup – dentist, doctor, mechanic.
* Keep it simple.

In working years:

Good job! You do it, and do it well. There may not be a fanfare and drum-roll but you feel good because you did good ... and that's more than good enough. You see a smile on people's faces when you surprise them with a helping hand, or a care basket, just when they needed it the most but didn't dare ask. Your work improves; your health picture is pretty impressive, even if you had that 'problem'. Look at you go! You can touch your toes, your metabolism is running high and happy, and everything somehow just fits right into place. It's amazing how it feels being comfy in your body and at peace with the world. A pat on the back is due you for being on the ball, on how you saved the day by spotting the mistake and fixing it before it got worse. From the computer crash you saved a friend from having (that pesky virus) to the remedy you passed on to another friend that meant they were well enough to take that vacation they'd be banking on for months. You seem to be the one who saves the day, more than a few times. You finally have the chance for that clearout yourself – from the junk at home, the old clothes, to a thorough scrubdown at home, office, under the bed, in the garage. Your kitchen has never looked cleaner. Your bedroom now has boxes to store your stuff and you can actually find things (once you get used to where their new places are).

And to top it all off, your plants are thriving and you can't resist the pooch or puss you see giving you the sad eyes at the local street fair. You drop money in their box to support this great cause, or give in and take a furry friend home with you, to love and cherish for all their days (and get bushels of love in exchange). Things may not be perfect, you've certainly seen *that* this cycle, but you know that you can handle it. You can overcome. You can get by. You can make it, if you just keep plugging away, one foot in front of the other, one problem at a time. As you continue to work hard at smoothing the rough edges and taking care of what you have to take care of, life offers you incentives to keep going.

And chamomile tea has never been so useful.

In shirking years:

You know you need to visit the gym but you have fifty other things that needed to be done yesterday. Of course you'd rather sleep in and not bother. Laundry piles up, you have overtime (when you didn't even want it, but someone else got sick and you have to cover). Bills need to be paid and you'll no doubt miss the party because you're overworked and rundown. On your way to work the car starts acting up and it'll take days to repair. On top of that, the computer shuts down in the middle of working and you forgot to save the document you were working on. And that ache – where did that come from? You have no choice – it's a trip to the dentist or doctor to find out. You just don't have time for all of this! Just when you need all your time (and hands) to get one job done, another presents itself as more urgent.

Your extra critical eye is causing you heaps of trouble. Don't people realize you have the best intentions? If they would they'd not give you such a hard time after all you've done (don't they see all the hard work you do, how you try to fix everyone's problems, how you try to be so polite, so 'proper'). But wait … did these people actually ask you for help or do you continually jump to rescue people, thinking you know how to do it better? Maybe you do, but you only end up creating your own problems. Some could call you neurotic. Others would say you're never happy, it's never good enough, you're never satisfied and your standards are set way too high.

You do need to focus on one thing – yourself, and your own mess. You need a maid (to keep your place from being condemned), a trainer (to keep you from seizing up), a nutritionist (to keep you from settling for pizza), a yoga instructor (to keep you limber enough to keep going), a personal chef (so you can actually relax when you get home), a therapist (since you're fixing everyone else's problems, who else has time for your own?), an accountant (because it's take a professional to balance the books with all the current demands on you), a secretary (to take calls and messages when you simply don't have the energy to deal with them) and a better bed/neighbors (because you're going to need a good night's rest).

Stop. Breathe. No 'buts'. The issue isn't that you *have* to fix everything at once. The problems are showing the weaknesses, and with a little continuous effort (bit by bit, day by day, moment by moment) you can get through this. It won't last, it never does. Yes it does seem to all come at you at once, but that's the whole joke. It's only as serious as you make it out to be. Do what you can, and then leave the rest till another time.

And become acquainted with chamomile tea and Epsom salts, to soothe those frazzled nerves and soak those achey bones. Just because you're going through it, doesn't mean you can't pamper yourself a little. You'll get better, and be back on track again. You really will. Feel it. See it. Sense it. Enjoy it. Picture what you'll do and how you'll look and feel when that time comes (which it will). Nice huh? You'll appreciate things *so* much more by then. Just get through today. And you'll get there soon.

Cycle Lesson

Without regularity life quickly becomes chaotic, things break down and our bodies reflect that lack of wholeness within ourselves. You probably don't need half the stuff you have, half the habits you've picked up and half the daily activities you're currently participating in. Streamlining and simplifying gives us the clear space (mentally, physically, emotionally) to realign with our basic principles and needs. We get to work on the nuts and bolts of our daily lives, strengthening the things that work by safeguarding them to continue working for us, and we get to improve our service to all areas of our life and others we come into contact with. Things that no longer work remind us where our attention is needed, so instead of complaining about 'bad fortune', see it as a blessing because it actually is. Work on the weak parts and you can only get stronger, be stronger and experience more strength across the board. Health (emotional, physical, mental and spiritual) is the key.

Celebrity Spotlight

- *National Pet Memorial Day* on September 14 falls in Cycle 6.
- *Take Your Dog to Work day* is celebrated in the UK also in September.
- The US celebrates *National Healthy Aging Month* in September/Cycle 6.

Tips to successfully navigating your Cycle 6 Reparation

- Clean up your junk.
- Scrub the bath or shower.
- Empty drawers.
- Start a new or better gym (or fitness plan).
- Analyze your daily life – is it healthy and is it efficient?
- Streamline and simplify.
- Be of use – help someone out.
- Serve – give someone a neck rub, carry someone's load.
- Edit – from written work to what we say – is it useful, is it true and is it kind?
- Find a new job or work lead.
- Give coworkers a hug or confront them about how to pull their weight (or both!)
- Stop binging.
- Quit smoking or other habits you've picked up.
- Do sixty push ups a day (or ten to start)
- Drink more water.
- Set a great example.

⊙ Give someone some extra care and attention.
⊙ Go without, for a while.
⊙ Start a detox program; fast for one day.
⊙ Clear your mind more.
⊙ Have a checkup.
⊙ Give your time/energy/money to someone who needs it.
⊙ Get some bodywork done.
⊙ Dust!
⊙ Check out feng-shui.
⊙ Clear a space in your life and home for contemplation and nothing else.
⊙ Be minimalist.
⊙ Clear the decks.
⊙ Look after someone's pet.
⊙ Give your own pet a checkup/ extra squeezes/treats.
⊙ Aim to do better, be better.
⊙ Find natural ways to heal your ailment.
⊙ Simplify, streamline, downsize.

Surf Cycle 7

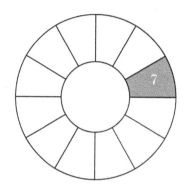

Time to Connect,
Compromise and Cooperate and
Find Beauty in Balance

Reflective Reminders from:

Your boyfriend/girlfriend/husband or wife
Your 'lover'/your ex(es)
Your sidekick/ally/partner or 'enemy'
Your best friend
Models/the beautiful people
Expensive department store staff
Your 'bit on the side'/your 'significant other'
Your fiancé(e)/your blind date
Business partners/clients
Wedding planners/romantics
Beauty industry specialists
Lawyers/judges/legal eagles/justice seekers
Snake (or people) charmers
Therapists/mediators
People who look like you
People who are the total opposite of you
Relationship experts/dating agencies
Your niece/nephew
Your grandma/grandad
Flower sellers
Feng-shui experts/window dressers
Etiquette educators/fashion experts
The indecisive
Libra people
Dancers, designers and decorators
Architects, sculptors
Painters, musicians

What you'll need:

A spirit level for balance
A firm, friendly handshake
Your winning smile
Etiquette lessons
A copy of your legal rights

You're not alone. You're never alone. At this time of your annual Cycle, your attention turns (or life turns your attention *for* you) to other people, to your relationships (or lack thereof), and your overall connection to other folk. Maybe you begin thinking back to a past love. Maybe a new one arrives. Maybe your current lover has something important to share with you. Maybe you want more from them or they from you? Maybe you shake hands on a new deal and land not a romantic partnership but a business one. Maybe you have to sit down and lay out a new contract and agree to the legally binding terms? Maybe it's time to 'check-in' with someone?

Maybe you just realize you need more company.

Cycle 7 brings you into contact with new and old people in order to: balance you out, give you another side to the picture, remind you of who you are (often by showing you what you think you're *not*) and what you want (via things you're not currently getting from others), help you see yourself reflected in others (you're more similar than you think) and to help you navigate the rapids of relationships with other humans. All of this and more.

Somehow, somewhere and in some way, in Cycle 7 people find you – and they have an important message about you. Your interactions with them will reveal a lot about how you see yourself, what you like about yourself, don't like about yourself, deny about yourself, repress within yourself. You'll discover your strengths, gifts, challenges, how you sabotage yourself, how you are this or that or could be; your internal conflicts, what you desire or fear and what you feel you're worth (for better or worse).

RETRIBUTION OR RESOLUTION?

Is it fair? What? Love? Life? You tell me. I guess it depends on your point of view, your 'rules of engagement', your code of conduct; and your contract.

What do you want?
What are you willing to give in return?
What does it say in the small print (either on paper or in your heart?)
Are you both half-hearted or are both parties in it 100%?

Cycle 7 bring us to a midway point of sorts where a lot has been said, a lot has been done, a lot has been thought about and now we need to find some sort of harmony with it all. We need to make peace with things. And that doesn't come without a bit of work, as you probably already know. Life becomes something of a tennis match, however subtle, where lines are drawn, sides are taken and rules are hashed out on how to play the game (whether in business, romance, the personal or professional) – or more importantly, how others should be playing *your* game, and whether you can play by their rules too.

Love, relationship, harmony, compromise and balance are the themes of this solar Cycle so if you start out entering it **wondering why life is so off-kilter** or why you have anything *but* balance, don't worry. That's why you're here now, to begin the juggle, to start sticking things in the scales and weighing up your life. Soon you'll know where you stand, what you want and how other people can help you (and where they fit into your picture), when you get clear about what it is you want from them – and how you can be of assistance to them in return. It's a give-and-take time of year. You can't run away from that concept and you probably already feel it, as certain relationships and unions are firmly under your celestial spotlight.

Most years, this Cycle puts the emphasis on your people skills. It's the one major playground (or battleground) where we get to face our own issues – through other people. We cast them in our inner dramas and dialogues, unknowingly. And they reflect them back to us. How do you know what 'stuff' you have to work on until someone comes along perfectly aligned to trigger you?

Meditate on that awhile.

How harmonious are your relationships? Is the peace and quiet really the calm before the storm and would a face-to-face clear the air? What is coming up for you to embrace? What type of relationships do you need now, this year, at this point in your life? Look to the sign the Sun is currently moving through to see just what type of energy is most suited to your style of bonding.

If it's Taurus season, for example, then it means you need Taurus-type relationships (not necessarily with a Taurus but this is the energy you are trying to incorporate into your life, to find balance and harmony within). You'd do well to bring Taurus energy into your unions – trips to nature, cooking together, mutual massages and so forth. Try this with the sign you find yourself in right now – bring more of this energy into your union. (Visit **www.SurfingYourSolarCycles.com** to determine which sign is active during your cycle 7 and what the attributes of that sign are.)

Whatever is happening is for a specific reason with a message for you – so don't just brush it off. You get a chance to learn a bit more about how well you do with other people, how to be better at relationships (or how great you already are in this area of life), how to treat yourself fairly and also let others be themselves too.

Stay alert to at least one Libra who appears to pass on the lessons of partnership (for better or worse) – either by revealing their own love lessons, teaching you some directly, or being the ideal sounding board for where you are with your own relationship (or what you truly desire in one).

FIGHTING YOUR REFLECTION:
What you see must be within you.

Is conflict bad or merely a way to connect on a deeper level? Are you truly asking for what you need? Are you smiling while resenting someone's unfairness? Are you giving someone a chance to have their say? Storms create the freshest air afterward, so could the magic you're seeking be found at the tail end of a confrontation?

It seems that in Cycle 7, it always, somehow, somewhere, comes down to conflict. Even if you're single, you're in a relationship with someone – everyone you meet in fact – be it the cashier at the local store or the person sitting next to you on the bus. In the presence of another, you're in a relationship, for a moment, a minute or a decade, doing the dance all humans do – giving, receiving, offering, taking. Peace-war. War-peace. Defining the self. Defending the self. Accepting another. And in today's world, the themes are likely to be clear, obvious and ridiculously predictable.

This Cycle has one meaning it'll make plain to you if it has to scream it in your ear:

Play Fair!

Without that, the game is lopsided and it's over before it has begun. No one wins any karmic points by cheating (and I don't mean in the relationship sense – always a strange concept when you think of cheating as implying the playing of a game). Politeness and civility are necessary tools to getting by on Earth. We're all animals looking for food if we don't follow one simple Law:

treat people as you would like to be treated.

Sadly, in this Cycle we often find ourselves treated how others treat themselves (which may be poorly) or find ourselves treating others as we treat ourselves (which may not be altogether healthy, either). Or, others are reflecting our own self-treatment by how they interact with us! This is why it all becomes about balance – you have to step outside of your comfort zone in this Cycle.

How much you take care of yourself
is in direct reflection to how well you treat others
and how well they treat you.

Hmmm ... but hang on, could this be why we have relationship problems, still? If we don't respect or even like ourselves how can we like someone else? What we see in others this Cycle is a clear indication of what may be dwelling within ourselves, as partners (business and personal) reflect issues *we ourselves* are tackling. Read that again – others act as mirrors to us during this Cycle, so what you *think* you're seeing as *their* problem, is actually yours. Listen to what you say (and what others say this month) and – it may be hard, but give it a go

192

to see how it sounds/feels – replace "he/she" with "I". It'll be an enlightening experience.

It's not *"why are they doing this or not doing that?"*, you should be asking yourself or viewing as the problem, but *"why have I brought this into my life and why am I fighting this battle?"*

What's in it for you? Have a second look. Maybe it's simply a distraction from another feeling. Fighting another is better to some people than accepting that you have to let them go – just watch any TV court show.

And if you find yourself disagreeing here, thinking "but s/he's the one being selfish, while I give give give, so how can being selfish be my problem?"....

...Think again.

The message could be that *you're not being selfish enough!* 'S/he' plays the role to show how unbalanced you are. You're allowed to take too, you know! Or perhaps you're being so selfish, by always giving because you have a problem asking for help or depending on another or not allowing yourself to receive what you're owed. It's selfish (and a form of control) to only give and never allow another to give to you. Again, selfishness perceived outside is still rooted firmly on your insides. Same goes with any other theme you care to replace it with (honesty, organization, reliability, caring etc).

**Whatever 'issue' you have with someone right now,
trace it back to your over or under-doing it (in a healthy way)
in your own life,
or denying within yourself.**

The key is balance. Anything *out* of balance now in your psyche and thus in your life, will reveal itself to you.

As the title of this section explains, what we see must be a reflection of what is within us – especially where a judgment is present. If we had no attachment to it, why would it hold such an emotional 'charge'? It's either that we strive so hard not to be or it's something we know we could be, or actually are, deep within. And if you still disagree that what you see reflects what is within you, then remember that whatever you witness triggers that same energetic vibration within you. Interact with a stressful situation or person long enough and you'll begin vibrating to that level; you'll feel irritation welling up in you. Don't rude people get your back up? How many times have you been drained by people who continually look on the bleak side? If you're around something long enough, you start operating on the same level – unless you put your focus on something else. (That's the principle behind girls sharing the same home, who end up on similar menstrual cycles). Like attracts like: a vibrating tuning fork soon has nearby tuning forks vibrating to the same resonance.

So when someone does something that annoys you, instead of focusing your lazer-beam attention on that, focus on something else, so you can avoid activating that energy within you. How many people have become the very thing they despised, by simply obsessing over *not* becoming that. Focus attracts people, events and things to us.

Sermon over. You're free to roam the cabin.

LOP-SIDED LIAISONS and UNFAIR UNIONS

Those who treat you unfairly when you truly believe you've committed to being there for them, and for yourself too, will probably be phased out of your life at this time of year. It happens. (Note: Are these people truly being unfair or merely saying things to you that reflect your inner opinion of yourself ... i.e. the truth hurts?) You may decide to cut out some people because there truly is no middle ground anymore. You feel bullied, controlled, manipulated, used or overlooked. Perhaps someone feels the same way about you. No matter. New people will find their way to you during this Cycle, but although you have ditched certain faces from your life, or vice versa, the themes of conflict and conflict-resolution may remain with you in the form of energy imprints from which you'll attract similar people (or if you've done your homework and cleared away these patterns, new balanced people based on the new balanced energy you're carrying).

You'll see how healthy you're treating yourself based on who you now attract. It may be an eye-opener. Perhaps you need a wake up call on how you're treating yourself, based on what you're attracting. Are you beating yourself up? On a downer? Like always attracts like. And misery loves company.

Where you can, then, resolve the disputes, whether internally (accept your part in any drama) or externally (giving or accepting apologies or hearing someone out or letting them know where you stand). The best way to end an argument is to release one end of the rope (and release resistance to being right/demanding fairness/showing others the error of their ways etc). Watch how others relax when you do. They are all mirrors – of yourself! You may not make friends now, you may even make 'enemies' as we'll see, but it doesn't matter. It's more about being as fair as you can, and accepting nothing less than that same treatment back. Everyone deserves it.

ATTRACTION IN ACTION

You're a magnet in Cycle 7 – that's the beauty of this time of year. You're magnetically attractive, and **attracted**. And that's not just in the classic 'looks' department. If you're angry about something and are hiding this from yourself, it'll arrive in the form of someone who somehow senses it from you and who is also pissed off about something. You both wind up fighting and get to relieve some necessary stress! If you want something and won't let yourself want it, you'll find someone else acting it out (then you get to blame *them* for wanting it, because you were fighting yourself about wanting it!). What an interesting time of year.

So be careful and be aware – casting others in our own internal disputes is a surefire way to make Cycle 7 a heck of a dramatic mess (but still a lot of fun if you like that sort of thing). However, it just means there's more to balance out before you plunge into deeper and darker territory in Cycle 8.

So, to recap, as far as relationships go:
Singles: It's a fantastic time to work out what you need to balance out in yourself. Calm, quiet and stable usually? Throw some crazy energy into your life. Reverse it. Turn it on its head. Extroverts – spend more time analyzing your own feelings and asking for opinions and guidance. Balance out time-wasting superficiality with some serious study. Introverts – get out and connect with more people, or just be around others more. Balance out depression with a daily dose of humor.

I remember as soon as one Cycle 7 phase kicked in for me, one year, I realized I had no photos of my friends up on the wall at home and went about asking others to send me some. I wanted them around me when I was home alone, working. I needed that extra company. In another year, I ended up moving in with someone, in the woods – with fewer people around, so I was still 'alone' to a degree, which suited me just fine.

If you're single you have more time on your hands to be a good friend, so cash in on the opportunities to make yourself available to others who in turn will do the same for you. And why not get out with some pals? You're more likely to meet a healthy, happy someone when you're radiating and having a good time yourself. Try it. There's nothing more attractive than someone in a place of joy.

Newly Dating: Okay, so you're the one most likely going through Cycle 7 if you're reading this. If so, the Sun shines the spotlight on the *other* in your life. What about them? Are they going through something major? Maybe you need to be there for them, through a big shift or a tough time. Maybe you're working something out? Deciding to get closer and begin the process of sharing space/money/more time etc. Maybe you have to cheer them up, cheer them on, brighten their day or help pick them up? Or just love and applaud them (just like you needed way back in Cycle 1 the 'all about you' chapter of your annual story).

So whatever it is, look at the other person. Is this 'the one'? That's easy – yes, *this is the one for you right now*. Today. They'd not have shown up if it wasn't to show you something. You invited them in, energetically speaking. Whatever soul agreement you both have is something to look at, now. Maybe you're giving your power away and letting them dictate how *you* feel. Maybe their needs are beginning to come first? Are they dominating you too much? Are you letting them? Are they helping you or are they hurting you? Are you trying to control them for some reason? Is there mutual respect? Mutual care? Mutual effort? There's that key word for this Cycle – **mutual**. Are you as into them as they are into you? How do you know? Can you be honest and open? Are you balancing out time apart, with as much of this intense time you're spending together?

Since it's the early days, you may want to note the **Red Flags** (see next section), and track the feelings you have and take things as slowly as you can, so you can ease into this new union in your life.

Couples: Time to renew vows, or celebrate your togetherness by seeing how far you've come, and planting new seeds for new directions of growth together. What new bonds can you create? Any projects, plans, ideas you can work on as a team? Where is the 'we' factor? Can one of you pick up the slack while another focuses on another part of your current challenge (we each have different strengths, which is yours and which is theirs?) Quit fighting against each other and work together. Issues that come up now remind you that you're still two separate individuals, even though you're part of a team. Is it time to let others into your world or keep them at bay and salvage some alone-time together? Any conflict can now be worked through by looking inwards first at the separate triggers and histories that led you to this moment, where you risk parting due to personal issues and not what the other person is or is not doing.

You met for a reason, work out what.

Yes, it's possible your ex comes back into the picture or something someone does that's similar makes you react; a timely reminder of where you've been, ***the emotional ground you've covered to date and how you handled it then.*** We all seem to carry at least one form of relationship problem or addiction or dysfunction that we're drawn to like moths to a flame or that is drawn to us, but which never ever feeds us and only leaves us feeling empty and frazzled.

So, if your old flame does come back, perhaps you can resolve some things left unfinished. Maybe you get to continue where you left off. If so, congratulations. You deserve it for the work you've done on yourself (and will continue to do together). Keep in mind that, whatever the case, it's worth working out if the reconnection is to warm you or to draw you in for another ride around the emotional burn-out roller coaster. Energy seeks like energy, and often people are just looking to feast on emotional attention (any kind will do) just to know they exist.

No matter how long your current partner has been around, you'll get a check-in on how well your union is going, and old issues may creep back onto the scene that weren't resolved/faced 'way back when'. Maybe it's the different ways you both handle stress (one of you goes inside and withdraws, the other seeks outside expression to relieve stress; you both have different home needs, sexual desires or different ways you consider the art of loving).

You'll get a second (or third, fifth, eighth) chance to rework and revision, cooperate, compromise and find a middle ground – where 'I' meets 'You', 'Mine' meets 'Yours' and 'Me' versus 'Them' to create this strange creature called 'Us'.

Business Partners: All of the above still applies to professional deals, contracts, client relationships or business deals, so you can read the above sections from a purely work-oriented perspective, replacing sexual dynamics for other entanglements such as financial sharing/management and so forth.

RELATIONSHIP RED FLAGS

We all see them, sense them and spot them. We sometimes just choose to ignore them, when rose-colored glasses are on and we're giddy with 'love'. Red Flags are those annoying things that pop up that really jar you with someone and don't fit with how you live your life (or want to live it). You've had five magical dates with the most amazing person you've ever met and then, on date 6, you're out with them and they do something appalling. How could they? What kind of person would do that? Or, you discover that someone has been lying to you. You feel betrayed. Or that when they are with you, everything is wonderful, but they treat all their friends so poorly. A red flag goes up to show there is something that is causing you discomfort, and it is likely to pop up again, later on.

However things begin, are usually how things will end. It's a strange thing but it's the foundation of astrology.

> *The things that reveal themselves in the early days*
> *are a foundation for what is to come.*

Movie writers understand and apply this concept (the really good ones). In my university days studying the craft of screenwriting, we were trained how to set up scenes early on as a mirror to what would happen later. The audience wouldn't pick up on it all until later but they'd have a certain sense of satisfaction when things played out as they did. 'Foreshadowing', they call it. Horror movies use it a lot (notice how many times someone early on warns a character "someday, that tongue of yours will get you in a lot of trouble" who later on winds up with their tongue caught in a machine and ripped out. Charming!) Often life is way more subtle, but you get the point. If someone brings up a red flag in you (you feel uneasy, you get a pull in your stomach etc) then it's something to pay attention to. You can hope, dream, wish and want but it's something that is likely to become a point of contention down the line.

If you're bringing the opposite of what you want in, it's because you're not aligned with what you want and not focusing on that. If you can, bring up what you *do* want, mention it or at least be honest with yourself about what you now want, after being presented with something as you do *not* want it.

Use the do-not-wants to quickly ascertain and affirm what it is that you do want.

Each dislike should be used as your immediate springboard to your next new desire. To be treated better. To feel happier. And so forth. Energetically, we meet people where they are and can't change them. Do they blend well with us, do we fit where they currently are, where we are? Are we just enjoying the fact they like us and make us feel good (because we don't feel so good inside, about ourselves) and are we selling ourselves short in the process?

This goes for business connections too. Relationships are relationships and in Cycle 7 you get to see those red flags early on so you know who you're dealing with. And if we ignore them and don't bring them to our conscious awareness, we act shocked when, down the line, these people reveal their true selves. No one suddenly does that. The messages are there from day One. Pay attention and all will be well. Your feelings are the guidance to understanding if you're in alignment with who you are and what you want. Then you can't act all deflated when someone does what they've been doing all along: *just being themselves.*

Maybe, when it comes to long-term satisfaction, peace or harmony, you're just not the right person for them and vice versa?

It happens.

Don't chuck the towel in just because someone disagrees with you, argues with you or makes you face something in yourself that you don't like. Often the ones who press our buttons and help us grow and evolve (however uncomfortably) are the ones we'll look back on and see as our greatest soul mates. If someone upsets you, they're helping you learn something about yourself.

Relationships also move cyclically. It's how we handle the 'down' cycle that determines how our partnership evolves. So the next time you enter a stressful period in your union (whether romantic or business), step back and realize you're being given a chance to get closer by working out the kinks.

Be sure that you're behaving the way you want someone else to. Like does attract like. To attract someone into your life who does A or acts like B or does C for you; you have to be sure that you do A and act like B and do C for others. In Cycle 7, you get to meet yourself time and time again. Be what you wish to discover through others.

ASTROLOGICAL SYNASTRY

Astrology has much to say on relationships. In fact this is one of my favorite areas and one I've come to specialize in, specifically because it's what most people come to me regarding. Does he love me? What is he thinking? Why does she behave this way? Why do I always attract this type of person who does this to me? What do I really need in a relationship? Do we have a soul connection? And so forth.

Love never brings us true lasting happiness it seems, except in fairy tales, and even then it's laced with tragedy. (You have to die to be happy like Romeo and Juliet, or you'll not be able to live until you are kissed by a prince as in Sleeping Beauty etc.)

From all my years in this field, working with clients across the globe, there seems to be a common thread:

Karma Mates: the people we meet whom we clash with in order to learn an amazing lesson and retrieve some fantastic skill we never knew we had. They are the people you cling to who let you down till you finally realize you're actually okay being independent. Or the ones who withhold affection to show you just how much you're actually an affectionate and loving being (who deserves the same). They are similar to 'Reminders' (see below) but they usually come with that karmic price: **It hurts**. The theory is that you have a soul-agreement with the person pressing your buttons. Because no doubt you're pressing theirs too. Like attracts like. (Let that be a consolation when you feel trapped or stuck in a karmic knot!)

The funny thing about karma mates? They're so damn attractive to you! It's nature's cruel (and clever) way of getting you both close enough to do the cosmic contract thing. It gets it off the ground. Which is why so many people feel so torn. Attraction doesn't always mean bliss. It means *there could be some work to do behind the scenes.* Keep that in mind the next time you go head-over-heels for the amazing person you just met. When the magic pink smoke clears, will you be facing some ugly truth about yourself?

Now, karma doesn't always mean a bad thing – you could have helped someone out in another lifetime (because karma mates nearly always are people whom we've known before). Maybe you took something from them and they never forgave it. Back you both come to replay something. Anything left unresolved (from an emotional standpoint) is fair game in this current lifetime. Can you forgive – even yourself, perhaps? Maybe this is the only way to alleviate the karma. And perhaps even more importantly (to at least one of you), can you say "Sorry" when it's needed, and even when you may not think it's warranted?

It's incredible how much karma is dissolved and resolved by simply asking for forgiveness. Getting it doesn't seem to matter. **Saying sorry**, seems to be an amazingly powerful step to wrapping things up – or doing the best you can to help heal any damage you caused (which could be why you're stuck in a miserable situation, as some form of penance you laid on yourself because you felt Oh So Guilty). But don't let it become an excuse for staying put and accepting pain. That's just silly.

Stalkers, the ones you love who don't love you back, the ones who love you then stab you in the back, the ones you lose painfully, those who belittle your ideas and tell you "You're not good enough", and the ones you allow to keep hurting you over and over – these are your difficult karma mates. And the reason you love them so much is because they're helping you grow and evolve by getting clear on what you want, who you truly are (and the skills you didn't know you had until they came along and dragged it all out of you) and what you're willing to accept on the path to happiness.

And the ones who come and help you out in the nick of time when they don't seem to really need to, are your good-karma mates. No good deed goes unnoticed in the eyes of the universe. Your cosmic bank account pays interest on everything done unto others, both helpful and not. And you know the difference.

Buffers/Fluffers: We discussed these in Cycle 1, so you can also refer back there. You find these people in each Cycle and each bears a different message. In relationships, buffers and fluffers are usually very welcome, but they don't often remain permanent fixtures in your life. They come in with a breath of fresh air as they open the door to new horizons, possibilities, tastes, experiences and feelings. And then they go. Job done.

Buffers show you that new world by helping you out of the rut you're currently in. Daring you to give it a shot. To break out of jail. To quit a job that's boring, end a relationship that's sour. To take that dancing class. To let your hair down. Buffers do it by either *being* they way you'd like to be, or they have access to the things they just *know* you'd like (life is the master creative conspirator). They know the people, places and the times that events are happening. They won't do it for you, but they'll go with you, send you the invites and hook you up with the people who can help. They remind you that there is more out there and that you don't need to settle for less. That you're actually freer, or more attractive, or stronger, or more capable, or more talented than you think you are. They're wonderful. And the funny thing is, they're merely reflecting back to you who you already are (but being your self-critical self, you just don't see it yet or appreciate that you actually *are* that awesome!).

Fluffers are your ultimate pep talk squad, your cheerleaders. Fluffers support you by telling you that you can do it. They'll see you through, cheer you on even when you're tripping up and making an ass of yourself in rehearsal late through the night, and still find time to be there at your opening performance. They believe in you. They see something in you that you don't.

They hold your hand through it. They somehow sense where you're going and they do the job they came to do – to tell you you're right in wanting this. You are. But sometimes, without someone else butting in and telling us, we simply don't take the risk. Fluffers are the ones who really are your best friends, even if they're the ones sleeping next to you each night.

Reminders come in various forms. Mostly they are people who remind you how you *used* to be. Maybe they do silly things you did before you got wise. Maybe they look like you used to before you changed your style. Maybe they represent times and places you've been in the past, to remind you of where you came from and how far you've come. Maybe to remind you of who you are, beneath the glitz and glamour. Maybe they bring the best out in you, maybe the worst, but it's just that – *in you.*

So they're good markers of your spiritual progress through life. Other reminders are those people who remind us of who we'd *like to be.* We want to be like them. If only we were as patient as them, or as daring, as conversational or funny, or confident enough to go for it; no apologies. They come around to reflect back to us that we actually *are* that way and can train to be like them. How? Because they would not appear if it wasn't a potential already inherent in us.

And then there are those reminders (often annoying) of who we *actually are.* The people who remind us by their own actions how we despise selfishness (because despite our appearance of giving we're actually pretty darn selfish). Or we see through them and their actions, how it hurts other people when they don't listen (just as you do, yet don't realize). Good or bad, these reminders will shove in your face *every* thing about yourself you've forgotten, refuse to see or quite simply don't yet realize you are. They're true mirrors and until you get their message, you'll see their behaviors over and over until you correct or re-align *your own.*

Like always attracts like. Even if you don't believe it's in you yet. These people help remind you of what you desire, often by not being it or doing it, or by being and doing the very same things as you (to either frustrate you out of it, or to reinforce that you're on the right path).

Twin Souls seem to be one person in various bodies. Sounds crazy, but this is the science behind those instant recognitions, those familiar connections, the people who feel like family and lovers all in one. It's natural. It works. You know each other so well because you *are* the same person – occupying different bodies so you can learn a heck of a lot more.

It sounds incestuous but it's an interesting theory to chew on. Why are you so familiar? Past lives together may produce love-at-first-sight folk in the present, the ones you instantly recognize and go nutty over. But many twin souls find they don't or can't stay together. Being the same person means you don't get to learn as much as you could or should or planned to this lifetime.

Yes, you can share the same roof or bed and be vastly different enough to teach each other new tricks (the ideal) but it can equally mean that you wind up being stuck at a plateau of comfort where you both become so similar that all perspective is lost. That's when twin souls usually part ways (and agree it's for the best) so they can continue learning new things in different parts of the country, city or globe. You always know they're out there, you just don't need to be in each other's pockets and they never really leave you because … weirdly enough … they are you. It's kind of comforting really.

Soul-Mates are the ones we feel complete us. They have things we want, they do things we want to do, and they represent the parts of our personality that if *only* we could be more like, we'd run better (like vastly superior machines). *Reminders* get mixed up in this category. They are the jigsaw puzzle piece that seems to encompass all we yearn for, which is grand when you learn to incorporate their traits into yours. But when you start relying on them to play that piece so you can stay the same, that's when trouble brews. And they won't stand for it. You're two sides of the same coin that came together to learn the other side. So often soul-mates begin to switch over in each other's presence – receptive become a bit more assertive, assertive become a touch more receptive. And so on.

You'll often see soul-mate relationships at play when the individuals are vastly different in one vital area – together they truly are a perfect blend of the ideal person: tall/small, fat/thin, confident/shy, polite/rude, givers/takers, fast/slow etc. Polar opposites often. If you're in this sort of union, you'll notice already that as a team, you really work. Keep learning, keep your eyes and ears open. Ask. Try. Train. Then you become better, and even more whole, as you each become more like the other, yet still retaining what makes you different.

Soul-Mates don't complete you, they give you a sense of who you are as a complete person. And reflect it back to you. Allowing you to access your own completion and self-acceptance. It's not always about them; it's in you too. True love, reflected in their eyes, of yourself. Beautiful. Like a mutual fan club. Open, growing, evolving. Romantic bliss. Physical merging. Two different energies that will never be the same again because they came together to create something totally unique.

Often, we find these various types showing up within one union itself, through one significant other. Someone can play our Soul Mate one day and the next be a Karma Mate, helping us to evolve by reminding us of our 'buttons' so that we can evolve beyond the triggers of a painful past.

Astrology presents an amazing array of possibilities when it comes to analyzing relationships, through a process called synastry. Your chart meets someone else's chart (with clicks and clashes) and creates a third chart of the relationship itself (called Composite).

Also check out Jerry and Esther Hicks *The Vortex: Where the Law of Attraction Assembles All Cooperative Components* book or CD series for a deep understanding of how the law of attraction can help you attract the right relationships into your life and affect the ones you're already experiencing.

BALANCING ACTS: Male/Female, Passive/Aggressive, Overt/Covert

Since things are often uneven by the time we reach Cycle 7 and are in need of a tweak in a few areas, you may spot some of these patterns making themselves known in your life. Yin-Yang issues are common. How in balance are your male and female sides? Did you forget you have both? Many people do. We're not talking about sexuality, although that area is often an easy target. Are you a "straight-acting" gay man? Are you a straight man in touch with your feminine side? Are you a woman who's becoming 'masculine' and aggressive? This is perhaps a little too simplistic but you could do with adding a little of the 'other' into your palate so you're not painting life one shade of color the entire time.

If it scares you, there's likely to be an imbalance at play in your life.

> *Those who are truly comfortable with themselves*
> *put others at ease also by just their mere presence.*

They seemingly are giving other people permission to be themselves. That's why they are so attractive to us.

If you're overly one thing, you'll need (or find attracted to you) a piece of the opposite. This is where the relationship see-saw begins. Pushy meets passive. Quiet meets loud. Clean meets dirty. They're really all just labels, so be careful how much you cling to one label because you may wind up in someone else's shoes someday. It's almost inevitable.

Yes we really do just meet ourselves throughout life (and then are shocked or repulsed or deny it or even turned on when we do!) but things that are seemingly 'opposites' do attract to neutralize each other. That's where the phrase 'two sides of the same coin' came from. Life is ultimately about the handling and juggling of polarities, fragments on the path to remembering our wholeness. You can't say you're explicitly one thing unless you want to do just that – split yourself! And then the part you disown finds you through another. What a great game!

Take a look around and see just how many opposites and 'different-sides-of-the-same coin' things, people or situations there are. Try and play both or accept you *can be* both and you'll attract an honest reflection of this in another human who is 'whole' and not playing a role.

For example: don't attack those who seem to want an open relationship with you. If you continue to attract those kinds of people, it is probably because somewhere in you is the need for space or the exact same thing (a desire to want to experience other people as well as your partner). Or a fear of not being loved enough/lovable enough. By repressing it, you bring others into your life who don't want to fully commit to you (if that is what you see as a sign of total devotion).

Is someone doing something you used to do? Met someone who reminds you of who you were and where you were (or what you wore) three months ago/last year/before you were reborn into your new life? Role models on who *we were, are and want to be* appear now, as do those who remind us of things we *don't want to be.*

Call them soul mates, psychic markers, beacons, messengers, 'they' all help us bring ourselves back to ourselves – because this journey is, don't forget, all about *you* and must be walked alone. But be careful, the more polar opposites you both have in a relationship, the more your chances for conflict as you both play out a certain role and get stuck in it. ***Couples who seem vastly different are always working on bringing that new facet of the other person into themselves.*** Enjoy differences, but seek sameness on a fundamental level if you're to be happy, or at least be willing to adapt and adjust (another theme now) to what you may wind up perceiving as a major pain just because someone does it differently to you.

DECISIONS, DECISIONS ...

Weighing things up during this Cycle could see you sitting on the fence a lot; becoming indecisive as you try to work out what's best for any given situation – what you actually want and what you're willing to give or do, or put up with to get it. Everything has a price, and you will find you have certain things that need to be paid for or unlocked in your heart in order for your desires to become manifest. So whatever you're juggling, give it some time, and you'll finally come to the conclusion that *one path in particular feels better.*

There is no 'wrong' decision, so don't let that keep you from choosing. Reality has a weird way of shaping itself around the decisions you make and your beliefs about them (and we make our decisions often based on what we believe) and not the other way around. Don't worry that if you choose Path 1, you'll wind up messing up and Path 2 is doomed forever as 'the road you should have taken, but didn't'. That's nonsense. Life isn't always so black and white but will always bring you to what you need on any path chosen; it's just a change of scenery. ***It's how you feel about your choice that's most important.*** So use your feelings as the barometer for how on track you are when faced with any decision-making choice.

Weigh your options and then commit to at least one.

MIRROR, MIRROR ON THE WALL ...

You're in an attractive Cycle, whether you know it or not. Your magnetism is so strong, so be aware of what you wear and how you dress and act when you're around other people. Even alone, you may find yourself dwelling in the mirror (another reflection) and wanting to primp and preen. Go ahead. Be vain! You're beautiful and you're allowed to say it. Try not to let your emotions pollute your surroundings during this time; better to remain placid and peaceful – it'll get you further. That's not to say you should avoid all ugly confrontation – but the way you say things has a marked bearing on the ways things pan out.

True, it's all about the 'look' now, at least at the beginning (first impressions and all that jazz). Not to sound superficial but this Cycle covers fashion, hair, color, style, feng-shui, design, make-up and beauty in all its forms. Even for the guys. Who cares if you're classically un-beautiful (in your opinion), you are your own model, so make the most of what you have. Accentuate your assets. Your ugly part may be another person's dream come true. And you have what they don't have. Supermodel Tyra Banks (born with Venus [the planet of beauty and connected to this Cycle] in her 7th house/Cycle) was told she'd have a hard time modeling with such a large forehead – something she purposefully emphasized in her photos shoots and which became her 'signature' and part of her ultimate success.

Stay alert; others notice you – which is why it's such a fabulous Cycle to meet someone! Or to get your way. So stay sharp, look your best, dress to feel good and these good vibes will be noticed. See what happens. Cycle 7 is a great way to test these Cycles out for yourself. Someone is sure to compliment you at least once during this time. Smile knowingly, and don't forget to dish out a little flirtatious compliment back in their direction. And don't forget to say thanks.

There's really never any reason to dwell on things that make you feel lousy. It drains your energy and sucks you back to old places. This Cycle in particular is about letting others enjoy the brilliance that is You. The Universe *wants* to team you up with someone else or a whole bunch of others, if you yourself are ready and willing. You deserve the best, even on bad days, in bad years.

Be beautiful, because you are.

THAT'S YOU, NOT ME!

Cycle 1 puts the solar influence on the 1st house of your astrological chart wheel. That's the time when you get to say "*This is me*". Directly opposite, is Cycle 7 (the 7th house) and it deals with "*All things not me*". However, there is an illusion at play that is worth noting so you'll get smart with what's really going on. As soon as you say "I *am* ...", you energize, attract, or bring into play somewhere, the opposite of that, something that is different to that which you say you are. How can we know day unless we have night? So be careful – the more you fix your personality as This or That, the more you chance attracting others to play out the 'not you' – the parts that reflect the opposite of that which you claim to be. Helpers always wind up attracting those who need help. Followers wind up bringing in leaders. Those with low self-esteem attract those who treat them poorly. And there's nothing inherently wrong with that – it's the Law of Attraction at play.

What you're really going for that will bring you the longest and most deeply satisfying experiences is true balance within. To realize that we all contain a myriad of personalities and options on what to make bigger and what to downplay and that we all have the potential to be light and the potential to be dark. So instead of locking yourself in with point-blank statements such as "This is who I am" go for more honest ones like "This is who I am choosing to be, and the parts of the whole I am choosing to focus on and develop". You get to choose. To be honest or deceitful. To love or to not to love. So be careful if you're pointing the finger a lot at him/her/them and judging. It can only say, ultimately, more about you and your inner issues than anything else.

YOU YOU YOU: Relationship Reality-Check:

Are you getting your needs met in your relationships? What *are* your needs? Are other people feeding your sense of comfort and safety and beauty or are you left hungering, hankering and hopeless? This Cycle lets you iron out the wrinkles in your relating, or else you'll jack in a union that's not working (as far as you're concerned). You may find a parting of the ways is in order if neither of you gel, jive, mesh or flow naturally. Sometimes it either works or it doesn't.

Relationship questions abound and it's your job to ask them and seek answers outside of yourself (if you can't come to some resolution within your own heart). *If in doubt, find out by asking.* Don't assume! *Never assume*, in Cycle 7. Ask around. Go straight for the bulls-eye; look in the horse's mouth. It's not just romantically but the business deal or handshake you want with the local firm, company or corporation. Remain open. Find out.

Whoever the relationship is between, it's a Cycle full of "is so-and-so staying with Mike? Is Sheila breaking up with Matt? How do Tom and Tyler remain so committed after all these years?" Should you stay, or are they going? Are they worth your time? Is this equal?

What's the state of *your* contracts? From signing a phone plan to renewing vows. Weddings, divorces, engagements, mergers, deal makes-and-breaks are all headline news this season and you'll have to get clear on:

1. what you want
2. what you're getting and
3. what you're willing or unwilling to do, to find satisfaction.

The media I am sure will be abuzz as always at this time, in reflection of what *you're* going through. Along with your friends. Throughout this book, **the reality around you always has a message** for *you* about *you* no matter what is going on, down the street or on the world's TV screens. This is *your* version of reality, and how you perceive it all says more about you than the thing you're perceiving. Symbols, themes, messages are all around you, that will reflect 'you' back to you.

So ... who's with who? Your life is ablaze with all of these questions, queries and quandaries. Look around yourself and you'll get an education in the whole arena of relationships.

The whole issue of the 'you' in our lives (as opposed to the 'I' of ourselves) is paramount now as your focal point, learning curve and teacher.

<blockquote>

**Experience will reflect back to you,
your current issues,
thoughts, feelings, problems, desires,
repressions, judgments, fears,
lacks, needs, blockages, illusions,
and strengths.**

</blockquote>

Everyone reflects ourselves back to us. Or to be more precise where we are with ourselves. Our alignment with ourselves.

<blockquote>

**The strongest points of attraction now
just have a more emphatic message for you –
on something inherent within you that needs
acknowledging, accepting, embracing, releasing or clearing.**

</blockquote>

Allowing, and then deciding what you want next, is the way to move ahead.

WHENEVER YOU POINT, THREE FINGERS POINT BACK AT YOU

The blame game just isn't worth it, this Cycle. Give it up. Your relationships say more about you than anything else. You can't hide from yourself in the presence of another. The very fact that another is interacting with you says a lot about you. They came into your experience for a reason (by way of that magical and eternal Law of Attraction). Even the infamous person we all know who cuts us off on the freeway. Enjoy yourself, and love yourself and you'll see the face of love everywhere and in turn be loved in equal proportion. Simple when you realize that is all that's needed. If you don't like something, work on it within, and turn your focus to something else.

<blockquote>

**By focusing on anything, you're including it in your vibration –
whether you're saying *I Like This*, or *I Hate That* –**

</blockquote>

and whatever is active in your vibration, will seek you out
by way of the Law of Attraction.
There is no such thing as No.
Focusing on only that which you want to see,
or reaching for the best in all you encounter and experience,
will determine the quality of your reality experience.

Reclaiming forgotten pieces of yourself is an amazing journey; no wonder relationship questions are top of the list during astrologer-client sessions. We want to be plugged back into who we are, like who we are and share that self-like with someone else who likes themselves so we can both like each other and create a whole abundance of liking. Call it a mutual fan club.

If they are in your life, they have come in response to a vibrational signal you have sent out. In other words, they'd not have arrived if on some level of your being you had not invited them in. It's kind of like vampires. That goes for the people who bring you joy, as well as the suckers that drain you. Whose name is tattooed on *your* neck? (And remember, you're tattooing them there by talking about them, saying No to them, and anything else that involves giving them energy – pulling *or* pushing).

SHIFTING THE SCALES
New rules in your current connections are also likely to pop up – what are your relationship boundaries; your business working partnership commitment terms? Who does what, gets what and wants what?

It's time to negotiate.

The deeper questions are: are you seeking someone to fulfill something in your life that's 'missing'. If so, you'll keep on chasing your tail, or bring someone in who seems to fulfill your every need, until you discover they are only playing a role in your life that you cast them in: 'strong, supportive savior' or 'fun and feel-good firecracker'. Roles are roles – and unauthentic.

CALLING THE KARMA MECHANIC
The scales of justice and judgment fluctuate at this point of your year as you begin weighing things up – indecision reigns supreme as you find yourself stuck between two paths, two people, two possibilities, two potentials. Which is best? Are you leaning more heavily on A ... or B? What if A doesn't pan out? Is it more about looks or personality? Frivolous or practical? Short term or long term? Money or freedom? Help! As the scales of karma fluctuate too you'll find life may intervene and seemingly force a decision out of you by having someone else make the decision *for* you (in the form of a judge who gives their verdict).

You may have to lie down and take it, since karma (you'll meet this notion again in Cycle 9) has decided for you. Whether it's for you or against you, you'll have to face the decisions made. (Whoever said there were only two options was a drama queen; if in major doubt, seek a third option and choose that until further notice).

This is where playing 'fair' or 'by the book' comes in. But if you don't like the book, feel free to re-write parts, as long as you get others' input also. If there are rules and you choose to break them, you have to be willing to pay the penalty for this. Of course, some rules are meant to be broken, but for every action there is an equal and opposite reaction. Repercussions abound, from things you set in motion earlier this year to things last year that you've forgotten about. And how you've treated people to date. During Cycle 7 you get to learn all about how the universe gives and takes away, with the hand of universal karma; the ultimate balance. No judgment, no punishment, just an eternal book-keeper who makes sure everyone gets their turn, their dues and ultimately… (here's where I swallow)… we all get what we give out eventually.

Simple as that.

If you're in a crazy Cycle 7 year, finding balance is a major quest when you start realizing your life is really off-kilter. So you'll have to make some snappy decisions on how to moderate things to restore some form of sanity, and it's going to mean listening and involving other people because during this month, **it's not just all about you**, I'm afraid. And you need people, as you'll see. And … finally … *they* need *you*, did you forget?!

YOUR CHARM FACTOR

With all this tricky stuff to navigate, you do (as always) get a blessing to use towards passing your current Initiation. Your current gift is the art of charming. Your ability to smile and be nice can only work *for* you in your personal 7-Cycle. And yes, at times, drawing the line and being decisive and direct, also works. But your abilities at getting along with other people are tested at this point of your annual journey and you'll get to see just how well you can play the game of social graces.

Use honey, not vinegar. Kill them with kindness. Smile at sourpusses. Refuse to lower yourself to anyone's level. Maintain your own composure. Be your own peace. It all helps in Cycle 7, bringing in greater equilibrium. And you get to enjoy good vibes while others can choose their own darker path. It's all personal choice – you get to set your own vibration, always.

And that's all life is: **energy and vibration**.

What's your default vibrational level currently and can you raise it?

PLANETARY SIGNATURE: VENUS

The last time we were working with the energy of Venus was during the earthy Cycle 2 (the time of 'nice stuff' and getting comfy). Venus in Cycle 7 is airy, reminding us of the pleasure (Venus) within the mental (Air) realm. Communication. Sharing ideas. Connecting with people. Reaching out. Here we use the energy of Venus to share: to give and to receive. To keep the lines open for that synergistic two-way flow of energy. We gain by this coming together. And we'll enjoy it. Love blossoms now, when two unite to create something new. And two heads are better than one.

BRIDGE BUILDING OR BURNING?

Think really carefully before you write someone off this month, because you can't cross back over burned bridges and ruined roads. Well, you can, but the potholes of pain and mistrust can take years to seal over. You never know when you may need a favor from someone who may have hurt you. And what a beautiful chance for them to level some karma and give *back* to you then, and for you to learn it's okay to ask *and* receive. It doesn't so much matter where help comes from or goes to, as long as it's given and received. Offer it. Accept it graciously. Spread the good vibes around. Angels don't walk among us, we *are* each other's angels down here. Cut people off and you cut off another doorway and pair of hands (or wings) that can help you.

We're not saying you have to put up with mistreatment (Cycle 7 as we have seen may be the perfect time once and for all to put your foot down and give a message out to all and sundry that you will no longer tolerate being treated poorly). Where you can, move on and try *not* to cut off major parts of your life in a stubborn cut-throat way. Distance is fine; space and time do heal. And a chance at reconnection on any level is always appreciated. Maybe it just is a matter of time and space, and Cycle 7 being an air-phase (the element traditionally associated with this time of your year) is a good moment for everyone to breathe. So back off to your corner if need be, and let others do the same.

In the game of life, *we teach others how to treat us*, by what we allow.
**Setting our own standards now in Cycle 7
is a great way to attract better energy in the Cycles ahead.**

I remember reading a quotation somewhere that went something like this:

**We all are one-winged angels.
Alone we are incomplete;
by embracing each other,
we fly.**

MAY I HAVE THIS DANCE?

With a constant monthly theme of sharing, agreeing, merging, reaching, connecting, joining, attracting, mixing, balancing, doubling, teaming, compromising, cooperating, confronting and combining (phew), you have to work out what it is you want, so you can look at what you're attracting to see if it's in line and on track with your desires. No use complaining about it down the line when you didn't find it to your tastes at the beginning. Anyone you meet and decide to share with is a *dancing partner in life* and it's far better to know your partner, because it's a quick two-step tango from fun-friend or luxurious lover to ruthless rival, which is when the mirror starts showing you things you don't want to see and you begin hurling missiles at each other from the trenches. Which leads us to:

THE ENIGMA OF 'ENEMIES'

In some years you meet someone you could label your 'enemy' (if you want to give them enough power over you as to warrant such a dramatic title, that is). They certainly appear to have it in for you. Fighting this foe could swallow up a lot of your time, but a deeper look will show that some issue between you is keeping you chained together because you're both more similar than you think. Why else 'do the dance of drama' (which is all it is) with them? It's like you're dating, or married, spending so much time making someone else your life's work.

Why wage war with someone and keep yourself stuck with them for the duration of the battle? To regain fairness, what is rightfully yours? Or are you the bully dominating the scene to get more of something you feel is your right? Who is right? Maybe you both are – from your individual points of view. What can't you surrender and let go of (not to save face but save your sanity)? You're both in it together, and the best way to get out of it is to do just that – get out of it! But can you? Or is your addiction to the person/object/situation/place so strong that you'd rather be stuck fighting it than let it go and be – alone – without it…?

Maybe it's best to give the power back to someone to level the playing field. Notice how refunding money to someone who is causing you conflict in a business deal often alleviates the stress and pressure and lets things flow again (and gets that bad energy off your back and out of your life).

Cycle 8 becomes even more intense if you can't deal with this now in Cycle 7, so try if you can to tie it all up before you're forced to later on.

Those who oppose us are often our greatest teachers, pointing out where we are not in alignment with who we really are. We get to see what we want and what we want to become. Fighting them doesn't help (it often just reveals our own weakness and insecurity); just being yourself at the level you want to be is all that's needed.

Suddenly, 'enemies' dissolve away as the lesson is complete.

SOLO AND SMILING OR SOLITARY AND SAD?

Being alone ('all-one', whole) is such a strange concept in Cycle 7, but *those who can be at peace when alone with themselves make the best partners* who can be at peace and whole when with another. Maybe this year, during this Cycle, you can finally find the balance between time to yourself and space for another, between *maintaining you, while embracing them.*

All fighting with foes can only teach you something about yourself, your shadow, what bugs you, what you need and what you're willing to accept, put up with and tolerate. No blaming, no finger-wagging; either deal or quit. All interactions ... unless legal (which we'll go into next) ... are by choice.

LEGAL EAGLES

Sometimes your relationship theme will take you into legal channels where you're either taking someone to court or trying to, or they're issuing you with papers. It's the same symbolism – you need to learn to play fair, work out what the rules of engagement are, what your side of the deal involves and whether you've overstepped your mark or someone else is going too far. Again, what is your contract?

Maybe you'll be helping someone determine what their rights are as a tenant or dealing with the pressures or trying to break a lease due to a breach of contract (things need repairing, it wasn't what you thought it was, you were landed with a lemon, etc). Maybe you're helping someone else navigate the legal rights of another – or consulting a professional to help you. Maybe as a landlord, you're figuring out the same stuff. The small print in all its glory is sure to raise its head. Some years justice prevails. We get what we deserve, and our fair share. In other years, we wind up on the flip-side of karma and have to learn what unfairness is (with a view to being a bit smarter down the line). Everything you do is put on the scales of karmic balance and you can't ever truly get away with anything that is unfair in your own eyes, whether it's this life or, for reincarnationalists (of which astrology seems to highlight as a given), in another lifetime.

Balance is balance and the scales are always rectified *eventually*. Good to know, right? When you think about taking the law into your own hands, or issuing someone a form of karmic payback – revenge does often figure in Cycle 8, your next one – it's simply not worth it, because what you give out ultimately comes back. Keep your end clean and things will get better – guaranteed.

SUPERFICIAL SWEETNESS

Since all Cycles have their downside, and Cycle 7 is all about balance, we had to finally end up here. The flip side of this Cycle is the desire to keep the peace at all costs, become a smiling, sugary sap who charms others to manipulate them into getting what they want, or just becoming smarmy-charmy in order to avoid any ugly scene or confrontation. Beauty turns to vanity when you are so concerned about the appearance of something you lose the substance beneath. You'll know you're veering into this if you start worrying about how others are seeing you (are you playing a role as opposed to just being you?) and so begin buying/wearing/doing/saying things to impress others. Then you've lost the plot and somewhere they'll probably ditch you because they psychically feel you're not really genuine, authentic and, in short ... Real. How unfair *that* may seem.

Be nice, but if you're unhappy say so; we'll appreciate knowing there's at least one person around we can rely on to keep it real. Just be sure wherever possible to keep it polite too.

BEAUTY and its BEAST

We desire beauty now – from hanging artwork, to buying nice things, to sharing good times with great people, to loving unions, and exquisite surroundings. Maybe we desire a beauty treatment, and go pamper ourselves, or give someone the same gift. We want others to treat us beautifully and we want others to share in the joy of life by showering them with feel-good compliments, genuinely felt and meant.

So... you may find in some Cycle 7 years you're faced with the 'not so beautiful' and this is a different concept to everyone ('beauty is in the eye of the beholder' etc). You may see ugly surroundings, unclean, unsavory or unbearable situations or people. The growth initiation is still the same – you get to set your standards and decipher and determine what it is you desire and what you find beautiful, and also whether you feel worthy enough to have and enjoy it.

THE PURSUIT OF PEACE

The possibilities for peace are endless. It starts with each individual on the planet resolving their own internal battles – especially the ones that show up for us in our personal 7-Cycle. And you're a major player in this Cycle, by how you handle yourself during this time. Your energy in Cycle 7 sends out shock waves or peace waves. Don't underestimate the power you have in how you handle all people and conflicts. My recommendation for this chapter of your life: 'Drop whatever you're fighting and back off'. You can always resume it, picking up where you left off, but for a moment, for a day at least, all weapons are to be discarded. And all players return to their corners.

This Cycle affords you a fantastic opportunity to gain another perspective on your daily dramas. They're only as strong as you make them. Fueling the fire only helps them burn brighter. Ever seen what happens to someone when the other person lets go of the rope in a tug-o-war? Or when the other person suddenly hops off the see-saw?

Peace isn't an eternal principle – all is in flux. But it's a more achievable constant, when we remain constant – *in honoring our feelings in any given moment.* Cycle 7 thrives on beauty, and yet often the most 'ugly' (in the eyes of the majority) is in so many ways the most beautiful. The regular guy or girl we pass on the street who beams confidence and humility, compared to the magazine model who treats others like scum. Suddenly, what's classed as typically beautiful is anything but. You'll see that a lot, during this Cycle.

What is beauty to you? Are *you* beautiful?

By focusing on finding, creating and being the beauty we are so drawn to, we suddenly find there is little space for conflict. We're 'full', and it's mostly empty hearts that make idle hands and lots of trouble.

CYCLE 7 INVITE
You're invited to the Be Beautiful Ball.
Be sexy, be stylish. Be seen.
Dress code: As you are.

CYCLE 7 ACTION PLAN
* Evaluate all your current relationships – patterns, apparent differences, similarities, pros and cons, points of contention and ways to compromise.
* Improve each relationship (clear the air, lay new ground rules, talk things out) or move on.
* Have a make-over, physically and in attitude.
* Be more open. Be kinder.
* Team up with someone else.
* Beautify your surroundings.

In a sharing year:
You commit, you get married, or you divorce and end up meeting someone who sweeps you off your feet. You're offered a special deal or golden handshake and are cashing in after accepting the opportunity of a lifetime (or at least the best offer you could ask for right now). You charm someone with a smile and suddenly they're your Public Relations manager and doing a better job than you could have done alone. You bump into someone who offers to share half the workload and you get to split the profit.

For everyone you lose, someone else arrives to take their place. For everything you lose, something else appears to replace it; better than before. It's 50-50 or even better, and they don't mind giving you 60-40 or 70-30! You make it up with someone you had a major fight with. Harmony prevails, after what you thought would be an unresolvable dispute. People just seem to be there for you. Life is simply beautiful. A surprise reconnection comes with an apology, when you did nothing and said nothing.

You get a chance to level the playing field and offer something to someone that really helps them out. You scratch their back, they massage yours, with a view to scratching yours and enjoying a nice massage down the line – or better yet, with no expectations, debt or IOUs involved. Love is the golden chain that connects you to others.

You create and are surrounded by beauty. You get your fair share, aren't afraid to stand up and be counted, and you wind up respected by those who matter. You end up the mediator in numerous conflicts and always find a way for everyone to be happy, or at least content they got something they wanted. You're nothing if not fair, and it shows in everything that happens to you. The scales of justice balance themselves out and life just works. Ahh...

In a wearing year:
You lose the deal, the lover, the help, the support. You give the shirt off your back and get a kick in the teeth. You give someone your parking space and are ticketed five times in one week. Life's a bitch – or were you just rotten in a past life? The scales of justice tip against you. Why?

You have to go solo, or you'd rather do it alone when you're landed with a contract, client, relationship that's everything you could do without. Karma seems to trip you up at every turn. Either someone is draining you expecting you to over-give without getting anything decent back for yourself, or your demands at someone else to pull their weight falls on deaf ears. It's not fair. You wished you'd read the small print because what the hell did you get yourself into?

Somehow, you're trapped in a karmic chain of pain. You want a recall, a re-vote, you want your money back, you want justice, you want revenge, you want to re-write the small print. Someone issues you with paperwork to cancel your contract suddenly. You move across country and the house isn't ready or the landlord has changed their mind. You don't see eye to eye with someone and because of your differences they (or you) pull the plug. What would have been a great union falls apart and you both walk your separate ways. Life is anything but balanced, it's more like a glass plate spinning in a moonlit circus show. One door closes and yet another one. You open your door and a passing truck soaks you or takes the door off by the hinges, and your insurance paperwork hasn't gone through yet.

Everyone seems to want (or be) something you don't want (or are not). Does life have it in for you? People just aren't reasonable, they're unfair and selfish and you're left to pick up the pieces when it all hits the fan or falls apart. And let's not talk about manners. They seem to fly out the window. A friend has the nerve to talk down to you. Family give you a lecture. A new lover reminds you of all the things you hated about life and yourself (or your dating life) when they replay and repeat actions and words that old lovers used to –

or they're just up to their usual games/tricks again! Telling them only creates further spirals. How could it get so unfair? You fall for someone who looks like an old flame, and ultimately get burned. Or everyone else is coupled and you're single. It's like you won a season-pass to the Ugly Awards, winning top billing for Loser of the Year.

Cycle Lesson

You're only as strong as your ability to handle the ups and downs of life – especially the downs. Bring your unique vision to others to receive their input since you can't manifest your Dream Vision alone. Sharing, then, becomes life's ultimate goal and challenge for you now, where the point is not to agree completely, but to allow for two energies to combine to create something new and something better than had you just stayed the course without aid.

Remain open, and prepare to extend your awareness to where others stand. You need input, and life brings many chances to incorporate these new vantage points into your awareness. As you share – both the beauty of your vision and the (in your self-judgment) ugly parts of your opinions/personality – so others gain and as you allow them to share, you gain too. They learn about you, you learn about them. Together you get stronger and can pave the way ahead with more clarity. It's all out on the table, and nothing lurks in the shadows waiting to trip you. Both parties are 100% present, aware, understanding, compromising, the rules of the game are understood and all parties can agree. Win-Win.

Celebrity Spotlight

- ⊙ In a nationally televised White House news conference during his Cycle 7, Bill Clinton claims he "did not have sexual relations" with Monica Lewinsky.
- ⊙ Judge Judy (famed for her US television show where she presides over a small claims court) is born with her Sun, Mercury, Venus, Mars and Neptune in Libra (Cycle 7).

Tips to successfully navigating your Cycle 7 Connection

- ⊙ Reach an agreement, whatever it is – even to 'agree to disagree'.
- ⊙ Charm your way ahead with sincere smiles and genuine flattery.
- ⊙ Don't underestimate the power of appearances.
- ⊙ Enjoy a dash of vanity, be beautiful.
- ⊙ Bring more beauty in – whatever that means to you.
- ⊙ Calm down – peace begins when you let go of conflict (inner and outer).
- ⊙ Listen to the other side.

- Find common ground, build bridges.
- Team up with people you resonate with instead of forcing others into boxes of your creation.
- Weigh up the pros and cons.
- Mediate – when faced with two options, create or choose a third.
- Refuse to take sides For or Against.
- Fence sit for a while.
- Start a new relationship – go on a date, agree to a business deal, handshake, merger, joint effort.
- Celebrate differences and diversity.
- Remember it takes two to tango – so dance or sit it out.
- Find a partner – to go to the gym with, or go dancing/shopping/sitting/thinking with.
- Enjoy company anywhere, anytime.
- Flirt freely – everyone loves a lover!
- Beautify at least one part of your life – your kitchen, bedroom, your office desk, a wall, your closet, yourself.
- Makeover time!
- Use symmetry, balance, harmony in all your work and in all you do.
- Refuse to bow to others' pressure, anger or aggression.
- Watch out for unnecessary people-pleasing – if need be, smile and draw a line.
- Learn some feng-shui and make your home space more 'auspicious' and 'fortuitous'.
- Tidy up at least one room; make it smell and look good.
- Wear brighter colors/learn color therapy.
- Tell someone how much you love them.
- Spend time with one person you can be yourself with.
- Be yourself with anyone you meet.
- Have an astrology reading.
- Ask advice from someone you trust.
- Go dancing with a partner.
- Do anything with someone else – two heads are better than one.

~ Surf Cycle 8 ~

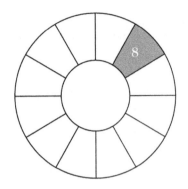

Time to Dive Deeper,
Give It Up (and Get Back Up)
and Pursue Passionate Purpose

Darker Detours courtesy of:

The elusive tall, dark, handsome
    stranger
The bank, creditors, tax office
Government agencies
Undertakers/funeral directors/the
    dying
Gay, lesbian, transgender, transsexuals
Accountants/investment advisers
Tantric teachers/energy workers
Income Tax/Internal Revenue System
Private investigators/researchers
Occult specialists/psychics
Debt consolidators/ collection
    agencies
Sex columnists/advisers/escorts

Relationship experts/counselors
Exterminators/plumbers
Scorpio people
Shady, mysterious or powerful people
Those who live close to the edge/
    danger
Your father's friends
People who 'talk to the dead'
Recycling junkies
Goths/vampires/late night lurkers
Witches/wizards/wiccans
Hypnotherapists/hypnotists
Your partner's accountant or
    divorce lawyer
Brokers/ bail bonds/ loan sharks

What you'll need:

An X ray machine/night vision goggles
Bedroom eyes in the back of your head
A secret stash of tax-free cash
Gas and a lighter
Breadcrumbs to find your way back

218

The Eight Initiation is your time of transformation, when you, yourself, your life, and the people and things in it, are moving from one state to another. Nothing is allowed to stagnate by remaining rooted in its present condition, and how can we have a new beginning if we don't take care of the old stuff hanging around?

Something needs to 'die' now, or be left behind and this Cycle will bring about the energy to allow for a chapter change. Just as midwives help us birth something, we now need those who can aid us in letting go – but who teaches us this? Who's playing funeral director in your life, this month? In some years, you'll look to play this role in others' lives helping them turn over a new leaf and move on while some years you'll see others appear to help you with this process yourself.

Ah, there's an important word: **process**. All is a process – don't expect to magically let go of everything that has to leave now. It's our nature to hold on, to dig our nails in to retain some sense of a status quo in our lives, but this particular stage of your annual seasonal Cycle shows it's tough to do that. Something has to go, something has to change, something has to die and be reborn. It doesn't necessarily have to be a person or a possession (although that's still a possibility if it's a necessary stage in your development) it could just as easily be a way of life, a habit or something else that isn't aiding you any longer.

So accepting that something has to give, is the first step to embracing the theme of your month ahead. Got it? Great. Now breathe…!

Overall, this Cycle is kind of like your personal Halloween – when you get to creep around in a mask and hide your feelings from everyone (or your motives, your secrets or parts of yourself and your life you'd rather not have in the tabloids, or spread around your coworkers), or you get to unmask people and situations in hiding *or* find *yourself* unmasked – standing naked before someone, with your most valuable physical assets dangling there or your most hideous side (and feelings) hanging out, for everyone to see. It all depends how much you can cope with, how much the 'dark' scares you, and how much you don't really like about yourself and your current circumstances that will reflect the lengths you'll go to protect and hide it all. If you're happy, you'll fear little in Cycle 8. Those brave enough to be vulnerable will find some amazing treasure buried beneath the layers of rubbish.

Those with something to hide are powerful and formidable enemies (as are those who think others are hiding something). So it can all get a bit creepy, shady, cloak-and-dagger, horror-movie stalker-special this Cycle if you're not careful. And you could end up on the nation's most wanted billboard, or six feet under. Either way, when it's done, it's done.

But was it worth it?

See this as your 'taking out the trash' phase of the yearly journey you're on, whether you're just bagging up clothes you're clinging to that are clinging to you since they're two sizes two small (but which you love so much), tossing out stuff from under the bed, or more serious things like working on the major temper you have, the seething jealousy you've been feeling lately, the forgiveness you can't quite reach in relation to someone who hurt you, working out if a relationship is squeezing the life out of you, or even a tumor that needs removing from your body.

Stuff that's 'built up' in your life has reached boiling point somewhere no doubt, and it's time to make some decision of what will stay and what must go! Grab your trash bags, bleach, sieve and prepare to get dirty!

DARK KNIGHT OF THE SOUL: aka SURVIVE THEN THRIVE

Intensity ripples through your life; it always does when big stuff is happening. For one, we go into survival mode. Ever seen a snake shed its skin? It crawls away somewhere quiet and temporarily goes blind, its vision impaired as it outgrows its old, restrictive skin and casts it off. A friend of mine who owned a snake told me it's dangerous to approach one at this time, as it's likely to thrash about out of self-protection and you're virtually guaranteed to be bitten.

Apply that to humans and you have a sticky scenario waiting to happen somewhere this month.

Survival mode means hormones begin flying. Adrenalin. Frustration. Anger. Rage. Fear. This Cycle you're likely to need sex a lot more than usual, or at least you'll be thinking about it. But since this period also is about extremes (survival mode means fight or flight), maybe you'll go completely the other way and totally shut down, or swear off any sexual contact altogether as a form of self-control (or controlling another). The last thing we want is to be vulnerable – but that's exactly what this Cycle 8 Initiation is asking of us! Understand that point and you'll have this Cycle in the bag, and cruise through the dark alleys of your soul and life experience with a beacon of hope instead of a sharp object in your hand.

Whatever the case, sex (one of the most vulnerable expressions of the self) is still becoming a major issue for you – as are any situations involving an emotional charge. Intensity comes in many forms. And that is what you're seeking, consciously or otherwise. Maybe you're just seething with anger, hate, envy, sexual hunger, revenge. You name it. Maybe you're ready to explode. Maybe you're faced with someone ready to 'unleash' – and you're in the firing line. Whether it's you or someone else, the theme is still the same – the healthy purging of unhealthy 'stuff' that's reached a peak and needs to come out. How it comes out will dictate how this Cycle unfolds for you. Getting caught in the dark energy that rises up from your depths is a challenge you may face, and which may spiral out of control quickly if you don't get a handle on it.

Power games abound and you may find that keeping this chapter handy just saves you from possibly losing something precious. Face the dark and then prepare and expect to face the dawn. Nothing lasts forever. No matter how long the 'night' feels. And without the other (the light or the night) we have no reference point, no way to know which direction to move. Life loses all meaning.

Many of you will notice the age old emotional fears welling up inside you at one point during Cycle 8 (or repeatedly) which can be boiled down, according to Gregg Braden in *The Divine Matrix*, to one of three universal fears: **1: Separation and abandonment**, **2: Low self-worth** and **3: Surrender and trust.**

⊚ **Separation and abandonment** issues surface when someone does the death thing for us and cuts us off, leaves us, runs away, betrays us and otherwise ditches us. We're pulled from the safety and warmth of the womb again. It never gets easier. It hurts. Time helps but the initial cut goes deep and scar tissue must be built up. Allow then for your defenses to grow back by being gentle, going easy and nursing yourself as you would a small child who feels shut out in the cold. Separation and abandonment issues always appear to show us where we have abandoned ourselves by not honoring our feelings, listening to ourselves, fulfilling our own needs or voicing them and so forth.

⊚ **Low self-worth** issues are always reflected back to us when others treat us badly. They mirror how we feel about ourselves, whether we care to admit that or not (or even know it yet). We somewhere sense we deserved it or why did it happen? We beat ourselves up and then allow others to do the same. That's the pattern that emerges now for you to acknowledge and then free yourself from, by remembering that it's how you feel about you, that forms the basis of who and what you'll attract into your life. Everyone is equal. Humans are bags of emotions and we all want the same thing. To feel good. And we all deserve it. Start there and stop focusing or chasing things that make you feel bad. Low self-esteem issues always appear to remind us that when we don't feel good, it's because we're not treating ourselves well and thus we have a choice to change direction or tack.

⊚ **Surrender and trust** issues are usually brought up by the above two issues. How can you be open and allow others in when you've been hurt before? By realizing that it was your opinion of yourself that was a major part of the puzzle. By re-evaluating who you are and what you're worth (and giving up that awful energy of guilt – forgive yourself or another to truly free yourself now!) you can then trust and surrender knowing full well you have your own back, because you can only meet how you see yourself – through the eyes of another. Trust yourself. Surrender to yourself. And those who truly love you for who you are will find you, because, finally, we love ourselves just how we are too. We're not perfect, we're human. Love yourself as the package deal you are. You're perfect for someone out there. Guaranteed. First you've got to be perfect for *you*.

How you handle each and every small frustration or trigger (when your button is pressed) is likely to be related to one of these. And of course, underlying it all is the fear of death: the fear of the ultimate ending.

DRAWING OR DEALING THE DEATH CARD:
Deep destruction and reaching for rebirth?

You may want to shy away from the whole death thing but you really can't in this Cycle. It finds you. From movies on life after death (think *Ghost*), to talk shows dedicated to the subject, from books you read to dreams you have, to what your friend says to you on the phone. Maybe you hear that someone you know has died. Then the next question becomes how did they die and 'why?' Was it an accident or did they die naturally? Why is death such a shock when it happens? What's the whole death thing about anyway, you ask. Maybe the death is not literal but symbolic – someone is going through a divorce and a relationship has 'died', maybe you're quitting a job or moving away to a new location (with all the inherent stress of these big experiences).

Whether the Grim Reaper actually tries to take a swipe at you and you end up having an out-of-body experience, or whether you end up in a body-bag at the morgue, you'll notice the theme of death hangs around you like a bad smell (or maybe you won't because you're actually in the body bag, in which case you have nothing to worry about anymore ... kidding).

In some years (not all thankfully) the not-so-nice side of death comes to the forefront and you get to see firsthand what happens when someone transitions over to the other side, and you're left wondering what it all means. Like one Cycle 8 when I was sitting in a restaurant and ended up being forced to listen to a TV show playing on the TV screens above me and across from me, about a woman whose body was weighed down with bricks and thrown into a river. Nice viewing to eat to. Or how about my friend who in his own 8-Cycle, heard his father had turned a gun on himself because things got so bad (thankfully his father was fine but it gave him my friend a good scare).

In every Cycle, we either get to experience the theme directly or we are surrounded by holographic representations of the theme. So while reading the material in this particular Cycle, keep in mind that the lessons are passed on either via direct experience or involvement or through witnessing others going through their own Cycle 8 transitions.

You may be thankful, then, that you're reminded how fragile life is and how grateful you are for the people still in your life – and if you're not, you may be humbled by the experience of losing someone and then – too late, understanding just what it meant to have them around. The saddest thing is to not be able to say goodbye or I love you to someone you care deeply about, who leaves.

Maybe you're drawn to skulls, skeletons, and other symbols of death. The Grim Reaper himself. Perhaps you get close to people who were or are close to the edge themselves – either through failed attempts at suicide (I passed a balloon and note tied to a bench on the pier in Ventura, from someone who had obviously lost their life there, and on the same day earlier I had seen a large procession of cars with 'funeral' labels in their back windows, escorted by police officers on motorbikes, snaking along the freeway following a hearse containing the coffin). All during Cycle 8.

Some people may be trying to overcome a dangerous habit or addiction or losing themselves to it. Others may just be close to the theme of death like I was – perhaps someone you know nearly lost their dog, or was raped or robbed or suffered an accident and survived. Hospice or hospital patients. The elderly. Or those who just faced a break-up. Whatever it is, it all teaches you one thing during this Cycle – that *we're vulnerable, that we can protect ourselves but when our time is up, it's up. So we may as well make the most of everything since no one is really 'safe' and the best experiences (the stuff we take with us when we go) are really all about those key times when we allow ourselves to be vulnerable enough to grow.*

In the Tarot, the Death card (the one bad movie writers love to wheel out as an 'ominous sign') actually doesn't represent death as we know it. It doesn't mean someone will die. It means that a transition has just taken place (past) or is taking place right now (present) or is about to take place (future). A transformation. A resurrection. A metamorphosis. A baby is about to be born that changes someone's life forever. A move to another country shifts everything. A caterpillar on the way to becoming a butterfly. A relationship begins or ends and nothing will remain as it once was. Life is full of big stuff and massive change. Total and complete. Cycle 8 teaches us just how to handle this, and how we are able to handle it, often by witnessing how others handle it.

The beautiful thing to remember during 8-Cycles is that nothing, absolutely nothing, happens to you in this physical lifetime that you're not on some level equipped to handle. You'll get through this, you'll see.

THE TANTALIZING TASTE FOR TABOO

Creeping around in the dungeon of your soul (or someone else's) or poking around in the dark shadowy places leads you to a sudden (or re-ignited) interest in taboos, which may surprise you as you unleash your darker side. What do we mean by 'dark side'? You don't need to don your Darth Vader mask or take up serial killing. Everyone has a shadow – the part you don't talk about over breakfast, or you pretend you don't have.

The little voice inside you that wants to get back at the person who pushed in front or took your parking space. The little man or woman inside you that wants to murder the noisy neighbor or kidnap their dog as punishment.

You may be shocked, but save it. We all have these possible people inside of us. The side you think others will reject 'if only they knew'. Not everyone is open to the idea of telling others they are heavily into spanking. Did you know some women (and men) hunger to feel a rape scenario? I know some of them personally. Whatever secret thing you are feasting your dark-mind on, is sure to come back for another go at you, to remind you of your lusty desires, your carnal nature and your reptilian brain – the animalistic side of yourself.

Maybe you'll find yourself or someone close to you scouring the internet for 'death' related subjects and information or sexual stuff (yes, we'll keep coming back to that theme so get used to it). I know, I know ... we're not taught to talk about these things (let alone secretly want them) but this Cycle is about blowing the lid off all parts of your psyche, leaving no stone unturned and digging down under it to see what dwells there. If you repress it, it'll come back during other Cycles to bite you (and who needs a sex obsession when you're in your 2nd Initiation trying to make money?) You'd be surprised how often the two go hand in hand, and we do know that sex and money have long been connected.

Right, so let it all out now, while you can, while the air is ripe (oh yes, a lot is ripe, right now) and possibly on the verge of being rotten, and the season of sex is upon you.

SEX SEX SEX SEX SEX!

That heading is for those of you reading this book in a public place. I like to give something to the person next to you on the bus, something worth spying over (and spying is a Cycle 8 theme too). Cycle 5 was also really about sex (for fun) but Cycle 8 makes it more important, more urgent, and potentially more dangerous. With intercourse/ making love (or whatever you want to call it) becoming such a prevalent theme in 8-Cycles, watch for sexual 'issues' that may pop up if you're going overboard and using sex as a means of control, self-esteem building or manipulation. Power can also come swinging back as the pendulum clunks you in the head this Cycle if you're abusing your position. Sexually transmitted diseases, and other embarrassing personal problems, could be a warning not to take your body (and what you do with it, and with whom) for granted. Blockages in the body are also a sure sign you're not doing your duty of letting things go. Watch out for signs.

In some years you're going to feel as sexy as hell and other people will notice. Sometimes you're going to feel like no one wants you, or you have some form of sexual dysfunction. Bad feelings can degenerate into stress in relationships when there's a sexual imbalance – is your partner oversexed and you don't want any? Maybe you're both not on the same page during this Cycle. Where do you stand on infidelity? Is it 'cheating' if you're not playing the game? Do you really and truly trust (yourself and others)? Often we forget we're capable of the exact same things we're so worried someone else is doing (why else would we worry that they were doing that to us?) Conceiving of a possibility means it's well within your own reach or you'd not have even thought of it as an idea.

It's a bitter pill to swallow, but one you'll have to digest at some point. We judge the darkness in others that exists within ourselves. How will you resolve these issues if and when they arise? Can you be open, and transcend the darkness you feel by bringing it into the light of conscious awareness? Cycle 8 gives you the chance but *only if you're willing to try*.

LET IT GO – ATTACHMENT ACHES
Let's get back to this 'letting it go' theme – what is it this time around, this year, this month, this week, you could live without, do without and make your life easier by tossing out? Maybe you just need to accept that something is over and has been for quite some time. Maybe someone lands a bombshell at your doorstep that it's over because *they* say so (and you have no recourse). Maybe it's taken from you, ripped from you in fact, and your soul feels torn along with it. Pain, during this Cycle anyway, comes from fighting the change of tide and holding onto what could have, would have, should have happened. If it's gone, going, dying, dead or about to leave (or you're leaving), then accept it as some cosmic clock that's chiming its chapter change or closure, and know that it's as it should be.

You can't lose what is yours, really and truly. So breathe. If it is meant for you, it'll return. Sometime, somewhere. And if it goes, then kiss it goodbye and smile with appreciation that you actually had it in the first place for a time, on loan as it were, from the universe (even our bodies are only ours for the duration, until our lease is up!)

So, you're getting rid of something (spiritual weight, I like to call it) but what then? What is coming to replace it? Your next Cycle after this is going to bring those answers so let's not get ahead of ourselves. Your next task is to decide *how* you're going to transform. Pour gas on yourself and flick a lighter? Ditch everything, move to Spain and change your name?

You can try these techniques but you may want to go for the less strenuous ones – like meditation, or yoga, or some form of detox plan. Simplifying your life and going *without things* may be useful too. Or divert your passion into something you really enjoy. A change of appearance could be on the cards as you decide to shave your head or radically alter your wardrobe. It helps you change your viewpoint again (as you did in your first Cycle).

Holding on will cause you pain in Cycle 8; a necessary time of shedding, and yes you *will* gain by losing, however much outer appearances or feelings seem to point to the contrary. Let's say that again – in 8-Cycles **you will gain by losing**. Attachment is all about Cycle 2, the polar opposite of this one. You can't maintain, you can't keep it the same, you can't dig stubbornly and push, you can't harbor anything, or it comes out and rears up in front of you snarling when you reach your Cycle 8.

Wow, it can get pretty ugly, pretty nasty. You may feel like destroying yourself, tearing your skin away, murdering someone or just sitting crying (a healthier alternative to the former choices).

You won't want to give in, to surrender, to let someone else have the power in Cycle 8. Sometimes maybe you shouldn't (like letting someone at home beat you up every night). But at other times, fighting only prolongs the pain and keeps you from the real issue, that something has to die and be reborn in a new form for you to be reborn in a new phase of existence yourself. Evolution is painful sometimes. We see that a lot. Seeds crack out of hard shells (that can't feel good), babies cry when teething. Snakes as we have heard, freak out when they shed a skin. And ask any mother what childbirth feels like. Something so wondrous and beautiful. It hurts like hell. Even bones ache when they grow. Ouch.

Life can be painful.

Well, the pain is increased the more you resist change and try to keep things the same. That should bring you some relief when you find yourself pushing against current events in your life.

In *your* Cycle 8 you have to feel it all intensely, one last time, fully, with all of your being until you die ... meaning you reach the end point. Literally perhaps and you exit your body. Or hopefully more symbolically. You die to one way by forgiving, or you decide to forget or simply move on and keep walking ahead and leave it behind you, as your old self crumbles in the ashes along with everything about yourself that you were (or thought you were) yesterday.

Cycle 8 is pretty complete. It's emotional (like Cycle 4) but what wasn't left behind at that point really has no choice but to go now. By choice or by force. And the magical part you'll come to learn soon enough, is that you never needed it and you can live without it. You can. You'll see.

THE URGE TO MERGE

Cycle 8 is an amazing time. What? After everything we've covered so far! Yes. Don't get me wrong, Cycle 8 isn't always about losing, and separating, it's also about coming together (ha, what a pun for a major sexual Cycle). It's about merging. Assets, bank accounts, our minds, bodies and souls. Our resources are shared. We feel a hunger to join on a deeper level, to go beyond the honeymoon into the fire and through it and out the other side, where all the dross is burned off and all that is left is the pure, untouchable stuff: loyalty, affection, care; all names for love.

The power of deep change is felt through this merging. Not only do we find power in numbers (two heads are better than one, two incomes are more powerful etc), but we find our own power through our emotions (we feel strongly about someone especially when we fear losing them). Trust becomes the necessary tool and safety and soul-space the incentive to getting this close. It's dangerous, it's dark, we have no guarantee we'll be safe. No guarantee we won't lose, or be hurt. But therein lies the ultimate magic of Cycle 8 – if we're willing to venture deeper, we'll reach the good stuff.

Surrendering the ego becomes the ultimate quest, when it's no longer just about you. You have the values, emotions, and life challenges of another to contend with. What they go through, you go through simultaneously, 'for better or worse' or for some, 'till death do us part'. And you can be sure that our partners are chosen on many levels because of these very issues and themes that we ourselves need to play out, compassionately played out by those we have come to be so fixated on, or head over heels for.

Often it's not the person we fall for but who they represent, energetically, in our lives. Some facet of their being, that reminds us so strongly of who we are, who we're trying to be and what we need ourselves, to work on. Attraction and desire pull us to them like a magnet (which began back in Cycle 7).

XXX POWER

You feel your power in moments when something surges through you, when something you feel grabs you and won't release you it seems. You feel your intensity. Like the build up to an orgasm. You feel how amazingly strong a sensation or zinging emotion it is. Overpowering in fact. Consuming. Entire. Intense. Passionate. Complete.

All.

That's when we reach a turnaround point in Cycle 8. Satiation (fully following something to its ultimate conclusion, filling yourself with it 100% so every fiber of your being is drenched in it) leads to a final understanding that we have to move on. That we've reached an impasse and something has to shift or we may as well shut up shop, hang up our life and say, "I won't go any further, I'm done".

If you're still here, then you're not done.

Build-ups of pressure are your ultimate lesson and gift in Cycle 8. They lead to explosions (life creates shifts on the outside – you lose a job, gain one, lose a lover, gain one, get ill, get better, things start over or end, new chapters begin, things finally reach a peak) or implosions (life creates shifts on the inside – you find out something bad through an x-ray, you feel depressed or angry). Inner shifts lead to outer ones with the same intents and purposes. To effect the same shift your soul seeks now – to release yourself from something you're chaining yourself to.

Either way, release is your mission. Whether you blow sexually, or whether you blow your metaphorical lid, blow your cover, blow the deal, release blood, release tears, release someone from prison, release someone from your life, release yourself from guilt, whatever it is, release will find you. But will you allow it? Either way it'll arrive. You'll find it. Somehow, or some way. You can't escape and nor are you meant to. Sweet release is yours and it's imminent.

Cycle 8 will seal the deal, close the door and nail the coffin on some things, but only ... only ... when you're fully done with it so you know you won't go digging it up again. Until then you'll be metaphorically on your hands and knees at 5am scratching at graveyards, dirty with a flashlight in your mouth or moon overhead, trying to dig up what was buried way back when you believed you were done with it, but discovered lately you haven't at all.

So don't be done ... until you're done.
And if it's done with you, it's giving you an out already. Take it.

You're the prisoner in Cycle 8 sometimes, and you're always the prison guard simultaneously. Why? Because you can choose to up and walk away from an emotion you no longer like feeling. Why keep yourself stuck? Everything present in your life serves a purpose, but it doesn't need to be forever. You have the final say.

You will go further, you will go beyond this point and you will continue growing. That's life. Cycle 8 is amazing at showing you your soul-grit, your strength of will and what you are capable of when the chips are down, counted or taken from you. Who are you, when all is said and done?

Prepare to be amazed.

WHEN IS ENOUGH ENOUGH?

Good question. So when has it ended? Is it ever really 'over'? Well, you get to decide in Cycle 8 or the entire phase helps you decide. Generally the theory is in a relationship that if you're *ready to run*, there's something you're probably *running from* within you that needs resolving via the relationship (or perhaps therapy). A button is being triggered. Cycle 8 is great at doing that. And you're virtually guaranteed to wind up running into it again in the form of another person and another relationship, perhaps more extreme the next time.

If you're ready to *walk*, peacefully, feeling you've done all you can and it's better for you to continue on ahead alone, then it is probably the right time to end the union. It may shift down the line but for now it appears the most peaceful solution.

Again, it's just a theory and only you can know what's right for you, but it's worth a thought.

Are you ready to run or walk?

QUIT IT!

It's worth pointing out again, that Cycle 8 is the polar opposite to Cycle 2 (the time when I said you should gorge). So Cycle 8 is about abstaining, quitting that bad habit, and trying to go without (for a change). It won't kill you. If anything it'll make you stronger when you realize you don't actually need it. You can live without it. There's a season to eat and a season to fast. Figuratively (or literally) it's your time to trim back to the essentials or face the penalty for over-fixating on any one thing. So now's your time to kick the smoking habit (if you're trying), lessen your sexual conquests, quit stalking that ex, cease holding a grudge, and so forth. If it's not healthy, this is your best time of the year to scrap it.

DIGGING FOR THE DIAMOND IN THE DIRT

Major change! That is basically what Cycle 8 can be boiled down to if you didn't catch that already. Some years you'll love the change before you, other years you just want to sit at home in your comfy pants and lock the world outside. Not this month. It's not always about death. So don't feel down if you read this and think you're in for one hell of a time. It all depends on your emotional response to life's events and you *do* have control over that portion of your human life adventure. It's really about *transition*. And death is one of the big ones.

You'll be aided in this quest by at least one Scorpio person who'll either help guide you through the darkness or the intensity or show you just what pitfalls to avoid if you want to steer clear of the more exasperating aspects of this Cycle, or teach you by example just how to handle the whole tricky Cycle-8-world with willpower, strength, relationship loyalty and a head held high.

On a lighter note, the theme of digging could see you burying a time capsule instead of someone you love; digging up dirt on someone or finding something from under the bed you lost, or scouring antique stores for a special find. You're peering in the nooks and crannies and it involves a 'mystery' – you never know how it will turn out; a lot like life itself, really.

SHARING THE SPOILS OR SPOILING YOUR SHARE

How much money do you have in the bank? Is it all yours? Are you sure? Hmm... This is another one of those money Cycles only this time you get to focus on money you have tied up in other things or other people – credit card plans, your partners bank account, insurance schemes, your joint account, the business venture you're sharing the rewards on.

Anything you have tangled up with someone else becomes a major focus of your attention. Maybe you and your partner are deciding on a major purchase and have to pool your money together. Maybe you lend someone some. Your partner suddenly goes through a major financial shift, affecting the monetary landscape of your togetherness. In other years you may be working out a last will and testament, receiving a trust fund, setting up an insurance policy (or changing the one you currently have because it's daylight robbery) or being audited because your tax paperwork is incomplete. Debts: the money you owe others, the things you owe others or the things they owe you, are also focuses in some years – what if you don't get it back? Can you let it go or will you set up a legal battle that becomes full scale in your Cycle 9 next month, or becomes a continuation of a battle begun last Cycle (see also the section on 'Legal Eagles' in Cycle 7)? Don't worry, it may actually be the best thing.

Now before you insist on thinking this Cycle is all about loss, and are about to put this book down, wait! We said this Cycle is about *transformation* – when things change form and when you deal with big intense stuff. From simple things like your car (which needs an overhaul), or having to buy a new camera because your old one breaks down. It doesn't need to be always so dramatic. This is an amazing time of year when whatever you're invested in can change to become something much, much more meaningful and rewarding! In some years, the relationship you're in goes into unchartered territory and suddenly you're picking up each other's thoughts, giving someone a key, or opening a joint bank account, because you trust, because they're a soul mate and because you'd die for them. Impressive stuff. Don't you really crave that sort of depth?

True, the flip side could be that you wind up in a shouting match or an actual physical brawl because anger has reached an explosive level and the dark stuff is pouring forth, and it's virtually impossible to control the pressure relief by then. If something needs to come out, it will, during this Cycle. If you can, be conscious of this and be ruthlessly honest with yourself – and others – and force yourself into that vulnerable place to let your fear/worry/darkness/anger out, before it builds in the secrecy and hidden depths of the shadows (where you repress it, try to ignore it, or rise above it). In Cycle 8, you rise above things and heal by letting the pus out – like a painful boil. It's ugly, but once it's released it heals amazingly fast and feels a hell of a lot better!

A business deal or merger can undergo a major overhaul and suddenly you're bringing in heaps of extra cash from your joint plans, programs, investments and financial wheeling and dealing – possibly even a lottery win (Cycle 8 relates to money that you don't technically 'earn' but which comes your way anyway). Bingo, literally! Out of nowhere. Whatever you're involved with (be it a person, company or group) it'll change form into something deeper, more intense, more passionate, more genuine and loyal – or in the flip years, it will turn into obsessive, cut-throat, manipulative situations and people who you can't wait to get rid of (but whom you may be addicted to for the drama and 'burn' they provide for you).

Which is it this year?

So, as you've gathered, you've arrived at a point in time and space that's anything but light. Whether you're stalked on the phone by the credit card or loan company, or you, yourself are stalking your ex (or new lover) to watch their whereabouts, it's all about what lies beneath – hidden feelings, buried treasure, hidden money, things behind/underneath or locked away inside. And it's your job to get to grips with what's going on away from prying eyes and behind the scenes. And to decide if it's worth your soul investment or if it's a vampire that's draining you dry.

The sweet relief you experience when you give up pushing, forcing control and trying to dominate your life, will be something you enjoy so much next month, when the dust settles ... but you can start today. Like an orgasm, a sneeze, a cough or a sigh – letting go is exhaling – you have to do it in order to take in new fresh air. It ultimately feels good, so loosen your grip and dive.

CAUGHT IN THE WEB

Entanglements are inevitable when you get involved with others, you owe them something, you sign contracts, you get into deals, you share your body, your house key, your bank balance. Yes, even germs sometimes. You share feelings, secrets, you become vulnerable, you lose power, you're at the mercy of another in so many ways. You have to lean sometimes. Or catch someone. Trust begins to develop. It may be betrayed, but you're open, raw, and you either let yourself experience this, or you clam up and brick yourself up and harden inside. It's a choice we are all faced with during our personal Cycle 8 passage. Remain open and grow, or clam up and keep the world out so we can't be hurt. Our choice dictates how our lives and perhaps our healing will progress.

RELATIONSHIP RIPPLES

Things always get heavier, darker or just more intense or serious, and during Cycle 8 you're likely to experience at least one major turning point, especially in close and intimate encounters. Maybe you both come out of the long, dark tunnel you've been stuck trudging through together and get to experience a deeper level of intimacy stripped now of the ego masks you put up to protect yourselves from hurt. Maybe you wind up *in* that tunnel, because you've avoided the deeper ramifications of your meeting or current situations and events (that may reflect past issues or personal hurts one or both of you carry inside), and the issues you need to work out together (or alone as individuals). Separation may figure in your path to give you the space and loss you need to gain insight and understanding.

'Stuff' comes up here also – especially that which has been building for a while. Suddenly, after the wedding and honeymoon, you have to deal with the less attractive things about the person you've come to know. And that includes yourself. Prepare to discover you may be angrier than you thought. That you seethe with the best of them. That perhaps you claim you're direct, yet you seem to do passive aggressive things, to get a reaction. That you're just as 'bad' when pushed. That your inner world isn't a bed of roses. That you also may have an inner murderer (although *you* may have the safety switch, others don't, and they can flip it before you flip out and pull the trigger). Either way, Cycle 8 pulls stuff up you may not want to deal with, but it's a time when your inner light is directed into the dark recesses of your psyche for a reason – *to clear out what is controlling you from behind the scenes*. That's why you want to probe other peoples' psyches too and worry if they are lying or wonder if you're right to be suspicious – are they cheating, stealing, swindling? You only feel this or wonder this now because of your ability to be and do these very same things.

If you're wondering what material may be ready to bust out of your repression closet, look to the sign your Cycle 8 falls in. Gemini could show you that the thoughts you keep under wraps, the way you view things or the way you communicate to others isn't altogether healthy and needs to 'die' and be reborn in a healthier way.

Aries could show that your ability or inability to express and deal with anger issues could erupt. Capricorn could show your control tendencies or feelings of being out of control come to the fore. And so on. (Refer to **www. SurfingYourSolarCycles.com** for sign attributes.)

Knowledge is power – it could just save you from a really ugly scene. If you've already gone through that ugly scene and are thinking 'wow, too late', don't worry – it takes two to tango and anything that manifests is a perfect opportunity for both people present to deal with their own individual darkness.

Issues relating to infidelity, betrayal, deceit, violence, backstabbing, secrecy, abuse, underhand actions and other nasties could surface for you to deal with. The dark side of human emotion is never easy, but it would help to use a bit more detachment in dealing with it all if something does indeed rise up. Tricky but not impossible. No one is perfect. Was the act to intentionally hurt?

And if so, can you forgive it (and yourself), because no one is perfect? Was it just simple human nature or error?

8-Cycles aren't so much about what other people are doing, but more about our own level of self-mastery, which we can work on to take ourselves to new heights. To learn to rise above the more base human feelings, and be unafraid to feel them but then to work through them, so they don't become our main fixation and focus. What we focus on does have a habit of becoming more important in our reality.

Can you rise above what's currently happening by taking a larger perspective and flying above the scenario instead of getting lost continually in the intricacies of the moment, down below?

Think of this quickly – the most peaceful, tranquil place you've ever been. Go there in your mind. It exists still (and hopefully in the real world too). Somewhere, peace and quiet still exists. Go there during difficult times. Let the dust settle then continue. As a popular poster my brother gave me says, 'Keep Calm and Carry on'.

All you can do is take care of your own power. Abuse it and you'll always wonder if someone is doing or will do the same to you. In many ways, karma is self-generated. See how it works? What you put out will always, always without fail, find you. Maybe just through a nagging worry or eternal guilt. If you do it, chances are someone else will or *could* do it to you. So you can tell a lot about someone from how other people treat them. Those surrounded by deceitful people need to understand if they are lying – perhaps even to themselves. We always attract what we are, in Cycle 8 it becomes exaggerated perhaps or more extreme and intense, so we cannot avoid it and smile and keep it sweet (that's Cycle 7!), we just have to face it.

Don't worry, this Cycle comes once a year and you get to squeeze the spot and release the pressure. I had a skin abscess healed with surgery during Cycle 8 one year, I won't go into the nasty details but suffice it to say that releasing yucky-stuff was the name of the game. And inevitable sweet relief! That really is all there is to it, but it may feel hard when it's happening and, yes, often painful.

But remember the relief that is waiting for you at the other side.

And the stuff that comes up doesn't necessarily need to be dark or 'bad', it could just as easily be beautiful. Yet it will always be tinged with something serious or heavy because the nature of the 8-Cycle is not to shy away from the big stuff. What happens to those who win the lottery? Intense emotions, nervousness, and often the issue of family who come out of the woodwork demanding a share! All key Cycle 8 themes. In the best of years, commitment deepens. Our love ripens. We show how truly there for another we are, often during some of the most difficult periods. We are willing to push through our intimacy blocks and get closer.

233

It's not easy, it's not safe or encouraged, but it's well worth it when we get to the other side.

ALL OR NOTHING – EVERYTHING OR BUST

You're either *in* or *out*. No middle ground. If you do find yourself straddling a fence, sooner or later it'll be blown over or someone will come along and bulldoze it and claim the land and you'll have to budge anyway. Cycle 8 reminds you that for all the compromising you did in Cycle 7, sometimes you have to throw it all away (the differences, the conflicts) and merge with what you desire, and become one with it. So who and what do you merge with (because by wanting to, you are saying you want to become like that)? Passion is the fuel to aid you in deciding that if it pulls you and makes you feel uplifted, follow it. If it pulls on you, feels intense and you feel depleted, drained or anxious, chances are it's not so nice a path. We're not talking romantic butterflies we're talking a feeling of inner dis-ease.

So ask yourself, are you going to truly *commit* now, and prove your allegiance to something, a path, project or person? Can you give all of your being, because to get 100% you need to give it now. Cause and effect. Your entire being is involved in this process, so no mediocrity, no middle ground, and no maybes and mumbling are allowed.

YES OR NO?

Extreme emotions are all good and well but if they lead to extreme behavior of course you can run yourself into the ground, or get thrown in prison too. Cycle 8 is a Cycle not a spiral (even though the symbol of the 8 is an infinity looping back on itself, take that as a warning). You may have to replay the past a bit more to see what works and what's rotten. And there we go again, Cycle 8 says take out the trash and separate out the potatoes that are starting to fester. Ever seen what happens to dying potatoes? I found a bag stashed at the back of my cupboard once that somehow had slipped into another dimension, and the bag was still sealed, and was full of maggots and flies (maggots grow into flies apparently). Taking out the trash is much better than dealing with the consequences of further disease down the line. (And for those of you saying, "What a messy Pisces" – no, I didn't know the bag was there). Okay, so shoot me. On second thoughts don't, this is Cycle 8, after all.

As in life, it's not long before bad stuff spreads and takes over the good parts and you have to throw the whole lot out or work that much harder at separating out what's salvageable from what is long gone.

Before your life gets that dirty and rotten, stop the spread of disease by focusing on the problem area long enough to relieve pressure, cut out the core of the problem, hit the roots where they sprout to stop further growth, or simply let it wither by *focusing your attention away from it*. Things are fed by energy – focus, attention, love, call it what you will. If you focus on it, it grows. Cycle 8 says do so (give it attention), to at least understand where you are, but do something about it or refocus away from it. Or you'll be stuck fighting dragons, bats, witches and other inner and outer demons and wasting your time, when you could be furthering your dreams by getting rid of anything that is blocking them from further growth.

Weed your garden. Your Life. Your space. Detox from drama. Don't dwell. Work out your inner shadows and why you keep playing out the same traumas. Work out where your pain is and why you need to keep picking and reopening the wounds. Do you want to truly heal or are you just defined by your darkness? Doing it for yourself helps others do it too, by example.

If you want to heal, you need time.
If you want to get better you need the right setting.
If you want to feel good you need to focus on feel-good things.

DARKNESS DELVING AND PROFOUND PROBING

Playing detective and private investigator works for you now, because you get to sniff out and research things that will help you improve your life by understanding the parts that currently keep on tripping you up. The nasty emotions. The replays. The painful stuff.

So probing into psychology, body language, astrology, self-help, therapy etc are all ways to look at what's going on underneath. No matter what is happening it's not about what's playing out on the surface. Ever. So much is happening if you just looked under the table. The infamous iceberg is mostly lurking beneath the water and is mightily misrepresented by surface appearances.

Don't miss a trick then and believe you're seeing the full picture. You don't know what's going on behind the scenes or closed doors. Whether you then vow to do so by climbing drainpipes to peer in, or tapping someone's phone, best stick to your own stuff and work out what's happening within *you* and why you're so obsessed/hurting/agitated or whatnot. Someone may be angry at you but they could be medicated. Then what? Someone may seem to have it in for you but they may have just lost their mother. Then what? There's more going on than you know, which doesn't mean you need to continue putting up with hurt, but know it comes from somewhere and it has a root cause.

Maybe you're present to help someone (and yourself in the process) heal the **key and core trigger and issue**.

For example – individuals with a core issue of violence/anger (whether repressed or overtly expressed in childhood), often find each other to play the core theme out over and over until it is risen above and no longer works or is necessary. Someone hurts the other. The other accepts it, feels they deserve it. One apologies, the other forgives. They work together on trying to heal the core pattern. Anger is challenged and expressed in healthier ways. Understanding creates a safe space to become vulnerable. The couple break through the core issue and heal. This is the best case scenario and one that lies there for all of us. What is your core issue? Others around you are here to help you work through this. And you are here to help them with theirs.

And it's worth mentioning that it's a good idea to inform those close to you that you are working on some things, and you may need more time alone, or to have patience while you do so. That way, they won't begin their own questioning of you or of your union with them (the last thing you need now is to be rejected). Others reflect back to us our Cycles so help them understand (as best you can) what you need and are dealing with in your personal Cycle 8. Your life will be all the better for it (and who needs extra stress right now?!).

Wanting to get to the bottom of something, the core, to truly work out how something works, is part and parcel of this Cycle. At the time of writing this paragraph, during my own Cycle 8, I found my study of reincarnation (life after *death*, there's that theme again), deepening as I wanted to get to the nitty-gritty of how to read this in the astrological chart. I didn't know why I had this burning obsession and drive to learn something new, on a deeper level. My friend, wise to the ways of astrology, asked me which Solar Cycle I was in. When I mentioned Cycle 8 he smiled and said, "There you go then. You want to deepen your study and get to the bottom of the mystery." He was a Scorpio of course (one of the messengers you'll meet during Cycle 8 as we've already mentioned). My desire became a driving force that led me to the specifics of karmic astrology; something I'd always enjoyed but now I wanted to study deeper into the past lives and present issues as seen in our birth charts.

You get a broader, higher perspective soon in Cycle 9 when you can put it all together to create a workable belief system or philosophy (your own truth of what you've amassed in the form of knowledge and information and experience), but for Cycle 8 it's about plumbing the depths of whatever it is you're looking into and dealing with the raw material and the nuts and bolts of how something operates. It's psychological, it's profound, and you don't get the juice unless you probe. No wonder sexual energy comes with Cycle 8s too.

A close ally of mine in this lifetime deepened his reading of depression, something he (and his family) had been dealing with for quite some time. Life after death, depression, abortion, rape, incest, loss or pain isn't light material, but that's Cycle 8. You get to look at some of the core issues of your life.

Did I mention the same friend bought the DVD *Twilight* during his Cycle 8? The theme: intense love encounters, obsession, and vampires. Love, desire, intensity and death. At the same time I was watching the entire series of *Buffy the Vampire Slayer* on DVD and I was in my Cycle 8 too – the theme; violence, death, life after death, obsessive love, loss and deep magic, deep power and deep emotions. Classic 8-Cycle themes. Oh, and his mother wound up at the emergency ward. She was fine but the scare of loss was still there.

WHOSE STUFF IS IT, ANYWAY?

Cycle 8 is one of those 'stuff' Cycles, specifically things that aren't yours. Stuff that no longer can be yours, things you have to hand over or give back. Like divorce settlements, tax or insurance payments, losing custody of your children, owing the library for the book you 'lost' – You get the picture. Or you're trying to get things that you're owed but which aren't in your possession. Like the stuff you left with an ex partner.

Loss comes in many forms – maybe it's you, maybe it's them, but suddenly the 'fairness' is gone in Cycle 8 (maybe it really wasn't fair in Cycle 7 and now you get to truly divide and conquer equally ... all is fair in love and war, and all that jazz). The spoils are divided. What is yours remains with you, what isn't ... departs. That's about the sum of it, in Cycle 8. So you can either fight for your share if you truly believe it's yours (or worth fighting for) or you can chalk it up to the big universal checkbook-balancing magician in the sky. What goes around comes around and then goes around once more.

Can you let it go? Is it worth fighting over? Is it about the stuff or the value/principle? Is it more emotional and an excuse to stay connected (i.e chained) to a part of your life that really died off and ended but which you didn't accept? Is this about control? Anything too intense is probably a trigger or hitting a button. If you have the strength to release your grip and relax your control, everything will flow again where it needs to, but you may have to swallow your pride or anger and anything else you're harboring to begin the process. Either way, you'll have to lose something, but only the things that aren't right for you. The sooner the better, eh?

Let it go – from things you no longer want or need, to emotions you no longer want or need, or people in your life who trigger states you no longer want or need. It's time to let it go.

JUST IN CASE...

This is a good time to cover all of your financial bases: update your will, write one if you haven't already, check up on your insurance policies and perhaps leave a note or document somewhere for your loved ones with your wishes after your death. Take a look around your home tonight and realize that one day you will leave this physical realm too, and all of your stuff will be there right where you left it. Maybe it's time to go through your possessions and clear things out, or at the very least make some preparation for the time when you won't be here.

Protect yourself and protect your money and protect those you love.

PSYCHIC BORDER PATROL

Whether to keep people out or let people in becomes another issue in Cycle 8, since it's another of the water/emotional/psychic Cycles. (Cycle 4 asks you to safeguard your home but let people into your emotional space, Cycle 12 asks you to dissolve your separateness to others and become whole but also protect from too much dissolution and escapism).

8-Cycles ask us to allow others into our psychic space but not to let them dictate and control us, due to fear we'll lose them, or fear of our own power. If we project our own power now, we'll attract those who suck us dry, or who appear to be more in control, and dominating and dangerous.

Our inner border patrol police are on high alert this Cycle for anything or anyone who seems to be trying to invade our space (like the ants that took over my kitchen during one 8-Cycle). And like antibodies at the ready for any sign of infection, we're likely to react by clamming up and shutting down or else lashing out to be sure no one can hurt us, or getting inside our protection shell or spell that we've built or cast, to keep us safe in such an uncertain and shaky time of our year.

Yes, we're vulnerable, but we'll be damned if we'll let others know this! Perhaps our dreams start showing signs of wobbliness, as death or insecurities surface to remind us of our worst fears. But dreams are self-created and we cast each player within them to represent part of ourselves. So this is a great time for self-reflection.

What are you trying to tell yourself?

Border patrol staff within you are very sensitive also to sexual encounters of course, because you have to let your defense mechanisms down to get close enough to another person, unless you're having empty meaningless sex (which is perhaps more of a Cycle 5 experience, just for fun). But Cycle 8 is about true soul contact. How can you expect to be changed, if you don't allow yourself to be open and vulnerable and close enough to be touched on all levels? Border patrol staff are given sedatives or given the month off during 8-Cycles, or at least long enough for you to let people cross over into your psychic terrain.

They still exist (the dragon in the moat, the guard dog etc) and they still do their job where need be. And they'll alert you to any danger if you pay attention to how you feel.

The same goes for financial deals – trust is the main theme that is reflected in all encounters. Safety may come from keeping others at arm's length, but it feels a lot better to have others wrapped in your own arms.

If you're feeling intensely about something, you've let it in. Congratulate yourself and now decide on how you want to feel and begin shifting your perspective. It's all a learning curve. Remain open to decide how close you want to merge with the object of your desire or disdain.

PLANETARY SIGNATURE: PLUTO

Mythologically, Pluto is Lord of the Underworld. You can see why he has domain over this particular Cycle. Who else is better at taking you by the hand and leading you into the spooky places. He doesn't even need a flashlight. He sees in the dark. And his mission is to help you dig in the muck and go where no one else is brave enough to go. Call him Guardian of Hell, or the Keeper of the Treasure under the Mountain. You have to use his energy and work with him to get anything worthwhile done during Cycle 8.

Pluto helps you strip things away. The soil hiding your vegetables. The rotten spot on the apple. The cyst on your skin. The cancer eating away inside of you. The nagging guilt you let eat away at you in the same way. If it's festering, Pluto wants to know about it. And he wants *you* to. So he'll show you. Someone will come along to poke at it. Hurt you where you're not strong. Then you can shore up the weak spots. Not out of fear. From survival, yes, but also for the sole purpose of bringing what is buried and unconscious to the light of your conscious awareness so you can use it. Knowledge is power.

He isn't just good at digging stuff up. He can also help you bury things – and give them a proper funeral. And to make sure they are actually dead, before you stick them in the ground. If you let Pluto energy strip from you what is unnecessary (no matter how much you think you need it, and hold on) you'll be rewarded with the real treasure, not the fool's gold you've been clinging to all along.

OCCULT MAGICK AND SPIRITUAL SURGERY

The idea of spiritual surgery comes with Cycle 8 in that we may have to transplant something (including ourselves) or cut something out of our life, or even our body, as we go in for actual surgery. (Invasive treatments often show up in Cycle 8 to correct an imbalance when no other method will: cutting something open, probing something, attacking something).

Deep spiritual and physical practices often show up now too. Perhaps you take an in-depth look at healing techniques (reiki, rolfing, reflexology for example), or even decide you want to become a doctor, or work in a hospice or emergency room, or a suicide/abuse hotline or emergency telephone operator. All deal with intense stuff of course, and all are helpful and healing in varying degrees.

Maybe you just face the ultimate anguish of suicidal thoughts within yourself or another. Maybe you just fear losing sanity, or dream about giving up on everything (the ultimate form of letting go).

Your ego *is* seeking to die right now, and as long as you know this, you can find the release you need in healthy ways and still continue this magnificent journey (and you don't want to miss out on Cycle 9, which is next up, because it is so much fun and makes Cycle 8 truly worthwhile). There *always* is a payoff to hard work!

Some get drawn to Tarot cards or occult practices, kundalini yoga (using energy to affect change in the body and mind), tantric sexual practices (again affecting change using sexual energy) or using their work to learn how to control something, someone or a state of being.

In the past, the word 'occult' meant *hidden*. It meant the knowledge was secretive, hence its relation to Cycle 8. Now anyone can learn techniques of self-mastery (hypnosis for example), and re-shape their lives accordingly.

The choice of whether these practices are to help or harm is a personal one, but we may get to learn in a future Cycle that what we put out surely will return to us in some form or another.

Best make it helpful, eh?

THE BIG BAD

With so much going on that could be called unsavory, or at least something most people would rather avoid, it can become problematic when you start only seeing, sensing or expecting the worst, the darkest, the most evil, the crappy. Lighten up! Not everyone is out to get you.

If you find yourself feeling this way, then you've stumbled into the flip side of Cycle 8 and you risk starting fires just because you've become so good at (or so itchy at trying your hand at) putting them out. The quiet moments then become the quiet before the storm. The bottom line is Fear. If you fear something is going to die, you may wind up stabbing it just to make sure, to get it over with in a timing of your own choosing, and to have some measure of control over it. We call it self-sabotage. Strike before you're struck, the best defense is a good offense. If the ship's going down, why not blow a few extra holes in it to speed up the process, instead of painfully waiting? That is the 'logic'. Control is the illusion. It's what you crave in Cycle 8 and so often what you lose ... but look deeper and you'll see you gain power by letting go of things that were *draining* your power.

So, stay alert to sinking into the dungeon of darkness and chomping at the bit to do battle with anything that *hints* at leaving or rejecting or abusing you. If you want to be pro-active, have a clear-out; recycle things (or give them away to charity). It may even be a good idea to watch a good horror film or read a murder-mystery, to satisfy your desire for intrigue, thrills and drama, so you won't go looking for it in your own life.

There's no way to clear the decks now unless you do just that – clear, cleanse and allow for a rebirth. Life goes on after death, and the best way to be fully alive is to continually strip your skin, shed a life and grow into your new skin. And the only way to do that is to lose one thing in order to gain another. The question becomes, 'do you trust that death will lead to new life?'

When the chips are down you'll be ready and able and willing, but don't sit and wait for them or turn the card tables at the casino over in order to spill them.

CYCLE 8 ACTION PLAN
* Look around you. What needs discarding?
* Hold a personal 'funeral' to honor and mourn your transition.
* When you hurt, face the wound. Focus on healing; not dwelling.
* If you or a situation is 'stuck', let it go for now.
* Recycle stuff, give things away, offload, shed.
* Face your core issue and trigger with a view to moving beyond it.
* Clear up any outstanding debts.
* Express passion and power, as honestly as possible.

In a top year:
You rise to the occasion. One door slams shut then blows off its hinges but another door screeches open like a secret chamber leading to a new labyrinth. It's not over yet! Even with no assurance you'll survive, you manage to risk it and discover a whole new field you can channel your sexy passionate energy into. Saved by the bell! Life catches you when you jump. You hurt but you manage to see it as an opportunity to heal and grow stronger. You help another out of their black pit also, by example. The darkness is soothing, without the savage beasts lurking in the shadows.

You forgive. You feel powerful, as though a higher power moves through your veins. Magic crackles from your fingertips. You read people; can sense their thoughts, feelings or motivation. You're ahead of the game. On top. A wolf with senses so sharp you outmaneuver your foe even before they know you're nearby. Your monetary deals come together nicely, and you see that there's power in numbers – literally! Why go solo?

Research digs up what you need to know, and your secret knowledge puts you even further ahead. By ditching what you didn't need, you wind up with more free time and free space and free hands to take on new things that seem to have appeared by magic. Apparently you passed some test of faith. Things worked out when you eased your grip. Your load is lightened when something that was beginning to annoy you was finally taking its toll, and then Poof! By magic it's removed from your life like an ugly wart. You wind up at a funeral, often for parts of your own life, but it feels right and you accept it and look good in black. You celebrate what's still here and you see the new chapters ahead and appreciate all that came before. You're stronger now, you rose back from the ashes and rise higher, ever onwards and upwards thankful to all who have helped you climb to this amazing vantage point. Without the tests, how could you ever know just how powerful you are and how you create your reality by the focus of your feelings?

In a bottom year:
You rise to the bait, not the occasion. You're stalking shadows or you get hooked onto something that really isn't good for you. Your soul seems unable

to escape. Or maybe you just like the pain. It hurts. Real bad. You become an *S & M* expert, someone well-versed in negatives and quite willing to dish a few out yourself. The clouds overwhelm you with no way out. Ghosts of regret, pain, bitterness and personal evils (done to you or by you) haunt your every moment. It's truly the Dark Night of your Soul.

In some years you're just obsessed and seething. Enemies abound. You're screwed over royally and vow revenge. Someone hurts you, betrays you. Whatever the case you just can't get past it, and can't accept it. You feel dead on the inside. Your funeral hurts, and you're asked to attend a whole string of them but you don't and can't let it go. The cruelty of it all. The injustice. The disappointment. And oh, worst of all – the loss ... Part of you is killed off (or someone is trying to do that, it would seem). The graves pile up or the issue from your dubious past you thought was buried and gone, rises up once more.

Or are you on the prowl ready to do someone in yourself, scouring the internet for secret information to nail them with?

Nonsense, it means you're hooked on something you can't let go of and you're chained to pain. Until you can cut your losses and focus on the light, you're doomed to stray in the shadows. For now, the night is unending – because you won't seek the dawn. You replay the moment you were stabbed or you're sticking the knife in another and twisting. Repeatedly. No matter what someone did or did not do, it's the feeling you're meant to overcome and transcend, to grow stronger and perhaps closer (if not to them, to yourself, perhaps both). Isn't it time you freed yourself by moving on and moving through this?

Cycle Lesson
Something needs to change. Life forces you to do just that, by arranging things so that you can no longer put off the inevitable growth; cutting the dead wood from your life, energy and your Dream. It's time to shed something so you can grow stronger, taller, brighter, free of the shadow obstacles of ego, played out in all various forms of fear. As Linda Goodman once said, "If it was negative, it didn't happen. Except in the world of illusion". Delaying this process impedes your evolution and weakens you. Release your grip and let the pieces arrange themselves accordingly. Like a young fragile seedling, shake off the dirt and reach for the light.

Celebrity Spotlight
- *The Titanic* sinks in the 8th Cycle from its launch date.
- Princess Diana marries Prince Charles.
- Capricorn Dolores McNamara wins Europe's largest lottery jackpot of €115,436,126.
- Freddie Mercury is diagnosed with AIDS.

- Monica Lewinsky reveals all to Barbara Walters on ABC's *20/20* programme before 70 million Americans.

Tips to navigating your Cycle 8 Transmutation:

- Face the darkness and know this is a temporary path.
- Realize what's keeping you chained to pain, and give it up.
- Talk to a professional to help you let go.
- Look at your addiction to the dark stuff.
- Begin some recycling scheme.
- Clear out things you no longer, use, value, need or like.
- Be open to intimacy and going deeper.
- Seek support, give support, pool resources, talents.
- Face your fear and move through it (what doesn't kill you makes you stronger).
- Meet your shadow (maybe it's your issue not theirs).
- Shed a skin and don't look back.
- Be honest about the seething emotions you now feel.
- Exercise your power of healthy choice and if you can't, choose not to act, just yet.
- Watch horror movies, and notice the symbolism of facing your fear/demons.
- Investigate, research, uncover, probe.
- Ask for a loan, extend credit, seek financial advice/support.
- Accept it's *over* (in its current phase or form, anyway).
- Use passion to move mountains.
- Take your anger, rage, jealousy, hatred and channel it into something positive.
- Enjoy sex with a soul-connection.
- Learn tantra.
- Visit a sex shop, indulge in erotica, discover your hidden desires.
- Take a kundalini yoga class.
- Accept and embrace your power – power 'is', it's what you do with it that matters most.
- Undergo hypnosis, surgery, counseling.
- Visit a graveyard and feel the peace that surrounds death.
- Talk about taboos/Share a secret.
- Reveal your vulnerabilities/fears.

~ Surf Cycle 9 ~

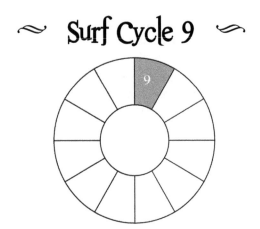

Time to Seek Higher, Wider and Further
and to Grow Through New Experience

Expansive Encounters with:

Travelers, travel agents
Out of towners
Students/teachers instructors
Judges/legal eagles/barristers
Authors and publishers/
    mass media types
Internet service providers
Gurus/experts/lecturers/promoters
Airline companies and employers
Migrants/immigrants/foreign
    -influenced/born
Border patrol/immigration service
Map-makers/travel professionals

Bus/train/taxi companies
Spiritual leaders/soapbox preachers
The religiously inclined/sceptics
Passport providers/jet setters
Sagittarius people
Cultural collaborators
Bookwoms/'brainiacs'/bookstores
The adventurous/knowledgeable
Seekers, nomads, gypsies
Athletes or outdoor folk
'Eat, drink and be merry' people
Language professionals, librarians
Ethical thinkers and philosophers

What you'll need:

A good idea of where your north is (and water)
Hiking boots for rough terrain
A translation kit for every language
A ready-packed knapsack by the door
A massive dose of adventure and optimism
A working sense of humor

Okay, you ... where now?

After the heavy-stuff-sorting of Cycle 8 (told you it wouldn't last forever), you get to enter the fresh fields and greener pastures of Cycle 9. You'd not be so free now if it wasn't for where you've just been, so accept, acknowledge and try to find appreciation for all the darker elements that popped up during your last Cycle. You got to see them and bring them to conscious awareness so they were no longer blocking your progress or controlling you by remaining in the shadows.

Now, you get to go on a hunt – for more, bigger, better, further. You're reminded (if you can remain open regardless of what happened during your last Cycle) that life is full of a bounty of some sort and that life always opens a new door, clears a road or space and asks us, "Now where?"

Did you forget you're in the driver's seat?

We can't all be millionaires at the same time, we can't all be happily married or dating at the same time, and we can't all be taking vacations at the same time. There is no fun in a world without duality, difference and variety. That's how life is set up currently on Earth. We get to pick and choose what we desire. So even though we may not have it all at the same time, we *can* have it all, if we realize that life is infinite and that our chart represents a moment of time – we are ambassadors of that moment in time. Everything we do affects that moment of time that we represent, and in changing our lives, in each choice we make, we change the very moment we are. The moment of our birth. Yes, we change the past ... all from the present moment.

Who says you can't time travel?

One choice now could change everything for you. That's the power of your 9-Cycle and nowhere is the possibility of great things more apparent than during this phase – the time of grand schemes, amazing dreams and mighty adventures. Shoot for the moon and you may just land there. And never judge a story until the final page – and even then, how do you know it's really truly over?

It's a *big* world out there. Sometimes we forget.

I visited the Natural History Museum in Los Angeles, California, during one 9-Cycle and was blown away by just how many species of bird there are in the world. Mind-boggling! It's a fact that massive lizards roamed the earth with claws as long as your arm. It humbles you. You realize you're pretty small compared to what else is out there. And that no matter how wise you may think you are, or knowledgeable; you don't and can't know everything.

I'll never forget the unbelievably long eel they had on display, which still exists in the oceans' depths. You thought Jaws was scary?! There's a lot out there we have no clue about because we haven't stumbled across it yet. It doesn't register as 'possible', because we haven't yet experienced it and therefore have no frame of reference for it; no context.

Lack of experience accounts for most of the world's habit of dismissing things that seem too far fetched, too 'out there', solely on the reason that there is no backlog of personal experience with which to understand it.

There are some pretty amazing things and people and places and experiences out there, waiting to be met, visited or embraced. Things you've never felt yet – but if you did, you'd absolutely *love* them (and wonder how you didn't find it/them earlier).

That's the key to this current Cycle. It's time to make your world bigger.

SUPERSIZE YOUR SPACE

It *will* get bigger whether you choose it or not – even if you stay at home, you will end up connecting more widely with the world through the internet, television, DVD rental, or maybe a magazine subscription or library card.

You wind up with more at your fingertips, during 9-Cycles.

Maybe you'll spend your days reading, thumbing through bookstores and your nights chatting to people on foreign shores (or in other cities) who are doing things very differently to how you do them (a cultural revelation). How about eating your lunch outside instead of stuck at your desk, behind your computer or in front of the TV? Maybe the travel channel piques your interest to see new shores or something you read in a magazine gives you new ideas on new horizons to explore?

The number of shows I caught one Cycle 9, when I merely had TV on in the background, relating to travel and new experiences was astounding – shows about chefs attempting to eat the biggest burger, scouring the world for the 'best pizza experience', shows about where to go to find the 'fastest roller coaster', 'longest waterslide' 'biggest pepper-tasting convention' and even the most expensive ice cream sundae (which in case you're wondering, and at the time of writing, is the *Frrozen Haute Chocolate* sundae that comes with edible 23 karat gold leaf. Price: $25,000). You name it, these shows were about more, bigger, or going further.

Your world may be bigger temporarily to give you a taste of width, breadth and spaciousness by spending time somewhere other than the possibly cramped home or lifestyle you've been adjusting to, as of late. Like the Cycle 9 year when my friend went out of town for two days and let me stay at his place, which was about five times bigger than mine, cooler in temperature and in a better area. It's amazing what a new perspective provides you in 9-Cycles, if you're open and willing to go on an adventure.

Perhaps you'll run into someone from out of town, with an accent (or from back in your hometown, to remind you of how far you've come), someone with a different skin color, who eats different meals at different times and sings songs and enjoys music you've never heard. I knew someone who began looking up online classes in changing their accent, during this Cycle. Suddenly you open your mind to new possibilities, ways of living, different cuisine, music. Maybe you'll broaden your physical space by just buying a mirror to give the feeling of expansiveness at home (which I discovered I'd done without consciously thinking about it, one 9-Cycle). The ritual of day to day living becomes something entirely different. Maybe someone new moves into your home. Maybe an extension is added. Maybe next door is knocked down, and you end up with an amazing view out of your bedroom window. Maybe someone sends you information about a cheap plane or train ticket.

Sometimes you just need the perception of growth, space, distance and expansiveness.

Whatever happens now, or is offered now, is all to *expand your bubble, beliefs, insight, mind and experience*.

More – you're about to be given *more* of things (more information, life experiences, reasons to be hopeful, ways to have faith, numbers of people or things – your 'reach' is about to be stretched).

So how will your world get bigger now? In any number of ways and it's all your choice – you could get out on a road trip and check out another city. Or grab your passport and venture overseas. Don't have one? Get one! Maybe you'll find yourself renewing your passport application at this time. My partner bought me a new passport cover during one Cycle 9 and that same day we ended up sitting by a park and the make of the car parked next to us was the Honda *Passport*. Perhaps you'll start studying. How about an online class if you don't feel like the drive to your local college? Or teaching. Can you share what you already know? Or you could start learning a new skill again, or taking an old one to new heights. Guitar anyone?

BROADENING YOUR BUBBLE

Your waistline? Your horizons? Your database of facts and figures? Your contact with other people and their ideas and lifestyles? What will you make bigger (or a bigger deal) now? Which aspect *of your Cycle 11 Dream Vision* are you going to blow up and make bigger? You tell me. Something *has* to get bigger and expanded (even if it's just your waist size from stifling your hunger for experience and satisfying it in other ways). Which aspects of life would you like to enjoy more of? Focus on those, this Cycle. Feed the Dream. Stretch further but be careful not to overstretch or you may wind up falling victim to the flip side of Cycle 9 which we'll read about later – over-stretching, over-reaching, overdoing, over-blowing, over-investing and over-promising.

Stick to finding out more and enjoying doing something with what you already know. What you learn now (or rediscover you already knew) sets you up for success later. Maybe you'll go through a process of 'un-learning' – emptying your mind of things that no longer hold true for you – experience has proven otherwise, perhaps. So you may find you wind up back in a classroom, taking exams, or studying, reading, learning and navigating new terrain in preparation for something up ahead. Or polishing up an old base of knowledge. Life is an adventure, a university or a school of hard knocks, delivering more of what you feed/seek/focus on.

You'll be aided in your quest by crossing paths with at least one Sagittarius who reminds you what it is to be a gypsy on the road, creating your own philosophy as you go, experiencing all life has to offer without taking any of it too seriously (yet offering some profound wisdom along the way). From over the horizon, to over-the-top promises, you'll see what this Cycle is all about through their eyes. Soak up the sights.

Maybe you want an extra qualification, or you need to receive your certification before you become an expert yourself? From driver's tests to speaking new languages, your new desire to enlarge your brain capacity can only help you out with what's to come.

You could be one of the lucky ones to come out of your 9-Cycle with a degree, qualification or certificate. Maybe you'll just read widely, expanding your awareness of a particular topic or field of study. Maybe you'll be giving a class, teaching others what you already know? Perhaps you'll come to see that direct experience is the best teacher, and you can never fully understand everything just from books and study. At some time you have to take a test drive and see for yourself.

Does it work for you? And is it true to *you*?

So go for it – take on more. Learn more. Develop more. Experience more. See more. Try more. Discover more. Dare to be more. Seek more. Pass on more. Keep emptying and then filling up with yet more. You can't overdo it when it comes to experience – because:

everything teaches you something.

MAKING YOUR ROAD A TRIP

All is valid in the wide wondrous world out there, and all it takes is curiosity, choice, focus and desire to drive you to your destination. So as you can see, this Cycle is so big that not even a whole book could cover the possibilities.

You can broaden your horizons physically by moving around more (going horse riding would be a perfect symbol for Cycle 9 since it relates to Sagittarius the centaur), by covering more ground, or putting on weight from sampling more food.

You could broaden your mental horizons by stuffing your brain full of new and interesting theories or opening your mind to new possibilities (optimism/hope/great expectations make a comeback).

You could broaden your emotional horizons and understanding by venturing further into the heart, and all its intricacies, or the human psyche (Cycle 8 surely taught you a lot about psychology, how you work and how humans work in general). Many people expand their spiritual sense of life's meaning by exploring new philosophies or strengthening their faith/religious convictions.

9-Cycles ask you to sort through what you know (or think you know) and now make sense of it. It's less about learning new stuff ultimately and more about putting what you have amassed together to create some framework through which to view life by, some personal ethic, some code of conduct, some belief system to live by – that works for you. That gives you freedom, hope, optimism, and inspires your adventurous spirit.

Making sense of it all is really your ultimate mission this Cycle.

FANNING THE FLAMES OF YOUR DESIRE-FIRE

Cycle 9 is another fire Cycle, but this time, unlike Cycle 5 (when we were asked to fix our focus and burn bright), we get to unleash our inner-fire and spread it around a bit. Think of a forest fire and that's how you are to be and feel during Cycle 9; spreading wildly, untamed and running free like the centaur; the symbol of this time of your year.

See your bigger picture. Forget the small stuff and don't sweat the details. Stand back. Gain perspective. Climb a hill, take a breather, look beyond the current time frame of circumstance and find the bigger meaning. The larger concept. Feel ahead to the rest of your story. Stop fixating on life 'as-is' and look at how it could be, how you want it to be. Where do you want your Dream (and life) to take you next?

There's no reason to get bogged down in chilly feelings or emotional potholes now, that was last Cycle – the road of life is showing you a new horizon, a new exit, a detour to a new place.

The question then becomes: Are you 'present' enough to see this?

SEARCHING, SEEKING – QUESTING QUESTIONS AND ARRIVING AT ANSWERS

Somewhere over the rainbow ...
... somewhere in another town, city, village, state, country or continent ...

Somewhere in another book, in another relationship to another soul...
... somewhere in another mindset ...

Somewhere other than where you are ...

... is your answer.

Or if not *the* answer, then a whole new set of life experiences to help you re-frame your question, feel free and begin a quest for something new. There is no endpoint in life (we always reach a new vantage point and thus a new desire) but you can at least get to *further what you were pursuing back in your Cycle 11.* Maybe what you desired up until this Cycle was not really what you wanted. You may feel itchy now to shift it around.

9-Cycles help you do just this.

Whatever search you get to go on, it can only be to expand your bubble and push back the boundaries and borders of your world. If you feel you've been living in a snow globe, trapped behind glass or bars, squeezed between unsatisfactory options (or neighbors), dwelling on dark matters or dealing with things you wish had left your life long ago, then this is your time – to get out, break out, and test things out. You may find you end up searching for bus schedules to get out of your town and go on the road. Maybe you're filling up your car for an actual road trip. You could be preparing to fly off to a special class being offered across country. Perhaps you're all set for school or higher education somewhere other than where you were born.

Bon Voyage! The adventure begins right here as you carry a new map with you of the new terrain, or if you are map-less you begin crafting your own, based on whether you enjoy the experience or not.

The only way to know ... is to go!

ADVENTURE AWAITS: TRAVERSING NEW TERRAIN

Whether you wind up buying a physical map for yourself or someone else or trekking across unknown lands, through strange neighborhoods, towns, cities, country landscapes, business fields, emotional realms (you name it, you can traverse it this Cycle) you'll at some point have to plot a new course and learn a new way of interacting with your environment. You may begin learning a new language and the rules of the road in that department, perhaps reading music (for those who are new to it, it certainly looks like a foreign language). No matter what it is, you'll find you have to stay hyper-aware of where you are and the road you're on (as opposed to Cycle 3 when you just cruised through your environment absorbing it all on auto-pilot).

This Cycle comes with a purpose. Sure, you can take a tour or play tour guide somewhere, but you'll get more out of 9-Cycles if you decide what it is you'd like to experience, find out where to go for that, and then plot an itinerary to get there and some idea of what to try when you arrive.

Don't forget during this fun time of your year, that it's never really about the destination and more about the journey there. The new people, scenery and things you learn on the way. You get to see a lot more than you'd normally see, and learn a lot more than you normally would in order to make better and bigger choices for yourself. Otherwise you'll cram yourself into a box, and that's just no way to be living your life. Cycle 9 gets you out and about, opening your mind and expanding your options and possibilities.

Opportunity knocks for most people in 9-Cycles. You have to be ready to live life on the fly. New stuff comes when you're open to it and ready for it, on some level.

Isn't it time to prepare for your life to take off?

ADD MORE MORAL FIBER TO YOUR DIET

How will your Cycle 9 end? What will be the theme of your story, this month? There's always a moral to every story. Or at least some deeper meaning, like the message you take away from a book or a film: 'Love conquers all', 'Believe it and you can achieve it' etc.

Stay alert to messages relating to justice (the law, judging people or being judged yourself, 'right from wrong', society's 'shoulds', communication highways and cultural byways). How different slices of society do things differently: think differently, eat differently, act differently and treat others differently. In fact, it's the differences that aid you in Cycle 9 as you open up to variety once more in order to adjust your compass point on your way to the top.

For those who have already read Cycle 11, the Dream and Vision you created then gets a new angle, a different perspective as you expand it and take on new perspectives and possibilities on the road to manifesting it.

Everything that happens to you now is to aid you in sculpting your personal beliefs and philosophy of life. It is for the purpose of *choosing new roads on the way to your Dream Vision* by scheduling meetings with interesting people, ones you'd not normally hang around with, or even give the time of day to (who'll also show you how they are creating their own realities based on what *they* believe), and by bringing you into contact with new experiences that widen your scope and enlarge your potential. All these things will show you more of the world than the small chunks you may have been digesting lately.

Everything has a meaning. Everything is symbolic. Things happen for an important reason. Go to a music concert you'd not normally go to but get a feeling you *should* check out, and you could run into an old friend from eight years back who has a key piece of information that your life path is missing so far, and which you could really use if you're to blossom towards your Dream Vision. Or you wind up talking to someone who just so happens to have a tattoo of something inherently symbolic to your own life path (as I did one Cycle 9). You're meeting your dream through others, and seeing yourself reflected back. You catch up with the current of synchronicity that's been surrounding you but which you've been out of sync with because you've been fussing over unimportant matters.

You venture to a bookstore and run into someone important, or perhaps a piece of knowledge that reshapes your entire point of view and reality structure. Boom! Your world explodes and you're off on a roll, into a much more exciting and dynamic future.

It can happen in major ways or small ways, but it'll happen. How it ends is up to you and how far you're willing to go to soak up life's new sights. What could life be trying to show you? Is there a moral to your story and is there a meaning you keep missing that keeps getting bigger and bigger so you can no longer ignore it?

GET UNSETTLED

Unrest is your ally during Cycle 9, when you are fidgety and fired up to do something. If life has become too familiar of late, it's a sure sign you may be still swirling around old Cycles, trawling through Cycle 8 material when it was really time to move on and try something else by turning your attention away from the shadows into the vibrant colors surrounding you, and the possibility of a better road up ahead.

The best way to improve your life (and the fastest way to shift stagnation and overcome roadblocks) is to be open to trying a new approach, taking a new route, going a new direction and learning new things.

BELIEF RULES YOUR WORLD SO EXPECT A MIRACLE

Prepare to pack your bags, as you're off on a trip. Maybe it's literal and you're heading out of town, even out of the country? Life will arrange whatever you need to wake you out of your slumber or depression. If you're not on the go physically, you'll get to do some traveling in your head or on paper (brainstorming, reading, learning). But whose ideas are you ingesting?

You'll get to look closely at your own version of 'truth' – of right and wrong. Does it fit your new worldview or are you clutching to old beliefs? Could a new perspective or frame of mind alter your entire life's landscape?

Cycle 9 teaches:
'what you believe, you will
see, experience, find, meet
and get to live with and through'.

It's worth meditating on that point, as it sounds simple yet it's the key to this entire Cycle.

It sounds like a lot, doesn't it? But it's operating in your life right now (and always has and will). You're constantly proving your rules to yourself – and it *begins with expectation.*

Belief rules the world and it's never clearer than now *that what we believe, we seem to get* – **we're living under a self-fulfilling prophesy** and in Cycle

9 you learn something new to help you make a leap into a new world, based on new energy and less on traditions and beliefs you have held just because it seemed like a good idea in the previous year.

You're ready to open a door, throw open the window and explore the world at large. It's so vast, yet we forget as we move from one box (our bed) to another (our home) to another (our car) to another (the store) to another (the office cubicle) to another (the bus) to another (the coffin!)

In all seriousness though, it's worth considering where your freedom is this Cycle – and if you can venture past the city limits of your own comfort zone again (the ones you should have departed from in Cycle 4). Feeling stuck, trapped, bored? Good – this Cycle has a lot to offer you. Again, it's time to get up and move on somewhere new, like a nomad. Even if you just begin flipping through travel magazines, looking at photos of distant lands, or begin planning your long distance trip or overseas voyage.

We're all students and teachers at the same time – we receive messages and pass them on, unknowingly.

Choices open up and once again we see just where our freedom and power lies – in choosing the best for ourselves. You cannot fool someone out of the truth, it's felt in our heart and guts and souls as a bell chiming inside. Truth seeks truth and finds it this Cycle – so the question becomes:

Are you living the life you were born to live?
Anything else is a lie. Honesty isn't the best policy, then.
It's the *only* one. And assurance (and insurance)
of bliss, guaranteed.

WHEN YOUR KARMA RUNS OVER YOUR DOGMA

Belief is a funny thing. Listen to those around you while you make your way through your larger-than-life 9-Cycle and you'll hear a lot of people spouting what they believe as though it was ultimate fact, ultimate truth. 'The only way'. "But this is how it is!" they'll scream. And then they'll pull out a million facts to back it up. "It *is* true, see?" You may even try doing the same! The courage of their convictions may be enough for some people to totally buy what they're selling. But the trouble with 9-Cycles (and beliefs in general) is that everyone is creating their own reality based on the baggage of beliefs they carry around with them. Everyone is right, in their own way (or at least within their own heads).

When we energetically vibrate to a specific thought for long enough, it becomes an ingrained thought and finally a belief (and repetitive thoughts are all beliefs really are, anyway).

And, by the magic of the Universal Law of Attraction (the principle that 'like attracts like') we pull to us people, things, thoughts, situations and events that match that energy. We find proof of our convictions. We have even *further* evidence to plaster people with. Talk about a never-ending spiral. But it doesn't mean it's true for everyone, unless they believe it too.

So listen up now, if you can. You'll see a lot of people around you trying to make you swallow the belief they themselves have been chewing on for some time. This is your mirror that you may be doing the same, without even realizing it. The more passionate the crusade or belief, the more preachy the message, the longer they've been feeding the thought. And soon it snowballs to become a total life philosophy. Look at Martin Luther King, born with the Sun in Cycle 9 or Gandhi, born with Uranus (the planet of freedom and independence) in Cycle 9, who played a major part in the Indian Independence Movement. Strong beliefs can effect massive change and bring others into the fold.

You just want to be sure it's something you want to believe in.

If anything, you'd be wise to **believe nothing now but entertain options, ideas and possibilities**. If could be true, but do you want it to be true for you? That's a better question, before you buy into any version of reality life tries to sell you through the mouths of those you come into contact with (during 9-Cycles especially).

You'll hear a lot from the horse's mouth, but is it a healthy horse?

Don't become so convinced of your convictions that you create your own dogma.

Dogma: 'established opinion, belief, or principle'.

Life has a funny way of running over that with slingshot karma.

Karma: 'the good or bad emanations felt to be generated by someone or something'.

If you expect the bad, you'll often get the bad, especially the more you focus on it. Basically, the stronger you push your beliefs, the more likely you are to karmically attract someone equally as sure of themselves who gives you a good run for your money and their belief (likely to be in contrast to yours) is stronger than yours (Doubting Thomases listen up), and they end up bowling you over with their belief or 'facts' or ideologies.

Did you know that science has proven we change the result of an experiment by the simple act of our observing it? Check out *The Divine Matrix* by Gregg Braden for more information. Our expectations also affect the outcome of events. That's huge – it means things happen because of our interaction with them. Nothing is random, and life shapes itself to our observations.

Who wins in the belief challenge (which basically means who gathers more 'proof')? Maybe one, maybe the other. Maybe neither side, **since the only belief that matters is our own**. And beyond that, the best beliefs are the ones that allow for true learning, true growth – that we don't know everything, there's always more to learn and everything holds part of the truth. Together it all makes sense; pull it apart and it won't. Life is like the jigsaw puzzle, Cycle 9 says, and now it's time to decide which picture you want to prove when you put the pieces together. Because you will, but is it a picture you'd like to see?

Have you become rigid in your beliefs and are you trying to force others to conform to them? If so, you're probably hiding your doubt and skepticism behind blind belief. The best way to show us what you know is to stop telling and start showing.

Get out of the pulpit and live by example, not by your whipping cane.

THE TRUTH, THE EXAGGERATED TRUTH, AND THE BEST PLACE TO HIDE A LIE

You can't seem to escape it, in Cycle 9: The truth (cue dramatic music). Now, we're not talking generalized truths that could be considered more bias/ opinions/subjective than purely objective fact, we're talking things that you know unequivocally to be true. Tricky. Again, it's still a personal bias. When someone asks you if you like their hair, or if their artwork is any good – and it isn't (in your opinion) – do you tell them?

Are white lies okay in Cycle 9? Don't ask me. I think a general rule of thumb (I'm trying to steer clear of any dogma or belief here) is that if it won't hurt anyone and you won't feel guilty for it, then you can get away with appeasing someone and being gentle. If you feel you want to be fully 100% in-your-face honest, you're probably not going to be shot down either, if your *intention* is pure (in other words you're not trying to cause trouble or pain).

Yes, you may be caught out in a lie this Cycle, if you've been, as they say in England 'telling fibs' (lies), or you may be one to uncover someone else's less-than-frank behavior. How you handle it is up to you, but you can't very well give someone the axe because they've lied if you've ever done the same thing. That would be hypocritical. Are you really that saintly? Understanding helps. Maybe you were meant to uncover the lie so you could blow it out into the open.

If you attract deceit, it's a sign you're not being fully honest with yourself or another too. Like attracts like. Why the need to deceive? Perhaps to find greater honesty and clarity periodically? One thing is certain now – becoming more honest is a great way to clear the road ahead and live a better life. Lies take work. Honesty is much easier in the long run. Growth is *seen* in Cycle 9, so things happen to give us an opportunity to really feel that growth. Cycle 9s are great for this – exploding myth and getting to the real reasons behind things or the real reasons to hide behind anything anyway (be it fact or conscious fiction).

Asking "*Why?*" is a fantastic way to spend your 9-Cycles. Why are you doing or saying something? Why is another? You may get varied answers, but then you can at least make a more informed opinion, yourself. More information is better than assumptions or guesswork. Still, don't think that everyone will agree nor even listen to you in your Cycle 9. At the end of the day, and your physical lifetime, some people will always believe certain things about you, or about life. And nothing you can say or do will change that. And that may sound frustrating but what can you do? Everyone is entitled to their own opinion. And if you want others to respect yours, you're going to have to respect theirs.

Exaggerations are also common during this time. You can elaborate and tell a good story (a tall tale) and not even know you're doing it; or listen to others and think "what embellishment!", which is great if you're writing a novel, giving a toast or entertaining others with what happened to you last Friday night, but in general day to day life it may win you the reputation of 'un-believable'. Oh, there it is again – belief. Wow, there's just no escaping the concept at this time!

You may be asking, why the message in the title of this section? Where to hide a lie? Where do you think that would be?

Where better, than sandwiched *between two truths*, of course.

It works in politics, it works in advertising. Once you hook someone with the truth, you can slip in a lie and it's more likely to be swallowed whole, by the hungry. If Part A is true and Part C is too, it's somehow easier to believe Part B must be true as well. We believe the source of our information. The media uses this technique a lot to skew things to their own bias. That's why you're best to follow your own intuition than take anyone else's word on anything.

Whether you lie, find someone else has been lying, and whether you're unsure what is truth anymore, all that matters in your Cycle 9 is about whether you trust yourself to be as above-board, honest, and genuine as possible (thus lessening your chance of attracting or worrying that others are being less than honest with *you* – after all we fear what we know we are most capable of). As they say, those who find it hard to trust are the untrustworthy ones.

Integrity counts for everything. You're not here to judge in 9-Cycles (though the temptation is strong), but to be the best you can be. Set your own standards. And if in doubt, maybe it's best to have an honest talk with yourself on how you feel about what you've done, and forgive and forget instead of chasing people on witch hunts or condemning them for failing to maintain standards you really should only be setting for yourself.

Like attracts like. If you bring in something shady, it's only because somewhere your light wasn't as strong as it could have been.

SCHOOLS OF THOUGHT

Belief could lead some of you into church this Cycle (after all where else can you preach, promote and parade your beliefs with so much welcome?). Cycle 9 seems to bring in religious elements probably because it's based almost entirely on faith. You may wind up in several conversations, arguments, or debates over God (whether it's a 'he' or 'she' or whether 'it' exists at all). Some of you may be invited to a religious building, a chanting ritual or some other place connected to spirit. Maybe you just light candles and pray or visit an altar or temple. Or get into deep conversations about life and what it all means.

Some seek knowledge in dusty libraries or the expansive halls of education in their 9-Cycles, and prefer to find out the truth for themselves instead of sitting before someone on an altar preaching their version of the ultimate truth. Some take to the world, using traveling and experience as their ultimate teacher. It all depends on what you're after. Where you go matters not because somewhere, you're going to find whatever it is you're seeking.

Everyone has a bias. What's yours?

I found myself listening to a lot of online lectures regarding the universal laws, in particular the Law of Attraction, reshaping my personal belief systems to allow for a greater creative control over my life. You may find yourself doing the same; amassing a lot of information 'right up your alley' as they say, to help you progress on the particular path you've chosen. Side-streets often take you to better places than the main routes you're used to. Entertain the possibility you may not be fully correct, and that there's more information out there to help you align with what it is you *really* want.

Expect then at least one detour this Cycle on your road ahead to aid you in taking another direction. You won't lose track of your destination or goal, but a new viewpoint and new scenery may just provide your soul with the refreshment you truly need (and you may get wind of something else you can add to your picture of how the perfect life for you would be).

Everything and everyone has a role and has a place, but does it (or they) have a role and place in *your* story? Read the book or watch the film of the fantasy tale *Inkheart* by Cornelia Funke, for more on this theme.

BELIEVE IT AND YOU'LL SEE IT

Yes you read correctly. Not 'see it to believe it' as it is often expressed but 'believe it to see it'. Your mindset is really key in Cycle 9. Ideas held long enough, coupled with the power of emotion, create repetitive patterns inside of you that are broadcast outside of you, magnetically.

A belief is really a thought that's been thought repeatedly, gaining ground and power over time. You may find you have to reprogram out of your mental hard drive some of those negative beliefs that you've amassed and ingrained over time with dramatic dedication, when you keep interacting with situations that don't please you (especially in Cycle 3 when you began taking on new information and making judgment calls on what you did and didn't like).

Now all this labeling has brought you to this point – you've created a picture, a philosophical structure of how your world is operating and will continue to operate ahead.

Cycle 9 says 'change the tape and re-record for relief'. Retrain your brain.

Ask yourself this: Is the world a great place full of people ready to help you out? Or is it full of greedy hounds you need to protect yourself from?

I say it's better to believe the world is full of people ready to help you at a moment's notice, and full of possible and potential friends in the making. That belief would get you further than believing that people are out to get you. What you believe, you're most likely to perceive, and then experience. *What you believe, you'll prove to yourself*, especially during your Cycle 9. You'll seek out proof and find it everywhere you look – but it's only true for you. When you believe it, you're almost certain at some point to see it.

When you look, you'll find it – especially during 9-Cycles. So, what will you choose to look for, in life's buffet?

BANISH THE BLUES WITH GREENER PASTURES

Oh yes, the grass *is* greener and it's time to hop over the fence and find a fresh field. New horizons stretch you and show you more, and Cycle 9 is here to help you do just that.

You're really shifting your meaning of life. What's it all about to you, what are *you* doing, what is your meaning, your personal purpose? You can become your own truth – a happy person, a helpful person, a kind person, a grouchy person. Who do you want to be and how do you want to live? You perfect it now, ready to show off publicly in Cycle 10, coming up next.

Life will continually bring you into alignment (or conflict) with: people very different to you, cultural connections or confrontations, things to discipline your mind by constantly expanding its muscles, being honest and demanding nothing less from others, justice, finding out for yourself, taking to the road or hitting the books, what you do or don't know, your intelligence level, IQ tests, looking into encyclopedias and bookstore/libraries, becoming a guru of some field or other, tours of sites of interest.

DREAM PROMOTION

Remember your ideal world, your new goal, your *Vision List* that you created internally in Cycle 11? Where are you at now, in relationship to it? Let's take a look at it. I'll wait while you go and dig it out …

How does it look? Do you still like it? How is it shaping up for you? Are there areas you can give more emphasis? Be more specific? Maybe you already have seen things grow and you've altered your perspective on them. Perhaps you need more of something? Cycle 9 provides a platform from which to springboard to advertising it, to make it bigger and to help it reach more people (including the ones who'll help you market it or take it to the next level).

Would a website help you at this point, to reach a wider audience? A radio appearance? Television? An online ad? Classifieds in a magazine? A free local or nationwide paper? Maybe it's time to talk to everyone you meet about what you do and envision? Could asking others to help you out, be the true advertising you need? Is it time to take it abroad?

Seeing it from another perspective (to find an angle you may have missed) is possible when you give your dream wings and let it fly you to somewhere new. You can't help but magnetize the new people to you when you hold true to the vision. Just don't get cramped up in a box or dwell on the dark stuff (like last Cycle). Keep the hope going, the trust and optimism and faith that all is well and can only get better.

FAITH, PROOF AND PERSONAL TRUTH

What is faith? Do you have it? Even if there's no evidence yet that things will be okay and work out well? If you don't, or you're struggling, Cycle 9s are good times to remind yourself that in the past things have been more challenging and you got through them. So if you're in a tricky 9-Cycle, that should give you at least some measure of hope that things can only get better again as they did before. It's all a conspiracy now to help you find new vantage points and new viewpoints in order to feel something different, and be *open* to something different.

If you've been low, prepare for new adventures that will lift your spirit. Stock up on vitamins, protein bars and energy drinks as you may need them, with all the possibilities and quests life has planned for you (or that you're planning for yourself).

Other people, new information and insights, pour forth to meet your expectations and thus prove to you that all that matters is your personal truth, not what anyone else says is true, or important. It's how *you* feel about things you do and the things that happen to you, in your own life.

REDEFINE ROBOTIC RITUAL

Repetition is boring when it has no meaning. Religion – one of the topics of this Cycle (how many clashes of belief will you be witness to this Cycle, I wonder?) – faces that challenge; repeating rituals that for many have become empty and meaningless. No matter. Your challenge now is to try and create your own meaning. Why do something unless it's personally important to you? When our actions are imbued with meaning they take on a whole new power. Like the true act of prayer perhaps invokes a higher power. Stuff happens. Call it magic. Miracles. The act of showering, with the intent of clearing away negative energy from your energy field or body, as the water washes over you, has the power to do just that. That's the whole purpose behind 're-birthing' or 'christenings' where babies' heads are washed, to symbolize the washing away of 'sin', according to the Church. Believe it and you can achieve it. People also burn sage at home to clear away negative energy. How about visualizing what you'd like to happen? Lighting a candle every night to focus your mind and create a peaceful energy at home.

How many of us truly create work-out programs that are ritualistic (and not just moving the body)? The number of people I saw in Los Angeles at the gym who were running on treadmills while absorbing the nightly negative news on TV monitors or chatting away on their phones (thus imbuing their health program with unhealthy energy) was pretty amazing. Or those who are arguing while eating, thus swallowing the stressful energy along with their food?

The act of wanting to be happier pulls happier things to you. Intention sets the energy blueprint and life shapes itself to that. The ritual of cleaning, with the idea it is clearing energy and preparing you for something new, aligns you with your desire. It never fails. Intention has power. Cycle 9 reminds you that you're the walking prophet, creating your future by your focus.

Try if you can, then, to redefine what ritual is to you and if there's a place for it in your life. Not a boring routine. Not something for the sake of it. Not superstition, but something that's personal to you. Your own personal magic. A spell. A chant. A mantra. An action, that each time you repeat it, adds more power to your original intention. Make it something symbolic and something intentional.

Where will you continue in Cycle 9 to cast the seeds of your dream vision?

BYPASSING YOUR BOX AND BORDER

Take it further, one step further; go the extra mile and you'll be amazed. As Wayne Dyer says in his book of the same name, "It's never crowded along the extra mile". Most are content to do what is expected, and nothing more. The act of going a little bit further has the power of creating some astounding and speedy results. Sometimes we are on the verge of a major breakthrough, just beyond the point where we are ready to give up.

Author Stephen King was rejected sixty times (he papered his walls with the rejection slips) until he was finally published. Frustrated with one of his stories, King threw it away until his wife Tabitha rescued it, read it and convinced him to continue. *Carrie* became a hit and the paperback rights were sold in 1973 for $400,000 with half going to King himself. From trash to $200,000? Not bad.

Just when you're ready to give up, go a little further, and you may be pleasantly surprised. Cycle 9 rewards those willing to go further out, further afield and try.

Remind yourself that you won't know, if you don't go.

PLANETARY SIGNATURE: JUPITER

Astrologically, Jupiter is the biggest planet (so far). That's why you'll find this energy connected to this Cycle – which is namely about making things a big deal. Blowing stuff up to bigger proportions. Giving you more of something. Jupiter is the lord of abundance. So it's during good times that we can look to this planet. Yes, we may go over the top, but excess leads to wisdom. We expect the good stuff to flow and indeed it does. And we share our bounty, thus promising plenty. Our well is always replenished. Use Jupiter to explore and adventure. To find meaning in all we have experienced and all we have learned and collected, thus far. What does it all mean? This energy helps you to connect the dots and find meaning – and thus, wisdom … and finally … your own truth.

TALK TO STRANGERS

The list of interesting new people you *could* meet now is pretty extensive, but like everything, you have to be in a prime position to actually meet them! True, your postal delivery service may have a special message for you along with a parcel, but you're more likely to run across others from different backgrounds in coffee shops, bookstores, clubs, venues, events, on the street, on the bus, at the supermarket – everywhere and anywhere people go. Just think of the possibilities.

Stepping out of your door during Cycle 9 leads you on many new adventures. Watch how you suddenly run into women from Russia, men from Peru, kids from India, adults from Nepal, families from Brazil, your new lover from Indonesia, your new business partner from San Francisco, visitors from Spain, your teacher from London. And the contacts and connections *they* have for you blow open even more doors!

You can't help but become global in Cycle 9 and the world cries "Try it, you might like it!"

If you're invited, go. If you get a number, call it. Overbook yourself if need be, but go out on a limb and make the contact. See where it goes. Maybe it's not about your immediate contact but about *who they know*. Again, you don't know if you don't go. 9-Cycles will remind you of this time and time again. And you don't want to miss out on the story when others come back from the adventure to tell you all about it, do you? What better souvenir to have from the trip than your own memories and new friends in the making.

You may notice everyone around you suddenly going on trips too. Friends up and fly to Australia, buddies have tales/photos of their latest voyage and colleagues are heading out of town on a road trip. There are no limits and the possibilities are endless, if you're open and ready to make things a bit more fun, bigger, wider and more expansive. The universe wants you to become a global citizen and it will do its best (if you're willing and show readiness) to open up your world and get you out, get you connected and get you circulating in new scenes.

Ever heard of turtle racing? Neither had I – until someone took me to an event, during Cycle 9.

I wound up in different bars, meeting new friends (who were always from somewhere new), coming across people from out of town or out of the country, meeting fascinating people with knowledge beyond my own, and I was out and about every day going to new places. One new friend I was with during a Cycle 9 even ended up chatting to a woman in a coffee shop whose name matched the very same one tattooed on his ring finger (his ex wife). What a conversation that was. Life will find anything to help you connect. People just want to meet you, talk to you, get to know you, under Cycle 9. And you can choose to stay home, or you could go along for the ride.

TEACHING, PREACHING

How do you go past the city limits of your knowledge and experience? Simple. You just do it. You go. You sign up. You drive, walk, bus, fly someplace new. You ask someone for more information. You give it a shot. You stop worrying or questioning your possible success or possible failure and instead question what the point and purpose is of keeping things the same.

Be prepared to pass on what you know many times over during this Cycle. Many people you meet in Cycle 9 are crossing paths with you because somehow they sense you're in a dissemination cycle, a time when you're well placed to pass on information, knowledge, advice or wisdom that they need to hear. You have access to just the right jigsaw piece that will complete their picture or at least give them a greater perspective on something they've been struggling with.

It works both ways. Sometimes it's a mixed year – you get to learn something from someone who passes your way, and you get to understand more. It's amazing the growth and expansion that knowledge gives you, just from simple conversation this time of your year. The number of times I hopped on a bus or train to visit a new friend in Cycle 9 years is astounding.

Cycle 9s are not about limits. How can you expand when you're stuck in a rut or fraternizing with the familiar? I guess you could say that Cycle 9s then, paradoxically *are* about limits – in the way they show you there truly are none, only the ones you impose upon yourself.

FIND YOUR FUNNY BONE
Don't take it all too seriously, this Cycle. Life is like a tide. Business goes up and down. Meeting people is a numbers game. Emotions ebb and flow. You win some; you lose some. Life's a game. Gamble some and see what happens. Don't base your entire life on the feeling you're feeling *right now, where you stand*. It's only one page, one hour, one moment, one phase, one Cycle, one moment in a grander story. And things, as you may or may not have learned already, have a habit of changing pretty quickly, depending on what you're thinking about and how you're feeling about it!

If you can, be 'footloose and fancy free'. Refuse to be tied down. Kick up the dust. Try things out. Be a nomad. Keep moving. Refuse to be tied to any commitment or decision unless you're sure this is something that will encourage growth in your life. Does it feel exciting. A new opportunity?

Go on a hunt or an adventure. Pick and choose. Don't let the seriousness of others get you down. Don't let your light be dampened or put out. Have faith it'll work out magically. Every cloud has a silver living. Expect a miracle and you're sure to see one.

Feel better. That's your starting point, and doing whatever you can to feel better, however slight, will create the shift you've been seeking and the shift that Cycle 9 is wanting to provide for you.

In *The Luck Factor*, Richard Wiseman reminds us that if everyone we know, knows at least fifty people on a first name basis, just chatting to one new person a week would give us access to the fifty people they know and the fifty people their friend knows and so on. Imagine the potential. Your Dream Vision could be given wings pretty fast and take flight with all the connections you can make in your 9-Cycle.

Make your own luck, then. All it takes is knocking on doors, tapping someone on the shoulder, turning to the person near to you and making the contact – being open, friendly, curious, and relaxed.

The rest will take care of itself.

TOO MUCH OF A GOOD THING?
Excess is your enemy in Cycle 9, or could be. Overdoing it (too many parties, late night, drinks, pills, sexual partners, commitments, balls in the air, loose ends, anything) will no doubt land you worse off than you were when you started. Things get exaggerated in 9-Cycles as things blow up out of proportion (the good stuff becomes amazing, the bad stuff becomes dreadful). It all depends upon which fire you're feeding. Be sure to throw logs in your dream furnace and you'll be warmed with fierce flames.

Choices open up and once again we see just where our freedom and power lies – in choosing the best for ourselves. You cannot fool someone out of the truth – it's felt in our heart and guts and soul as a familiar bell chiming inside. Sagittarius is open spaces, big adventures, high energy, freedom, independence and big ideas! Since it's also the sign of religion, overseas, law and education, look to new doors opening in these areas – from new laws introduced to unite countries and people from differing belief systems, to the delivery of more old-world concepts and archaic principles. Sagittarius is also the sign of the holier-than-thou preacher!

Movies are often released at times that relate to the Cycles they touch upon. *The Chronicles of Narnia* was released on December 9 during the sign of Sagittarius (its author C.S. Lewis was born with six planets including the Sun in Sagittarius). This sign is the 9th sign and thus corresponds to Cycle 9. The story is full of Sagittarian principles – independent children, vast open land, horse riding, the issues of honesty and nobility.

During your Cycle 9, a new opportunity awaits. A door opens – or at least you get to see a new one. Freedom. More independence. Enjoy wherever this next adventure leads you. And don't forget to keep an eye out for those folk listed at the beginning of this chapter, as signposts along the way!

CYCLE 9 ACTION PLAN
*Find ways to expand your horizons – physically (go somewhere new), mentally (learn something new), emotionally (take a risk and leave your comfort zone) and spiritually (believe in no limits).
*Bring back optimism and hope – there's always a silver lining, even if you can't see it yet.
*Do more, expect more, adventure more, experience more, desire more. Get more.
*Cross the cultural divide – go global.
*Bring humor back – rent comedies, laugh more and see the sillier side.
*Treat life like a road trip – enjoy the journey and quit worrying about how to get to your destination (or if you ever will, or even where that is yet).

In traveling years:
You get the key to the city, or better yet a round trip ticket to the country or continent (or planet) of your choice. Life just feels good. You win the lottery, or simply a toaster at a local church fête. Someone offers you a ride – or you're giving someone else one, to the next city along, and you're free to go. Did someone say, "Road trip?" You're in! Or the flight is cheap, the hotel more of an international hostel but comfier and there's a free breakfast (of something you can barely pronounce but wished they served back home). All you need do is pack a few things.

Suddenly a book drops in your lap with such an amazing passage you photocopy it and stick it on the wall and in your wallet and broadcast it to the world, because it's awesome. Your online blog takes off and everyone seems interested in what you have to say, so much in fact you're offered a gig teaching or promoting.

You're big. People want to know what you know. What's your secret, oh wise one? Doors open, your internet connection takes you to other cultures and the number of foreign-born or accented folk coming your way is unbelievable. And your new accent is pretty impressive! But then with the stream of foreigners and out-of-towners giving you tips on where to go, what to see and what to do (and how to do it), you can't help but be a pro. Who needs sleep when you have conversations and possibilities such as these?! And don't even mention the book deal – the publishers love it.

They want more, more, more – can you put aside the drink, food and good times long enough to get any work done? There's always one more party, one more hour, one more meeting, one more adventure and one more side street to check out. But there are only twenty-four hours in one single day so pace yourself. You're juiced up, ready to go and things truly haven't looked as good as this in ages. Freedom calls!

In unraveling years:
You're either overbooked or undercooked. Your travel plans fall through and you're stuck at home, or in an unknown country with no guide book or translator. Nothing makes sense and no one is listening, so how the hell can you make progress? Paperwork is wrong, or you need border patrol's permission to gain access, but you're wearing the wrong shoes or your t-shirt is too controversial. Beliefs get in the way – so much so that life takes on political intrigue – some don't agree at all with you and others want to worship you as their guru, and you want neither. Can't people stop listening to the loudest voice? But wait, can *you* stop shouting? It's hard to pass the test or exam when you're ill prepared and since there's always one more party to go to, you wind up overdoing it and out of commission for some really important work.

For now – you may have worked it out already but it's all your darkest repressed stuff bursting out – your biggest phobia, fear and worry.

Somehow you have so much to do, never enough time to do it and you're overindulging in things that simply won't get you anywhere. You're exhausted. But some of it is hard to resist: the invite to stay out till 6am, the extra glass of wine, another slice of cake. And don't even talk about the splurging – when are you going to replace the money that's gone out? True you may get lucky, but you may just get mucky when you trip over and don't come up smelling of roses. Too much, too fast.

You're overstretched and over-burdened, or feeling trapped in a tiny cell, with a view of a brick wall. First step – visualize yourself into a bigger and better place, learn something new, begin a course of study, plot a new adventure, and take a journey inside or outside. Anything is better than this, and you really can't go wrong. All roads lead home – it's just time to take a new one.

Cycle Lesson

Every thought when thought enough soon becomes an ingrained 'belief'. It's not too long before we become dogmatically trapped in a limited perspective (more commonly known as a narrow mind). The same goes for us physically. Without exploration, we cannot learn what is beyond the city gates of our limitation. Without the pursuit of 'more' we are trapped in the familiar and risk becoming lost in the fragments of thoughts inside our heads. A bigger picture is needed. Whether we move physically or open up intellectually and emotionally, we can only grow when we go places we haven't been, discover things we don't know, understand things we never tolerated before and try things we have never experienced. Our growth comes when we gain a wider perspective, a deeper understanding and a more open mind.

It's only through these new windows of opportunity that the questions we are asking can find the answers they seek.

Celebrity Spotlight

- Michael Palin completes his television travel series *Around the World in 80 Days*, during Sagittarius Season (Cycle 9) in 1989.
- Passenger aircraft *Concord* celebrates its retirement long-distance voyage on November 26, 2003 (Cycle 9).
- Cher's single *Believe*, is released during Cycle 9 in the States (November 24, 1998).

Tips to successfully navigating your Cycle 9 Expansion

- Take a l-o-o-o-o-o-n-g trip: throw a dart at a map randomly and go.
- Go horse riding, hiking, exploring. Jog, walk. Get outside!
- Visit the local bookstore or library.
- Take up a night course or college class.
- Travel overseas – renew your passport *now*!
- Buy a guidebook (even for the town you've lived in for ten years).
- Promote a cause you really believe in.
- Sit in the back of the local church and enjoy the sights, sounds and smells – regardless of whether you're a 'believer' or not.

- ◎ Aim big – (you never know if you don't go).
- ◎ Laugh often – at nothing in particular.
- ◎ See the cosmic joke and the funny side to everything, even the worst stuff.
- ◎ Be the free spirit you truly are: stretch your horizons/limbs.
- ◎ Play darts, paint-ball, archery, laser-tag, anything target related.
- ◎ Eat, drink and be merry.
- ◎ Expand your world: connect to the internet and other countries.
- ◎ Gamble – someone has to win, right?
- ◎ Enjoy a current spell of good luck (it's your turn this Cycle).
- ◎ Expand space – move clutter, give yourself leg room and elbow space.
- ◎ Allow others their own space.
- ◎ Redefine your belief system and don't get caught up in holy wars.
- ◎ Promote and advertise yourself, your message, your ideas/products.
- ◎ Bridge cultural divides.
- ◎ Stop preaching (unless you can walk your talk) and start teaching.
- ◎ Tell the truth no matter how difficult it is.
- ◎ Reach for a dream, star, better situation: seek greener grass.
- ◎ Be optimistic, reconnect with your inner faith.
- ◎ Renew your religious or spiritual vows or connections.
- ◎ Try to see the Bigger Picture.
- ◎ Publish a new book or get writing.
- ◎ Be an example, even if no one else is doing it.
- ◎ Have faith in the silver lining and the light at the end of the tunnel.
- ◎ Find a new vantage point high up a hill/mountain/building.
- ◎ Enjoy the journey simply for what it is.

∼ Surf Cycle 10 ∼

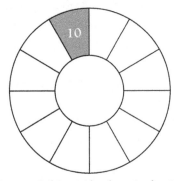

Time to Achieve Absolute Authority
Upgrade by Getting Real and Respond
and Determine Your
Next Direction

Instructional Introductions from:

Your boss/principles/authorities
Your employers
Your parents
Colleagues and clients
People in uniform
Job contacts/job fair staff
Capricorn and serious and sober
types
Your cousin
Your father or step father
Your mother's new husband
Executives/headhunters/judging
panels
Hotshots/professional admirers
'Wise elders'

Agents and personal promoters
The people upstairs
Chief executive officers/corporate
managers
Timekeepers/clock-watchers (or
makers)
Control freaks/tyrants
The one you're trying to impress
Captains, sergeants, sheriffs,
presidents/ kings
Leaders, rulers, higher-ups
Business clothing staff
The elderly/more mature
The one who lays down the law
Government officials

What you'll need:

A head for heights
A compass and a reliable watch
Classy clothes
A pole to vault any hurdle
A candle to burn at both ends

HARVEST TIME – crop or crap?

Did you manage to pick up a copy of this book prior to this Cycle? Were you able to do what was asked of you way back in Cycle 11?

If you were, stay tuned.
If you weren't, don't worry. That Cycle is coming up next.

You already have put your wishes out there by what you were focusing on and secretly desiring during that time, with or without the aid of this book.

If you *were* one of the *consciously* creating ones back then (which if you weren't, you'll be better equipped now to be during every 11 Cycle for the rest of your life!) then whatever you envisioned, crafted, and planned for way back in Cycle 11 – when you planted your ideal/vision/wish-seeds/hopes – has either arrived, is ripe for arrival/well on the way to manifestation or failed to manifest. Simple. In the space of your annual Cycle this is the point where you wind down as you come to the final unveiling and showcasing of what was originally just an idea; a seed. You're not ready to rest *just* yet, you're not quite done, but you're at the last leg of one particular journey.

Keep going. You're truly, nearly there.

Even **if you weren't a conscious creator** (because you forgot, didn't know what Cycle 11 was all about or hadn't come across this book yet), don't worry, you missed nothing except the awareness of what was taking place. You'll still see results, but your focus may not have been as sharp and therefore the results may be less defined.

Maybe you've just about lost the weight, finally built the company, married your soul mate, quit the habit, sealed the deal. Maybe you've just stayed healthy or stayed out of trouble.

Maybe you didn't.

Achievement is relative to the individual. But the effort was there (hopefully) and possibly this year wasn't the one that saw you succeed with flying colors. But the good news is that at least, now you know. And you can move ahead onto grander goals and new heights or you can have another go, with all the wisdom you've amassed from last year.

Plenty of time, and no mistakes. Just pathways, possibilities and experiences.

Either way, you're wiser now. You have more life experience. And if you continue to use the structure laid out in this book (tell your friend to buy their own!) each and every year of your life, you'll find you can only gain and the game gets a bit easier to navigate and possibly, understand.

So in your Cycle 10, **enjoy your harvest**. Something is either ready, is here or isn't working out. Here's a short breakdown to help you locate yourself in your very important 10th Cycle:

Something is Ripe for Arrival: A Vision from Cycle 11 (almost a year ago now, or from Cycle 11s further back in your history) is ready to burst onto the scene. Through preparation, the steady focus of your energy and the intensity of your focus, along with unwavering dedication, love, hope, commitment and faith (along with all the other lessons and gifts of each of the previous Cycles that led you here), you are within close proximity to seeing your Vision reach completion. How does it feel?

Some of you may be nervous that it may not pan out. Understandable. Some of you may be 100% sure it's a done deal. A nice feeling. All that is asked of you now is to stay the course, to see out the final stage of your planning, and that is to maintain your dedication, commitment and discipline to the Vision, the Dream, the Goal. All else is insignificant. This has become bigger than you. Congratulate yourself on getting this far, and for all you've done through each of the tests and challenges, and for arriving where you currently stand. So much potential and so much to anticipate.

As astrologer Linda Goodman said, "Expect a Miracle".

Something has Arrived: This is it. You got it. You won. You arrived. You make it. You achieved! How does it feel? Amazing, yet it's already over in some way, and you sense a need to now take things to a new level, a new height. Aren't you ever satisfied?! No. We're living a human life and there is no final destination point. It's a work in progress. You get something, then say "Okay now what?!". But first give yourself a major pat on the back and allow others to do the same. Blow your own trumpet. Celebrate your success! What you dreamed up in Cycle 11 has come to fruition and completion. That is spectacular! Is it how you envisioned it? Are the photos you collected in Cycle 11 mirroring where you are now? Maybe it's even better? Maybe you could have been more specific. Now you know what to do during your next Cycle 11 coming up ahead. Fine tune your details and focus. Ask for something clearer. You know you can do it, nothing can stand in your way. Do it again. Only this time, do it even better! Congratulate yourself for being a master manifester!

Remember too, you may have been successful in manifesting something you didn't want. The rules still apply. With focus, dwelling, obsessing, and fussing over something long enough, you draw up an energetic blueprint for its final physical manifestation. As a creator, that's your job. You're good at it. So if something shows up now that you didn't want – a fear, an illness, something you always hoped and wished and prayed (that's commitment and intense focus!) would never happen to you, see this as a reminder and proof that these principles work. You can undo these things with a commitment in a new direction if you are willing, or you may have to run with it and focus on new areas and chalk this up as another growth experience.

You'll be aided yourself no doubt by at least one Capricorn who appears by magic during this Cycle, to remind you of the clock (either that you have plenty of time, or that time's running out), to show you that even under the heaviest burden you can still carry on and overcome, and how doing your duty and putting playtime to one side for a time can bring its own rich rewards. Through good or bad, Capricorns will show you what it is to keep on climbing, even when you lose the feelings in your legs due to the cold, a fracture or fear. A lesson you can't learn in any classroom.

Something failed to manifest: You dreamed it up one Cycle 11, but by Cycle 10 it collapses or never appears. Did you try hard enough? Maybe it's just too early and more work is needed before it's ready to manifest. Like a university degree program. Maybe you're not done with the workload yet necessary for the final achievement of your goal/vision. But you had multiple visions in Cycle 11 so don't fixate on only the ones that haven't arrived yet. We could sit and sulk or beat ourselves up if we see ourselves as 'failing' but it doesn't matter. This gives you an enormous opportunity to re-shape your Vision, or keep going (who says it needs to manifest this year only?). If you're truly committed, this won't stop you. If you truly love it and value it, you won't stop now and you won't quit or give in.

Outer success is achieved through unwavering inner commitment. Is your ideal really *ideal* for you? *If* something didn't manifest, then that is great because it gives you the chance to focus on something new. You gave it a shot and maybe, just maybe, you don't really want it with all of your being anymore. In which case, now's the time to prepare the way for a new goal. Ah, now you're feeling excited? Good. Great. You're off for another shot at another dream. That is life. That is how we play the game. Congratulate yourself on living to tell your story, living to see another day and for another chance at creating something even better.

Something is ready to change. That is for certain. You already feel it. It's time for new goals, mapping new terrain and planning ahead for a new phase in life.

Regardless of where you are, or think you are, or feel you are, or appear to be ... something *has* manifested in your life. Even those of you who sit and think "Wow, that year was a total failure", think again. It wasn't. You touched lives, you made friends, you loved, you got up out of bed, you learned lessons, overcame obstacles, worked around challenges, fell out with friends and made up, decided what you *really* wanted, drew some boundaries, opened up more, risked, loved, you got ill and better, stood and fell. You're here another year, to read this book. You survived. Pat yourself on the back for that. No one else may give you an honor, medal, trophy or mention in the paper (or they may) but that's an achievement with the state of the world right now, isn't it? In short, you were playing the human game of life in all its glories and defeats.

Pretty great stuff.

So ... as in all Cycles – don't judge your entire life by this one. Cycle 10 is an end point to some degree (is there ever such a thing as an 'ending?'). It's more a final presentation of something already set in motion. To show you if you really want what you wanted all the way back in Cycle 11, consciously set out for yourself or otherwise.

Well, do you? Do you still want what you set out for yourself back in Cycle 11? (Take out that Vision List you stashed away in preparation for this moment.) Or did your plan change along with your needs? It's okay to change your mind. You can spend a year, or longer, pursuing one thing and realize when you get it that you never really wanted it after all; it doesn't satisfy you or you no longer want to chase it.

WHAT IS SUCCESS TO *YOU*?

It's not the attaining of something that will bring you peace and inner happiness, but **the process of attaining it.** That's where the hard work pays off, and the hard work is the pay-off in itself. Anyone who ever worked for something felt so much better achieving it than when it was handed to them; if it *was* handed to them their insecurity kicked in because they didn't know if they were truly worthy or could handle it. Did those born into money and financial success ever have it easy on the personal front? Look around.

Your feelings of happiness come from knowing you pitched in, not from the final attaining of something. That's just the cherry on the top.

You can make, in Cycle 10, one further push for more power, authority, control and a new vantage point if you want to take on more power, and responsibility, and feel ready for it – and why the hell not? Chances are you'll get it, if you've paid your dues. Cash in on that now with a final bid to scale higher. Be proud, bold, talk to those higher ups and act like one, because you're an authority yourself.

However, if you want more freedom and a new vision and to try your hand at something else, something different to what you've been investing your time, energy or money in to date, then Cycle 11 is coming up, and this is the time. You can release old pursuits and projects and move into fresher pastures, by planting new seeds again. Right now, though, you get to see everything for what it is. Reality seeps in. You get a reality check, and a chance to review what you've been doing and therefore where you find yourself.

Cycle 10 gives you an opportunity to look at yourself and look at the life you're living and to see if they match. If not, you have a major chance to reinvest back into yourself and re-navigate your life's direction. It's *never* too late.

For now, enjoy what Cycle 10 is also about. And whether you choose to participate or not, even this too shall pass.

ACHIEVEMENT: INSPIRATION MEETS PERSPIRATION

In perfect universal synchronicity, I received an email that had this at the bottom, this morning, while working on this chapter. It read,

Success is not final,
Failure is not fatal,
It is the courage to continue that counts.

As a recap, Cycle 10 arrives and asks you:

Are you on top of things? Or at least prepared to get on top and sort things out?

Are you in the driving seat of your own life or ready to grab the wheel?

Do you have a new or continued direction/ goal and some plan to get there?

No matter where we are, there's always further to go, on the path. This Cycle brings in a new burst of energy to wise-up, mature and decide where we want to move next.

Immaturity is swept aside when we realize that it's up to us to get us where we want to be. The driver on life's highway, the author of our own story. How's yours going?

Cycle 10 is all about achievement and brings a newfound urge to *do* something, *be* something, *stand* for something and *succeed* with something, someone, some avenue, some quest, some goal.

At this point it's either about getting to the top, or crumbling on your way to the bottom in preparation for a new attempt.

First of all, find your harvest, whatever it is (most likely some 'result' of your efforts: be it an honor, object, congratulation, praise, adoration, love, green light, sum of money, relationship etc.) Or it may be one of those dud harvests when it's only just 'effort' you see as your outcome, even if it seems to have yielded nothing. It may be hard to push against the tide. What you set in motion, your vision/dream/wish-seed in Cycle 11, is here. Right now! This month comes the payoff. Or the almighty realization that it failed. It didn't manifest. Oops! Better luck next time. When is that? Now! *This time.* You get to stand on stage and see if you get a gold, silver, bronze or whether you weren't even invited to the award ceremony!

So you made it. Here. Wherever that is. At the bottom; at the top. Somewhere in the middle. Fine. Now its time for a new conquest, a new challenge. A new goal or mission.

Can you see it, define it, name it and ... Are you ready once more to climb?

THE CLIMB

Chances are you've already started wondering about your future career path or the direction your life is taking or 'should be' taking. Where is everything leading? Where are you leading yourself or disowning your power and letting yourself be led? Talks about (or with) bosses, authority, leadership, getting on top of things, upgrading, stepping up your game, taking charge, having more control, office politics, positions of power and climbing the ladder and making an impression; all permeate the air either through you or the people around you. It's about power, control, authority and mastery; how could it not be? The time is ripe to ask yourself: What am I good at? What am I a pro at? What does the world need to see through me as an example of excellence? How can I show my stuff? Do I believe in myself (belief being something you learned in Cycle 9) enough now to unveil just how great I am in Cycle 10, my public presentation phase of my annual voyage?

You want power in life again, yes; you want to stand tall and in control of yourself with no boss or parent sniffing down your neck, yes. You want to stand above others somehow, you want authority, you want mastery, yes. You want to get to the top and stay on top. You want people to look up to you. You want your career to take off. You want to be good at something; the best. You want to manifest a great work of personal accomplishment. Yes?

Of course you do.

Right. This is Cycle 10 and this is the launchpad for this and more.

You may feel inadequate reading these words in some years. Hard work seems to have landed you with nothing. You're worn out, weak, depressed, dreary or just down. We'll get to that.

Some Cycle 10s give you a hint at an upgrade: Is it promotion time? Could well be. This is the time of your annual Cycle when you get rewarded for hard work and hoisted up a notch or three in a good year, or wind up fired, quitting or downsized if you've a few lessons still to learn. It's all about being in the driver's seat, carving your own way, showing others just what you're made of. Yes, mountains will appear, greater heights you must soar to or scale over (by tooth and nail maybe – is that why dental work often gets done in Cycle 10?) but who said the reward is sweet without a few obstacles? How can you truly say you 'made it', if you didn't have at least some form of resistance, roadblock, someone telling you that you couldn't, or some feat you weren't forced to overcome?

You'll need a backbone now, if you didn't grow one in the other Cycles. You simply need a strong structure to keep you in place (like your skeletal system and spine), to have the nerve (and courage and audacity!) to stand tall, stand straight and face reality (the reality you're creating) head on.

Successful people have an edge: the confidence to stand strong and perform, even in the face of fear or adversity. Quitting just isn't an option. You keep on because it's who you are.

Pitting your wits against the stresses and strains around you now sets you up for major success (or major failure if you can't even set foot on the road that leads to the pinnacle). Like Frodo Baggins, you stand at the threshold of Mordor – will you enter, will you face the Dark Lord, the only one left who has potential power over you? Or will you turn around defeating yourself at the final hour? It's the last stage of one journey – a lot is left to karma, you've set it all in motion so now you await the season of your crop. It's harvest time or you'll have to sit out the feast and banquet until another better day.

STATUS SHIFT

Prepare for an imminent status shift. Perhaps you're getting married, changing your name, becoming part of a team. Maybe you're offered a promotion and thus an entirely new set of credentials, duties and responsibilities. Perhaps you suddenly become a parent, having to navigate this new life role. Just as Cycle 11 allows us to shape our new life role with visions of 'what will be' (and what can be), Cycle 10 is the final step where we *become* a role, we achieve a life status.

Maybe you've squandered resources, lied on the job (or not even tried to work), given up halfway through a project or not yet even started it. Your life status at Cycle 10, for a society who judges often on our external status-symbols (cars, homes, bank balances, relationships etc), looks pretty shabby. You're a 'loser', a 'bum', whatever your version of amounting to nothing may be. You may be faced with judgments (whether from outside, or actually from within your own mind).

Whichever way the pendulum swings (we'll explore both a little later on), you're faced with lessons, challenges and gifts. Nothing is set in stone forever, especially in how you perceive it. Is it a curse or actually a blessing? You often won't know until further down the line, when you look back with Cycle 10 wisdom and insight.

Since you're here now, take a final look at who and what you were, who and what you were doing with your time and energy and focus and mind and feelings in Cycle 11, and look at what you became. Your new status. Did it improve? Did it get worse? Did you achieve anything (surely you triumphed in some area). Can you try again? Start over? Continue the climb? Try a new angle/possibility/direction in Cycle 11 next up?

Evaluate where life has brought you, in this, your Cycle 10. And then decide where you'd like to go next.

ARE WE THERE YET? CAREER-LEADING CHEERLEADING

Are we careering out of control? Or in control of our career? What we truly want to do with our lives is inescapable at this point. Our mission. Our destiny. Our direction. Our destination. It's time to redefine this, and put at least one foot on the path we desire to be on.

Forget 'getting there' ("How do I make it?!") All we're asked now is to take *one* step towards it. Want to start yoga? Search for a class, grab a book. Call a studio. Simple. Don't get overwhelmed with the 'bigness' of your idea. Just one step towards it is all you need.

Need better management/organization? Same thing. Look online at free articles on how to re-arrange your life. Buy a calendar. Map out one day of your life and follow the plan. Go to the library, ask someone you respect who has what you want, and see how they do it. Want a pay rise or promotion? Ask for it! Tired of your job? Seek a new one. Begin the work of *looking*. Instead of sitting bemoaning your current dead-end situation.

Forget achievement – the achieving now is in the **doing, allowing and being open to change.**

We climb the ladder this month and make it, or slip trying (or stalling) – and we can allow the process to unfold or fight against it. Therein lies our real success. Life wants something better for us and fully supports all actions that are invested in this intention and this intention only: to better our lives.

Not bad, eh? Yes it involves work, but we truly can't afford to remain where we are, permanently.

Life helps those who help themselves, in Cycle 10.

Everything is a *work in progress*. Everything. Help your own work of art along by giving it structure, a plan, and solid support. Don't skimp, don't quit. Plug away. Little by little. Effort is all you need to give it.

Under a 10th Cycle, success is guaranteed if we invest in ourselves and our true desires, backed by unshakable determination. **And again, all we need is the desire to better ourselves and our lot in life.**

Avoid the snakes of doubt,
and continue climbing the ladder!

WHO'S IN CHARGE?
Tips from the Top: Dad

Many find their first authority figure marches back onto the scene at this time – Father. Or some father figure – possibly your mother if she was the only one around or who set the rules at home. Authority is anyone who reminds you of the rules of the game and your limits. And the duties of life. Do they badmouth you now to push you to 'prove yourself' or do they help you up? Either way the only way *is* up, if you choose to go.

Often wisdom comes with knowledge and maturity, but just as many times it doesn't. Does his/her return bring a sense of stability, or does it rattle your cage that s/he's still throwing their weight around and doing a bad job of showing you how authority *should* be?

You may receive a phone call, letter, email or visit from them, in person or just in memory, or perhaps via a dream. Perhaps you'll end up arguing that your father was never for you. That you don't respect his life choices. That he's not doing enough to help you. Or you're commending him on his success, or thanking him for being there when you needed him. Those who pop up now are around to show you that really it all boils down to parenting yourself in this Cycle, being your own grown-up and standing tall no matter what's hitting the fan. It would be nice to lean on someone and indeed maybe you'll have the opportunity, but on those Cycles when you have no one, you have the memory of those who have gone before you and have made it to the heights to carry you through.

Is yours another rags to riches story (or riches to rags and back again?). Maybe it's time to check in on how those you really respect did it. How did they make it?

Tips from the Top: Mom?

Okay so some of us don't have Dads. He left when we were young or he was never around or we lost him. For some of us, Mom was the boss. Or grandparents. For others, an orphanage or surrogate parents. If Mom was your authority, then she'll be the one who will star this month and you'll find she either gets in your way, points the finger or helps you higher up. You'll see how she deals with things and whether you can 'one-up' her and emulate her or whether you would be wise to do things a little differently. Either way, don't forget that mothers can be bosses too, and in many households that rings true.

For the rest of us, whoever played boss to you is likely to show up again now – either in person themselves, or people who act like they did. Which will either frustrate you or comfort you, depending on how they were at handling the responsible job of being a healthy grown up themselves.

Tips from the Top: Boss

Are you the boss? If so – lucky you! Or perhaps not so lucky, if you have stressful employees to deal with. A promotion at this time could weigh heavily on you if you don't feel prepared. Or you may just eat up all the new power and responsibility bestowed upon your very capable shoulders. Maybe you'll be barking "Off with their heads!" and firing someone. Of course, you may be the one being fired during this Cycle. Watch what you say and watch what you do, there's always someone with more power than you. Even if it's just Mother Nature.

More weight falls on your shoulders now whether from extra responsibility or from a personal internal pressure to 'be more, do more or have more'. Maybe you're noticing an infamous Cycle 10 reaction of "Wow, at this age this is all I have to show for myself?!" Work wise, and life direction wise, you may be facing an upgrade where your company grows and you are shoved into the limelight. Or if you've not been working hard enough you have to pull out all the stops to make ends meet. Either way, as the sole controller of your life and career, it comes down to how hard you work, how much you do, how committed you are and how disciplined. How's your schedule? Are you dedicating yourself to achieving? Where are your goals? Are you crumpling under the weight of fear? If so, what small steps can you take to get out of it?

Setting goals and achieving (or breaking them) feels good. Even if you're feeling lazy, Cycle 10 affords you a special moment in your annual voyage to step up your game. Divide up your days or hours to accomplish something (don't forget some downtime as a reward, though. It makes the climb and work all the sweeter).

If you *have* a boss, then they may suddenly figure strongly in your life, with a message for you. A sudden phone call could land you a fantastic new position (like the wonderful time my boss called me in Cycle 10 and asked me to appear alongside him on the radio). Often, they'll shine a light on some part of you that really needs it now (as a reminder of how great you are hopefully). Maybe they need to check in with you on an idea you were pushing way back when, that suddenly now seems to be the right time. A green light. A thumbs up. A golden handshake. Congratulations!

Some years you may find you're called into the boss' office, or that of the principle/headmaster or mistress (if you're at school or a student) or a government official, because you did something wrong: you're being suspended, investigated, fired or put on probation.

Those who symbolize authority (maybe they wear a uniform, maybe they just have a big chip on their shoulder or the life experience or qualifications to make you sit up, pay attention and give them respect) always venture across your path as a reminder of where you *could* be, where you *should* be, where you'd *like* to be, or where you had better change your ways to *avoid* being or becoming.

So, pay close attention to the signs and messages that crop up now from those around you in a stronger position that you. They can help you, if you let them. Ultimately they are external representatives of your inner authority – the part of you inside that knows it can do better or be more. How healthy is your connection to your inner parent and inner boss? Now's the time to see that and perhaps tweak your discipline, and reach for a better position in life.

Tips from the Top: The Elderly
Experience doesn't always bring wisdom. My clients have ranged from 70-year-olds who weren't able to let go of a grudge they held back in their early years, to 20-year-olds who have learned some of the most valuable lessons a human can. Age just means you've been alive longer.

But sometimes you do come across a wise elder, especially in this Cycle. Whether it's your grandparents, an old man standing behind you at the checkout, an elderly lady at the post office, or someone else's older relatives, you could find in one Cycle 10 that you're visited by someone with the wisdom of their age (or the Ages).

That's just what happened during one of my 10-Cycles, when I found myself standing on the western-most edge of the United States coastline, staring out to the vastness of the sea, beside an 80-something-year-old Capricorn (the sign associated with Cycle 10). I asked her what her wisdom was, her philosophy of life. She said it was that "the Creator is real. Everything is so beautiful and I'm glad I was created as I am". Her smile twinkled like the glimpses of light reflected off the ocean lapping the cliffs below us.

She saw something bigger in all of this. Losing her mother at an early age, battling five years of depression and countless other (very Capricornian) setbacks, delays, frustrations, burdens and responsibilities when very young, she was able to triumph, because her spirit saw something bigger through everything that had happened. She felt blessed.

Just as I was, to be standing beside someone so chronologically old, yet spiritually youthful. And just as you may be, if you keep an eye out for the wise elders who appear (like cosmic clockwork) during our Cycle 10s.

THE RULES: CLIMB THE LADDERS; WATCH THE SNAKES
Remember the game Snakes and Ladders mentioned earlier? To win you had to move ahead on the board and avoid the snakes, whose bodies would lead you slithering further back down to where you just came from, and hopefully climb the ladders to cut corners and make it to the finish line. Life's like that: 'Ten steps forward five back'. Sometimes it's ten forward, ten forward and two back .

Whatever the case, the back-steps are always useful, and often the best things that could happen to us as they teach us much: resilience, patience, discipline; and often wind up putting us in the right place at the right time (didn't Cycle 9 teach you anything?!) So lucky breaks can come from these slithering snake scenarios. Obviously it feels better to climb the ladders but often true success involves a redefinition of those moments that would for all intents and purposes outwardly seem like 'failure'. What is failure or rejection anyway? It's all in the eye of the beholder. Keep that in mind, this Cycle. The tough times could be saving your bacon when you don't even know it. Or reserving you for something greater.

Which leads us to the concept of *Rules*. The system always 'gets you' in this Cycle. You get a ticket for speeding (or a broken light like my friend did one night in my own Cycle 10). Or you get audited. Or you meet red tape or a big *No* from the government or your parents or someone you're trying to impress. Again, it's a test, a challenge. Do you give up and opt out? Or does it shape you and help sculpt your new disciplined efforts at climbing further ladders?

You'd be wise in some Cycle 10 years to see it as high time to try something else. Maybe you've beaten your head against one wall one too many times. How do you know if that's the case or if you're *just* about to reach that saturation point where success truly is just a step away (even though you can't feel it, see it or even sense it)?

I've seen it happen countless times. **How much do you want it?** That's the question. Would you be willing to die trying? Not that you need to, but is your *commitment and dedication* fully behind it? 100% will always get you there. Or somewhere even better. Always. Without fail. Can you believe and conceive of that? Remember your Cycle 9 beliefs? Perhaps this is a good time to revisit your 9-Initiation with a quick re-read so you can whizz back here and continue on. Do so, if you need a recap; it's worth it.

Can you commit right here today as you're reading this paragraph to see everything that's happening or just happened in your life or is about to happen, as a conspiracy to *help* you get further ahead on your path? Even the crummy stuff? And can you commit to what you want, and know you can have it and that you're allowed?

And can you accept that just somehow, life may know your plans and be arranging and lining something much better up for you, and is shifting your well-laid plans right now, making it seem like a major inconvenience?

Patience, my friend. Patience. It pays off. It's Cycle 10. It may be serious, but things can get seriously good ahead. Remember you have no way of knowing if you're nearly there or not in some years. All you have is your commitment and desire.

Whose rules are you following? Work with the system, let the system work for you. Stay with it a while. Jump through the hoops and you may find a loophole. Rise to the challenges, and you'll get stronger. Follow the rules laid out and you can eventually create your own. Just don't fall victim, if you can help it, to the rules of fear that say you can't do this or this isn't likely to work or that never worked for such and such, or the economy won't allow that. Self-fulfilling prophesies were in play in Cycle 9 (and throughout each Cycle) and in Cycle 10 you get to work with the ones you really want to see play out. Be a walking, talking, living breathing example of the best ones from Cycle 9. Believe it. Know it. Live it. Walk it. Talk it. Commit to it. Regardless of any outer signs of 'success' or 'failure'.

The chess pieces of your life are moving, and it's all being aligned perfectly.
Patience...

YOUR NEW LIFE RULES

Write yourself a list of **New Life Rules**. Stick it up somewhere on the wall (yes, print it out or write it down. Effort!). This way you won't forget your **Prime Objectives**. You'll see how worthwhile it is. What would you like to achieve or complete this month? Write that down too and put these somewhere you'll see them every day. Somewhere you work preferably. This is your new action plan. We all need a **Mission Statement** and Cycle 10 is the best time to craft one to remind you of your focus. Then you can't be knocked off or sidetracked as easily. Try it, and see.

S-T-R-E-T-C-H-!

Yes, yoga would help. You may have begun to notice a little rigidity (both mentally and physically) creeping into your life. Possible back or joint aches, tension, shoulder strain or knots, a stiff neck, teeth issues or other skeletal problems. You don't want to be so rigid and uptight and work-oriented that you turn into a wall. You need to bend like a tree. Put down roots this Cycle but stretch your body as well as your spirit. You'll feel the difference right away.

If you're feeling stuck, go somewhere and stretch. On a yoga mat. In the sunshine outside. In fresh air. On your deck, patio. At the gym. In the bath. Just out of bed or just before going to bed.

It works for cats. And it works for us.

CLOCK-WATCHING

Patience and clock-watching. Who hasn't stood at the checkout line or sat in traffic and felt like screaming? Your concept of time is set to change in Cycle 10 or it becomes another odd theme that appears now – you'll notice clocks, watches, microwave LED displays, calendars and other timepieces making their way into your world. Noticed time going really fast, or suddenly it's at a crawl? Need to keep asking what day it is? Does two days ago feel like two years ago?

Are you like the white rabbit in *Alice and Wonderland* screaming "I'm late, I'm late, I'm late"? Or is the boss reminding you of it? Is someone around you messing up for the very same reasons? Did you miss an important meeting or event that was scheduled this week? Perhaps it's everyone else who seems two hours behind. Or are you finding yourself ahead of the game, on time or with extra time on your hands? Are you getting up earlier or crawling out of bed late in the day?

You may end up buying a new watch or clock this Cycle, or someone gives you one. What a beautiful symbol and psychic reminder to yourself to use your time more wisely. What type of watch or clock is it? Does it have a symbol or picture on it? Is it a specialized one? Is it fun (reminding you to spend more time having fun) or a serious time-keeping device for your office (urging you to be more constructive with the hours you have)? Play with the themes and you'll be surprised what you're trying to tell yourself through gifts you give yourself, others give you, or you find yourself stumbling across or having to purchase now.

Each day we're covering a whole lot more ground now than ever before, as the Earth continues to undergo a major transition. Clocks won't show this – it's a feeling we have inside. Time seems to shift, we miss time; we feel as though we're in two places at the same time.

No, you're not going crazy. You'll feel it since this is your 10-Cycle. Time reintroduces itself to you. You'll have to iron out your time-management skills this Cycle if you're to get anywhere or achieve anything of note. Those who do well, know how to manage their resources (as little as they may have to begin with), and time is one of the most valuable.

Don't put a price on time, but spend it wisely. This Cycle is an open door allowing us to take charge of our own use of energy – how we use time. Are you 'killing time', 'wasting time' – how are you 'spending' time? (After all, it's a currency of sorts.)

THE EXTRA MILE

Hard work – what does it mean to you? Extra hours, overtime, burning the candle at both ends? By all means get up early, stay till late. Put the time in now and you'll surely be rewarded. But that may just be with burnout and a long stint in bed. Becoming a workaholic and an overachiever is the pitfall of Cycle 10, so be careful you don't become Jack Torrence in *The Shining* (Moral: All work and no play could make you an axe-wielding freak or seriously upset the people around you). Sometimes success comes naturally and you don't need to work your pants off to attain it. If your childhood message was 'you get nothing unless you work yourself to the bone', then you may just try and prove that rule (remember 10-Cycles 'rules'). Maybe you can redefine your interpretation of success, achievement and 'making it' and what that entails. Many people out there have done amazingly well and haven't worked themselves into the ground doing it. It is possible, and possibilities are all we need entertain to open doors of further possibility.

PUBLICITY: ANY NEWS IS GOOD NEWS

It's time to be more public now – and chances are you won't be able to help it. Stuff you do seems to attract attention. This phase helps you realize that age-old dream of 'what do I want to stand for, what do I want to be when I grow up, what is my purpose, mission and how do I want people to remember me?' Or you realize fame by something terrible/outrageous/naughty/amazing that you did, or got involved in seemingly against your will, out of the blue.

One thing you *do* have control over is how you handle what comes your way – how you respond and handle what transpires. Your responsibility is being tested for strength or signs of weakness (your response-ability). Deal with the slings and arrows now and you'll progress higher and get stronger, (and find yourself in a stronger position and situation). Refuse to deal or stand strong and you'll collapse and suffer a fall from grace or a great height. Ouch!

Who cares if you're 90, what you say and do stays with people a long time, all starting within this Cycle, so watch it! Okay, so answer the question above. Here it is again:

> what do I want to stand for,
> what do I want to be when I grow up –
> what is my purpose, mission, and
> how do I want people to remember me?

Well? Why aren't you working towards that today? Therein lies your choice, free-will and ultimate power, this Cycle.

As you carve your way in the world, trying to make something of yourself, making a name for yourself in a world of big business and corporate climbing, you'll have to spend more time away from home – either on the phone, on the internet or actually out and about doing public presentations. Good. Hiding at home isn't the greatest of plans since no one can see you and say "Hey, you need to be star in my next movie!".

You have to be out mingling with the rest of the world to get anywhere or if you work from home, you'll have to reach people further afield – if you want the help, put yourself out there. Head-shots, business cards, emails, postings, ads, talks with people who are further up the ladder than you are.

Look at websites such as *Facebook* to get your message out and tell people what you have to offer and what you're doing. Try *Twitter* for the same purpose. Create a new website for yourself or your business using unique templates and designs, contact radio stations, tell journalists in the magazines you like that they can interview you (or have your own questions and answers ready to mail them!), use online ads, internet postings, newspaper classifieds, local groups sharing similar interests, seasonal meetings and mixers.

Have you ever done a search for your name online? Try it and see what you're 'known' for. Or your email address. It's amazing what people can discover about you, purely from these details. From comments you've left reviewing books and movies to postings at online chat forums.

Do what you can where you can to *put yourself out there*. Celebrities know this – so much so, they'll often call the paparazzi and tip them off that they'll be at a specific location (anonymously of course). Bingo! The press gets their snaps and the celebrities remain in the public eye. Advertisers use this to push their products at any opportunity they get – movies, game shows, commercials, billboards, flyers, restaurants, posters, newspapers, magazines and car bumper stickers. Just to remind you they exist and to stick in your mind, with the subsequent hopes you'll buy their product. Retention = sales. For pop singers, actors and any company out there, make them remember you and they'll remain loyal. Or at least give you status, energy, attention and publicity (any kind will do), even if they don't like you!

If you have to be home, then use your time wisely – be more disciplined. Use the internet and phone, hold interviews or bring important people in your field there, invite them for dinner, or offer a trade of sorts.

Make your life more professional.

Showing off, strutting your stuff, looking good and being the best is the best way to attract those who'll notice you and want to give you even more of what you already seem to exude masses of – **Power**. You may have to 'fake it till you make it'. If you believe in you, others will too. It's that simple. The illusion of power may attract those who have it, so can you pull it off? Can you be your own PR person and agent and play the game; work the system? Can you risk losing by playing for bigger stakes? Power is inescapable now. Those who want it and have some to begin with seem to get more. Like attracts like.

That last magical thought is probably the key to all Cycles in this book but in particular this one. ***If you want to make it, you have to be making it now*** – maybe not materially, but at least in your head, actions, energy and way of being. Even if you're not where you want to be, start living as though you have the things you want, the position, the job title, the matching salary. Create a life where you feel and act as if you have the position you want. Even if you work from home, dress sensibly as though you were at work. Be polished. Be the best. What a way to treat yourself! If you do go to an office, act as though you're the best one there (with integrity and respect, not lording over others with arrogance, of course).

Don't be sorry for being so great. Don't apologize for your mastery. Don't lessen your light. You are big. You are great. You are fantastic. You earned it. Let yourself have that right.

Being a master at your job means living it today, not waiting for the world to give you a million and a medal to show you how good you are. You need to be the best today. Try it. Feigning confidence now could boost your self-esteem enough to effect a massive change. Acting as if you have it already (whatever it is you want) makes the universe magnetically reflect that back to you, with situations and people lining up to give you whatever it is you're wanting.

GRACE UNDER FIRE OR FIRING GRACE

Just don't become the next tyrant or you'll fall as many have done during this Cycle through overconfidence, cockiness and the fear of failure – which attracted just that. Many people of note have hit the big time in Cycle 10 only to have it snatched from them when they thought they could control the world (or everyone in their own world). You may be witness (or play a role in) the demise of others from their own pedestals, during this time.

You have much to gain in 10-Cycles. From the crops of seeds planted last year, to the fulfillment physically of what you've energetically been carrying around for the same time (perhaps longer). And that is an amazing thing to witness, let alone experience.

Be serious, but be stylish. It's not always about winning, it's about being the best you can be and letting others see that. What is true success? ***Living the life you want to live***, when it all comes down to it, right? Once people see you're trying your best and handling all life throws at you, how can they not help but *help* – by giving you more responsibility, work, respect, applause or power? You can handle it, and what's more attractive than someone who can handle it all.

Yes, you want to become stronger, more powerful, more capable and more on top of your game. And anyone who tries to take charge of you or control you is going to be in for a surprise. If you give your power away and expect others to live your life for you, you're asking for trouble. Control freaks abound in Cycle 10. Do what you know you need to be doing, should be doing, and don't expect others to fall in line. Then you'll get all the help you need, when you least expect it.

If anyone is trying to control you, in Cycle 10 it's a sign you yourself are not taking enough control of your own life. Get the message.

WAIT – DO YOU HAVE A FEAR OF SUCCESS?

It's a strange question, but one you'll have to face head-on this Cycle. It may sound crazy, but some people actually do fear success because they equate that with things getting too big, too good and then losing their freedom to a sense of responsibility, stress, obligation and the worry that people will need them to be on call 24/7. And not to mention the extra hours, the lack of free time ... etc etc etc. So, they sabotage their success at this stage of their journey when they see just how powerful they could actually become, or have become. Watch this tendency – it could be operating behind your back.

Maybe you're scared to arrive because once you get what you want, the fun phase (of longing, desiring, dreaming, hoping, wishing) will be over. Think about that. Often we get hooked on the 'it might be'. We chase the ones we can't have. Because maybe, just maybe ... we might be able to have it. Longing is a lonely companion but for some of us, it's enough.

Being in control and at the top means you get to set your own limits, rules and regulations. And free time. Or at least you can negotiate. A foot in the door is worth more than you could ever dream of. That is the payoff. Most of the top dogs in the world may work hard but they don't work as hard as the ones at the bottom usually, who slog away for minimum wage day in, day out. The success of those at the top takes care of itself. The work getting there is worth it, in the form of nice bank balances, tropical vacations, fancy cars, eating out at 5-star restaurants. Maid service. Mansions. Endless boxes of chocolates. Personal assistants. Personal shoppers. Expensive clothes. Feeling better about success now?

Why knock so hard on any door only to walk away from it when it opens, for the fear of what may happen when you step through it? Think on this – if you do succeed, you always have the option of returning to your old life of having less, doing less, being less. But chances are, you'd probably not want to. Once you upgrade in life, you get a taste for the new level and come to love that. We set our comfort zones with each step.

But let's skip back to the idea of walking away from doors that open for a final moment – which people do, you'd be surprised. If you're feeling this way, try the following on for size:

> ***you'll never get landed with more than you can handle,***
> ***in any field that you thoroughly love.***

So stick with what you enjoy, and take it one step at a time. And just think of all the good you can do and nice things you can buy with the money you make from your new position of power. If that wasn't an incentive to at least give it a shot, what is?! The nice apartment. The bigger space (with extra storage). The new stereo or TV (with surround sound and crystal clear quality). The new car (that is so smooth you could live in it). The personal chef (so you can come home to gourmet meals). Whatever you like.

Nothing lasts forever, so ride the success train as far as it'll take you now; you deserve it.

Everything will pass, so do it while you can.

REALITY CHECK, MATE!

You have to mature in your Cycle 10. Life often throws you some tough questions or challenges that you need to work through, pitting your wits against some of life's big stuff. Nothing is handed to you in Cycle 10 that you haven't been heading toward for quite some time.

Reality has a way of seeping in to remind you that you are at *the mercy of certain laws, in the physical world.* Like gravity. Aging. Red tape. Bureaucracy. That your knees don't bend backwards. That you need to look after your body because without it, all the success in the world is useless. That you're not in control of everything. That there's always someone else who can one-up you or surpass you or hold you back if you piss them off. That you have to do your best and not try and control others, who are on their own path (and at their own pace, working through their own individual Cycles).

So, something may come down on you and seem harsh or dire or depressing, during some Cycle 10 years. You feel in a vice, put-upon, over-stretched, over-worked or under-appreciated. Your behavior seems judged by everyone, nothing you do is private. You're in a global goldfish bowl with all eyes trained on you. Or in such dreadful isolation (at least emotionally). But your emotions are still broadcast around you, by your lack of light or vitality.

Cycle 10 gives you a chance to see how bright your light is, and how much you may be stifling it or how much you're letting others do that to you (by how down you feel). Your light then becomes as evident in how dark things have become (everything is in balance). The good side of this is that it helps you to get your act together. Cycle 10 demands that you get real. You may have little choice if you're to make any logical headway.

Are you ready to take care of some of the important stuff in your life?

BE A BETTER ROLE MODEL FOR YOURSELF

Parenting yourself is one way. Setting your own structure and limits. Giving yourself a stern but loving talking to. Disciplining your days. Setting standards. Reaching for something other than another soda or slice of pizza. Becoming something. Amounting to something. Having a purpose. Gearing up for your goal. Committing. That is Cycle 10. Your life has a foundation (which you laid down in Cycle 4), now it's about building something worthwhile on top of it. Reach for the sky. Your castle, your dominion, your place of power. To get over what's going on inside of you, and establish something on the outside. To show the world who you are.

So expect some form of a reality check in your life. No, they can't always be avoided. They do us a service – by revealing to us how things are, not as we want them to be, hope them to be or dress them up to be in some way.

Maybe you just have a realization one day that you're wasting too much time/energy/emotion/money on something or someone. You snap out of it. Or perhaps a way of living. It no longer works; it depletes you more than feeds you. Reality comes and bites you from behind when you're painting it in pretty rose colors. If you've been doing that, watch it. Harsh, uncaring, cold facts sometimes land at your door during 10-Cycles as a reminder of what is.

It doesn't need to be depressing, but the wild gleeful days of passionate abandon and carefree cavalier craziness and liberated luxuries of Cycle 9 have drawn to a close to give way for a more lean, structured way of life in Cycle 10. You can fight to revisit the glory days of then, but you'll find it so much more satisfying to put work first and pleasure second (and then you'll have the reputation and money and power to boot).

That is your prime motivation or should be – disciplining yourself instead of seeking an easy out, a quick fix or an escape from what you really seek – structure and seriousness. It comes but once a year, so try and enjoy it as you belt up, knuckle down and actually find a way to be a bit more frugal in all areas. Cycle 11 is coming up ahead and you can burst out again, but for now lay a structure in your life that works for you. That helps you manage yourself better. That gives you something to lean on. Something that supports you, and something to be proud of.

Are you proud of how you're handling your life? Would you be okay bringing a camera crew in *today* to show the world your life? We're not talking about your bathroom habits, but about how you carry yourself through your world and what you're doing with yourself.

To some that will be frightening (if that's you, now you know where your work is, in Cycle 10) while to others, that idea is bliss. And you might just find some producer knocking on your door asking you to star in your own Reality Show.

People become famous in 10-Cycles.
Just make sure it's something you truly want to be known for.

PLANETARY SIGNATURE: SATURN
Saturn is the border-patrol of boundaries and barriers – from physical ones such as our skin and bones, keeping our internal organs in place and secure, to walls, barriers, restrictions in our world that force us to knuckle down and focus, by narrowing our horizons by choice or by force, to help us get something done that we need to.

Time is one of the biggest, also ruled by Master Saturn. He keeps us on track if we work with him. Or if we succumb to his lie, we feel we can't progress and we prepare to give up, to quit, opt out and let ourselves fail to even try. Giving ourselves a structure helps enormously. A plan. Being a little more robotic, for a time. A regular schedule. Clock-watching. Setting standards and goals. And being systematic about following them and ticking off what we have achieved.

Saturn helps us stay the course and stay on track by keeping us firmly tied *to* the track. We know when we're off base and going the wrong way (for the creation of our Cycle 11 Vision) when we feel listless, drifting, without purpose and depressed. Crack out your Saturn action plan (see end of this chapter) and you'll feel better in no time. And it remains with you long-term. Results are guaranteed with Saturn. Hard work always pays off.

CONTROL AND CONTROL FREAKS
Self-control is a tricky thing for many of us. Being the driver, the manager and boss of yourself (or others) means responsibility – your ability to respond

(response-ability) to life's challenges, pressure and deadlines with a whip in hand and your sleeves rolled back, ready. How hard that can be, can be laid out for you by anyone who has ever worked from home. But that's where you currently find yourself: in a place that necessitates some form of self-control (like those annoyingly tricky balancing postures in yoga, if you've ever taken a class).

When does that way of being cross the line to becoming a micro-manager – a bossy, pushy annoying invasive tyrant who abuses others (or the self) because it's never enough or good enough, and it's all about climbing to the top and never being happy?

Is it worth it if you 'make it' and no one likes you? Or you despise yourself? Or are ill, depressed and out of the race? Or you have all the accolades and trophies and no one to share them with? Imagine looking back after you claim your prize and having everyone turn the other way, even the one handing you the award? Ouch! What's the point?

Success is empty if it's not fought and won the most valiant way – when others can turn to you and shake your hand even though you beat them, did a better job or snatched victory from their hands. Not everyone can win or be a winner, not when we're all at different stages of different Cycles. That's the beauty of your life. This is *your* Cycle 10, so act like you mean it.

Don't be afraid of your success as we said earlier, or your bigness, your amazing abilities and what you've done. You *are* better than some people, maybe the *best* in the world. (Did you run for Mr or Ms Cosmos? No? Well then, there may be someone out there better than you. In which case find them and learn from them!) Be open to being better, and next year you can scale higher. Really, the best you can do in Cycle 10 is find a way to top your previous best, to beat yourself at your own game, to step it up, to play higher stakes. Why the hell not? We get bored if we get everything we want. It's not fun without competition.

INSECURITY EXPOSED: THE NEED TO BE IN CONTROL

It's worth reminding yourself that 'control' is an illusion. You can't control your partner, your friends, your employees, your boss or your neighbors. Well you can. You can manipulate or play games of all sorts to get someone to do your bidding, so that you'll feel better. But only insecure people, or those going through an insecure moment we should say (to be completely honest – who hasn't had a weak moment?) are more at risk of wanting and feeling the need to control another.

Those with any sense in Cycle 10 will see control for what it is. The need to keep something the same or the desire to have someone do as you wish so that you'll feel good. And no one was born merely to please you. So give it up. Concentrate on setting yourself new rules and boundaries and then letting others know what you need from them, thereby giving them a chance to see if they even want to play. Your rules aren't necessarily right for anyone else. At work it seems easier – bosses get to set the structures and everyone else has to jump if they are to keep their jobs. But in emotional relationships, who gets to decide what is the right or wrong way to handle anything?

Partnership is just that – a joint effort. Go back now and re-read Cycle 7 if you're having difficulties in relationships during your Cycle 10. Maybe it's you who needs to redefine how hard you're being on yourself, and thus making others suffer in the process?

Control is overrated. It tires you out, and others can always rebel and mess up your best laid plans. Do the best you can, respect others and they'll more than repay it in it mutual respect.

Instead of control – try focusing on what this period is really all about. Cycle 10 says: Find a new goal, find a new way to do what you do even better, even stronger, even more solid, even more public, even more lasting, even more structured, even more capable, and inspiring to everyone who looks upon it. When they look upon it, they look upon you. Even just by being the best you can be, at anything – honesty, patience, integrity, helpfulness. It doesn't need to be an actual achievement that people will pay you for or applaud you for outwardly, but inwardly where you're looked upon as a role model. That is true immortality. You inspire the rest of us to achieve more, and really work on our own Cycle 10s.

CYCLE 10 ACTION PLAN
*Congratulate yourself on getting this far.
*Tense all the muscles in your body. Now let go of all that tension!
*Map out an action plan based on your end result (what you want to achieve), your next steps (to work towards it), and a priority list
(of what's most important).
*Wheel out your new life rules.
*Manage your time better with a stronger, structured schedule.
*Beef up your CV, resumé, press kit and show off – you're one of a kind!

In a sunny year:
You get the promotion and the big job. Your name's in lights. Someone notices you. They want to help boost you higher. You did it! They see your glory and want others to notice you, as well. You become famous for a day, an hour, fifteen minutes or an entire television season. Perhaps infamous. For good or ill. You earn a title. You climb your way to the top and have such power as to control and influence the lives of one or the many. And it feels good. People stand up and take notice of you, and – even better, respect you. Wow! It feels amazing. After all you made it. You got yourself there. With your hard work

and commitment to yourself. You won. You earned your right to have us bow before you, triumphant. Applaud yourself, you deserve it.

You surpass old records, or ones you had from last year, or take on extra responsibility and do so without complaining (maybe, quietly!) and with total dedication. You're on top of your game. You may be working every day but it means something, and it's making something of you.

In good years, doors open and people arrive to help hoist you up the ladder of society's snakes and ladders game. Maybe you just did a great job. People are talking about you. These are your 'Up' years when there's more ladders than snakes, and more signposts to aid you in your quest for the top. Not that the climb isn't hard, but the way is shown and you have the energy and courage to overcome all blockades, barriers, and challenges that litter your path.

Your earn your way with every stepping stone crossed and every obstacle overcome and every mile walked. And boy has it been a journey. Sometimes power is thrust to you and your status changes, you get married, you become a parent, someone helps you onwards and you wonder how or why. Enjoy it, it means life wants to see what you can do. The powers-that-be (bosses, parents, authorities, God, whatever you want to call them) want to offer you a gift, a reward, a test. Who knows and who cares; it all works out beautifully. You're ready to step into the light and step into yourself. To reap a harvest for a job well, well done. No one can do it better than you. You deserve every ounce of success.

In a crummy year:
Another growth experience in the School of Hard Knocks. Life's a bitch. The company folds. The boss is on your back. You're fired. You don't get the job or are laid off even though you worked so hard to land the job in the first place. No one notices you. Or someone else gets credit for something you did. There's seemingly no reward in sight, and you're back slogging away trying to not only gain old ground but to climb even higher than your previous plateau. It's all sneaky snakes, with barely a ladder in sight (not to mention the snakes who seem hell-bent on tripping you up, blocking you and otherwise making life hell for you). Or you're too tired or depressed to even bother trying to climb them – they seem so tall anyway.

A vacation would be nice from all obligation, duty and responsibility and the really heavy stuff going on. Whereas you may have liked control in the past, now too much is in your hands – namely, making your own way in a world full of brick walls and people with more power than you. You've got toothache and you smash your knee on something or twist your ankle, and you've already got a bad back. Your father is a nightmare to deal with, or he's simply no longer around to bail you out like he used to. And others are heaping piles of you-know-what on you, for not doing enough, doing too much, failing, or simply not measuring up to certain standards you don't even know about.

Don't be fooled. You deserve everything that happens now. Imagine that. Ouch! How can that be true? The structure of your life is shoddy at best and non-existent at worst. You're under or overdoing the whole control issue. You either have too few rules or too many. Too many balls in the air, or not having the balls to even dare juggling. If things weren't hard enough, now you're to blame too?! Okay, let's re-define that. Life has dictated that what it is dishing out to you, is what you have dished out. Call it karma. Call it things catching up with you. Or call it a taste of your own medicine. Or you haven't laid a strong enough foundation, covered your bases or put in the effort necessary, and now it's too late. The dam bursts, the roof collapses on you.

Maybe it's just time to give up and move on to new pastures. You can't wallow forever. If you have messed around the past year, abused your position or power or failed to bother trying to achieve, you'll experience little (if any) praise, respect, or pats on the back. However, if you have put the time in and still nothing great seems to be happening, you're being tested on your ability to carry on, carry the weight, to try hard on your own, in short to be your own boss with no outward sign of support. It's kind of like being your own parent.

Depending on how insecure you may feel, you're seen as a controlling micro-manager, or find others are doing the controlling. You feel powerless or forced between a rock and a hard place. Life doesn't seem fair. Your job situation is bad and you have to contend with an evil boss, a tyrant official or some other major red-tape that blocks you. You're against the clock, the State, your parents. Anyone who has an ounce of power over you seems to loom large swallowing you in their smug shadow.

You're forced, therefore, to smarten up, straighten up and toughen up. Time may not be on your side (actually it is) but you'd better put it to good use working out some plan of action to get yourself out of the wasteland you're currently in. It's serious, it's somber, but it's just one part of a bigger Cycle. Since mastery and authority is the name of the game now, you may have to do it alone; but do it you shall.

The climb appears harder this year, or the distance between where you want to be and where you are is achingly wide or seemingly too far. What are the odds of success, what's your chance of making it? If you give up, it's a done deal. You stick it out and you're already one step ahead, and one step closer to your goal. In 'down' years you have little energy to get moving or you fail to summon up the courage to overcome all blockades, barriers, and challenges that litter your path. Or the way is clouded, and you feel stuck, blocked or up against all manner of problems. Don't worry – these are all karmically scheduled to come your way to test you out. (What will you do to get to the top? How committed are you? What is your definition of success?)

Some years you may topple from a great height if you've become full of ego. Everything you built may seem to fall. Maybe you'll just notice these things happen to people around you, as you stand and watch the people in power suffer some form of loss. Life is a business now, and you won't win points from being upset over what didn't work out. You need a plan. Long hours and elbow grease become your greatest allies.

Expect some form of change in the chain of command in your life, family, or within the field you're working in. Maybe it's best to team up with those who have more clout than you. Some years a company may push you up the ladder and you're not prepared, or else it's a slide lower down the ladder (maybe you want less hours to find what you really want to be doing with your life, instead of selling out to a big company). Is a new title headed your way?

This is an 'eye for an eye' year where you're treated as you've treated others, so if you've been a bully, expect others to give you some grief back! Getting a career path plan or some form of counseling may help – you need a step by step agenda on putting yourself back on the pedestal you belong. But you'll have to prove yourself. Try the tips below to help you get back on track:

Remember Cycle 11 is just up ahead, and with it the promise of all the fresh air you need, lots of new things, people, events, places, activities, life situations. If things seem hard and there seems no end in sight, you can be sure there is a shift promised. Cycle 11 will bring that to you, but you first have to face this sometimes-difficult Cycle 10. Buckle up, knuckle down, straighten and sober up and do what you know you should do under this Cycle and the rewards will be forthcoming. And if you didn't do so well on this go around the wheel, vow to try harder next time, and learn from the lessons that presented themselves during this time. There's always another chance to do it better, get it right and improve on your performance. That's what life is – multiple chances every day to do it differently and do it better. And morning always follows night.

Cycle Lesson

Our life is our responsibility, ultimately. Our parents do what they can for us, but there comes a time when we have to accept that we pilot our own plane, sail our own ship and drive to our own destiny. The more we can step up to this job, the more success we face, the higher we climb and the sweet success of the summit and its magnificent vistas await us. No one can force us to make the effort, but we can be pushed down by the weight of guilt, obligation and the internal feeling that we're not measuring up to the things we know we came here to do. Life is a job. You are your manager. Stand tall, strong and proud and make something of this special life you have in your hands. Now is the time.

Celebrity Spotlight

⊚ Scorpio Sun Prince Charles has a status change after marrying Princess Diana during his Cycle 10, the same cycle that saw his engagement to Camilla Parker Bowles 24 years later. (Synchronistically, the announcement fell during Camilla's very own 10-Cycle).

⊚ The TV Show The Apprentice first airs on 8 January 2004 during Capricorn (Cycle 10) season and American business magnate Donald Trump, (born with his Sun in Cycle 10), becomes known for his fateful catch phrase "You're Fired!"

⊚ Walt Disney, born with Neptune (planet of fantasy and imagination) in Cycle 10, opens Disneyland to the public during his 10th Cycle.

Ways to succeed during your Cycle 10 Manifestation:

⊚ Go hiking.

⊚ Climb a mountain.

⊚ Take in the view from the top.

⊚ Give yourself a break for getting this far (life's not always a bowl of cherries).

⊚ Do something and applaud yourself for its masterful completion.

⊚ Control yourself (instead of others).

⊚ Put in a few more hours on something worthwhile.

⊚ Give yourself a pat on the back for each accomplishment, however small.

⊚ Decide what you want to be known for and begin doing it publicly.

⊚ Remember that each setback is really a conspired move to move you ahead.

⊚ New ideas from bosses are worth following.

⊚ Implement your new life rules and regulations.

⊚ The elderly coming to the forefront (for a second burst of youth?)

⊚ Enhance your CV/resumé – polish, perfect and be proud!

⊚ Print new business cards, buy new clothes and emanate confidence.

⊚ Create new relationships with authority figures or professionals.

⊚ Re-define parent roles – release yourself from unhealthy discipline.

⊚ Plan your next move strategically.

⊚ Become more disciplined.

⊚ Stretch more – to ease joint stress.

⊚ Manage your life, become your own personal assistant.

⊚ Hire a personal assistant!

⊚ Climb the ladder, don't give up.

- Talk to the head honcho about a promotion.
- Do it yourself.
- Organize.
- See it as a test and vow to pass.
- Get serious and real.
- Promote your agenda.
- Fake it till you make it.
- Wake up early and work till late.
- Go public.
- Front a project, head an office.
- Be your own boss.
- Get to know your boss more.
- Put up your achievements on the wall, desk, shelf or create an altar dedicated to your successes to date.
- Give yourself a pat on the back for getting this far.
- Have a shoulder rub.
- Check in with your father, if he's not available go one better and impress yourself instead of seeking approval.
- Be a 'pillar of the community' no matter if no one else seems to care.
- Buy new dress clothes, a runway outfit or just power dress.
- Show us what you've got – don't play it shy, get in the spotlight.
- Blow your own trumpet; toot your own horn – contact a newspaper and get them to write an article about you.
- Sell yourself (just don't sell yourself short).
- Make a public appearance.
- Pretend you landed the job of your dreams – act, talk, *feel* it!

⌣ Super Surfing ⌣

Now you know which Cycles you move through under your zodiac sign. If you want to locate which Cycles you're also moving through as the *unique* Pisces, Cancer or Sagittarius that you are (since no two individuals lives or birth charts are the same) you can do that now.

Your Personal Solar Cycle gives you even more accuracy to unravel the mystery of you and your life. This is the most personal method of using this book, tailor made for you and your individual birth chart. Use it to see which Cycle *you* are in aside from everyone else born under your sign.

Both Cycles (the one for your birth sign and the one you'll now learn relates to you specifically) are relevant to you. Use the Solar Cycle Combinations further below for ideas on themes.

If you're a Cancer currently in Cycle 3, and the Sun is currently in Cycle 8 in your birth chart, read up on Cycle 3 and Cycle 8 combined. Your life at the moment will be a combination of both Cycles' themes.

You can gain this extra insight and accuracy if you know your own astrology chart; that way you can locate the exact day you enter a new Cycle. You can calculate your own *individual* Solar Cycles free at my website (you'll need your time of birth for this).

Just visit **www.SurfingYourSolarCycles.com** and you'll also find an option there to have this done for you. You will also find a special document you can print out to keep track of your Personal Solar Cycles so that you can use them every year alongside this book.

As you track the movement of the Sun through each of your twelve Cycles for an entire year, make a note of the dates as they will be the same for you every year.

These are your own *Personal* Solar Cycles.

Your Lifetime Solar Cycles...
...correspond to the sign your Sun was shining in (Aries, Taurus, Gemini etc) when you were born, along with the *house* it was found within. Together these form your Solar Cycle Duo and this combination dictates the main Solar Cycles of which you're trying to 'crack the code' in a big way, this lifetime.

They could be areas left in the dark from another lifetime.
They may be areas you need to build your confidence in.
They are guaranteed to be Cycles essential to your soul evolution.

Say you were born a Cancer with your Sun in the 9th house of your birth chart. In other words, you're a 9th House Cancer. You'll find that your life is a continual learning curve around Cycle 4 (Cancer) and Cycle 9 themes.

Use the table below to determine which two main Solar Cycles your life will revolve around.

Your Sun Sign	The house position of the Sun in your chart
Sun in Aries is Cycle 1	Sun in the 1st House is Cycle 1
Sun in Taurus is Cycle 2	Sun in the 2nd House is Cycle 2
Sun in Gemini is Cycle 3	Sun in the 3rd House is Cycle 3
Sun in Cancer is Cycle 4	Sun in the 4th House is Cycle 4
Sun in Leo is Cycle 5	Sun in the 5th House is Cycle 5
Sun in Virgo is Cycle 6	Sun in the 6th House is Cycle 6
Sun in Libra is Cycle 7	Sun in the 7th House is Cycle 7
Sun in Scorpio is Cycle 8	Sun in the 8th House is Cycle 8
Sun in Sagittarius is Cycle 9	Sun in the 9th House is Cycle 9
Sun in Capricorn is Cycle 10	Sun in the 10th House is Cycle 10
Sun in Aquarius is Cycle 11	Sun in the 11th house is Cycle 11
Sun in Pisces is Cycle 12	Sun in the 12th House is Cycle 12

Solar Cycle Combinations

These combinations of Solar Cycle themes are by no means exhaustive but are given here to pique your interest, open your mind and to give you the flavour of the energies of the Cycles combined. Locate your Sun Sign Cycle and Sun House Cycle below. Some descriptions may relate to you directly, some are just ideas whilst others may give you more insight into your lifelong themes, desires, skills issues or challenges. You can also use these combinations to look at your current Sun Sign Solar Cycle alongside your Personal Solar Cycle for ideas on possible themes currently active in your life.

Cycle 1 and 1
Trailblazer, butting heads, new beginnings, first in line, ignition spark, warrior armor, angry action, what you see is what you get, fools rush in, bangs and bruises.

Cycle 1 and 2
Asserting self-worth, enhancing physical appearance, touchy-feely, stop and go, red rag to a bull, proving yourself, financial fights, being practical.

Cycle 1 and 3
Direct words, appearing curious, 'what I say goes', as you think so you become, self-talk, verbal confrontations, new phone, constant commuter, walk your talk.

Cycle 1 and 4
Anger in the family tree, pursuing comfort, assertive mother, finding time alone, feeding the need, being the caretaker, heart on your sleeve.

Cycle 1 and 5
Fun-loving, self-proclaimed creative artist, confident lover, 'look at me', strutting peacock, taking the risk, self-PR, going for broke, sun in a cloudy sky.

Cycle 1 and 6
Staying in shape, fasting, self-criticism, working on confidence, caution versus recklessness, 'if you want something done, do it yourself', you are what you eat.

Cycle 1 and 7
Defining self through relationship, aggressive partners, being beautiful, fighting for peace and justice, drawing boundaries, fair play, looks do matter.

Cycle 1 and 8
Beginnings and endings, courageous research, life after death, being mysterious, ego death, all or nothing, fearless of the dark, wearing a mask, deep-sea diver.

Cycle 1 and 9
Soapbox sermons, boldly going where no one has gone before, eternal scholar, being in the know, know-it-all, more more more, seek and you shall find, gaining weight, credentials.

Cycle 1 and 10
CEO, following the leader, control freak, being on top, mastering the self, controlled anger, calculated risks, new title, public spotlight, pursuing power.

Cycle 1 and 11
Iconic, fiery friendships, going out on a limb, one of a kind, free spirit, everyone's friend, freedom fighter, oddball, party of one, new computer, being the change you would like to see.

Cycle 1 and 12
Pursuing peace and quiet, being sensitive, dreams of conflict, going with the flow, projection screen, personal smokescreen, wizard behind the curtain, more than meets the eye.

Cycle 2 and 2
Touchy-feely, natural is best, satiate the senses, large appetite, quality and quantity, comfy slippers, simple pleasures, gourmet connoisseur, art appreciation, musical maestro, dig your heels in.

Cycle 2 and 3
Money talks, gift of the gab, putting your money where your mouth is, multi-purchase, practical thoughts, sales pitch, stubborn tongue.

Cycle 2 and 4
Home improvement, family money, working from home, creature comforts, security conscious, nest-egg, back to basics, cozy home, practical mother.

Cycle 2 and 5
Risking for gain, financial show off, enjoying your earnings, artistic skill, food lover, buying the best, only the best, lucky lottery ticket, physical fun.

Cycle 2 and 6
Conserving funds, simple appreciation, sensible spending, health purchases, tip jar, eating disorder, budget cut, counting coins, financial aid, practical favor.

Cycle 2 and 7
Love of money, spending on partners, appreciating beauty, financial fairness, pleasant voice, spreading the joy, stress-relief, balancing the books, buying love.

Cycle 2 and 8
Financial settlements, lost objects, enjoying the occult, not what you own, sex sells, what's mine is yours (and vice versa), large inheritance.

Cycle 2 and 9
Buying books, overseas landscape, beautiful views, stubborn beliefs, money lessons, big spender, law of attraction, stay or go, five star travel.

Cycle 2 and 10
Managing money, appreciating authority, financial goals, spending on PR, tools of the trade, gourmet connoisseur, business guru, Fortune 500,

Cycle 2 and 11
Oddity collector, fiscal friends, humanitarian spender, financial freedom, sudden expenditure, quality electronics, saving for a rainy day.

Cycle 2 and 12
Psychic talents, lost wallet, non-materialist, appreciating feelings, buying magical artifacts, enjoying the ocean, seashells, universal abundance, stolen goods.

Cycle 3 and 3
Think before you speak, double entendre, crossword puzzle, nicknames, busy bee, Peter Pan, as you think so you become, sales tactics, neighborhood watch, sibling rivalry.

Cycle 3 and 4
Family talks, sharing feelings, emotional writer, photo album, heart and head, busy household, journaling, chatting about the past, trips down Memory Lane.

Cycle 3 and 5
Creative writing, mouthy show-off, chatting to children, thinking about love, infectious laughter, fun limerick, romantic note, risky reasoning.

Cycle 3 and 6
Mental health, carefully chosen words, efficiency books, crosswords, critical thoughts, whining, trivial pursuit, editing, 'how-to' manual.

Cycle 3 and 7
Heart to hearts, chatty partners, agreeing to disagree, legal documents, saying 'I do', snake charmer, polite words, eye for beauty, verbal sparring.

Cycle 3 and 8
Speak-no-evil, hypnotic words, powerful speech, dropped call, more than meets the eye, reading between the lines, in the doghouse, talking to the dead.

Cycle 3 and 9
Overseas emails, travel magazines, language learning, tall tales, witty humor, standup comedian, old books, questionnaire, positive thinking.

Cycle 3 and 10
Public speaking, talks with the boss, controlled words, ambitious siblings, pessimistic thinking, off-limit topics, public presentation, important message.

Cycle 3 and 11
Friendly conversation, weird words, shocking speeches, social hub, fast thinking, change of scenery, new words, rewiring, latest technology, switchboard.

Cycle 3 and 12
Poetic mind, daydreaming, lucid dream, lie detector, meditation, secret thoughts, invisible ink, head in the clouds, scream therapy, subliminal messages, space cadet.

Cycle 4 and 4
Home sweet home, feather your nest, all you can eat, comfy pillows, apron strings, location-location-location, hungry mouths, licking wounds, memory lane.

Cycle 4 and 5
Fun family, lineage of performers, stage mother, home decor, needy for love, family pride, emotional outbursts, party at home, big heart, 'feed me!'

Cycle 4 and 6
Housework, domestic repairs, family faults, memories of criticism, perfect cook, picky diet, scheduling personal time, tough love.

Cycle 4 and 7
Living with lover, parents' relationship, needing harmony, family fairness, birds of a feather, partner's family, need for beauty, hugger.

Cycle 4 and 8
Black sheep in the family, digging up the past, burying the hatchet, private home, uprooting, intense mother, stalker, memory like an elephant, emotional manipulation.

Cycle 4 and 9
Overseas home, religious relatives, need for adventure, somewhere over the rainbow, all-you-can-eat buffet, home on the road, needing to know, home truths.

Cycle 4 and 10
Need for rules/goals, controlled emotions, sensitive boss, working from home, caring career, weight of the world, family business, keeping the tradition alive.

Cycle 4 and 11
Need for change, family of freaks, odd home, unique past, futuristic feel, earthquake underfoot, caring friend, hostel, back to the future, cool mother.

Cycle 4 and 12
Hidden home, underwater haven, past life regression, emotional whirlpools, transcending the past, saying goodbye, psychic feelers, quiet time alone, bleeding heart.

Cycle 5 and 5
Superstar, child at heart, thrill ride, laughter is the best medicine, sunbathing, Drama Queen or Queen Bee/King of the Hill, grand romance, look at me, making love and art.

Cycle 5 and 6
Perfect performance, showing skill, expressing criticism, practice makes perfect, children's health, taking pride in a job well done.

Cycle 5 and 7
Showing off (or show-off partner), name dropper, artistic talent, enjoying company, compliments, beautiful creations, child with manners.

Cycle 5 and 8
Dark art, femme fatale, dangerous liaisons, cutting kids free, fatal attractions, edgy art, secretive children, pain as pleasure.

Cycle 5 and 9
Drama queen, large canvas, adventurous children, foreign date, art teacher, hungry for the unfamiliar, double dating, gambler's rush, outdoor fun.

Cycle 5 and 10
Creative career, star manager, artistic goals, studious child, playing with the boss, award winning, calculated risk, keeping up with the Jones's.

Cycle 5 and 11
Rebellious kid, strange tastes, unique talent, crazy date, being different is best, look but don't touch, proud oddball, fun friend, party animal.

Cycle 5 and 12
Closet artist, intuitive gamble, pleasure addict, creative daydream, broke gambler, stage presence, the 'It' factor, creative high.

Cycle 6 and 6
Squeaky-clean, filing cabinet, pill-box, granting favors, healing hurt, fix-it, worrywart, fault-finding, constructive criticism, elbow grease, practice makes perfect.

Cycle 6 and 7
Work-out partner, helping others, getting the look right, critical reflections, beautiful technique, apprenticeship.

Cycle 6 and 8
Surgery, sexual health, quitting bad habit, health obsession, helper/healer, minimalist, cut and dried, the bottom line.

Cycle 6 and 9
Working abroad, seeing the forest and the trees, exaggerated errors, fact-finder, big is better, outdoor workout, yoga class.

Cycle 6 and 10
Award for excellence, simple is best, cutting to the chase, healthy limits, time-limit, manager, employee of the month, office politics, pleasing father.

Cycle 6 and 11
Working with friends, odd coworkers, improvement groups, helpful pals, perfectly weird, electric upgrade, strange schedule.

Cycle 6 and 12
Confused criticism, private plans, in the zone, charity work, imperfections as perfect, working hard and playing hard, healing sleep.

Cycle 7 and 7
Fair's fair, me versus we, shake on it, agree to disagree, small print, mirror mirror, peace symbol, artist's eye, win-win, honey not vinegar, fake smile, snake-charmer.

Cycle 7 and 8
Intense intimacy, dark lovers, joint bank account, loss of love, moth to a flame, financial entanglements and settlements, till death do us part, killing them with kindness.

Cycle 7 and 9
Love of the unknown, summer fling, justice seeker, legal diplomat, adventures in love, lover in every port, law books, knowing your rights.

Cycle 7 and 10
Following the rules, public surveillance, celebrity couple, high taste, status shift, misery loves company, old reliable, arranged marriage, public unveiling, high profile client.

Cycle 7 and 11
Free love, social circle, unusual partner, social causes, the beautiful people, love of space, socially popular, everyone's friend, team player, group effort.

Cycle 7 and 12
Clandestine affair, dreamy beauty, all things rosy, blurry boundaries, shared soft spots, victim of love, past-life lovers, peaceful sanctuary.

Cycle 8 and 8
Halloween, deep sea diving, under the carpet, basement boxes, secret finder/keeper, graveyard, undercover, hypnosis, joint account, all or nothing, rising above, investigation.

Cycle 8 and 9
Legal settlements, occult knowledge, religious extremism, learning to let go, foreign dangers, psychic teacher, releasing prejudice.

Cycle 8 and 10
End of the line, researcher, sustained passion, public revelation, serious business, going all the way, harsh reality, spotlight on shadows, all under control.

Cycle 8 and 11
Hot and cold, 'frenemies', on and off, friends with benefits, fetishes, social clean-up, friends in transition, sexual experimentation.

Cycle 8 and 12
Sexual fantasy, hidden subtext, hypnotic lures, private investigator, letting go, basement boxes, trauma therapy, final farewell, cloak and dagger, fear of the dark, ouija board.

Cycle 9 and 9
Gypsy, in my opinion, honesty is the best policy, globetrotter, bookworm, translator, clumsy, seeking the silver lining, funny bone, mass media, foreign correspondent.

Cycle 9 and 10
Working overseas, respect of ritual, public opinion, satirical humor, business trips, official passport, professional author, teaching program, father knows best.

Cycle 9 and 11
Overseas connections, foreign friends, sudden trips, weird knowledge, religious rebellion, strange groups, sudden windfall, eclectic classes, progressive ideals.

Cycle 9 and 12
Exotic enticement, grass is greener, psychic knowing, adrenalin junkie, grand visions, couch surfer, dreamy drifter, we are one, oceanic adventures, cosmic consciousness, conspiracy theory.

Cycle 10 and 10
Head Honcho, follow my rules, suit and tie, following father, clockwatching, powers that be, hierarchy, going for the gold, fine wine, keeping up appearances, reverse-aging.

Cycle 10 and 11
Humanitarian goals, social control, friends in high places, crowd control, lasting friendship, business goals, shaping the future, rebel father.

Cycle 10 and 12
Power behind the throne, public gossip, doctored CV/resumé, well known psychic, sloppy authority, gentle leader, delusions of grandeur, public isolation.

Cycle 11 and 11
Everyone's friend, people-watching, mad genius, square peg, struck by lightning, save the earth, rebel without a cause, weird is wonderful.

Cycle 11 and 12
Shady friends, social outcast, psychic rebel, galactic federation, local pub, drug dealer, alone in group, futuristic dream, erratic sleep, sudden insight.

Cycle 12 and 12
Ocean by moonlight, stiff drink, 3D glasses, dream journal, save or suffer, sensitive soul, divine inspiration, floatation tank, lost keys, charity work.

When you're *weak, uninspired, bored* or *lacking in light*, your Sun is turned *off*. Turn to the Cycle and read what to do to turn yourself back *on* again. That is the surest way to plug back into your source: Cosmic Central. You'll be powered up again in no time.

When you're *bright, buzzing, shining like a star* and *receiving applause*, you're turned *on*. Congratulations. You're doing your Sun Cycle right. You're nailing it. Scoring a bull's-eye and you can go on to help others with this specific area too, by setting an example of how to shine your light,

by being the best you can be.

CELEBRITY SOLAR CYCLES

These famous people were born with the Sun in the house corresponding to each Life Cycle – in other words those listed in Surf Cycle 1 had the Sun in the 1st house of their birth chart – and their lives stand as a testament to the themes outlined throughout this book, for better or worse. Look up the names of the celebrities under your Solar Cycle and you can compare your life with those sharing your Lifetime Solar Cycle theme.

Surf Cycle 1
Steve Allen, Pamela Anderson, Julie Andrews, Adam Ant, Victoria Beckham, John Belushi, Bjork, Nicolas Cage, David Essex, Dalai Lama XIV, Emily Dickinson, Matt Dillon, Robert Englund, Sally Field, Samantha Fox, Dave Gahan, Jennifer Garner, J. Edgar Hoover, Harry Houdini, Steve Jobs, Scarlett Johansson, Grace Kelly, Jude Law, Heath Ledger, Bruce Lee, Abraham Lincoln, Steve Martin, Freddie Mercury, Ralph Nader, Paul Newman, Olivia Newton-John, Eva Peron, Matthew Perry, Brad Pitt, Arnold Schwarzenegger, Peter Sellers, Barbara Streisand, Jean-Claude Van Damme, Gene Wilder, Kate Winslet.

Surf Cycle 2
Ansel Adams, Ludwig van Beethoven, Tom Brokaw, Sandra Bullock, Ellen Burstyn, Maurice Chevalier, Agatha Christie, George Clooney, Robbie Coltrane, Billy Connolly, James Dean, Ellen Degeneres, Robert De Niro, Cameron Diaz, Leonardo DiCaprio, Thomas Edison, Errol Flynn, Maurice Gibb, Robin Gibb, Alfred Hitchcock, Billie Holiday, Rock Hudson, Diane Keaton, Lisa Kudrow, Jay Leno, Harpo Marx, Karl Marx, Michelangelo, Spike Milligan, François Mitterrand, Elvis Presley, Christopher Reeve, Joan Rivers, Tim Robbins, Frank Sinatra, Elizabeth Taylor, Tracey Ullman, Walt Whitman, Oscar Wilde, Tennessee Williams, Oprah Winfrey.

Surf Cycle 3
Ben Affleck, Hans Christian Andersen, Lauren Bacall, Justin Bieber, Bono, Jeff Bridges, Pat Buchanan, Jim Carrey, Fidel Castro, Sir Winston Churchill, John Cleese, Russell Crowe, Cameron Diaz, Christian Dior, Walt Disney, Cary Grant, Merle Haggard, Jim Henson, Paris Hilton, Jeremy Irons, Mick Jagger, Elton John, Stephen King, Lulu, Bob Marley, Dean Martin, Bob Monkhouse,

Roger Moore, Luciano Pavarotti, Vincent Price, Patricia Routledge, Beverly Sills, Britney Spears, Sting, Jimmy Swaggart, Elizabeth Taylor, Lily Tomlin, Rip Torn, Denzel Washington, Hank Williams, Shelley Winters, Tammy Wynette.

Surf Cycle 4

Woody Allen, Jennifer Anniston, Neil Armstrong, Marlon Brando, Jeff Buckley, Naomi Campbell, Julia Child, Patsy Cline, Phil Collins, Bill Cosby, Michael Crichton, Aleister Crowley, Ted Danson, Neil Diamond, Carmen Electra, Michael J. Fox, Lady Gaga, Robson Green, Melanie Griffith, George Harrison, Jennifer Love Hewitt, Victor Hugo, Tom Jones, Annie Lennox, Liberace, Martin Luther, John Malkovich, Rupert Murdoch, Lee Harvey Oswald, Pablo Picasso, Julia Roberts, Dennis Rodman, Diana Ross, Albert Schweitzer, Martin Scorsese, Sandie Shaw, Sissy Spacek, Bruce Springsteen, Jimmy Stewart, Nikola Tesla, Tina Turner, Tiger Woods.

Surf Cycle 5

Louis Armstrong, Candice Bergen, Halle Berry, Shirley Temple Black, William Blake, Jon Bon Jovi, Sonny Bono, Pierce Brosnan, Sir Richard Burton, Carol Channing, Hillary Clinton, Kevin Costner, Joan Crawford, Leonardo Da Vinci, Bette Davis, Marlene Dietrich, Placido Domingo, Faye Dunaway, Larry Flynt, George Foreman, Aretha Franklin, Tommy Lee Jones, Liberace, Marilyn Manson, John McEnroe, Joni Mitchell, Mozart, Richard M. Nixon, Peter O'Toole, Dolly Parton, Sidney Poitier, Franklin D. Roosevelt, Teddy Roosevelt, Charlie Sheen, James Spader, Ringo Starr, Gloria Steinem, Mae West, Malcolm X, William B. Yeats, Paramahansa Yogananda.

Surf Cycle 6

Muhammed Ali, Fred Astaire, Tyra Banks, Kenneth Branagh, Rory Bremner, Joseph Campbell, Charlie Chaplin, Kurt Cobain, Richard Dreyfuss, Bob Dylan, Morgan Fairchild, Greta Garbo, Ava Gardner, Dick Gregory, Jean Harlow, Rutger Hauer, Dennis Hopper, Whitney Houston, John Hurt, Eddie Izzard, Vivien Leigh, John Lennon, Joanna Lumley, Matthew McConaughey, Roddy McDowall, Ian McKellen, Julianne Moore, Barack Obama, Dan Rather, Robert Redford, Vanessa Redgrave, Christina Ricci, Charlie Rose, Carl Sagan, Martin Sheen, Cybill Shepherd, Maria Shriver, Suzanne Somers, Steven Spielberg, Ben Stiller, Justin Timberlake, Sigourney Weaver.

Surf Cycle 7

Warren Beatty, Belinda Carlisle, Courtney Cox, Billy Ray Cyrus, Doris Day, Clint Eastwood, Sigmund Freud, Peter Gabriel, Mel Gibson, Daryl Hannah, Katharine Hepburn, Hermann Hesse, Adolph Hitler, Dustin Hoffman, Gustav Holst, Anjelica Huston, David Icke, Peter Jackson, Carl Jung, Jack Kerouac, Heather Locklear, Mario López, Madonna, Charles Manson, Ricky Martin,

John McCain, Joseph McCarthy, Martina Navratilova, Liam Neeson, Gwyneth Paltrow, Lisa Marie Presley, LeAnn Rimes, Isabella Rossellini, Diana Spencer (Princess of Wales), Sylvester Stallone, Sharon Stone, Sid Vicious, Dionne Warwick, H. G. Wells, Prince William, Bruce Willis.

Surf Cycle 8
Buzz Aldren, Lucille Ball, Truman Capote, Edgar Cayce, Cezar Chavez, Deepak Chopra, Glenn Close, Sean Connery, Howard Cosell, Wes Craven, Jeffrey Dahmer, Matt Damon, Bo Derek, Shannen Doherty, Farrah Fawcett, Bobby Fischer, Larry Hagman, Prince Harry, Buddy Holly, Jesse Jackson, Elton John, John F. Kennedy, Nicole Kidman, Kris Kristofferson, Sophia Loren, Shirley MacLaine, Bette Midler, Demi Moore, Sean Penn, Sylvia Plath, Prince, Richard Pryor, Susan Sarandon, Alicia Silverstone, Mother Teresa, John Travolta, Harry S. Truman, Rudolph Valentino, Raquel Welch, Stevie Wonder, Renée Zellweger, Catherine Zeta-Jones.

Surf Cycle 9
Paula Abdul, Brigitte Bardot, Cindy Crawford, Tom Cruise, Marie Curie, Catherine Deneuve, Céline Dion, Robert Downey Jr, Zac Efron, Melissa Etheridge, Bob Geldof, Richard Gere, Whoopi Goldberg, Al Gore, Mata Hari, Eric Idle, Dr. Martin Luther King, Peggy Lee, Courtney Love, Steve McQueen, Michael Moore, Willie Nelson, Nostradamus, Conan O'Brien, Jacqueline Kennedy Onassis, Sean Penn, Burt Reynolds, Molly Ringwald, Roy Rogers, Roseanne, Brooke Shields, Aaron Spelling, Gwen Stefani, Martha Stewart, Uma Thurman, Robin Williams, Barbara Windsor.

Surf Cycle 10
Christina Aguilera, Drew Barrymore, Kim Basinger, Kathy Bates, Napoleon Bonaparte, Charles Bronson, George H. W. Bush, Karen Carpenter, Ram Dass, Albert Einstein, Jerry Falwell, Harrison Ford, Jerry Garcia, Goethe, Vincent van Gogh, Tom Hanks, Larry King, Heidi Klum, Jessica Lange, Jennifer López, Paul McCartney, Kylie Minogue, Mary Tyler Moore, Jim Morrison, Jack Nicholson, Al Pacino, River Phoenix, Burt Reynolds, Condoleezza Rice, Rihanna, Kenny Rogers, Mickey Rooney, Eleanor Roosevelt, Kurt Russell, Meg Ryan, Claudia Schiffer, Kristen Stewart, Martha Stewart, Igor Stravinsky, Donald Sutherland, Natalie Wood.

Surf Cycle 11
Harry Belafonte, Sandra Bernhard, Michael Caine, Jackie Chan, Cher, Bill Clinton, Jamie Lee Curtis, Salvador Dali, James Dean, Johnny Depp, Danny De Vito, Kirk Douglas, Michael Douglas, Mia Farrow, Jane Fonda, Barry Gibb, Goldie Hawn, Ernest Hemingway, Jimi Hendrix, Julio Inglesias, Angelina Jolie, Kim Kardashian, Kevin Kline, D.H. Lawrence, Jayne Mansfield, Groucho

Marx, Marilyn Monroe, Mandy Moore, Friedrich Nietzsche, Nick Nolte, Michael Palin, Robert Pattinson, Gregory Peck, Joe Pesci, Della Reese, Chris Rock, O.J. Simpson, Meryl Streep, Oliver Stone, Donald Trump, Peter Ustinov, Gore Vidal, George Washington.

Surf Cycle 12
Evangeline Adams, Giorgio Armani, David Beckham, Tony Blair, Robert Blake, Orlando Bloom, David Bowie, George W. Bush, Camilla Duchess of Cornwall, Mariah Carey, Joan Collins, David Copperfield, Divine, Henry Ford, Jodie Foster, Mahatma Gandhi, Judy Garland, Hugh Grant, Anthony Hopkins, Elizabeth Hurley, Saddam Hussein, Janis Joplin, Henry Kissinger, Queen Latifah, Rush Limbaugh, Tobey Maguire, Mystic Meg, George Michael, Liza Minnelli, John Nash, Michelle Pfeiffer, Keanu Reeves, Jessica Simpson, Patrick Swayze, Taylor Swift, Randy Travis, Liv Tyler, Andy Warhol, Orson Welles.

THE CYCLE OF ELEMENTS
Every Cycle relates to a specific element and its corresponding energy. Some Cycles urge us to do, some direct us to be, others inspire us to think, whilst others move us to feel.

The Fire Cycles – Action
Cycle 1: Self-initiation
Cycle 5: Creative expression
Cycle 9: Expansive growth

Go your own way (1), expressing yourself in your unique style (5), to continually expand and evolve (9).

The Earth Cycles – Manifestation
Cycle 2: Worth/value/pleasure
Cycle 6: Healthy/holistic functioning
Cycle 10: Status, self-mastery, outer achievement

Prioritize your desires (2), perfect and purify them (6) and experience their successful unfolding (10).

The Air Cycles – Thought
Cycle 3: Circulation
Cycle 7: Synergy
Cycle 11: Future Vision

Sift surrounding data (3), attract others to enhance direction (7) and map your new vision/goal (11).

The Water Cycles – Feeling
Cycle 4: Security, stability
Cycle 8: Intimacy, truth
Cycle 12: Surrender, submission

Nurture your gut feeling (4), transforming unhealthy patterns of energy (8), to access intuition (12).

IN CASE YOU'RE WONDERING...

Can you live through certain themes outlined here
when you're not in a particular Cycle?

Of course you can! The more you follow and implement specific change during each specific cycle at least *once* as you go around the zodiac wheel as outlined in this book, you'll then be well placed to enjoy the fruits of your labor during any of the Cycles mentioned. So just because you don't achieve your financial dreams in Cycle 2, or meet your soul mate in Cycle 7, doesn't mean you won't reap the rewards at another point in your annual adventure, *if you first do the work each Cycle asks of you.*

Whether you are consciously working with your cycles or vehemently resisting their messages, they're *always* in operation. Their main function is to serve as a way to peek at everything happening to you and find your place within it, to make sense of it, to make peace with it and ultimately give you something to work on and work towards. Because there is a higher reason, a bigger picture, a vaster story than the one you can currently comprehend from your limited perspective (like those times when you hike and look down over the land and see how small everything seems from this high up, how peaceful it is and how it all just 'works').

Maybe you'll find acceptance here. Surrender. Confirmation. Some new piece of information to help you see a new vantage point, to get to that hiking summit. Maybe you'll glimpse the beauty of life's clockwork majesty and laugh at the whole thing. Maybe you'll appreciate the up-turns by embracing the down-turns and ride your Cycles out to ultimate bliss and success.

Other planetary activity may cloud some Cycles, and you find it hard to see whilst in others you'll be amazed how crystal clear it all is. They work. Keep an open eye and an open mind and you'll see it.

We live stories within stories, Cycles within Cycles, chapters within chapters. And just because one may seem like a major headache or pain in the rear one year, it doesn't mean it won't shine as a glorious example the following year of

310

how things can turn around. Nothing is set in stone. You do have a say. It is after all, *your* story you're writing.

Life is a Game. Play well.

Love,
Neil D Paris
October 22, 2009, The Autumnal Equinox

Draw your Astrology Chart for free, calculate your own Personal Solar Cycles and discover other ways to use this book at:

www.SurfingYourSolarCycles.com

Also by The Wessex Astrologer - www.wessexastrologer.com

Patterns of the Past
Karmic Connections
Good Vibrations
The Soulmate Myth: A Dream Come True or Your Worst Nightmare?
The Book of Why
Judy Hall

The Essentials of Vedic Astrology
Lunar Nodes - Crisis and Redemption
Personal Panchanga and the Five Sources of Light
Komilla Sutton

Astrolocality Astrology
From Here to There
Martin Davis

The Consultation Chart
Introduction to Medical Astrology
Wanda Sellar

The Betz Placidus Table of Houses
Martha Betz

Astrology and Meditation
Greg Bogart

The Book of World Horoscopes
Nicholas Campion

Life After Grief : An Astrological Guide to Dealing with Loss
AstroGraphology: The Hidden Link between your Horoscope and your Handwriting
Darrelyn Gunzburg

The Houses: Temples of the Sky
Deborah Houlding

Through the Looking Glass
The Magic Thread
Richard Idemon

Temperament: Astrology's Forgotten Key
Dorian Geiseler Greenbaum

Nativity of the Late King Charles
John Gadbury

Declination - The Steps of the Sun
Luna - The Book of the Moon
Paul F. Newman

Tapestry of Planetary Phases:
Weaving the Threads of Purpose and Meaning in Your Life
Christina Rose

Astrology and the Causes of War
Jamie Macphail

Astrology, A Place in Chaos
Star and Planet Combinations
Bernadette Brady

Flirting with the Zodiac
Kim Farnell

The Gods of Change
Howard Sasportas

Astrological Roots: The Hellenistic Legacy
Between Fortune and Providence
Joseph Crane

The Art of Forecasting using Solar Returns
Anthony Louis

Horary Astrology Re-Examined
Barbara Dunn

Living Lilith
M. Kelley Hunter

The Spirit of Numbers: A New Exploration of Harmonic Astrology
David Hamblin

Primary Directions
Martin Gansten

Classical Medical Astrology
Oscar Hofman

The Door Unlocked: An Astrological Insight into Initiation
*Dolores Ashcroft Nowicki and
Stephanie V. Norris*

Understanding Karmic Complexes
Patricia L. Walsh

Pluto Volumes 1 & 2
Jeff Green

Essays on Evolutionary Astrology
Jeff Green Edited by Deva Green

Planetary Strength
Bob Makransky

All the Sun Goes Round
Reina James

The Moment of Astrology
Geoffrey Cornelius

The Sacred Dance of Venus and Mars
Michele Finey

The Insightful Turtle - Numerology for a More Fulfilling Life
Gillian Helfgott

Lightning Source UK Ltd.
Milton Keynes UK
UKHW021256010719
345363UK00003B/298/P

9 781902 405827